A CONCISE HISTORY OF THE BALTIC STATES

The Baltic region is frequently neglected in broader histories of Europe and its international significance can be obscured by separate treatments of the various Baltic states. With this wide-ranging survey, Andrejs Plakans presents the first integrated history of three Baltic peoples – Estonians, Latvians, and Lithuanians – and draws out the common threads to show how it has been shaped by their location in a strategically desirable corner of Europe. Subordinated in turn by Baltic German landholders, the Polish nobility and gentry, and then by Russian and Soviet administrators, the three nations have nevertheless kept their distinctive identities – significantly retaining three separate languages in an ethnically diverse region. The book traces the countries' evolution from their ninth-century tribal beginnings to their present status as three thriving and separate nation-states, focusing particularly on the region's complex twentieth-century history, which culminated in the eventual reestablishment of national sovereignty after 1991.

ANDREJS PLAKANS is Professor Emeritus at the Department of History, Iowa State University. His previous publications include *The Latvians: A Short History* (1995) and *Historical Dictionary of Latvia* (second edition, 2008).

CAMBRIDGE CONCISE HISTORIES

This is a series of illustrated "concise histories" of selected individual countries, intended both as university and college textbooks and as general historical introductions for general readers, travellers, and members of the business community.

A full list of titles in the series can be found at:
www.cambridge.org/concisehistories

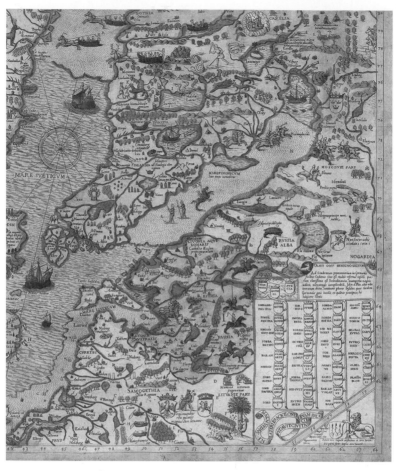

Fragment of *Carta Marina*, 1576. This famous "sea map" of northern Europe, created in Rome by the Swedish cleric Olaus Magnus, uses no borders in its depiction of the eastern littoral of the Baltic Sea.

A Concise History of
the Baltic States

ANDREJS PLAKANS

CAMBRIDGE
UNIVERSITY PRESS

CAMBRIDGE UNIVERSITY PRESS
Cambridge, New York, Melbourne, Madrid, Cape Town,
Singapore, São Paulo, Delhi, Tokyo, Mexico City

Cambridge University Press
The Edinburgh Building, Cambridge CB2 8RU, UK

Published in the United States of America by Cambridge University Press, New York

www.cambridge.org
Information on this title: www.cambridge.org/9780521541558

First published 2011

Printed in the United Kingdom at the University Press, Cambridge

A catalogue record for this publication is available from the British Library

ISBN 978-0-521-83372-1 Hardback
ISBN 978-0-521-54155-8 Paperback

To

Eamonn and Alexander

CONTENTS

PLATES

MAPS

PREFACE

The story of present-day Estonia, Latvia, and Lithuania must begin not at the time when countries bearing those names appeared on the European map, but when a group of stateless peoples settled permanently on the eastern shore of the Baltic Sea during the fifth and sixth centuries AD. At that time, to the south, the Roman Empire had already dissolved and, in what was to become France, the Merovingian and Carolingian kings were trying to form a successor state. Much later, in the medieval period, only one of the Baltic seacoast peoples – the Lithuanians – succeeded in creating a state of their own; the other two – the Estonians and Latvians – lost such political leaders as they had by the end of the thirteenth century and until the twentieth remained subordinated to German- , Swedish- , and Russian-speaking landowning aristocracies. The Lithuanians too lost their medieval state through a voluntary union with Poland that created a commonwealth in which the Poles became the dominant force politically and socially. Only after World War I did cartographers redraw their maps of Europe to include Estonia, Latvia, and Lithuania as independent nation-states. Twenty years later, they had to rework them again because the three countries were absorbed by the Soviet Union in 1940 and became soviet socialist republics. The redrawing exercise was not repeated until 1991, when the USSR collapsed and the three Baltic states resumed their independence. The political history of the eastern Baltic littoral thus contains far more discontinuity than continuity, many more years of war than years of peace, many more regime changes than periods of stable governance, and much more destruction than uninterrupted growth. The task of forming a coherent story from this fragmented history is a difficult assignment, and the achieved coherence is more likely to reflect the viewpoint of the historian writing the story than a coherence inherent in the past itself. Others would synthesize the history of the region differently.

Although political discontinuity appears to be the single most important facet of Baltic-area history, several themes recur throughout all periods and together provide some degree of continuity. These themes are location, language, statehood, leadership, and fragmentation; they appear in different variants and guises throughout the entire thousand-year period covered in the book. They will not be explored in equal detail in every chapter, and the chapters closest to our own day will do them greater justice. The book is a survey of limited length of a very long stretch of historical time, and the recent centuries contain more usable and reliable information about the peoples who in the twentieth century established the three Baltic states. As will be seen, for most of their history the Estonians, Latvians, and, considerably less so, the Lithuanians, remained, as individuals, mostly hidden from view. They themselves left only a sparse written record, and contemporary accounts written by the scribes of the political rulers of the region referred to the subordinated littoral peoples most often with various collective nouns (for example, peasants, serfs, non-Germans). Thus, for many centuries only a few of the subordinated emerged as unique individuals with names and fully documented life experiences. The "democratization" of the historical record began in the eighteenth century; by the nineteenth, evidence about people on the lower rungs of the social scale became a flood; and by the twentieth, people of all backgrounds – of high birth or low – could potentially be part of the historical narrative as full-fledged historical actors. The later chapters of the book thus cover a shorter time span because these centuries contain more usable and detailed evidence about all the inhabitants of the littoral.

The first chapter of the book deals with a long stretch of historical time from the end of the ice age in the eastern Baltic littoral and the first appearance of human settlements to about the year 1000, when the populations of the region had stabilized enough to be mentioned

by chroniclers as permanent residents. Chapter 2 takes up the arrival
into the area of crusaders and merchants from western Europe, intent
on Christianization and territorial conquest in a process some historians have referred to as the area's "europeanization." In these medieval centuries the region became bifurcated, with its northern part
(the later Estonian and Latvian territories) becoming the Livonian
Confederation governed by German-speaking political elites and the
southern area (the Lithuanian territories) emerging as a unified and
expansionist state governed initially by Lithuanians themselves.
Chapter 3 considers the eastern Baltic littoral in the early modern
period (1500–1800) as it experienced the secularization of the remnants of the crusading orders, the Protestant Reformation and
Catholic Counter-Reformation, and the changes wrought by the
littoral's becoming a component of the Polish-Lithuanian
Commonwealth, the Swedish Empire, and the Russian Empire, in
chronological order. Chapters 4, 5, and 6 deal with the region as a
"western borderland" of the Russian Empire from the mid-
eighteenth century to World War I. Various features of modernity –
agricultural reform, urbanization, industrialization, nationalism,
and population growth – arrived here through the opportunities
and the constraints created by Russian imperial policy, as the
empire sought to bring itself up to western levels. Chapter 7 exam-
ines the political, economic, and cultural consequences of the
national independence that the three peoples acquired during the
period of World War I, as a Union of Soviet Socialist Republics
replaced the Russian Empire. It was during the interwar decades
(1920–1940) that parliamentary democracy in the Baltic republics
lost out to authoritarianism, as similar political transformations
affected nearly all of the new states of the European east. Chapter 8
surveys the Baltic republics as constituent parts of the USSR
(1940–1991) after their occupation and annexation by the Soviet
Union during the course of World War II. Here the short-lived
occupation of the region by the Hitlerite Third Reich during the
war will also be considered, this episode having as one consequence
the simplification of the nationality composition of the Baltic region
through forced emigration and genocide. Chapter 9 describes the
post-Soviet years after 1991 when political independence returned
to the Baltic littoral following the collapse of the USSR and as

Estonia, Latvia, and Lithuania became members of the international structures of a new Europe. A listing of suggested readings primarily of English-language materials forms the last section of the book. The author would like to express his gratitude to the many people who helped in the creation of this book. Barbara S. Plakans not only provided insightful counsel about the contents but also reshaped and improved the book's first draft with her considerable editing skills. The Interlibrary Loan staff of the W. Robert Parks Library at Iowa State University helped obtain materials from other libraries. The gathering of the many illustrations characteristic of the "Concise History" series in which the book appears was facilitated by the following colleagues and friends: Toivo Raun of Indiana University; Vita Zelče of the University of Latvia; Alfred E. Senn, Professor Emeritus of the University of Wisconsin; Jānis Krēsliņš, Jr. of the National Library of Sweden in Stockholm; and Peter Wőrster of the J. G. Herder-Institut of Marburg, Germany. The author thanks them all. In Riga, Latvia, welcome assistance with illustrations was also provided by Uldis Neiburgs of the Occupation Museum in Riga; Viesturs Zanders of the Baltic Central Library; Guntis Zemītis of the University of Latvia's Institute of History; Anita Meinarte of the Latvian National Museum; and Z. Ciematniece of the Riga City and Maritime Museum. The book would have been poorer without their help. Finally, I am particularly grateful to my editors at Cambridge University Press, Michael Watson, Helen Waterhouse, and Chloe Howell, for their guidance and especially for their patience over the several years during which the book took shape.

Andrejs Plakans
Ames, Iowa

I

The peoples of the eastern Baltic littoral

A survey of the history of the peoples of the eastern Baltic littoral could start with the first mention of them in written sources, which would permit subsequent events to be described according to a recognized chronology. To begin much earlier requires that in this chapter we use a different time scale from that common among historians, reckoning the passage of time in tens and hundreds of thousands of years. The decision to start earlier was in part based on the desirability of underlining that the Baltic region was not empty space at the time major civilizations appeared, flowered, and declined in the Near East and in the Mediterranean basin; and in part to establish that human movement was from the beginning an integral part of long-term Baltic history. In the centuries when they began to appear by name in written historical sources – roughly starting in the first century AD – the peoples of the littoral were only the latest of hundreds of generations of migrants, some of whom left behind identifiable fragments of material culture while others disappeared leaving barely a trace.

All these comings and goings no doubt had turning points of various kinds about which we are unlikely ever to know very much. The one that was crucial for connecting the continuous human history of the Baltic littoral to the history of the rest of the European continent, however, came when writers in the existing civilizations began to assign names to the littoral peoples, imprecise and largely uninformative though these names were. The naming process was recognition of economic connections that already existed between the littoral and other parts of Europe, but at the same time the use of specific designations for these northern peoples piqued a curiosity about them that was never to subside again; with each century after about AD 800 sources about the Baltic littoral provide increasingly more detailed information that can be combined with the findings of archeologists to reduce guesswork.

No written sources from the littoral itself challenge descriptions written by outsiders because the littoral peoples did not record information about themselves in any fixed form or medium. Consequently, anything said about life in these preliterate centuries will always sound a note of uncertainty. Such descriptions rest on sparse mentions in the written sources of other peoples, on inferences drawn from surviving artifacts of material culture, and on contestable interpretations of the thought that lay behind identifiable customs and practices (e.g. the position of bodies in excavated burial sites). Thus, the littoral is no different from many other regions of the European continent, indeed of other continents, yet in some respects the painstaking reconstructions by modern-day archeologists of the living patterns of the littoral peoples are based on more reliable material than is available for other regions. Still, caution should be the watchword until the time in the past when the peoples of the Baltic littoral begin to testify about themselves directly.

ORIGINS

The thick sheet of ice covering most of northern Europe began to recede 14,000 years ago, leaving behind the physical features of the eastern Baltic littoral that have remained largely unchanged to the present. The withdrawal was slower than a snail's pace, uncovering first the territory now occupied by Lithuania, then that of Latvia, and finally that of Estonia. The ice retreated to somewhat north of the Arctic Circle in what is now Finland, and by the time it stopped moving, northern Europe had already become host to human settlements. What had begun as a large lake in the middle of this new territory eventually became what later would be called the Baltic Sea, and the fingers of ice on the southern edge of the receding ice sheet left behind very different landscapes. In the eastern littoral, however, these landscapes did not vary greatly overall: there were large river systems containing many smaller tributaries, medium-sized and small lakes, swampland, large areas of flatland and a few highlands (though not mountains), and porous soil interspersed with rocky patches. The post-glacial vegetation included large forests of fir, oak, birch, and beech; the climate finally settled to be rather damp and moderately warm, with somewhat harsh winters and a relatively short growing season.

Judging by skeletal remains, the first large animals of the eastern littoral were probably an early subspecies of reindeer that had migrated northward from areas on the southern shore of the Baltic Sea and from regions southeast of the littoral. These animals were followed by human beings probably from the same locales, whose remains attest to the first human settlements in the area (in what is now Lithuania) starting at about 11,000 years ago. These pioneering settlements, not surprisingly, were established on the banks of rivers and lakes; and from these very ancient remains, archeologists have surmised that early in-wanderers moved in bands of around ten to twenty persons. In this era the human settlements were not permanent; initially these hunter-gatherers followed the reindeer and moved on after the food supply in their immediate vicinity was exhausted. Most of what we can surmise about these early human populations comes from several dozen archeological sites scattered around the littoral, the earliest of these – in Lithuanian territory – yielding the oldest evidence from about 11,000 years ago and the most recent from about 10,000 years ago.

Among these early peoples, constant movement was characteristic, but relatively permanent settlements increased in frequency during the period archeologists designate as the late Neolithic (about 6,000 to 4,000 years ago). Physical evidence suggests that they became more numerous as time wore on, and were located close to either flowing or stable bodies of water. For a very long time, these settled communities, probably composed of farmers coming from the area around the Vistula River in Poland, shared the littoral with the hunters and gatherers. No doubt there was friction. The hunter-gatherers practiced their age-old traditions of moving over large territories, while settlers defended the locations in which they had invested time and effort.

Evidence about the activities of human beings is sparse in these earlier millennia, and analysis of the relics of material culture, no matter how carefully undertaken, involves a great deal of scholarly inference. Take the example of a burial site. Can the presence of certain kinds of seeds in it really lead to general statements about crop preferences? Or in grouped burial sites, does the slight physical separation of the grave of a man from those of women really point to the existence of a patriarchal system? The move from things to the thoughts behind things remains very difficult, verging on the impossible, in this long period of the past: it is simply educated and informed guesswork.

In the millennia before settled agriculture became dominant (that is, just before the era that began about 5,000 years ago) archeologists have differentiated the mobile inhabitants of the eastern littoral by reference to cultural features manifested in artifacts and especially burial practices. In the littoral these variously named "cultures," as archeologists refer to them when using the names of the places where artifacts were found, are the "Kunda" culture in the northern reaches of the littoral and the "Nemuna" culture to the south, with considerable overlap of the two in the middle. Moreover, the eastern boundaries of these "cultures" were located well within what is now Russian territory, and the southern boundary of the "Nemuna" culture reached into what is Poland and Belarus nowadays. Somewhat later, these "cultures" were joined by another – the so-called "Comb-marked/Pitted-ware" culture, a name derived from pottery decorations. Still later, carriers of the "Stringware" culture (again, from pottery decorations), also sometimes called the "Battle-axe" culture (from the weapon design), arrived on the scene without, it seems, completely displacing or replacing the others and bringing with them new agricultural practices. The postulated external boundaries of these "cultures" at no point followed the political boundaries of the present-day Baltic states, so their carriers can only figuratively be considered "ancestors" of the later Baltic-area populations. These "cultures" were separated in time from later eras by many millennia – by hundreds of human generations – as well as by the byproducts of the incessant in-wandering of other peoples from outside the littoral. It would be misleading, therefore, to think of these "cultures" as beads strung together at regular intervals on the string of time. There must have been chronological overlaps and cross-cultural penetrations, lending and borrowing of practices, since they all existed in a relatively small corner of Europe.

Still, after its first appearance in the eastern Baltic littoral human presence was continuous. Adaptation to local environments was evidently successful much of the time, and a good deal is known about how these peoples coped. When they stayed in one place, they built either small wooden houses with vertical walls and a roof, or structures (resembling the teepees of Native Americans) with thin tree trunks leaning against one another as a framework for an outer covering of hides and bark. They fished and hunted with tools made of bone or wood, adorned themselves with amulets of the same materials, and produced pottery with geometric decorations. The frequency of jewelry and the pottery designs suggest the presence of an aesthetic sense among the anonymous artisans who produced them, since decorations in and of themselves did not improve the efficiency of the artifacts in question. Weaponry was used for both hunting and self-defense, though there is very little direct information about actual conflict, territorial or otherwise. Perhaps population density was so low that destructive conflict arose only in the most extraordinary circumstances.

Thus, change of all kinds was ever-present but for the most part it was not cumulative in the technological sense. Small improvements in weapons, tools, and living quarters no doubt took place, but most such improvements made little difference to overall standards of living in the long run. The one type of change that was a true transformation and had the greatest consequences was the arrival and diffusion of settled agriculture: the cultivation of field crops and the raising of animals. These practices are associated with the carriers of the "Stringware" culture and date from the late Neolithic period. The dominant tool for these farmers was the wooden hoe. There followed a thousand years during which the old hunting-and-gathering practices coexisted with stable agriculture; but starting around 4,000 years ago evidence exists of the use of metals – bronze and iron – primarily in jewelry and weapons. Where knowledge of these technologies came from is not clear, but it is evident that in the course of time the use of metals and settled agricultural practices became mutually supportive. Fields measuring about 60 by 120 feet have been found; these were established on open land or after trees were cleared. Livestock was mostly of the multipurpose kind – sheep, goats, cows, and pigs – supplying milk and meat and yielding also large, strong bones, wool, and hides. The usefulness of this agricultural knowledge evidently diffused throughout the eastern Baltic littoral, leaving a great deal of archeological evidence. The instrument of diffusion must have been human beings, attesting to the fact that geographical movement of various kinds continued even in populations in which the advantages of being settled had become widely accepted.

Evidence from the centuries of the late Neolithic period shows clearly that building practices improved, since permanent fields necessitated residence for the long term and allowed time for learning by trial and error. Wood remained the principal material for the construction of housing, and stone was put to other uses: fields were often separated by fences of piled-up stone, and stone was also used for grave coverings, sometimes arranged in geometric designs. Occasionally one can find fortified places built to guard domestic animals, and this period – the late Neolithic – also provides the first evidence of the construction of wooden hillforts: village-like groups of residences surrounded by a high wooden stockade. Hillforts, however, became much more prominent in later periods. The desirability of metal implements of various kinds apparently translated into more frequent contact with outsiders, since eastern littoral gravesites from the period frequently contain crafted metal pieces of central European and Scandinavian origin.

The continuing use of metals eventually led to iron replacing bronze. This transition took place when far to the south in the Mediterranean basin the Roman Empire was becoming the largest polity in the European world of the time. Some evidence suggests that even before Roman expansion reached its zenith (in the third and fourth centuries AD) there were occasional trading contacts between the Baltic and Mediterranean worlds: Baltic amber was a desired good among the Romans, as were hides, and the peoples of the Baltic littoral were always in the market for metal goods. Probably the most active populations in these trading relationships were the peoples of the *southern* Baltic littoral, whose various metal objects made their way into the *eastern* littoral as well.

If processes of change in the littoral in earlier eras have to be measured in thousands of years, then starting about two thousand years ago economic and social change became more frequent and easier to date. One can speculate that settled agriculture improved the food supply, which in turn reduced infant mortality and increased life expectancy, and thus increased the population density of the region. A denser population put greater pressure on agricultural producers, which meant the clearing of more fields and the expansion of existing fields as well as more rapid diffusion of innovations. Similar dynamics of change in the regions surrounding the eastern Baltic littoral piqued the interest of neighboring, numerically larger peoples, who were looking for places into which to expand.

ACHIEVING RECOGNITION

We assume that during the same centuries when the Roman Empire to the south ruled the known civilized world, the peoples of the eastern Baltic littoral lived their lives in an orderly fashion, establishing rules of personal, social, and political conduct consistent with their values of what was right and proper. What these rules of life were is not known. Accounts of these centuries put forward much later in time by archeologists, however, use language suggesting that the population distribution of the Baltic region had achieved greater stability than ever before. These descriptions do not preclude the existence of movement, but the new context of movement had become a collection of peoples identified with specific areas within the littoral. This shift of descriptive language among later scholars looking backward draws in part on geographic accounts produced by writers of the classical world: it is in the early centuries of the "Christian era" of the Roman Empire that the very first written references to Baltic littoral peoples can be found. These references are vague, suggesting no deep knowledge of the area, but at the very least they signal a recognition by contemporaries that the peoples beyond the borders of the empire were not being thought of as an anonymous and interchangeable mass of barbarians.

The Roman historian Tacitus in the first century AD, for example, made reference to the *Aesti*, a people said to be living on the southern shore of the "northern sea." Similar references, carrying along the term *Aesti*, appeared in the writings of Cassiodorus and Jordanus in the sixth and Einhard in the ninth century AD; still other Greek and

Roman writers earlier and later than these four gave names to places and rivers around the Baltic Sea and referred to the sea itself as the "Svebian Sea". Such references were used by these writers as much to satisfy the desire to describe exotic European places as to point to the source of amber, which was valued by the Mediterranean peoples and imported from these northern lands. Though the term *Aesti* always appeared in these writings together with similar designations of other little-known northern peoples, the very fact that they were named at all was significant and indicated the growth of more specific knowledge about them.

Unfortunately, the terms used by the classical authors do not help very much in understanding the situation on the ground in the littoral. We can lay aside the practice of referring to these peoples by using such archeological terms as "makers of Cord-ware" and "the Battle-axe culture," but the question then becomes what to put in their place. In using such terms as *Aesti*, Tacitus and other classical authors were more than likely drawing on second- or third-hand travelers' accounts circulating among the learned of the time or borrowing them from earlier writers. It was recognition of a kind, yet there is no evidence that the people thus recognized called themselves *Aesti*, or of what they did call themselves. This really was an encounter between a literate and a non-literate people, with the former prevailing at least for a time. In addition, collective terms connoting peoples-in-place carry with them a strong suggestion of the cessation of population changes. It would be more sensible to assume that processes characteristic of numerically small peoples jostling each other for territory – assimilation, amalgamation, extirpation, expulsion, replacement – continued in some fashion even if we know nothing about them and the results of their workings. After about the year AD 500, however, references to the littoral's peoples-in-place began to grow in number: Scandinavian sagas of the ninth century contain descriptions using collective nouns, and Russian chronicles of the period include similar statements. From the growing frequency of these references, we can infer that population stabilization of some kind was occurring.

Many centuries later, particularly during the twentieth century, scholars writing about the Baltic littoral reached a kind of consensus about how to refer to the peoples of this period by using terminology coming from two different academic disciplines: historical linguistics and historical ethnography. Linguistic methodologies contributed general terms concerning language development and diffusion through the use of evidence from the language itself, but in this discourse what is said about the social history of the human carriers of the languages comes from cognate disciplines such as ethnography. Historical ethnography is concerned primarily with the nature and development of actual human groupings; it looks to evidence other than linguistic and seeks to identity differences among groups that might not be visible in the language domain alone. In the Baltic littoral, both disciplines have converged to offer a variety of names, some pointing to language groupings and others to population groupings. In neither case is complete direct evidence available, and such grouping terms are always to some extent speculative and at best hypothetical.

The categories of the historical-linguistic tradition are the most general, and therefore it is appropriate to start with them. Historians of European languages identify two broad categories relevant to the present discussion – the Indo-European and the Finno-Ugric – each category containing many different languages. The speakers of these language groups moved into European space from the southeast. Each group had an earlier version designated as either proto-Indo-European or proto-Finno-Ugric. By AD 500 each large grouping had already become associated with a location in the littoral: speakers of the Finno-Ugric languages were situated north of those speaking Indo-European tongues. Population movement was continuous in the central European regions during the middle centuries of the first millennium AD (sometimes this is referred to as the "wandering of peoples"), and others, particularly the Slavic groups (Indo-European language carriers), moved in from the east and south and pressed the existing populations northward. In response, Indo-European language speakers who had preceded them northward, in the process pushed speakers of Finno-Ugric languages ever more northward. These processes led to the latter occupying the territory of present-day Finland and Estonia, while the Indo-European speakers occupied the rest of the eastern Baltic littoral (the areas of present-day Latvia and Lithuania), as well as areas in the southern Baltic littoral (present-day northern Poland and Kaliningrad) and, judging by hydronyms (names of bodies of water), substantial portions of what is now Belarus and western Russia. When referring to these centuries, modern historians of European languages commonly use the term "Baltic" to refer to the Indo-European tongues on the eastern and southern shore of the Baltic Sea, and "Finnic" in reference to the languages farther north.

The terminology of historical ethnographers writing about the same period now commonly describes these Baltic- and Finnic-speaking groups by using a more differentiated nomenclature that frequently draws upon the names offered by Roman writers, Scandinavian bards, the compilers of early Russian chronicles, and the authors of later chronicle accounts of the thirteenth and fourteenth centuries. These ethnographers write with considerable confidence that in the centuries from about AD 500 to 1000 the peoples of the eastern and southern littoral of the Baltic Sea lived in territories sufficiently well defined to be depicted with boundaries when the region is mapped (see Map 1).

We shall be using, of course, the English-language versions of all these terms. The northernmost people of the eastern littoral were the Estonians, who occupied roughly the area of present-day Estonia, including the myriad islands off the Baltic Sea coast. Estonians used a Finnic language related to the language of the Finns who had moved northward across the Gulf of Finland, as well as to that of a number of smaller Finnic groups in the interior of what is present-day Russia. They were also related linguistically to the Setus, whose living space was southwest and south of Lake Peipus in modern-day Estonian territory and extended into modern-day Russia. The Livonians (or Livs) – also a Finnic grouping – lived in the lands immediately adjoining the now-named Gulf of Riga; their language was evidently somewhat different to those used by the Estonian or Finnish populations. Other Balto-Finnic-speaking groups – such as Ingrians, Karelians, Vepsians, and Votes – living in Russian regions outside the eastern littoral will not be considered here.

South, east, and west of the Estonians, Livonians, and Setus lay the territories of the peoples who spoke Baltic languages. Adjoining Estonian and Livonian lands lived the Latgalians, whose territory started on the eastern bank of the Daugava River and appears to have extended well into modern-day Belarus. West of them lived the Selonians, with the eastern border of their territory being the western

Map 1 The tribal societies of the Baltic littoral, twelfth to thirteenth century. The tribal names come from contemporary chronicles, but the internal boundaries have to remain educated guesswork.

bank of the Daugava. To their west, and directly below the lands of the Livonians around the Gulf of Riga, were the Semigallians, whose territory reached into present-day Lithuania. West of the Semigallians, with the western borders of their territory being defined by the Baltic seacoast, were the Couronians (or Kurs), who in the south also reached into present-day Lithuania. South of the Couronians and Selonians and still in the Baltic-language area lived the Žemaitians, whose territory occupied most of present-day northern Lithuania. Southeast of the Žemaitians there lived the Aukštaitians, with their territory lying around the upper Nemunas

River. Just west of these lived the Skalvians (around the lower
Nemunas River); and south of these the Jatvings (or Sudavians),
whose territory lay between the lower Nemunas and the Mazovian
Lakes. Just west of the Jatvings were the Prussians (sometimes
referred to as "Old" Prussians), whose territory centered on modern-
day Kaliningrad and who also spoke a Baltic language. On the other
side of the Prussians (in modern-day northern Poland) there began
the territories of Slavic-speaking tribes. Slavic speakers, in fact,
defined the southern borders of the Jatvings and the southern and
eastern borders of the Aukštaitians. Judging by place-names and
other similarly slowly changing direct evidence in the first centuries
of these population movements, the territories of Baltic-language
speakers extended far into present-day Russia, but the Slavic tribes
who came later had pressed westward, compressing the residence of
the Baltic peoples to the area around the Baltic Sea.

Several comments are in order about this inventory of peoples.
First, in the centuries under discussion (fifth to tenth centuries AD),
what we refer to here as the "Slavic speakers" could also be
disaggregated into smaller units, each with its own unique name.
But since we are concerned with the Baltic and Finnic speakers of the
eastern Baltic littoral, we will not do so here. Second, the names used
for some of the peoples of this era in later centuries became the
official names of entire modern countries (Estonia, Lithuania) or
sections of countries (Latvian regions: Kurzeme, Zemgale, Latgale).
We should not assume from this naming history, however, that the
premodern people who bore these names gradually expanded to
absorb everyone else in their vicinity. The history of territorial
naming in the eastern Baltic littoral differs greatly from the history
of changes in the population makeup of the area. Third, the question
remains as to what exactly these populations were – peoples, tribes,
ethnic groups, language groups, nationalities, nations? The use of
collective designations varies tremendously among scholars dealing
with the area, and there is good reason to maintain some distance
from designations that imply a great deal of collective consciousness
of unity among these peoples, largely because of the nature of the
available evidence. The "boundaries" indicated on Map 1 are
inferences from the distribution of archeological findings and
linguistic evidence and do not necessarily demarcate precisely a

territory that the people living in it were willing to defend as "theirs." Terms such as "peoples" or "tribal societies" are therefore more defensible than others because they are more neutral on the central question of group consciousness.

The problem of how to refer to the littoral peoples has an important variant: can they be thought of as political entities – as states? The difficulties are compounded by the fact that present-day historians of the three Baltic countries sometimes use even finer distinctions in describing the territory of the littoral. It is said that "ancient Estonia" consisted of forty-five "parishes" forming eight distinct "regions": Virumaa, Rävala, Järva, Harju, Läänemaa, Saaremaa, Ugandi, and Sakala. Latvian historians speak of the lands of the Latgalians, Selonians, Couronians, Semigallians, and Livonians, and, referring to later documents, claim that each of these "lands" contained numerous separately governed or administered territories. Lithuanian historians refer to "four traditional ethnographic regions" – namely, Džūkija, Aukštaitija, Žemaitija, and Suvalkija – and hint at the existence of yet further subdivisions. The earlier existence of these entities and sub-entities is sometimes deduced from a bare-bones mention of a place-name later. Sometimes the place-name is buttressed by archeological evidence, and sometimes the source contains considerable description suggesting that the writer had something like a state formation in mind. Scholarly debate continues over the exact nature of these entities in the period before AD 1000, and about how centralized and powerful they really were. Often historians resort to developmental language by using such terms as "proto-states" and "proto-nations," implying that it was only a question of time before these entities became full-fledged and well-defined political actors with governing elites, central administrations, recognizable boundaries, and rules about membership. With the addition of ethnicity to the mix of defining characteristics, this kind of speculation stops just short of the belief that before AD 1000 the littoral peoples were well on their way to becoming the kind of nation-states that emerged elsewhere in Europe only many centuries later. Available evidence, however, is too meager to demonstrate firstly the existence of developmental processes of any kind. One conclusion that can be drawn with some certainty is that the eastern littoral of the Baltic Sea after AD 500 was becoming an area of substantial internal differentiation and, as such, deserved to be described with a much more variegated nomenclature than outsiders, such as the classical writers and later travelers, were inclined to use. What this differentiation would lead to several centuries later is a question that must be answered by sources from that later period.

The available population figures for the eastern Baltic littoral during the century just before AD 1000 are all estimates based mostly on a calculation of persons per square kilometer. The approximate tenth-century populations of present-day areas are as follows: Estonia 150,000, Latvia 220,000, and Lithuania 280,000. There is no methodology for disaggregating these numbers for the subpopulations – the tribal societies – of each area. The three areas then had the same position in a comparative hierarchy as they do today: the Estonian area was the smallest, and the Lithuanian area the largest. These societies were entirely rural with no urban centers in the true sense of the term, though the predominant settlement pattern was village-like concentration interspersed with single-household settlements. Overall population density was low, and large forested stretches covered the unpopulated territory.

Food was obtained through cultivation of crops, hunting, beekeeping, and fishing, and the proliferation of tools, weapons, jewelry, and woven cloth suggests the presence of artisans of various kinds. Dwellings continued to be constructed of wood as in earlier times, and protective stockades surrounding them suggest a persisting fear of raids by neighbors and outside marauders. Hillforts had become a common and hardier form of protection, some of them being large enough to accommodate many people in times of trouble. Some fortified settlements were built on lakes with the surrounding water serving as a barrier against outsiders. The clearing of forest land was a continuous activity and yielded new farm fields for cultivation. No wheeled vehicles of any kind were in use, and roads were for the most part tracks created by continuous use. The fastest and most efficient internal movement took place on navigable rivers.

To gain a sense of population development over time, we must resort to models offered by historical demographers for societies of this kind, since there is no direct evidence. Natural population increase in these

1 Hillforts at (a) Lielauce, Latvia, (b) Otepää, Estonia, and
(c) Daubariai, Lithuania. Several hundred such hillocks dot the
eastern Baltic littoral, most of them sites of pre-Christian
hillforts and most still untouched by the hands of archeologists.

1 (cont.)

tribal societies was slow: both infant and adult mortality were high; periodic epidemics, warfare, and food shortages wiped out most of the population gains during a preceding longer period of peaceful development. As a consequence, life expectancy at birth would have been rather low, in the range of 35–40 years. Survival beyond infancy, however, meant that adults could live into their sixth and seventh decades. Rapid population increase in any given area within one generation could come only through in-migration, if new settlers were accepted and integrated into the existing population.

Since archeologists have sufficient confidence in their findings to propose boundaries for these tribal societies, the question arises of whether these "boundaries" were in any sense fixed in the modern sense. It is likely that they were not, since the people living within them had neither standing armies nor border guards to defend them. Boundaries are the creation of scholars looking backwards in time, rather than realities with which contemporaries had to reckon. More than likely these demarcated territories had core settlements, but the regions lying beyond the core, populated or not, were always open to raids and possibly to permanent occupation by strangers. Such dangers are testified to by the proliferation of fortifications of various kinds throughout the littoral, as well as by the fact that the mention by name of these societies in contemporary sources almost always takes place when they are being raided or are themselves raiders. The residents of these demarcated areas lived in constant danger from "outsiders," who were not necessarily people who spoke a different language. There was, in other words, no absolute guarantee against depredations by aggressive bands speaking the same language as those people they attacked. These dangers of everyday life should not lead to the conclusion that the tribal societies of the littoral were unusually warlike; in fact, only a few of them are noted in contemporary sources as being particularly belligerent. The Couronians used the Baltic Sea for piracy and long-distance raiding of settlements on the island of Gotland and mainland Sweden; and in Russian chronicles Lithuanian tribes are described as fierce. But the us/them dichotomy was flexible. Speaking a Baltic language was no safeguard against being raided by other Balts, and the Balts did not exhibit any particularly marked animosity toward Finnic-speaking peoples or Slavs. Prowess, might, and avarice were demonstrated not along language lines but against neighbors whoever they happened to be.

We cannot properly speak of "decentralization" of power in the littoral because that concept implies an earlier initial condition in which the opposite was the case. The littoral had never had a King Alfred (as in England) who in any sense united the tribal societies against an "outside" foe; the area was fragmented from the time its components began to be named. There were, however, political leaders and some degree of social stratification. In the chronicle sources of the thirteenth century these facts emerged in the use of such Latin terms as *seniores* (elders) and *rex* (king), making it plausible that similar differentiation among people existed even before the start of the second millennium. The chronicle sources used such terms most often in describing negotiations and warfare, and they generally do not dwell on what rights and responsibilities these leaders had among those they led. Nor do the sources describe any specific instruments through which leaders exercised their power or the geographical extent of their authority. Such information must be inferred from their structural positions. Also, in the last centuries of the first millennium, such leaders remain nameless; leaders are referred to by name only in the chronicle sources several centuries later. Thus, leaders remain something of a mystery; they existed, but whether they were elected (as among Germanic tribes to the south) or rose to prominence through lineage membership or intimidation is impossible to say.

Direct evidence from archeological findings in gravesites attests to the social strata in these societies. Some corpses were buried with many more material possessions than were others, some graves were set apart from other graves. Somewhat less direct is the evidence about the placement of housing: some homes in a community were built upon hills while others were concentrated at lower levels. Since the word "stratification" implies an ongoing process, even if available archeological evidence is from points in past time, it is plausible that differentiation by wealth was continuous. Strictly speaking, the evidence from burial sites – with some individuals having more and better quality weapons and jewelry buried with them – tells us only that at the moment of death they had more material possessions than others did, but that practice was common enough elsewhere for the inference to be drawn for the Baltic littoral as well. The evidence about housing is ambiguous because not all uncovered sites had the higher/lower distribution of residences; some of these tribal societies were likely to have been markedly stratified while others remained less differentiated.

Social distinctions based on material wealth could not have been great, because there is no evidence that in these societies, which operated close to a subsistence level, there was much accumulated wealth of any kind. Since the population was not divided between urban and rural, no urban places existed where wealth could be generated faster. Wealth differences among individuals do not immediately suggest social strata, because high status – the position of chieftain, or shaman, or elder, or rich person – could have lasted for only the lifetime of the particular person. We do not know about inheritance practices in these societies, and therefore whether wealth and prestige could have accumulated over several generations in a single family. Also, fixed and long-term social strata would have been vulnerable to sudden changes of fortune in societies as numerically small as these, where misfortune could plunge an entire society into relative poverty.

Such quibbles about social stratification, however, are not an argument for an undifferentiated social life, because there is plenty of evidence for considerable specialization of skills and for the presence of persons with special talents in metalworking, construction, and jewelry making; in short, those with the skills necessary to create the caches of material goods found in gravesites. These were skills that could be taught within families to the next generation. Extensive occupational differentiation, however, would have been something of a luxury for societies of this size; most individuals had to be successful farmers as well as, for example, skilled metalworkers, excellent beekeepers, and, when the situation required, good soldiers or even military leaders. The extent to which such markers of high status as titles were recognized throughout an entire population is also unknown, as well as whether the authority of, say, a military leader persisted over any length of time.

Finally, can change in these tribal societies be discerned to have a distinct trajectory? The available archeological evidence is at the individual case level from moments in past time: a skeleton with all his or her trappings buried at a specific moment in a specific place; a collection of unearthed wooden building materials that may have comprised a hillfort; the mention in a chronicle of a collective name of a people. To identify change as having taken place, each of these items has to be given an approximate date and be arrayed according to a timeline. All in all, the evidence for constant change is considerable because we can make a fairly educated guess about what the members of these societies ate and what they hunted, how large they were, what they built their homes from, how they decorated themselves, what tools and weapons they used, with whom they traded, what crops they grew, and whether they moved from place to place. Using the longest possible frame of reference, we can identify a long-term pattern of change that transformed these populations from hunter-gatherers to settled agriculturalists, from wood users to users of bronze and of iron. The shorter term is the more serious problem as we seek to discern a direction of change within the two or three hundred of years around the year AD 1000. Change in these centuries appears to have been more accumulative than developmental: more people and hence greater population density, more hillforts, more of the same kinds of weapons and decorations, of the same kinds of crops, and of trade in the same kinds of goods. Generally speaking, at some point quantitative socioeconomic change can become qualitative and a society can turn into what it had not been before. Had that happened or was that happening in the centuries surrounding the start of the second millennium? The evidence is ambiguous, and we may never know. What we do know is that change of the qualitative sort had happened a long time ago in other parts of the European continent, producing there societies that were developing in distinct ways. They had become more populous, more organized economically and politically; they had adopted belief systems in which territorial largeness and possession of land were considered absolute goods; these belief systems also encouraged expansion for various purposes: adventure, domination of others, conversion of others to new beliefs, the accumulation of wealth through trade and rivalry. These societies had a certain kind of militancy that went beyond mere exploration, commerce, and robbery; sometimes heavenly rewards were promised to those who carried out their mission successfully.

The tribal societies of the eastern Baltic littoral held few such beliefs, or at any rate beliefs that would have introduced into their behavior any major expansionist motives. They might have raided their neighbors, but only to return to their home settlements with booty; some might have moved to new areas and thus transgressed against understandings about such borders as did exist. But unending repetition of these activities did not result in the territory of these tribal societies growing in size. In the centuries surrounding AD 1000, however, the eastern Baltic littoral became increasingly an object of interest to those European societies in which expansion had become normal behavior.

BELIEFS AND BELIEF SYSTEMS

The recurring problem of lack of sources is only slightly less troublesome in the search for direct evidence about the belief systems of the littoral's tribal societies in the time around AD 1000. By definition, beliefs do not leave material traces when they lose their hold over the imagination; they simply disappear. Belief systems also change over time. What is known about the beliefs of the littoral peoples has had to be extracted from later chronicles by writers who were Christians intent on demonstrating the absurd ideas of the previously pagan peoples now under their tutelage, and by clergymen writing even later in time and complaining about "survivals" of paganism in their congregations. All this then has to be projected backwards in time. Another layer of information of somewhat dubious value came from the enthusiastic nationalists of the nineteenth and twentieth centuries (see chapter 6). These authors replaced the condemnatory description of the earlier Christian commentators with celebratory accounts of pre-Christian belief systems, complete with pantheons of gods and a priesthood whose center was supposed to be a place called Romove in the Lithuanian lands. These extravagant nationalistic imaginings were particularly marked among some Latvian and Lithuanian intellectuals, who were also greatly impressed by the size of the territory over which traces of Baltic-language place-names and hydronyms were to be found. They thought that it was only logical that this far-flung Baltic cultural space also must have had a mighty philosophical and religious system within it. The oral tradition – containing the Lithuanian *dainos* and Latvian *dainas*, both being types of folk poetry – was mined for pure examples of what the "ancient" Balts had believed. Few such claims, however, were made by Estonian nationalists during and after the nineteenth century; even in the earlier Christian centuries commentary about the paganism of the Estonian population was much more muted than for the Baltic-language regions of the littoral.

A decision to avoid anachronistic claims thus leaves relatively little direct evidence about the religious-philosophical beliefs of the littoral inhabitants in the centuries before AD 1000. Yet we have to assume they did exist. These tribal societies, which had identifiable occupations, an organized economy, and the capability of defending themselves, would have been strange indeed if these features were not accompanied by notions about the great dualities of all societies: good and evil, sacred and profane, life and death, justice and injustice, nature and the supernatural, sickness and health, justice and injustice, self and other, friend and enemy.

Looking backwards, specialists agree that such beliefs and belief systems were probably suffused with animism: the conviction that each visible and invisible object contained a unique spiritual force that added to its nature a dimension that was imperceptible to the human senses. Animism contained a reverential attitude toward the natural world and manifested itself in diverse acts of placatory worship of natural objects – trees, animals, rivers – with the use of foodstuffs and other small and sometimes valuable offerings. The spirits of nature could be made less threatening by such acts of obeisance, which would make the efforts of human beings less likely to fail. The spirit world was omnipresent in the natural world and through that in the world of human beings as they interacted with the natural world. These approachable spirits were sometimes likened to human parents: before plowing, the plowman thanked an "earth mother," to protect the home from destruction in storms, one called upon the goodwill of the "thunder father." A worshipful attitude toward the fathers and mothers of the natural world evidently led to cults for some of them, because the spirit world was understood to have its own hierarchy. Spirits could be disembodied, but could at times take corporeal form as well. There were guardian spirits of the home and hearth, and some animals – such as snakes – could embody a spiritual force. Spirits departed when the body died, and some anecdotal evidence in chronicles tells of dismemberment of enemies to ensure that their spirits could not return to their bodies.

Later chronicle sources also tell of special persons who had the power to intercede with the spirit world on behalf of other human beings, but it is unlikely that these persons were anything like the organized priesthood that was portrayed by nineteenth-century nationalists. People thought to have special powers were venerated as individuals but not as a caste. The presence of shamans, magicians, and healers of various kinds is an entirely credible assumption; other societies with animistic beliefs had them. There were also special places for worship and sacrifice – sacred groves and large stones in the fields. These groves were sometimes believed to be the permanent homes of certain kinds of spirits. There is, however, no evidence from archeological sites that these venues for worship and sacrifice ever became enclosed structures such as churches or temples, or that worship as such ever assumed a permanently communal form.

At the highest reaches of the supernatural world there were gods, some of whom retained a connection to particular natural phenomena while others embodied more abstract notions such as fate and fortune. These deities with interventionist capabilities could be persuaded by appropriate rituals to affect human affairs positively or at least refrain from damaging them. But such interventions evidently left plenty of room for human decision and exercise of will. It is very much an open question whether the belief in "gods" included a belief in a single supervisory figure or was polytheistic. Folk beliefs in Lithuanian communities much later in time apparently did include a supervisory god – *Dievas* – while in the Latvian territory, again much later, there was a similar figure with a similar name – *Dieviņš* – who was almost always referred to by the diminutive form of his name and was believed to take human form as a beneficent and stooped old man looking over the fields. Though ninteenth-century nationalists conjured up a "Baltic pantheon" of gods – a veritable Olympus – there is no evidence that the gods of the littoral peoples had anything like the natures of the rollicking deities of ancient Greece. The peoples of the Estonian areas may not have had any such gods at all, and the one Estonian-area "god" mentioned in the later chronicles – *Tarapitha* – remains a somewhat shadowy figure of uncertain function.

How exactly belief in the spirit world and in gods of various kinds translated into moral codes, at either the personal or collective level, also remains an open question. Rules laying down what constituted good or bad behavior may have been anchored in the world of spirits and deities, or they could have been generated by social experience over time: which of these was the case, or whether both of these domains were a combined source of behavioral norms, we do not know. Nor is anything known about sanctions visited upon transgressors of common morality. Although the concepts of "hell" or "eternal damnation" do not appear to have existed, burial customs do testify to a belief in an afterlife of some kind. Graves frequently contained material objects – weapons, jewelry, and foodstuffs – meant to be used in the hereafter. In the Baltic-language areas (as distinct from the Finnic ones), the gods do not appear to have a frightening or judgmental aspect. Even though they are portrayed as being "in charge" of various parts of the natural world, their responsibilities evidently did not include direct supervision of human relationships. Perhaps behavioral norms at the personal and collective level arose principally from the recognition of what was needed for individual and collective survival in a relatively harsh world.

Among the many unclear questions concerning beliefs around the year AD 1000 are those relating to their distribution and generational transmission. In other words, they have to be placed squarely in the changing social context of beliefs among believers about whom we also know precious little. Most frequently, beliefs and belief systems of the littoral have been investigated as generalized features of two large culture-complexes – the Baltic and the Finnic – with these complexes conceptualized as standing above the fray of everyday social life. As a research strategy, this approach has the advantage of simplifying the task, but it does not go far in explaining how beliefs informed action. The Baltic-area littoral was a region of many different tribal societies, human groupings in a constant process of change, some of which may have been transformatory and some not. There was no doubt communication between and among the peoples of these societies; they were not hermetically sealed against outside influences.

Does that mean that they drew from a common stock of beliefs and a common set of behavioral norms – the Balts from theirs and the Finnic peoples from another? This does not seem likely, given the absence of a littoral-wide priestly caste to systematize beliefs and of religious institutions to disseminate them across the land. The existing information from chronicle sources later in time suggests that beliefs were highly individualized, though perhaps not unique to each location. Some trees, such as the oak, appear to have been venerated by the Balts generally, but many other natural objects had sacred qualities attached to them in some places but not in others. The Balts, as noted, had a panoply of gods, while the Finnic peoples seem to have had relatively few. Later sources also leave the strong impression that the tribal societies fought against each other more for material purposes, such as territory or booty, rather than in order to impose their beliefs on neighboring societies.

We assume that these beliefs and belief systems changed as they moved through historic time, which poses the problem of the generational transmission of information and knowledge in non-literate societies. The littoral had no collections of sacred writings from which each new generation could continue to draw beliefs, which means that there must have existed some mechanism for transmitting such information orally. Undoubtedly this was so, otherwise we have to believe that each generation invented new gods and new beliefs. The world of nature staying the same suggests that characterizations of natural forces and explanations for them would have also remained more or less unchanged over the generations. But later chronicle sources also depict sacred knowledge as being the monopoly of special individuals; such knowledge, in other words, was not public knowledge. Some beliefs therefore were passed on through the normal processes of socialization: children learned from parents about the spirit world that existed within each visible or audible phenomenon, and about how to behave in concert with it.

Cures, incantations, proper forms of obeisance and propitiation, however, were more specialized forms of information and had to be taught directly by one individual to another. There is no mention in later chronicle sources of these processes of learning; even if some wise persons were accredited with special powers, it is not at all clear that these folk had apprentices. Orally transmitted information and knowledge, as a corpus, undoubtedly changed somewhat in the process of reaching a new generation. Some beliefs fell by the wayside as outmoded, some were simply forgotten, some were learned in altered form. New beliefs could be created when the necessity arose and new phenomena had to be explained in terms of existing understandings. Thus, the beliefs of the Baltic littoral peoples reported in chronicles of the thirteenth and fourteenth centuries cannot stand unquestioned as the beliefs they had eight to ten generations earlier.

INTEREST IN THE EASTERN BALTIC LITTORAL

The growing frequency of references to the Baltic littoral in classical and postclassical writings as well as archeological finds attest to a growing interest in the Baltic Sea region among contemporaries during the centuries after AD 500. Roman coins were brought from the empire to the Baltic shores either by traders from there or by intermediaries; the largest hoards, however, have been found in the *southern* littoral – in the region that later became East Prussia – rather than in the *eastern*. The southern shore was the source of Baltic amber, a commodity highly valued by the Greeks (who called it *electron*) and by the Romans and the Byzantines. The "amber routes" of traders stretched over land, through what later became Russia and Poland, but also up rivers to the seacoast.

To portray these trading activities as absolutely the first contact between the littoral and the "outside world," however, would not be precise, because the peoples of the Baltic littoral by AD 500 must have been used to incursions by "foreigners" from every direction, given the migrations characteristic of the area. Traders were simply one of many different kinds of in-wanderers, with the main difference being that some in-wanderers came and stayed while the traders came and left. It is probably also an exaggeration to talk of systematic "trading relationships" between the littoral and the "outside," because the arrival of the traders was sporadic and unpredictable rather than regular and systematic.

If traders became an unremarkable part of littoral life as the millennium wore on, so did armed raids for the purposes of plunder and pillage. The sagas of the Scandinavian Vikings of the ninth century mention incursions affecting mainly the peoples whose territories lay along the Baltic coast – Couronians, Livonians, Estonians, and to a lesser extent the land-bound Semigallians. Even though the saga stories describe some raids as aiming permanently to subjugate the defeated localities, it was primarily plunder and not long-term Viking settlements that resulted. Moreover, territorial conquest – an early form of colonization – would have necessitated subsequent administrative structures, for which the Vikings had neither the taste nor the manpower. A much more profitable arrangement was the payment of tribute, which was the aim of incursions from the early Rus' principalities lying to the east. From these state-lets – Polotsk, Pskov, and Novgorod – raids were made into the territories of the Estonians, Latgalians, and Livonians, with longer-term tributary relationships developing between the rulers of these littoral territories and the Rus'ian states. Trade was not precluded, of course, but these relationships were a substitute for annexation and the need for subsequent administration. In the west, however, the Vikings appeared to have had no such plans. They did, however, use the rivers of the eastern Baltic littoral as pathways to points farther east, which was easily done without engendering conflict with the tribal societies whose territories bordered the rivers. By contrast, the Rus'ian peoples had no interest at this juncture and perhaps insufficient resources to try to penetrate to the very shores of the Baltic Sea from an easterly direction.

A precise chronology of these diverse trading and raiding events is difficult to establish, but it is fairly certain that their frequency grew with every century after the mid-millennium. By the ninth and tenth centuries, the peoples of the eastern littoral had to have incorporated into their view of the world the knowledge that their own societies existed among many other similar entities populated by practitioners of different customs, who venerated different gods and spoke different languages. It was also quite evident that these "foreigners" were much more intent on extending their influence to the littoral than the littoral peoples were on expanding theirs. Though Couronians launched raids against Gotland in the Baltic Sea and even against seacoast settlements on the Scandinavian peninsula, and Estonians sent raiding parties into Slavic territories to the east, none of these adventures entailed using a military strategy as a stepping-stone to territorial control or stepwise further incursions. The favored pattern for the littoral peoples was incursion–plunder–withdrawal, whereas the surrounding societies – especially those to the west and southwest – showed clear signs of wanting to convert incursions into something more by the end of the millennium.

To understand why this was so, we need to have a brief look at what had transpired in Scandinavia and western Europe during the centuries after AD 500. The "time of the Vikings" had come and gone in the Scandinavian lands by AD 1000. Their raids and exploratory voyages had taken them to North America, the western European seacoast, and across the eastern Baltic littoral into the Rus'ian lands. The causes of their "sudden" appearance were numerous and they certainly included internal conflicts and the love of adventure and plunder. But above all there was a rapidly growing population, which meant that the Viking departure from their homelands had more the character of an expansion. Viking ships from the Norwegian territories took the so-called outer passage, raiding Scotland, Ireland, and France and even reached North America. The Danes followed the middle passage, raiding the British Isles, France, and the Low Countries; the Swedes headed across the Baltic Sea (the "eastward passage"), through the Baltic littoral into lands farther east and eventually into the Byzantine Empire. The end product of these excursions from the sixth to the tenth century was mixed: new territories were settled (especially in the Rus' lands), considerable fear was instilled in the affected indigenous peoples, but colonies did not develop in the sense of conquered territory administered by and beneficial to the various Viking homelands. Where the Vikings settled, they eventually merged with the indigenous population. By the tenth century, the population pressures in the homelands had eased, and the outward movements ceased.

The influences flowing from these adventures were not unidirectional, because through them other European peoples became increasingly acquainted with the northern lands from whence the Vikings had come. These were pagan lands, arousing the keen interest of the church; the first strong ties with Christian Europe were established in Swedish lands in the ninth century. By that time, politics in the Scandinavian kingdoms also had become more stable, and local dynasties produced a series of strong rulers who were able to defend their homelands against predators and develop something like national policy. Christian conversion in the Danish lands made substantial headway under Harald II (Bluetooth) and Sven I (Forked-beard) in the tenth century, and the conversion of Canute II (the Great) in the first half of the eleventh century completed the process. In the Swedish lands, Olaf Skutkoning, whose reign spanned the late tenth and early eleventh century, was the first Christian ruler, and all his successors stayed in the faith. Full Christianization came to Norway only in the eleventh century, when Olaf II (St. Olaf) completed the task.

Two things should be noted: first, the Scandinavian lands joined Christian Europe without experiencing the occupation of foreign armies and the armed imposition of a new faith; and second the christianization of Scandinavia, from the point of view of the existing Christian states and the church, represented a successful expansion and heightened their interest in the remaining "pagan" peoples of the European north. The inclusion of the Scandinavian lands into Christian Europe, however, did not engender pacific behavior, but just the opposite. The Scandinavians themselves, particularly the Danes and the Swedes, continued their earlier interest in the eastern Baltic littoral, but now they had additional motives for their expansionist efforts. Also, with internal consolidation and strong monarchical leaders, the Scandinavian lands continued to push against each other, as they sought to enlarge the territories under their control. They also had to ward off the efforts of the western Europeans who pressed northward as they followed christianization with attempts at political control. By the end of the eleventh century the Scandinavian states resembled the rest of Christian Europe: internally consolidated, with monarchical dynasties struggling to raise revenues to expand national governments and to retain their positions against power-hungry nobles; and with economies that were in the process of developing continuing long- and short-distance trade.

The christianization of the lands of western Europe, of course, had taken place much earlier; Gaul, for example, had been a part of the Roman Empire and had converted to Christianity when the empire became Christian. The collapse of the Roman Empire, which had been the most successfully expansionist power to date in the classical world, did not diminish the attractiveness of the idea that expanding control over new territories was an absolute good. The western European successor states, most notably the Carolingian Empire, continued their expansionary ways, but by the end of the ninth century Charlemagne had died and his empire had become divided into three parts among his sons, producing smaller though still energetic states. The royal dynasties in these states were to form France and the Holy Roman Empire of the Germans. Though nominally Christian (embracing the western variant of Christianity) these states competed fiercely with each other, and both were growing increasingly resentful of the efforts of the Roman papacy to be the overlord of all secular rulers.

Their development, however, did not follow a smooth path in the century approaching AD 1000. From the north, the Viking raids instilled fear, while in the east the empire of the Byzantines (the eastern half of the old Roman Empire) remained a rival of the western powers until it was overrun by Muslim armies. After considerable territorial gains that carried them into the Iberian peninsula, the Muslims succeeded to some extent in transforming the Mediterranean Sea into a "Muslim lake." By the tenth century, the European west had entered what was truly the "dark ages" by comparison with what had come before and what would come afterwards, and in sharp contrast with the admirable civilization of the Muslim territories. Domestically, the royal dynasties increasingly had to devolve authority to the powerful families in their realms: these were forming landowning nobilities whose support monarchs needed for governance and military adventures. The overall victor in this decline of secular power was the papacy, which, as an international institution, was concerned less with the territorial success of particular dynasties and more with the territorial spread of Christianity. The efforts of the church in the Scandinavian territories had been just one manifestation of this concern.

The eleventh century witnessed the beginnings of a reversal in the fortunes of the European west. A century of weak (though never totally absent) economic activity was replaced by growth, and population increase became a constant. In those regions where they had gone into a decline, cities and towns began to revive, with their associated economic and trading activity. Royal dynasties started to reassert themselves against their own landowning nobilities, against the encroachments of papal power, and against each other. Several centuries of decentralization were difficult to overcome quickly, but the trend was quite clear. The feudal bond – which tied powerful landowners to the king and to each other in a hierarchical fashion – remained strong but was not inviolable; and the seemingly eternal manorial system with its enserfed peasants could not be changed overnight, but could accommodate new forms of economic activity, especially long- and short-distance trade.

Even though commercial activities continued to expand, control of land (and of the incomes deriving from land) remained the principal motivating force in the affairs between states. Such control could be obtained directly by conquest or indirectly through dynastic marriages, and the monarchs of the new burgeoning Europe used both methods. Since the papacy could not use either means directly, it sought to enlarge its control by employing its monopoly over the salvation of souls – those of kings, nobles, and commoners alike. It had had to accept the presence of an infidel Muslim empire to its immediate south, but it did not have to accept the continued existence of pagan peoples elsewhere on the European continent.

Then there were the Slavic peoples who resided south and east of the Baltic littoral territories. They had taken up permanent residence in these regions in the two centuries immediately following the collapse of the Roman Empire (traditionally dated at AD 476), and not much more is known about their political history in the subsequent period than is known about the Finnic and Baltic peoples to their north and west. At that time the Slavs were not unlike the peoples of the Baltic littoral: small tribal societies jostling for territory, some with strong leaders and others with weak. One strong leader emerged in the ninth century from among the Scandinavian Vikings, who had been making their way into this Slavic territory by means of the rivers crossing the Baltic littoral. Termed the Varangians in later chronicles of the area, some of them settled and came to dominate the existing populations; among them, the most successful leader was Rurik, who appears to have ruled the principality of Novgorod in the 860s and is considered the founder of the strongest of the Rus' dynasties. Rurik's dynasty supplied the Novgorod area with a series of strong and active rulers: Oleg in the early tenth century and Sviatoslav somewhat later, Vladimir in the decades straddling the year AD 1000, and Yaroslav later. None of these rulers, however, succeeded in uniting the eastern Slavs into a single state, though each brought something to the development of the lands they ruled directly. Under Oleg, the center of Rus' political activity moved to Kiev; Sviatoslav was perhaps the most successful militarily, expanding his power to the south; Vladimir was responsible for establishing Christianity among the eastern Slavs, patterned on the church of the Byzantine Empire. Generally, the Rus' principalities oriented themselves toward the Byzantines and thus grew in strength out of the reach of the western European powers and the western papacy.

The similarities between the Baltic littoral peoples and those of the Rus' territories, however, were less important than the differences. First, the Rus' principalities were larger territorially, and in the centuries around AD 1000 may have been experiencing considerable population growth. Second, their leaders were expansion-minded and hungry enough for new territory to do almost constant battle against each other and against peoples living to their east and south. Third, they managed to establish dynasties within which political power could be passed from one generation to the next, thus perpetuating legitimacy of domination. Even so, unifying statehood evaded these peoples; dynasties were no more than individual families who had achieved power for a time but could be replaced by others when weaknesses developed. Even the strong rulers had to attend constantly to the plotting of relatively wealthy and power-hungry rivals within their own territories who were beginning to form a permanent class of *boyars* always ready to challenge sitting rulers. A unified Russian state did not develop naturally; it had to be fought for and in fact did not form until much later in time.

It is puzzling why the Rus' principalities adjoining the lands of the peoples of the Baltic littoral did not try to move westward in a determined manner. Perhaps a simultaneous three-front expansion (east, south, and west) was beyond their power, and perhaps the three Baltic littoral peoples directly across the western borderlands – the Estonians, Latgalians, and Lithuanians – appeared too ready to defend themselves. Thus, the Rus' principalities (and the littoral peoples in turn) settled for the status quo that involved periodic raids against one another (some looking initially like, but proving not to be, expansionist efforts). The Latgalians for a while paid tribute to the *kniaz* (ruler) of Polotsk. Relationships of other kinds continued throughout this period of military skirmishing: the Latgalians, for example, had their first experience of Christianity through missionaries from the Rus' principalities, and trading activity, while interrupted periodically, was never entirely extinguished. When at the end of the twelfth century more determined foreigners arrived from the west, the peoples of the Baltic littoral initially had no reason to think of them as anything other than yet a further troublesome group of in-wanderers.

2

The new order, 1200–1500

During the second half of the twelfth century, several interrelated chains of events transformed the eastern Baltic littoral thoroughly enough to produce what might be called a new order. The transformation, which involved western Europeans coming and staying in the littoral, did not take place overnight; in fact, it unfolded over a century and a half. To understand it properly, we have to step away from simplified models of what happened and consider the events in all their complexity. By the twelfth century, the peoples of the littoral had been familiar with strangers in their midst at least since the ninth century, when the Vikings were using the littoral waterways to travel east into the territories of the Rus'. Traders from the west and the east had come and gone, as had Christian missionaries from the lands of the Rus'. How these "others" had been incorporated into the worldview of the indigenous peoples we do not know, but the arrival of the German crusaders and traders could hardly have seemed like an unusual occurrence. Nor would their militancy have seemed extraordinary, at least initially. After all, the tribal societies of the littoral were themselves hardly peaceful and innocent farmers: for centuries they had raided and pillaged one another's territories, and taken captives and slaves. None of these forays had been manifestations of a determined expansionism, save perhaps those of the Lithuanians into adjacent eastern lands. But it would be a mistake to think of indigenous violence as purely defensive or retaliatory; indeed, it seems to have been a standard part of everyday life in the littoral. Hillforts were, after all, a favored form of settlement in the region.

The fact that the littoral peoples were not Christians even at this late date would alone not have been sufficient cause for attracting outsiders to the area. Although the Christian church in western Europe had motivated people from all socioeconomic levels to go on crusades of various kinds, the papacy and the secular rulers of the west were already involved in ongoing struggles for power among themselves. The desire to "christianize pagans" was only part of this larger conflict. By the eleventh century, the Christian west was surrounded by practitioners of "false" faiths – to the east, the heretical Orthodox, who owed their allegiance to Constantinople and not Rome; to the south, the Muslim kingdoms of the Iberian peninsula, North Africa, and the Middle East. Moreover, the popes and the nominally Christian rulers of western European states were each chafing under the others' claims to territorial supremacy; dangerous secularist elements were emerging in western European society in the form of cities that valued and sought to enlarge new forms of wealth (money instead of land); and the same Christian rulers were set on enlarging their own territories at the expense of their neighbors in a kind of giant zero-sum game. While the continuing presence of pagans in the northeastern corner of Europe would have been an irritant to the faithful, the latter most decidedly had other agendas, including personal ones, when they looked at the Baltic littoral and its peoples.

What they saw there was a vacuum of power. By the second half of the twelfth century, none of the indigenous tribal societies had emerged as dominant; none was sufficiently populous or predatory to want to lay claim to such a status in the near future. There were no powerful leaders bent on unifying their people as a first step toward domination of others. The littoral societies were not defenseless but were a tempting target for those outsiders who had already learned in their own geographical contexts how to obtain and wield power for personal, dynastic, or political purposes. In the second half of the twelfth century when the first western Christian missionaries arrived in the Baltic littoral, they perhaps unwittingly encouraged others for whom territorial conquest and the saving of souls were two sides of the same coin.

CHRISTIANS, TRADERS, AND CRUSADERS

The second half of the twelfth century marked the beginning not only of the continuous inflow to the eastern Baltic littoral of outsiders from central Europe. Also for the first time the history of the region can be described narratively with sequenced events, verifiable dates, and identifiable actors. The selfsame outsiders brought about this narrative – specifically, those few among them who wished to memorialize their victory over the Baltic-area pagans: Henry of Livonia and his *Chronicle*, which covered the events up to about 1230; the anonymous author of the *Livonian Rhymed Chronicle*, which covered the story to almost the end of the thirteenth century; the leaders among the victors who signed agreements detailing how the spoils should be distributed. Much of what we know precisely therefore is history written by victors, by those for whom the ultimate outcome was a sure sign that God was on their side. The voices of the losers were not represented in these stories because they did not write, and their reactions must be inferred from their behavior during the extended decades of subjugation.

The story has inauspicious beginnings as seen from the outsiders' viewpoint. Isolated instances of relatively restricted missionary efforts by the western churchmen began early: in the Lithuanian lands in the early eleventh century, in the land of the Couronians late in that century, and in the Estonian territory in the 1160s. All these forays came to naught. So almost did the efforts of two monks who used a water route – the prominent Daugava River – as their entryway into the littoral: an Augustinian named Meinhard in the 1180s and a Cistercian named Berthold in the 1190s. They worked among the Livs (or Livonians), who were only minimally receptive to their missionizing. Meinhard at least built a church in Ikšķile, some forty miles upriver from the mouth of the Daugava, having spent considerable time among the Livs. Berthold, however, was killed in a skirmish with the Livs soon after his arrival. Both of these pioneers had been given the title of Bishop of Livonia by the papacy which had approved their missions. The title clearly underlined the seriousness of the effort because at that moment the church had no flock to be tended nor territory to be claimed. These two thrusts into the littoral resembled more the earlier failed attempts than what was to come.

They were not even as successful as the conversion efforts of the Orthodox missionaries in the far eastern Latgalian territories of the littoral, where some of the local chieftains had already been converted, though perhaps not permanently.

The determination of the western effort became apparent in 1199–1200 with the arrival in the Daugava beachhead of Albert of Buxhoevden. A native of the German city of Bremen, Albert had received the title of third Bishop of Livonia from Pope Innocent III as well as the right to carry out his activities under the rubric of a Baltic crusade. He was clearly a strategist of a kind his predecessors had not been. His missionary activities were supported by a force of initially 23 and later 500 Saxon soldiers. Recognizing the strategic vulnerability of the Ikšķile location, he persuaded the Livs closer to the mouth of the Daugava to grant him permission (in 1201) to build a city – Riga, only ten miles upriver from the Daugava's mouth. Immediately construction of a kind of headquarters began there. Riga became a fortified place and a site from which expansion could be launched in all directions. Albert's second-in-command – Brother Theodoric – was as energetic as his master, being responsible for turning Albert's military contingent (both the original and later arrivals) into a crusading order called the Swordbrothers (more formally, the Order of the Knights of Christ – *fratres militae Christi)*, who were to follow the rule of the Templars. Grants of local land, wrested from the Livs, to these soldier-monks followed with dispatch.

Pope Innocent III also permitted the small merchant contingent among Riga's inhabitants to establish monopoly rights over trade moving along a substantial length of the Daugava. In short, Albert and his retinue – in which the clerical, commercial, and military elements were neatly combined – behaved from the start as though they already were masters of the territories into which they had just recently arrived. The response of the Livs – and it was only they with whom the outsiders were dealing in these early stages – was ambiguous. There was some armed resistance that was put down easily. But the Livs did not speak with a single voice in such dealings and negotiations. Moreover, Albert's forces used any means necessary – including hostage-taking, threats, bribery, and lies – to consolidate their presence.

2 Bishop Albert, depicted in a stained-glass window in the Dome Cathedral in Riga, Latvia. Albert was the first successful colonizer of the northern part of the Baltic littoral and the founder of the city of Riga.

At this juncture the newcomers had a choice: to launch out in all directions, since their now-fortified center of Riga was surrounded by pagan lands and pagan populations, or to follow a stepwise strategy of conquest. They chose the latter and set out to subdue the Livs completely. Albert's forces had already succeeded in converting several Liv chieftains, who now became the crusaders' allies against other Liv tribes. Following the Daugava inland, the crusaders

3 Pope Innocent III (1198–1216). Innocent saw crusades
against the Baltic littoral pagans as one method among many for
expanding papal power on the European continent. Fresco by
Maestro Canxulo from the second half of the thirteenth century,
Church of the Sacro Speco, Subiaco, Italy.

did battle against Liv settlements and hillforts until, by 1206, they
controlled both banks of the river. Each victory was followed by
conversion activities, the building of a church in the locality just
conquered, and the addition of the territory to the bishop's domains.
The thrust of the crusaders' drive continued in northeastern, eastern,
and southeastern directions. They progressively subdued resistance
in the rest of the Liv territories in the north, successfully occupied the
lands of the Selonians that lay south of the Daugava, and then moved
into the lands of the Latgalians immediately east of the Liv territories
and north into Estonian territory as well. The responses of the
indigenous societies to this drive varied: despite resistance, which

was overcome militarily, along the way the crusaders successfully recruited fighters from among the defeated populations to do battle against their pagan brethren. At least one of the Selonian chieftains fled to the Rus' territories for protection. By early 1208, Pope Innocent III announced the christianization of all the Livs, as well as large portions of the other tribal societies east of Riga.

These victories cleared the way for a continuing advance with the intention of securing for German traders the entire Daugava up to the approaches of the Rus' principality of Polotsk. Once this was accomplished, a similar drive with mixed motives proceeded in the direction of the nothern Rus' principalities of Pskov and Novgorod. As the inhabitants of the intervening areas were subjugated, local chieftains and the populations loyal to them converted to western Christianity. During these early years of conquest, the territorial question remained tricky: native chieftains and their populations, of course, lost all rights of possession, but among the conquerors two powerful sets of interests – those of the church and of the Swordbrothers Order – were in direct competition for ultimate control over the newly acquired territories. Both institutions had participated in the conquest in their own way, and the order was nominally a creature of the church. For the moment, the warriors were satisfied with the formula devised to solve the problem: one-half of the new lands came under the direct control of Albert, one-half went to the order. Later this allocation formula was changed, and much of the church-controlled land in any case was immediately granted out as fiefs to warriors of the order. But the rapacity shown by both sides so early in the conquest remained a principal source of friction, even conflict, for the next several centuries, making it very difficult to separate religious, economic, and political motives for any action by either side. By the early 1220s the church and the order fully controlled all the littoral territory east of Riga up to the Rus' principalities.

The triumphalist chronicles saw the hand of God at work and on that basis portrayed the victories of the crusaders as inevitable. Unfortunately we know little about the thinking of the overrun societies or their leaders at the moments when they succumbed. There was, of course, resistance, often fierce, and most of the conversion activities appear to have happened after military defeats of the pagan side, which leaves open the question of how thorough such conversions were. Tribal armies composed of those who had not yet been subjugated even made preemptive attacks against the outsiders: in 1210, for example, a strong army of Couronians attacked Riga but failed to take it. The crusaders were determined to press on until strong and decisive resistance was encountered; absent such resistance, they continued the conquest. Their military prowess, superior arms, and determination proved decisive in most cases. Also, some pagans showed considerable opportunism when they enlisted on the side of the crusaders against their neighbors, as yet unconquered. Expediency, bewilderment, and resignation were much more in evidence than concerted and organized opposition.

The march of the crusaders into the Estonian lands underlines the need to revise the simple "us versus them" model of the conquest – pitting littoral peoples versus German crusaders – because against the Estonian tribal societies the crusaders were able to enlist many Livs and Latgalians in their military forces. What motivated the latter? It is hard to believe that they also thought themselves to be doing God's work, even if they were recent converts. The chronicle accounts suggest that this was payback for earlier Estonian raids against the Latgalians and Livs. In any event, for the Estonians the enemy thus included not only the German speakers from central Europe, but Finnic people (Livs) and Balts (Latgalians) as well. The drive into Estonia began as early as 1208 with an attack on Otepää fortress, located due north of the already conquered Latgalian lands. An unsuccessful attack in 1210 by Estonians on the crusader stronghold at Cēsis (Ger. *Wenden*) – in Latgalian territory – followed and then an Estonian victory over the order and its allies at Jumara in the same region. The crusaders counterattacked in 1211 by laying siege to the fortress of Viljandi, deep in Estonian territory, with the order emerging victorious. The Estonians counterattacked again, driving far south into Liv lands against the Turaida chieftaincy, with the intention of attacking Riga afterwards. This plan failed to work, the Estonians were stopped, and an armistice was arranged. Simultaneously with these battles, the Estonians had to face another enemy, this time from the east. The chieftains of the Rus' principalities of Novgorod and Pskov, seeking either to aid the Germans or to preempt them (the chronicle sources are not clear), or simply to seize territory while the Estonians were preoccupied, invaded the Estonian lands in 1210–1212 by both crossing and moving around the southern end of Lake Peipus.

After a respite of about four years, these back-and-forth military encounters in the Estonian lands resumed in 1215. Neither side won decisive victories but the order captured sufficient territory to establish permanent settlements for launching ever-deeper campaigns to the north. Some of this fighting had a naval component: contingents of the Estonian forces came from the island of Saaremaa to the mainland by boat, while others attempted to block the mouth of the Daugava by sinking large ships there. Still the order and its native allies persevered and completed the christianization of Ugandi and Sakala, the two large Estonian regions lying just north of the Liv and Latgalian territories. This mass conversion finally revealed the potential German menace to the Rus' principality of Pskov, which began a major campaign in the adjoining land of Ugandi. The crusaders responded, this time together with the (nominally) christianized southern Estonians as their allies, and stopped the advancing Rus' invaders in Otepää in 1217.

Even after a decade of fighting, the northern part of the Estonian lands remained beyond German control, permitting two other aspirants for a regional presence to try their luck. First the Danes, who had manifested some interest in Estonian territory even earlier, arrived in 1219 with a large naval contingent at the site of the later fortress of Tallinn. After fierce battles with the Estonian resisters, they essentially established a beachhead and attempted to christianize the nearby Estonians, thus preempting conversion at the hands of German crusaders. For a while the Danish presence appeared to be becoming permanent. Then, in the summer of 1220, a Swedish army invaded Läänemaa, the Estonian region on the Baltic coast; this was a complete fiasco, and the Swedish effort to plant their flag did not last beyond the end of the year. The victory against the Swedes energized the Estonians, who successfully confronted the Danes at Tallinn with new forces; the Danes in turn overplayed their hand by invading the island of Saaremaa. The two victories against the Scandinavians apparently persuaded chieftains of the Estonian lands that the earlier territorial gains by the order were reversible, and the year 1223 saw a general rising everywhere in the Estonian territories against the order and its allies. In this effort, the Estonians negotiated for help from the Rus' principalities of Vladimir-Suzdal and Novgorod, the armed forces of which, when they entered the fighting, turned out to be more interested in pillaging Estonian land than helping to oust the German crusaders. By the summer of 1224, resistance by the Estonian forces – with or without Rus' allies – had come to an end, with the hillfort at Tartu remaining the only mainland territory still not controlled by the order.

Tartu and its environs were subjugated by summer's end, and the crusaders and their allies moved on to the large coastal island of Saaremaa, where Estonian contingents were ready to continue fighting. Saaremaa was invaded in January 1227, when the Baltic Sea between the mainland and the island had a thick ice cover. By the end of spring, Saaremaa was also taken, finalizing the crusaders' conquest of the territories north and east of Riga and allowing them to turn their attention to the tribal societies west and south of the city – the lands of the Couronians, Semigallians, and the Lithuanian territories beyond.

Before describing these campaigns, however, some generalizations about the crusaders' successes thus far will be useful. The chronicles, as noted earlier, tell the story as the inevitable unfolding of God's will, with a few flattering observations about the military prowess of the pagans. The Christian chroniclers could afford to be magnanimous in their descriptions, since they believed the campaigns had an inevitable conclusion. Was the outcome inevitable, God's will or not? The imposition of a 'new order' was not without costs to the crusaders: most of the pagan societies did resist in one way or another, and military encounters, some bloodier than others, that are detailed in the chronicles up to the end of the 1220s numbered at least seventy-five (over a thirty-year period). Crusader victories can be ascribed to superior military technology only in part, because their opponents adopted some of the same techniques and instruments in the course of the fighting.

The ultimate defeats of the Livs, Latgalians, Selonians, and Estonians can be explained by another aspect of the confrontations: the crusaders were driven by an ideology – admittedly a mixed one – in which the object of the struggle was portrayed as control over the entire littoral, while most of the time the littoral peoples were each defending their own territories. Even the seemingly coordinated Estonian rising in 1223–1224 was short lived; previously, cooperation among the Estonian lands had been minimal, and their overall fragmentation did not lead to long-term common efforts, even when the enemy was obvious. Furthermore, the littoral peoples showed a continuing tendency to import long-standing mutual enmities into current battles: witness the seeming ease with which crusaders enlisted some Livs and Latgalians against the Estonians and the Estonian incursions into lands to the south. The crusaders knew how to exploit these differences and used them to their advantage. The pagans appealed to other outsiders – the Rus' principalities in particular – who should have seen the dangers to themselves of ultimate crusader victory. But these potential allies showed more interest in expanding their own territory or at least in looting their neighbors' lands. The Danes and the Swedes, already operating from Christian states, revealed their venality on Estonian territory even though ultimately their efforts came to naught. Finally, none of the chieftains on the pagan side had sufficient general standing to command an armed force other than their own, and this played into the hands of such masterminds as Albert and the military strategists of the Swordbrothers. The crusaders had a long-term plan to subjugate under the aegis of Christianity; the pagans did not. Even if the littoral peoples had been able to hold the crusaders at bay or expel them from their Riga stronghold, it is at least doubtful that the experience would have radically changed the indigenous organization of the region. More than likely, these tribal societies would have returned to the *status quo ante* and to the endemic antagonisms of earlier eras.

Bishop Albert died in 1229 with the christianization of the littoral still uncompleted. But he had supervised the subjugation of a major part of it, and the chroniclers of the times, even before his death, had begun to use the term "Livonia" for the entire territory, implying that subordination and christianization of the remaining pagans was just a matter of time. As it turned out, the time in question was at least another generation, because the Couronian, Semigallian, and Lithuanian tribal societies proved to be harder to overpower. From the west, the Couronian chieftains had continually harried the now-crusader territories, even taking to the sea to do so, and initially subordinating them less by warfare than by treaty seemed a possibility. Both methods were tried in the early 1230s, but treaty-making brought out the rivalry between the occupying powers: one treaty made by the order was abrogated by a representative of the papacy which wanted its own, and there followed more direct and more successful campaigns against the Couronians by the forces of the order. Couronian lands were perhaps the richest prize to date, since they extended south along the Baltic seacoast into present-day Lithuania. Here in the south the Swordbrothers suffered a decisive defeat at Saule in 1236 as they led their own army, together with newly christianized Couronians, into Lithuanian territory. The peoples of the Lithuanian lands, perhaps observing the successes of the order to the north, had generated the kind of unity of purpose and common leadership that the peoples in the north had not been able to marshal, and this led to their victory over the order at Saule.

At this juncture we will simply note the entrance of two new combatants into this seemingly perpetual state of war: the Lithuanian state and the Teutonic Order. The battle of Saule was qualitatively different from earlier conflicts because of the Lithuanian ability to unify. After the defeat, the Swordbrothers, now severely weakened, placed their organization into the hands of the Teutonic Order, which had been consolidating its position in the Prussian lands (on the southern littoral of the Baltic) since the late 1220s. Organizationally, the Swordbrothers were subsequently known as the "Livonian Order," a branch of the larger Teutonic Order. Thus replenished, the Livonian Order continued to fight against the Couronians, and, by 1253, both the church and the order had almost completed that task and agreed to divide the Couronian lands between them. The experience at Saule, however, persuaded the Livonian Order not to start driving farther south into the Lithuanian lands, leaving the better-placed Teutonic Order to carry out harrying raids from their Prussian headquarters into the borderlands of the Lithuanians. The Couronians in the southern reaches of their ancestral lands continued periodically to revolt against their new masters, which gave the Lithuanians of Žemaitija an opening to weaken the Livonian Order. The Žemaitians defeated the order once more in a major battle at Durbe in 1260 when the Couronians refused to help the order. Not until 1267 was the

Livonian Order able to impose its will on the entire Couronian territory with a treaty of final submission.

While fighting surrounded them, the Semigallians did not remain passive. The chronicles document raids against first the Swordbrothers and then the Livonian Order, and also against Riga from the 1220s onward. These actions bought time for the Semigallians but no permanent security. In the 1250s, the Livonian Order began to focus on the conquest of Semigallia, using its time-tried tactic of subjugating a section of new territory and building a fortified castle there, from which to launch further campaigns. Numerous such castles were built on Semigallian territory, the most important in 1256 on the site next to the Lielupe River where the city of Jelgava (Mitau) stands today. The fighting between the order and the Semigallians continued well into the 1280s, with the order taking the last of the Semigallian hillforts in 1290. A large number of Semigallians went south into exile to join the Lithuanians in their continuing opposition to the forces of christianization. With the taking of the Semigallian lands, the church, the Livonian Order, and the city of Riga became the principal power-brokers north of the Lithuanian territories. While doing battle against the pagans, all three had been consolidating control over their new holdings, becoming independent centers of jealously guarded political power. Thus defeat of the northern pagans did not end violence in the littoral. In the "Livonian Confederation," as the new state formation would now be called, the conflict shifted from Christian against pagan to a seemingly perpetual power struggle among three ostensibly Christian entities.

Henry's *Chronicle*, the *Livonian Rhymed Chronicle*, and the treaties distributing conquered territories document a long process that has been termed variously the "christianization" or "europeanization" of the northern part of the Baltic littoral. Not surprisingly, central Europeans were depicted as the principal actors in the Baltic-area drama, and indeed they now took centerstage. But at the same time the chronicles also document the northern littoral's tribal societies fading into the background; ironically this was also the first time that these societies – and especially their leaders – were identified as flesh-and-blood individuals who had names and performed deeds. Their emergence from the shadows into written history was very brief, however. The chronicle sources sought to give these vanquished peoples credit for bravery and resistance, despite far fewer names of the littoral chieftains being mentioned in the accounts than there actually were. We learn about Kaupo, the Liv chieftain of the land of Turaida, who linked his fortunes with the crusaders; and Dabrel, another Liv leader who is remembered by no more than a name. Visvaldis, the Latgalian chieftain of the land of Jersika, also made a brief appearance in Henry's *Chronicle*, and his descendants are thought to have assimilated to the German-speaking population. The Latgalian chief Viescekis of Koknese evidently went into exile in Novgorod when his territory was overrun. Other Latgalian leaders included Tālivaldis of the land of Tālava, who was killed by Estonians in 1224; Rūsiņš of the land of Satekle, who fell in battle in 1212; and Varidots of Autine, who disappeared in a raid in Estonian lands. Among Estonians named in Henry's *Chronicle* the most prominent chieftain was Lembit, the only one able briefly to rally the Estonian tribes against the crusaders; there was also his brother Unnepewe, and Vytames of the land of Sakala. From the Couronian chieftaincy only one name – Lamekin – is referred to in the chronicle, although there must have been others; and among Semigallians the chiefs Viestarts and Nameisis are also mentioned. In 1281 after the defeat that sent some of the Semigallians into exile, Nameisis joined them in the Lithuanian territories.

The chroniclers are uncertain as to what titles to give these leaders. King (*rex, konic, regulus*), duke (*princeps*), elder (*senior terre*), leader (*houbetman*), and military leader (*dux exercitus*) were somewhat fumbling attempts to fit western European concepts to forms of leadership the chroniclers did not quite understand. Common sense suggests that these chieftains and their predecessors must have worked their way into these positions by gaining the confidence of their fellows, but how exactly this happened remains unknown. The same goes for the territories they "ruled," which in the chronicles have little geographical specificity. Did the borders of these territories constitute demarcations their rulers were prepared to defend at all costs? Or did they simply designate territorial space to which the rulers laid claim? The chronicle sources suggest that these rulers were able to gather raiding bands and sometimes armed forces, hinting that followers temporarily subordinated their own interests to some idea of collective interest. But how deep and lasting this loyalty was remains a mystery, as does the question of how power passed between generations of rulers. By the twelfth century the dynastic principle had become a central feature of successful states in the western European kingdoms, providing continuity to the exercise of power and to the state itself. Yet dynasties of rulers seem to be absent in the littoral societies, or at least they were so rare as never to be mentioned in the sources; in any case, if there were local dynasties, they ended abruptly during the wars of the thirteenth century when leaders and their sons were killed or left the littoral. Perhaps the power these leaders exercised and their extraordinary personalities were what brought them briefly to the fore either as opponents or, sometimes, as collaborators of the crusaders.

THE LITHUANIANS AND THE TEUTONIC ORDER

After the Swordbrothers were annexed by the Teutonic Order in 1237 and renamed the Livonian Order, the tribal societies south of Semigallia justifiably felt even more threatened. The Lithuanian lands immediately adjoining Semigallia – Žemaitija and Aukštaitija – responded to this new situation by continuing to launch raids deep into the territories now controlled by the Livonian Order; on their side, the two orders – the Teutonic west of the Lithuanian territories and the Livonian branch to the north – tended to view these and other lands farther south as the same kind of pagan territory they had already conquered. But the Lithuanian region was in reality more challenging for the crusaders. It was less accessible to easy movements of raiding parties and armies – with more intervening swamps and forested areas and fewer flatlands. The Lithuanians had strongly signaled that they were more likely than the northern tribal societies to offer fierce and consistent opposition to incursions. Such opposition was the result of a development that had not been present in the north: the appearance of a state both inhabited and governed by Lithuanians. Here the subordination and christianization of indigenous political leaders and the elites who supported them was bound to be more problematic.

State formation anywhere is a long-term process, and the chronicles recounting events in the twelfth and thirteenth centuries do not offer much precise information on how it worked in the Lithuanian territories. The starting point was the same as in the lands to the north: mutually antagonistic tribal societies with political leaders who were capable of marshaling temporary military support for raids against each other and against vulnerable territories surrounding the Lithuanian region. Exactly how many such societies there were is not absolutely clear: in addition to the largest named regions, Žemaitija and Aukštaitija, there were lesser groupings within and outside of these. In 1219, a treaty signed with Volynia – an adjacent land to the south – had the signatures of what later historians designated as "twenty-one senior Lithuanian princes," none of whom was named as leader over the others. Evidently, the most successful effort to unify the territories these chieftains controlled into something like a state was led by the chieftain Mindaugas (ruled c.1253–1263) of the Aukštaitian region, who thus reenacted the unifying role of King Alfred the Great in England three centuries earlier. Mindaugas' efforts are said to have borne fruit during the third and fourth decades of the thirteenth century, just as the Swordbrothers finished subjugating the Estonians in the north and were beginning to address the problem of the Couronians and Semigallians.

Mindaugas' methods of unification were frequently harsh: assassination or exile of rivals, and direct invasion of the lands of lesser chieftains and the transformation of them into vassals. He also was adept at incorporation through arranged marriages of relatives to potential rivals, thus creating an affinal kin network bound to him by both familial and political loyalty. By 1245, Mindaugas was being heralded as "the Grand" and as "supreme leader" of the Lithuanians; in 1251, even without conquest by the crusaders and in spite of his earlier resistance to christianization, he accepted Christianity and was baptized; and in 1253 he received the Lithuanian crown with the assent of Pope Innocent IV himself. Evidently, in Mindaugas' calculations, christianization was one method of warding off the threat of the Livonian Order and perhaps the continuing raids of the Teutonic Order from the west as well. Acceptance of Christianity bought him time to implement a variety of state-building measures: creation of a royal court, development of a central administrative bureaucracy, organization of a system of

4 Here depicted in an early twentieth-century print, the castle in Marienburg (Pol. *Malbork*) became in the early fourteenth century the headquarters of the Teutonic Order from which crusading knights repeatedly invaded the Baltic eastern littoral.

military conscription, even the introduction of a common currency. But there were costs as well. In exchange for becoming a "Christian king," Mindaugas had to surrender control of Žemaitija (the north-western region of the Lithuanian lands) to the Livonian Order and the church. His rough methods of unification embittered other prom-inent Lithuanian chieftains and their families, who believed they had as much right to the supreme office as Mindaugas had and whose loyalty was at best temporary. The Rus' principalities to the east did not particularly like Mindaugas' Christian conversion by the Roman pontiff rather than by the patriarch in Constantinople. Beyond that, it is doubtful that the christianization of Mindaugas and his court penetrated deeply into the general Lithuanian population; the con-version seemed more a political than a spiritual act. Realizing how much the papacy wanted a convert of his stature, Mindaugas had spent several years playing a cat-and-mouse game of promising to convert and then changing his mind, which had kept the papacy from proclaiming a crusade against him.

In any event, Mindaugas' career as a Christian ruler lasted only about a decade because of the Žemaitians. They did not fully accept the high-handed way Mindaugas had "transferred" them to the order and the church; continuing to battle with the order, they eventually turned back to Mindaugas for help. He complied, thus returning to his earlier status as an opponent of christianization or at least of the kind the order was practicing. The coalition he helped to form against the Teutonic Order and its Livonian branch, however, did not succeed militarily. Mindaugas was murdered in 1263, apparently by resentful Lithuanian chieftains. Whether he became an apostate in this last phase of his life is an open question, permitting the papacy to continue to refer to him as a "Christian king." But the state he had founded survived, even though immediately after his death it began to experi-ence the problems of succession. Treniota, the principal chief of the Žemaitians, followed Mindaugas as the supreme leader for a brief period; he was replaced by Vaišelga, Mindaugas' son, who in the interim had converted to Orthodox Christianity. A string of lesser leaders after Mindaugas cannot be followed with precision because of inadequate information in the sources, but clearly Mindaugas' legacy did not include the one element that could have strengthened the Lithuanian state, namely, a stable familial dynasty. The Lithuanian state's survival as a viable entity in the decades following his death is a minor miracle, considering the many claimants to his title from other families and the external threats which had not disappeared. By the turn of the fourteenth century, however, the political situation had stabilized because the throne had been successfully claimed by a family that was to become the long-lived Gediminid dynasty. How exactly the Gediminids became entrenched remains uncertain; Gediminas (d. 1341), who gave the dynasty its name and governed from 1316 to 1341, was apparently the third of the dynasty's rulers. He became, in a sense, the true successor to Mindaugas because of the quality of his statecraft.

One source of worry for the early Gediminid rulers was the Teutonic Order, which had repeatedly demonstrated its desire to expand eastward. This crusading organization had a history in the

5 Grand Duke of Lithuania from about 1316 to 1341 and a crafty pagan for much of his rule, Gediminas laid the foundation of Lithuania's expansion and was the first major figure of a dynasty that lasted for more than a century after his death.

Holy Land before it came and established a base of operations on the southern shore of the Baltic Sea in the late 1220s at the invitation of the Duke of Mazovia. The order's principal concerns were to establish its own state and to christianize the pagan Prussians surrounding it, and by the second half of the thirteenth century both of these goals were close to being met. Once the order acquired a Livonian branch (the former Swordbrothers, in 1260), it supplied them with the needed manpower and resources. As the Livonian branch continued to fight the pagans in the eastern littoral, the main forces of the Teutonic Order sought to expand its state eastward into the Lithuanian lands, experiencing in this prolonged endeavor both victories and defeats. With the growing strength of the Lithuanian state, however, the order's eastern prospects dimmed; the Lithuanians successfully blocked its expansion just as they had been able to block the Livonian branch's southward drive. At the same time, the growing strength of the Teutonic Order's state and its outward-thrusting foreign policy blocked any northward moves by the Polish dukes (including the Mazovian), who were seeking to move their territorial borders as close to the southern shores of the Baltic Sea as possible.

Thus the balance of power around the Baltic Sea at the beginning of the fourteenth century was as follows: in the north, the Livonian Confederation, where the church and the crusading orders had now subordinated the indigenous tribal societies, but which was blocked from further expansion; to the south, the new and energetic Lithuanian state, headed by an increasingly powerful ducal dynasty seeking to enlarge its domains; and to the west, the state of the Teutonic Order, which was bristling militarily but had a peculiar leadership – a crusading order rather than a familial dynasty. In this configuration, the weaker territories were to the east and south, which left the Lithuanians in an excellent position to try expansionistic adventures of their own.

The violent thirteenth century – about four human generations – in the eastern littoral of the Baltic Sea had witnessed the reduction of the main political entities from about a dozen to two – the Livonian Confederation and the Lithuanian state. Before we examine them more closely, we may also ask what else had been accomplished during these hundred years. Basically, in the northern part greater military strength and ideological drive had triumphed over weakness, defensiveness, and fragmentation; in the south, where the antagonists were more or less equals, a standoff had resulted. But at a more general level, the eastern Baltic littoral had been europeanized, this term being understood not as a marker of progress or regress but simply as a characterization of the transformation. By the beginning of the fourteenth century the process was not completed – Lithuania was still only nominally a Christian state – but change had gone on long enough for the fundamental features of the new status quo to have become irreversible. In the north, europeanization had rearranged power into a political and socioeconomic hierarchy not unlike those that prevailed in the western regions of the continent. The church and its servitors occupied the top ranks; military vassals (here organized as a crusading order) had obtained control over much of the land and chafed at having to take orders from their nominal overlords; and most of the rest of the population (the Baltic and Finnic tribal societies) had become minor landholders and peasants, whose rights were increasingly circumscribed with each generation. The cities – mid-sized concentrations of merchants, tradesmen, and administrators – were also seeking independence of action, following the lead of western cities which had started a similar struggle during the twelfth century. Embodying the basic principles of feudalism and developing as well a manorial system of land use, these arrangements were familiar to all from the European west, with two exceptions. The ultimate masters of the new power-holders of the littoral – the pope and the Holy Roman Emperor – were far away; and in the new hierarchy of power, an ethnic dividing line existed between the German-speaking and Latin-using top tiers and the now-subordinated commoners who were still speaking their ancestral Baltic and Finnic languages. Something similar existed in England with its Norman–Saxon divide, but in the eastern littoral lands, the top sociopolitical tiers continued to see themselves as missionaries and civilizers in a way that the Normans in England had not.

In the southern part of the littoral, the transformation had brought about a Lithuanian state that was easily recognized by visitors from the west – a polity with a determined dynastic leadership, whose main tasks were to hold together an ambitious but militarily indispensable second tier of strongmen, and to satisfy a distant papacy seeking ultimate rule. Here the hierarchy of power did not have an ethnic dividing line; in the Lithuanian territories, at least, the ruling dynasts and the common people could communicate in their ancestral tongue. One feature of this new polity – again not unprecedented in the western parts of Europe – was that its political leaders remained expansion-minded, in this instance toward weaker and smaller Slavic lands to the east. Nonetheless, here also europeanization had managed to replicate elements of the older part of the continent.

In short, a century after Albert's arrival in 1200 the eastern littoral looked very different. What its appearance would have been if western Europeans had not arrived is moot, but what is patently clear is that the events of the thirteenth century had drawn the eastern littoral peoples into historical processes – with many parallels throughout the continent – that would continue to set the course of their everyday lives in unpredictable ways. Their initiation into these processes was involuntary at first, but each passing generation adapted to the new realities of life. Although these macroprocesses were not inevitable, it is also highly unlikely that the peoples of the eastern littoral could have remained untouched by them. The sociopolitical and economic forms that carried Christianity with them had already been expanding northward into Scandinavia and along the southern littoral of the Baltic Sea from the tenth century onward, and there was no reason why the process should have stopped upon arriving at the borders of the last pagan corner of Europe.

THE LIVONIAN CONFEDERATION

In speaking about the Baltic littoral in the early thirteenth century, the papacy frequently referred to the area as "the Land of Mary" (*terra Mariana*), but in the course of time "Livonia" (land of the Livs) came to be used by all. Livonia eventually became a confederation of territorial powers: the archbishopric of Livonia, several bishoprics, the lands of the Livonian Order, and the city of Riga. No central government existed, but the Livonians showed themselves capable of unified military actions when external danger threatened. Mostly, however, these states within a state vied with each other for

Map 2 The medieval Livonian Confederation: a noteworthy
but fragile medieval political formation.

territorial control, often violently. In principle, such conflict should not have occurred, because the most powerful of these entities – the archbishop and the order – shared the pope in Rome as their external sovereign, and many of the large landholders were vassals who held their lands from the same liege lords. In feudal theory, vassals of the same lord were to live in peace with the lord and with each other. But during the late medieval centuries everywhere on the European continent, the order that feudal relationships were supposed to engender was typically breaking down, with self-aggrandizement replacing such virtues as long-term loyalty and fealty. Along with many other things, europeanization had brought to the eastern littoral the messy contentiousness among governing elites that had characterized western Europe for a long time.

Following the subordination of each of the indigenous littoral peoples and before the conflict ended, the crusaders made certain that ultimate control of the overrun territory passed to one or another of the participating corporate entities. By the end of the thirteenth century, therefore, the Livonian Order (previously the Swordbrothers) held about 67,000 square kilometers of eastern littoral territory, extending in a ragged pattern from the Gulf of Finland to the borders of the Lithuanian lands. The Archbishop of Riga controlled about 18,400 square kilometers in the former lands of the Livs and Latgalians. The Bishop of Saaremaa controlled the island itself and a portion of the Estonian mainland on the Baltic coast, the Bishop of Tartu an area southwest of Lake Peipus, and the Bishop of Courland three small non-adjoining areas in the western part of the littoral in the former lands of the Couronians. These bishops were, of course, subordinates of the archbishop in Riga. The city of Riga was the smallest of these territorial entities, controlling only the walled city itself and the landed property around it. Its real power and influence lay in its far-flung activities as a mercantile and administrative center. Indeed, for a time Riga contained the city's own government, the cathedral seat of the archbishopric, and the headquarters of the Livonian Order. The buildings housing the nerve centers of these competing corporations were within a half-hour's walk of each other. Riga's population at the end of the thirteenth century is estimated at about 10,000 persons, making it the largest urban center in the whole of the Baltic littoral.

With the exception of Riga, which sought and eventually did establish control over trade and commerce traversing the Daugava River, the other corporations – the archbishopric (i.e. the church), the order, and the bishoprics – based their relative strength upon control of land. When resistance to the new rulers from the indigenous peoples had ended through conquest or treaty, these corporations distributed territory to those who had fought on their behalf. Land thus acquired from the granting authority was to be "held," not "owned" in perpetuity by the recipient. The concept of private ownership of land was not fully operational with respect to land anywhere in medieval Europe. In return, the land-receiving vassals stood ready to provide military assistance to the lord from whom they held the land. Resident indigenous populations, of course, came with the land grant, and they had no say in the matter. Predictably, one major source of post-conquest conflict lay in the efforts of the vassals to make permanent the control over the land they held, most often by acquiring from their lord the right of heritability. During the lifetime of the confederation, many landholding families not only acquired their lands in perpetuity but held portions of them from various overlords, which was a fundamental misapplication of the principles of feudalism. Not surprisingly, by the fifteenth century the corporate principle – according to which authority was vested in a collection of corporate entities – was being displaced by a process of social stratification: land-based families supposedly loyal to their overlords were realizing their common economic interests and considering themselves as a new grouping – as a nobility. Power relationships were shifting from a vertical to a horizontal axis. These changes, of course, pertained only to members of the dominant corporations and not to the common people who worked the land.

In the Livonian Confederation, as in all medieval societies, rights and obligations were attached to groups rather than to individuals, and therefore the concept of corporations needs some explanation. The arrival of this basic idea into the Baltic littoral was another aspect of europeanization, and in the course of the thirteenth century it overrode whatever principles of group organization existed among the indigenous societies. In addition to the most important corporate entities – the church and the order – others came into existence as Livonia stabilized as a polity. Riga sought rights as a "free city';

within Riga, merchant and craft guilds also developed as corporations during the thirteenth century. Inequality was the key element of this basic social philosophy: different corporations had different rights, and which rights belonged to which corporation was contested constantly. Since the right to govern was attached only to some corporations, not all groupings could claim representation in whatever governing assembly existed. Similarly, the ownership of land was a contested right. Those with the most power were able to claim and defend the most rights, ensuring that the church and the order would emerge as the most powerful corporate groupings in the confederation. Moreover, rights were specific and concrete; they had to be received from a higher authority, agreed to in a treaty, fixed in some kind of basic document or legal code, or at least enshrined in custom. The entire thirteenth century in Livonia was therefore a long period during which rights and freedoms were being adjusted to the new distribution of power, and in that process the indigenous peoples were the ultimate losers. The fact of subordination eventually came to rest not on brute force, as it had immediately after final military victory, but on a new distribution of rights, freedoms, and responsibilities that together were spelled out in many different and sometimes conflicting codes of law. A further complicating factor was that configurations of rights could differ between regions; no one configuration applied to all localities. The idea of legal particularism went hand in glove with the notion of a corporation-based society.

The paucity of sources makes it impossible to tell not only how rights, freedoms, and responsibilities were distributed before the new order was fully established, but also how the subordinated peoples reacted to the new distribution. The regulations by which the latter lived were mostly unwritten; they comprised many differing location-specific "common laws" and customs. The chronicles mention small-scale landowners with special rights who must have come from the upper strata of the old tribal societies, suggesting that not all of the subordinated peoples were immediately driven into total powerlessness. But the diminution of earlier rights and freedoms was certainly their long-term lot. Since the process lasted some four or five generations, the losses would have been felt most keenly by the first generation, who personally experienced the change in systems.

Later generations would have gradually come to accept the new order as the natural state of affairs as the old societies faded from memory. Of course their resentment over a host of new requirements with which the new order burdened them did not diminish. But complaints gradually were based on notions of fairness rather than on the idea that liberties once enjoyed by their ancestors should be returned to them.

Political life in the Livonian Confederation was dominated throughout its entire existence by corporations capable of asserting their rights and strong enough to back the assertion by force of arms: this meant the church, the Livonian Order, and the cities. These corporate entities were also numerically the smallest; peasants made up the vast majority of the population – some 80–90 percent. They "held" the arable land allocated to them by their immediate overlord, tilled it, paid rent in money or in kind, turned over to the lord some of the harvest, paid taxes, and supplied much of the labor needed to till the land attached directly to the lord's family. Rights to forested land, lakes, and other non-arable lands eventually were vested in the local or regional lords. The constellation of a given peasant family's rights and duties differed between locations and landowning masters. The peasantry as a social grouping had no say in state-level politics, and precious little in the handling of local affairs; they did not have the right to participate in governance. A landholder had extensive freedom to develop the rules for his peasants, to ensure that they remained in place and formed a readily available labor force. The rights of landholders over peasants contained all the elements of a system of serfdom. In the thirteenth and fourteenth centuries, however, the rules had not yet coalesced into such a system; the peasantry remained sufficiently differentiated throughout the confederation to retain some of the regional peculiarities of the old order. There was simply too much variation in how laws were perceived for any kind of system to operate.

The absence of a central authority in the confederation did not mean, however, that the competing corporations were prevented from establishing effective means of governance over the territories each controlled. An administrative apparatus did not have to be created anew. The archbishopric and the bishoprics were already parts of a continent-wide and well-tried structure, namely the church, whose experience in these matters could now be put to use in the littoral. The archbishop and the bishops of the littoral were part of the hierarchy at the apex of which was the Roman pontiff, and within this hierarchy obedience to superiors was mandatory. Locally, the archbishop had a council in Riga composed of churchmen (*capitulum sancte Rigensis ecclesiae*) who advised him on governance; the bishoprics had similar advisors; and the authority of high church officials was implemented by hundreds of priests heading local parishes. Depending on their size and relative wealth, local parishes and congregations could involve more than a single priest. Church revenues flowed from the "bottom" upwards and eventually some part of them made their way to Rome.

The Livonian Order, being a branch of the Teutonic Order headquartered in the Prussian lands, could also draw on a wealth of administrative experience from the latter. The Livonian Order operated by a set of statutes (based on the monastic rules of St. Benedict) that were rigorously followed. The master (*magister*) stood at the head of the order's hierarchy; the second-in-command was the land-marshal (*marsalcus terrae*), who was among other things the principal military leader. Below him there was a layer of comturs (*commendatore*), who functioned as administrators of the order's castles (some forty-four in the Latvian section of Livonia). Below them were the brother-knights (*fratres*), at least twelve in each chapter (castle) (as Jesus had twelve disciples). Dozens of other jobs needed to administer the order's lands and castles were filled by functionaries hired for the purpose, but they did not need to follow the order's rule of celibacy. Revenues within the order also flowed from the bottom up, from the peasantry living on the lands of the order. The order could also receive inflows from the church for its service as a kind of military arm.

The city of Riga had its own institutions of governance consisting of a council (*consulatus*) which had twelve (later twenty) members, several of whom were chosen as an executive committee (*proconsules*) whose head became in effect the city's chief executive (Ger. *borger meister*). Other council members served as the treasurer (*camerarii*), the chief law-enforcement officer (*advocatus*), and the main secretary and record-keeper (*sindicus*). These offices sprouted a host of functionaries as the city's population and commercial activities expanded, and as it obtained control over land beyond but still adjoining its walls. During much of the thirteenth century, Riga's principal struggle was with the archbishopric. After all, Archbishop Albert had founded the city, the archbishopric had its seat in it, and these high church leaders were loath to surrender their formal and informal influence in the city to merchants and guild leaders. Riga's struggle for corporate independence from church control was the local variation of the mighty battle being waged in the twelfth and thirteenth centuries by new cities across the face of western Europe, as they sought to free themselves from the control of the secular and ecclesiastical landowners on whose lands they had been established. In their repeated skirmishes with the church and the order, the city of Riga and growing towns in the confederation (Cēsis, Valmiera, Ventspils, Kuldīga, Valka, Limbaži, Koknese, Straupe, Tartu, Tallinn) were strengthened by the prestige and great economic benefit gained from membership in the Hanseatic League, the consortium of northern European cities that dominated northern trade and trade routes from the thirteenth century onward.

By progressively enlarging networks of influence and control through ever-proliferating parishes and castles, the church and the order were in a position by the end of the thirteenth century to quell most challenges from the populations that did not belong to these new elite groupings. These networks also served as a magnet for additional immigrants from western and central Europe – people possessing military prowess, artisanal and literacy skills, administrative talents, and adventurous minds. The church and the order were in constant need of servitors of various kinds in the administrative centers as well as on the manors that were becoming the typical organization of agricultural activity. Riga and other developing towns could provide employment for many; and competition for these positions was not much heightened by energetic aspirants from the indigenous populations – now the peasantry – unless they were ready to assimilate to the new German-speaking elites. In any case, the assimilation process took several generations before peasant origins were forgotten. That the new elites remained a small minority – perhaps no more than 10–15 percent of the total population of the confederation – was not perceived as a potential threat. The balance between elites and non-elites was after all about the same in western and central European kingdoms, and it was from these that the ruling orders of the confederation took their cues about what was right and proper.

THE GRAND DUCHY OF LITHUANIA

By the fourteenth century, the Livonian Confederation with its rival components stood in sharp contrast to what was transpiring politically in the Lithuanians lands to the south. Here also the distribution of power was changing, but the process involved only indigenous peoples, not outsiders. Under the Gediminid dynasty, a Lithuanian state increasingly took on the appearance of the European states to the west, with a sovereign termed the grand duke (Lith. *kunigaikštis*; Lat. *magnus rex*), several layers of subordinate "aristocrats," and a large population of commoners – townspeople, artisans, merchants, and peasant farmers. Gediminas and his successors accomplished the transformation of potential political rivals into a stratum of *boyars* – local rulers who owed their loyalty to the grand duke and received their lands from him on the feudal model. This process in the core Lithuanian territories – Aukštaitija and Žemaitija – involved almost exclusively those who spoke the Lithuanian language. Eventually, as the Lithuanian Duchy (sometimes also referred to as the Grand Principality) expanded to the south and southeast, the sociopolitical layering came to involve a host of lesser Slavic dukedoms and principalities as well. By the end of the fifteenth century, the Gediminid dynasty and its successor Jagellonian dynasty (from Duke Jogaila [Pol. *Jagiełło*]), who ruled from 1377 to 1387) had succeeded in creating a multiethnic superpower with its eastern borders reaching the Grand Duchy of Moscow and the southeastern the lands of the Tatar Golden Horde and the Black Sea. Under Mindaugas the Lithuanian Grand Duchy had an estimated 300,000 inhabitants, with about 270,000 of these residing in the core Lithuanian territories; by 1500, the grand dukes ruled over a territory with about a million and a half inhabitants, with perhaps a third living in the Lithuanian lands. Through their standing in this large and complicated polity, the Lithuanian ruling elite had attained a position that none of the other peoples of the eastern Baltic littoral had managed to achieve, and as a result they

Map 3 The Grand Duchy of Lithuania, thirteenth and
fourteenth centuries. While in the northern littoral the
indigenous peoples were subordinated, in the south during the
late medieval centuries they created a mighty sprawling state.

also became important actors on a much larger geopolitical stage involving both central Europe and the Rus' territories. To retain a focus on the littoral peoples, however, we will be concerned less with the long and complicated history of the state Mindaugas and his successors created, and more with the history of Lithuanians within this state. As will be seen, the history of the Lithuanian state was not identical to that of Lithuanians, either in medieval or in subsequent centuries.

Why the indigenous peoples of the northern part of the Baltic littoral all became subordinates of outside powers while the Lithuanians did not remains intriguing and a source of disagreement among historians. The starting point was the same for all – namely, small tribal societies in the eleventh century – and nothing suggests that the Estonian, Latgalian, Couronian, Semigallian, and Liv peoples were inherently less capable (less martial, more quarrelsome, or less far-seeing) than the Lithuanian tribes in warding off foreign incursions. In part, an answer involves timing: the strategy of the crusading orders first subordinated the pagan peoples of the northern littoral, before moving to the south, which gave Mindaugas – the unifying grand duke – about twenty to thirty years to organize an effective resistance before the full intentions of the crusading orders were exposed. In part, the answer has involved the nature of leadership: Mindaugas and his successors evidently were persuasive and ruthless enough to overcome internal opposition to their determination to create a state, in contrast to the chieftains of the northern peoples, none of whom could establish a strong presence for sufficient time to take on the task; only Lembit among the Estonians appears to have had the potential for doing so. The chieftains among the others were short-lived rulers, uninterested and perhaps unable to obtain power over more than their own territories. In part, the answer involves location: the deeply forested and swampy Lithuanian territories were not as accessible to land-based invasions as were the territories to the north, as the repeated failures of the Teutonic Order to penetrate Žemaitija clearly demonstrated. By the end of the thirteenth century, when the christianizing invaders had finished their conquest of the northern littoral and could turn their full attention to the remaining pagans – the Lithuanians – the resistance of the latter was already based in a state that could muster defensive measures. When Grand Duke Jogaila finally converted to Christianity in 1387 and made it a permanent part of Lithuanian affairs thereafter, he did so because he found the step advantageous to his statecraft and not because he had just been defeated by outside crusaders.

Even though the Lithuanian state eventually grew to be powerful and influential, its sprawling nature made it difficult to defend in perpetuity. Initially, it was a compact land-based state; as it expanded to the east and southeast, it required continued military preparedness, high-level diplomacy, a growing administrative apparatus, and the mechanisms to suppress the normal centrifugal force of a feudal social structure. Under Mindaugas the Lithuanians had succeeded in keeping their territories free of foreign occupation, but that became an increasingly onerous task as the process of territorial expansion continued. The conflict involving, on the one hand, the Teutonic and Livonian orders to the north and northeast, and on the other, organized Lithuanian resistance manifested itself in the form of some one hundred military engagements over the course of the fourteenth century; ultimately, the Lithuanian state outlasted the order but at the cost of a continuing drain of wealth and manpower. To the east lay the diverse Rus' principalities, none of which was strong enough seriously to threaten Lithuanian authority until the late fifteenth century. Yet many of them continually launched raids into Lithuania's Slavic acquisitions. In the very south lay the lands of the Golden Horde of the Mongols, which by the fifteenth century no longer was the triumphant invader of earlier times but was still a threat. Immediately to the southwest of the grand duchy lay Poland, governed since the late tenth century by the Piast' dynasty and clearly intent on increasing its influence in regional affairs. Poland's aspirations were frustrated by the existence of the state the Teutonic Order had created to its north, and by a burgeoning Lithuania to the east.

These hostile and semi-hostile surroundings required the duchy to create what almost amounted to a standing army that could serve the needs of both defense and expansion, which was accomplished in the same manner used by all medieval states. The grand dukes enfeoffed the lands of their families and granted lands newly acquired to members of other potentially useful family groups in exchange for military service to the duchy. They also hired mercenaries and established temporary military alliances with other regional powers whose current interests were the same as those of the duchy. The military history of the duchy in these centuries suggests that it was successful in its endeavors and it suffered very few defeats on the battlefield.

Another method for reducing external threats was to annex, by force or treaty, those adjacent principalities and dukedoms that might have designs on Lithuanian territory. On this score the duchy was immensely successful. Annexation efforts by the ducal dynasties during the fourteenth and fifteenth centuries were aimed primarily at the relatively weak Slavic principalities to the east and southeast. By the end of the fifteenth century, Lithuania controlled virtually all of what is present-day Belarus and Ukraine. The grand dukes were intent on exploiting the military weaknesses of their immediate neighbors even if success created immense problems of administration. Such expansion had the consequence of placing the grand duchy at the center of a very diverse state – almost an empire – because the annexed populations were virtually all Slavic as well as Orthodox. After the Jagellonian dynasty permanently became Christian in 1387, it presided over a multilingual, multiethnic and multicultural polity, admirable in many ways but also containing prominent centrifugal tendencies.

What could not be accomplished by annexation could be brought about by diplomacy and dynastic marriage. The Lithuanian dynasts proved to be capable in using kinship networks and marriages to maintain the loyalty of subordinates and to bind potentially threatening neighbors to the duchy. The most fateful of these dynastic marriages proved to be the 1385 Union of Krėwe, a transaction by which Grand Duke Jogaila married Jadwiga, daughter of the Polish King Louis (d. 1382) and became the King of Poland. The territories controlled by the grand duchy at that moment were three times larger than Poland; the Polish nobility, which elected the monarch and was thus entitled to offer the crown, believed a personal union of the two kingdoms would clearly benefit Poland and argued that it would also be advantageous to both lands. Jogaila concurred, and the bond between the Polish and Lithuanian territories persisted until the end of the eighteenth century. Initially, the arrangement foresaw continuation of the office of the Lithuanian Grand Duke. Either the same person who was the Polish monarch would occupy it or another person appointed by the Polish monarch with concurrence of the Lithuanian nobility. Jogaila held both offices. At its initiation, this Lithuanian–Polish link was useful to both lands: Lithuania secured its western borders and established a permanent ally against the Teutonic Order; Poland no longer had to worry about Lithuanian expansionism, and the power balance vis-à-vis the Teutons also tilted in its favor. Both polities remained independent in name and governing structures, but were joined at the top.

The duchy's personal union with Poland and the expansion into eastern Slavic regions are good indicators of how the Lithuanian monarchs thought about territory. Maintaining the ethnic or linguistic uniformity of controlled land was never a worry, nor was the problem of administration worked out before a new expansionary move was attempted. The experience of both the Gediminid and Jagellonian dynasties suggests that neither of these challenges proved to be troublesome, because until the sixteenth century the grand duchy appears to have handled them well. Thus, ethnic and linguistic diversity became increasingly the main sociocultural characteristic of the enlarged state, even while the core of the realm – the original territory – remained largely Lithuanian in both respects. Even while it was a still a pagan state (until 1387), Gediminas had allowed, indeed had invited, the Catholic Church into its territory for the purpose of ministering to the Catholic populations already there; proselytizing, however, was strictly forbidden and if attempted was severely punished. This openness remained the grand duchy's policy despite the conversion of Jogaila upon his marriage to the Polish heiress (Poland had already become a Catholic state), and insistence on conversion of the rest of the population did not follow. Subsequent dynasts were quite accepting of eastern Christians, pagan practices, and even Jews in the lands they controlled.

BRITTLE AMALGAMS

The formation of European states in the later centuries of the medieval period followed no particular pattern. Some were self-described empires (e.g. the Holy Roman Empire of the Germans), some city-states (e.g. Venice), and some (e.g. Sweden, France) took intermediate forms that to some extent already resembled the nation-states of a much later period of European history. Very few of them resulted from *organic* growth – from a peaceful process involving the slow expansion of an initial core population through natural growth and the systematic assimilation of immigrants. The largest states added territory through annexation of adjacent lands (through conquest or marriage), and were familiar with having to govern culturally and linguistically differentiated populations. Although by these criteria most European states were composites of some kind – amalgams – some eventually proved more brittle than others. The two medieval states of the Baltic littoral – the Livonian Confederation and the expanded Lithuanian state – were far more medieval than modern and possessed features that placed them closer to the fragile end of the continuum. As it turned out, this fragility could be managed for a long time – formally, the Livonian Confederation lasted until 1567 and the Lithuanian state (after union with Poland) until the end of the eighteenth century. Yet from the beginning both polities had fault lines of differing robustness running through them, which by the end of the medieval centuries (about 1500) had hindered full internal consolidation.

Politically, the Livonian Confederation and the Lithuanian Grand Duchy each in their own way were plagued by incipient fragmentation. In part, the problem was the implementation of effective administration. In the confederation, missives and representatives from the ultimate overlords in Rome, central Europe, and even the Prussian lands where the Teutonic Order had its headquarters, took a long time to reach the littoral. The same problem became increasingly more serious for the grand duchy as it expanded its territory into the Slavic east and southeast. In the confederation, the absence of a single regional sovereign allowed the ambitions of the local corporations to flourish – especially the Livonian Order and the cities. For example, armed conflicts resulted such as those between the city of Riga and the order in the period 1297–1330 over the question of who controlled whom. The order's victory in this instance did not guarantee long-term peace, however, and the skirmishing continued throughout the next century. Or, to take another example, the crusading orders themselves, composed of celibate Christian brothers, were not immune to profound internal struggles. In the 1430s, the Teutonic

Order, headquartered in Prussia, sought to rein in the Livonian Order (its northern branch); the latter resisted such centralization, and conflict ensued. Not until the early fifteenth century did the warring corporations of the Livonian Confederation realize that their disputes might be settled through a regional quasi-parliament (Ger. *Landtag*) that included representatives from the church, the Livonian Order, the most important landholding vassals of these two corporations, and the cities. But this body, meeting sporadically, proved to be generally ineffective; the suspicions, jealousies, and resentments of the constituent parts of the confederation were too deeply seated to be permanently reduced through discussion.

The political fault lines of the Lithuanian Grand Duchy were different in form from those of the Livonian Confederation and revealed themselves more slowly. The process of consolidation of a Lithuanian state under Mindaugas had begun in the eastern region of the Lithuanian lands – Aukštaitija. The other important Lithuanian region – Žemaitija – lying between Aukštaitija and the Prussian lands of the Teutonic Order, took on the semblance of a poor cousin and was frequently treated as such by the grand dukes in their unending conflicts with the order. Though the prominent landholders of Žemaitija were also vassals of the grand duke, they remained, if not resistant to centralization, then certainly suspicious of it and had to be constantly flattered and pacified. Furthermore, the dynastic principle that was key to the long-term success of the grand duchy, especially under the Gediminids, did not necessarily work smoothly: bitter conflicts bordering on civil war erupted over the succession question in the later thirteenth, in the fourteenth, and then again in the early fifteenth century. Vytautas the Great, who was grand duke from 1392 to 1430 and earned his sobriquet by completing the eastward expansion of the duchy, came to power precisely as the result of such a succession struggle involving his uncle (the previous grand duke) and cousins. Clearly, the office of grand duke would not always be willingly surrendered by powerful magnates to a claimant simply because the latter appealed to the dynastic principle: there were always several competing branches in a governing kin group that traced their origins to a single founder, and each felt its own claims to be legitimate.

Two new fault lines developed in the Lithuanian lands during the course of the fifteenth century. Vast Slavic territories to the east and southeast – whose inhabitants were generally referred to as the Ruthenians – required attentive and imaginative administration, which characterized both the Gediminid and Jagellonian dynasties. Yet the addition of these territories to a core Lithuanian state did not involve cultural or linguistic assimilation: because of the tolerance practiced by the grand dukes toward differing religious faiths, various ethnic groupings, and indigenous cultures, territory was being expanded but not integrated. In the short run, this was a wise policy, but in the long run, effective control could be assured only as long as able administration was practiced and no adjoining states had designs on the Lithuanian-run Slavic-language territories. Unfortunately, not all the grand dukes were equally skilled in administering far-flung regions, and at least one rising state in the east – Muscovy – was developing its own westward-thrusting agenda. Furthermore, the Union of Krewe in 1385 and the merger of the offices of Lithuanian grand duke and Polish monarch meant either a single person would wear both crowns, competition for this more desirable joint office would double, or even that the two positions would have separate claimants. More turmoil was guaranteed at the very apex of the political hierarchy, at a time when a "Polish" agenda was becoming increasingly prominent in geopolitical strategy. The grand dukes of Lithuania, as Polish monarchs, now had to develop a savvy foreign policy toward territorially ambitious central European powers, adding to the burden of administering the Ruthenian lands.

Although another prominent fault line in the two polities lay in the domain of languages, much of what can be reported unambiguously on this subject remains in the realm of educated guesswork. The new masters of the Livonian Confederation had brought to the littoral two new languages – Low German and Latin – which they used for written communication and record-keeping. They exhibited no desire to use any of the littoral's languages in the business of governance at any level. This attitude meant that by the last centuries of the medieval period the common people of the confederation – especially the peasantry – had to reckon with a layer of cultural activity from which they were excluded. In addition, the languages the littoral peoples had spoken before the onset of the new order were themselves undergoing major changes. Among the Estonians, the dialects that existed were sufficiently similar not to be an obstacle to effective communication across regional boundaries and to further language uniformity. To the south, the Livs probably had better lines of communication with the Estonians – since the languages of both were Finnic – than with their Baltic-language neighbors (the Latgalians, Selonians, Semigallians, and Couronians). Virtually nothing is known about the Selonian language; the Latgalian population covered a large enough territory for their language to have several dialects; and some historical linguists believe that the Semigallians and Couronians spoke kindred languages. But as generations came and went within the framework of the confederation, these pre-confederation languages became increasingly less well defined. The written sources – produced of course by German and Latin users – did continue to differentiate among these peasant peoples (presumably on the basis of languages) long after the end of the conquest. During the fifteenth century, however, the term *Letten* (Latvians) or some variant was used increasingly for all of them. The term evidently derived from the name of the Latgalians. Alternately, the sources also used the terms *deutsch* and *undeutsch* (German and non-German) as if further linguistic distinctions in the confederation were of minor consequence. Looking back to this period from many centuries later, Latvian historians have hypothesized that during the fourteenth and and fifteenth centuries the conquered peoples south of the Estonians "flowed into each other" (Latv. *saplūda*), producing a *Latvian* population and something like a unique *Latvian* language. This colorful and suggestive metaphor, which implies the dynamics of amalgamation and mutual assimilation of rural populations, may indeed describe what was actually happening on the ground. But the only certain split developed between the confederation's governing elites and the peasant population.

That cleavage was neither inevitable nor natural. The Norman invasion of England in 1066, just a few decades before the coming of the crusaders to the Baltic littoral, also produced a socially, linguistically, and culturally layered society (Normans and Saxons). Yet a few centuries later a population had come into being in which the layers had merged to become *English,* speaking a common *English* (or at least an Anglo-Norman) language. Nothing like this happened in the littoral, and the only linguistic link between the German- and Latin-using upper orders and the language communities of the subordinated rural people were the pidgins that must have been created for everyday practical transactions.

In the Lithuanian Grand Duchy a very different linguistic situation unfolded: the government and court in the core Lithuanian lands continued to use Lithuanian, but at the same time tolerated Slavic languages that entered the realm as eastern and southeastern territories were added. Indeed a form of Church Slavic eventually became the official language of record-keeping for the Lithuanian state, while Latin and other western languages were used in official correspondence. Thus in the political entity that bore the name of Lithuania, the Lithuanian language was already losing its strength. And the marginalization of the language continued after the Union of Krėwe when Polish began to seem more attractive to the status-conscious upper orders. Among the peasantry in the core Lithuanian territories, especially Žemaitija, however, the Lithuanian language, though containing dialects, remained the principal instrument of communication even as the linguistic makeup of the sprawling territories controlled by the duchy became more complicated.

In the Livonian Confederation, linguistic stratification carried with it another fault line: a separation of the littoral's cultural life into "high" and "low" components based largely on language. The retention by the governing orders of close contacts with their places of origin in central Europe and the steady immigration from there to the littoral were mechanisms for continuing cultural europeanization even as the peasant populations – the Estonian and Latvian speakers – felt the progressive devaluation of their customary ways. The process of europeanization was unrelenting over the last medieval centuries owing in large part to the absolute conviction among the Livonian governing orders that they had "civilized" the pagan populations. On their side, erstwhile pagans responded in a variety of complicated ways that included the retention of some traditional folkways, but also acceptance, emulation, and absorption of the new. Though Roman Catholic Christianity became institutionalized, the depth of its reach into the hearts and minds of the governing orders and the common people varied considerably. Absolute loyalty to the church existed nowhere in the littoral by the fifteenth century. The increasingly powerful and increasingly secular Riga merchants fought against church control of any kind, and the Livonian Order repeatedly demonstrated its insubordination to the Archbishop of Riga and even the papacy. All this signaled that the salvation of one's soul (which the church controlled) was becoming less important as a motivating force, and in this the peasantry followed suit. Parish clergy complained repeatedly about and even condemned the persistence of pagan rituals and practices. Such complaints became a permanent component of clerical reports about their flocks for centuries to come. The Latin-language masses and the use by the clergy of imperfectly learned vernaculars in everyday dealings emphasized the distance between shepherd and flock, as did the "foreign" origins of the clergy. The church's unceasing condemnation of superstition and pagan practices – burial outside cemetery grounds, sacred groves or trees, sacrifices to the old gods, and continuing belief in the efficacy of magical incantations – meant that, if not abandoned, these had to be kept secret. In the Livonian Confederation Christianity remained associated with power, and the old ways with powerlessness. Yet some merging was inevitable. Some of the church's saints became indistinguishable from the holy figures of pagan belief, and some pagan holy days remained in the church calendar under a different name.

In the Lithuanian lands to the south, however, Christianity was perceived far less as an imposed faith than in the Livonian Confederation. The Lithuanian grand dukes, after all, had finally accepted the faith voluntarily and therefore Christian ways could not be associated with foreign power to the same extent as in the confederation. What fault lines existed in the cultural realm grew out of the situation and were not as clearly marked. From the beginning, there was always a shortage of Lithuanian-using parish clergy, and therefore the church recruited and the dukes permitted Polish and German clergy to fill the gap; Lithuanian origins were not at this time an obstacle to a church career. Among commoners, however, the Latin mass was no more easily understood than in the Livonian Confederation. By the last centuries of the medieval period the pagan past in Lithuania was not as distant and therefore folkways remained a refuge for rural people even as they participated in

Christian rituals. The complaints of parish clergy in the Lithuanian territories on this score closely resemble those of the confederation's churchmen. After the Union of Krėwe and during the fifteenth century, the growing closeness at the top of the Lithuanian and Polish royal courts and the gradual preference among the Lithuanian governing circles for the Polish language could not stir feelings among the common people of Lithuania of being governed by outsiders as was definitely the case in the confederation.

A line between high culture and low was also drawn by literacy in both the confederation and the grand duchy. Europeanization tremendously enlarged the place of reading and writing in the littoral's cultural world. The early peoples of the tribal societies must have been conscious of the existence of writing and of books, since some of them had had contact with Orthodox missionaries, who probably had texts. They may also have been familiar with the runic writing of the Scandinavians. Such modes of communication and storage of knowledge played no role in the littoral societies, however, at least not in the form used by the newly arrived European institutions. Yet now these instruments among the new governing orders in both the Livonian Confederation and the duchy had taken on exceptional importance in the form of sacred books, diplomatic correspondence, registers of various kinds, treaty documents, account books of merchants, tax rolls, and other instruments of record-keeping. How the common people responded to this literary component in their cultural milieu is not clear; the church did not encourage the development of literacy skills among the common people of their parishes, except for those few recruited for the priesthood; and, more than likely, landowners also feared that such skills would diminish the manual labor force on which they depended.

The domain of reading and writing was not entirely closed to common people, but until the end of the medieval centuries, it joined the superstructure of buildings (churches, monasteries, castles) and their interiors, forms of dress and personal decoration, and weaponry as the boundary markers between the governors and the governed, between high status and low. Cities and towns, with which literacy was closely associated, were also such markers. The urban centers of the littoral with their walls and restrictive residency regulations drew a line between insiders and the people of the countryside, signaling that the cities were far superior to rural customs and habits. The evidence was the growing wealth of urban populations in contrast to the rural areas, and the supply and trade networks that urban merchants created to acquire rural products. The city was increasingly the source of money, even though the monetization of Livonia proceeded slowly. Initially, cities – large conglomerations of people who did not cultivate land – were a new experience for the littoral. But with each generation, the presence of these centers became increasingly normal, until the oral tradition of the period came to view cities – especially Riga in the confederation – as objects of celebration and admiration, even if their residents differed culturally and linguistically from those in the rural areas and in spite of the fact that city merchants were also thought of as swindlers and sharpies.

In sum, by the fifteenth century these two medieval states – the Livonian Confederation and the Grand Duchy of Lithuania (in its extended form) – had become important powers of the new europeanized littoral. They had absorbed and redefined the indigenous peoples and marginalized paganism. Like other medieval polities, these two states were not internally cohesive. The processes of merging, linking, and integration of their populations had not been thorough or cumulative. Structural weaknesses were kept alive by corporatism in the confederation and tolerance of diversity in the duchy and its extensions. Common purpose was generally the temporary byproduct of the will of strong leaders who cajoled their followers into joint action. When the personal ambitions of rulers subsided, so did common efforts. Consciousness of class (in the modern sense) was rare. The St. George's Day uprising (1343–1345) in the Estonian lands, which involved an effort by the Livonian Order to expel the Danes and by large numbers of Estonian peasants to expel both, was anomalous. Such peasant uprisings were virtually non-existent in the Latvian and Lithuanian regions of the littoral throughout the medieval period; dissatisfaction among peasants was mostly characterized by flight from their holdings rather than direct violent action. The people of these polities were protectors of their niches: the upper social orders, of their status and landed properties; the peasantry, of their local communities and local traditions. Movement was continuous but small in scale.

Involvement in trading and commercial activities transported some away from the localities of their birth into new areas. The growth of urban economies created the need for workers in numerous support occupations – carting, building, cleaning, maintaining – and the city employers did not care where the labor force came from. The main power-holders continued to engage each other militarily and needed to raise armies against invasions and raids. Many of the infantry were recruited from the peasant population, regardless of origin. Landowners also moved their peasants around to obtain a better distribution of the labor force under their control. The cumulative results of these small-scale movements of the peasant population were that besides the permanent populations of the countryside, people came and went and settled anew, bringing with them new languages and dialects and in effect penetrating the normal isolation of non-mobile communities. Nevertheless, particularism remained the chief characteristic of the Livonian Confederation, and the determined efforts by the Lithuanian grand dukes to promote greatness through territorial expansion and dynastic marriage simply resulted in a larger stage on which particularism could play out.

3

The new order reconfigured,
1500–1710

The Europe into which the eastern Baltic littoral was drawn from the thirteenth century on was itself undergoing major changes. The grand struggle between secular rulers and the papacy over ultimate allegiance was resolving itself in favor of the monarchies, and by the fifteenth century, the monarchs had begun to realize the importance of dynasty and effective internal administration. As old feudal ties between lords and vassals and sub-vassals were eroding, lords could no longer expect loyalty from their subordinates on the basis of a personal bond alone. Military servitors to whom lands had been granted were refashioning themselves into land-based aristocracies, discovering at the same time the benefits of heritability of their holdings and the advantages of binding "their" peasants to the soil. Cities were becoming an increasingly powerful and independent political force, while long-distance trade and commerce established new forms of personal wealth.

The western church still remained in charge, at least nominally, of the salvation of souls, but, as an institution deeply involved in secular affairs, its activities were being questioned by reformers such as John Wycliff and John Hus who were greatly dismayed about ecclesiastical corruption and the spectacle of a very wealthy church. A conciliar movement (Constance, 1414–1417; Basle, 1431–1449) sought to pacify the reformers, but their disquiet continued. Wealth was being redefined to include more than land, but the impulse to control territory remained strong at both the personal and state levels. Indeed, expansionist tendencies were growing stronger rather than weakening as European states continued to vie for greatness through territorial expansion and to look at control of adjacent and even distant lands. The states on the eastern Baltic littoral – the Livonian Confederation and the Polish-Lithuanian union – were now part of the larger European system and therefore felt these changes variously in their own affairs and had to react to them. But the common people on the Baltic littoral, especially those in rural areas, felt them only at several removes; their everyday lives, suffused as they were with the repetitious cycles of the agricultural year and the demands of their low status, were conducted at a much slower pace and experienced breaks in customary ways only when these were thrust upon them by their overlords.

The location of the Baltic littoral on the edge of western Christendom made it vulnerable in the fifteenth century to the territorial ambitions of several would-be powers. One was the principality of Muscovy to the east, which was coming to dominate the lands of Kievan Rus'; another was the empire of the Turks, which took Constantinople and brought to an end the long history of the Byzantine Empire in 1453. Of the littoral peoples, the Polish-Lithuanian polity had the most reason to worry, because the earlier successful eastern and southeastern expansion of the duchy had thrust deeply into the territories now coveted by Muscovy. If the drive of the Turkish Ottoman Empire were to continue northward and overrun Hungary, Transylvania, and Moldavia, the Turks would become an unfriendly southern neighbor. The threat from the south and east was at this time much more worrisome than that from the west; there the empire of the Germans appeared satisfied to stay within existing borders at least for the time being.

Even so, the western European states were by no means practitioners of peaceful statecraft, and, in addition, their populations and territories were large. By the mid-fifteenth century, European populations had recovered from the Black Death a hundred years earlier and the major states were experiencing substantial population growth. The population of England at the time was about 3.5 million, that of the German Empire of central Europe about 20 million, and of Sweden about 750, 000. These numbers dwarfed the populations of the eastern Baltic littoral. Using the calculation of number of persons per square kilometer, the population of the Livonian Confederation (*c.*1500) stood at about 654,000 – including some 360,000 Latvian- and some 250,000 Estonian-speaking people. The Lithuanian numbers require three calculations: there were about 500,000 Lithuanians within the boundaries of the Grand Duchy of Lithuania, with the duchy itself having about 1.3 million people; the combined territories of Poland and Lithuania (*c.*1500) held just less than 4 million. Such figures are all speculative, of course, since there were no censuses, but they are useful for comparisons of relative size. They also suggest that the hardships of the period 1200–1500 had reversed continuing population growth. Estimates for the mid-thirteenth century put the numbers at about 150,000 in the "Estonian" territories, about 220,000 in the "Latvian" lands, and about 280,000 in the "Lithuanian" regions.

Perhaps more important than absolute numbers are the internal dynamics of these populations during the medieval centuries, the most visible of which was the continuing interplay between depopulation and repopulation. These populations were never static, even though primarily rural, and they reveal a pattern of incremental growth in the long term. Within that long-term growth, however, periods of rapid loss followed period of rapid gain. The frequent warfare described by medieval chroniclers killed many and laid waste large areas of the littoral, but this destructiveness did not prevent relatively rapid recovery, usually within a generation or so. Even though written sources often picture entire localities devoid of people, such usable space did not remain empty for long and was resettled by farmers moving (or being moved) in from less affected places. Another mechanism of repopulation was in-migration, which appears to have been continuous for the entire littoral. The Grand Duke Gediminas in Lithuania explicitly recruited new residents to the duchy by using the method – already popularized by German rulers of eastern territories – of offering lighter taxation and labor norms to new settlers. Both the church and the Livonian Order in the Livonian Confederation continually recruited settlers and soldiers from the German lands of central Europe, and the trading activities of the Riga merchants also brought ambitious new people to the littoral, many of whom decided to stay.

There was also the process of assimilation: the Semigallians who were said to have left their native territory in the thirteenth century for Lithuania to escape christianization presumably assimilated to the Lithuanian population; later, as Latvian serfs fled north and Estonian serfs fled south into each other's territories in search of better economic conditions, presumably they assimilated to the local populations where they finally settled. Arrivals from the Slavic lands steadily trickled into the confederation, because economic conditions were reputed to be better, and they also presumably assimilated to the local populations. The losers and gainers among the different ethnic-linguistic groups in these processes are impossible to name because the original numbers are suspect. Some long-term population growth – more births than deaths – was always present in premodern populations, and new arrivals, though small in number in any given year, enhanced natural growth in the long run.

Demographically speaking, then, the centuries from the thirteenth onward never experienced population booms in the littoral, but continuing repopulation always produced an increase at the end of any given century. The one characteristic of the littoral populations that achieved something like stability was the urban–rural distribution. Well-organized cities such as Riga maintained strict control over their populations, in part for reasons of residential space and in part because they could not absorb economically all those who might have wished to enjoy city life. Despite possessing the superstructure of all medieval states – cities and towns, castles, courts, churches, and monasteries – the confederation and the lands of the Polish-Lithuanian territories remained primarily rural (upwards of 90 percent) in terms of population and predominant activity, even though contemporary descriptions emphasized the more interesting non-rural part.

THE COLLAPSE OF THE LIVONIAN CONFEDERATION

Although the year 1500 saw no significant event in the confederation, its internal history was altered just before and just after that date. Throughout the fifteenth century the confederation had continued on its quarrelsome course governed by the Livonian Order (which controlled about 67 percent of the territory), the Riga archbishopric (about 17 percent), and four particular bishoprics (Kurland, Tartu, Saaremaa, and Reval – together about 16 percent). The order's system of governance rested on a network of fifty-eight fortified castles scattered throughout the northern (Estonian) and southern (Latvian) parts of the confederation. The church, in turn, extended its influence throughout these same territories with a similar network of eighty parishes. Lines of authority were anything but clear, and the flow of revenue from the general population to the highest levels of both controlling corporations was a continuing source of friction. The order held land from the church but always sought greater autonomy; the church, having no independent military force of its own, relied on the order for defense but at the same time asserted its spiritual authority. The three most important cities of the confederation – Riga (about 12,000 inhabitants), Reval (Est. *Tallinn*, about 6,000), and Tartu (about 4,000) – retained vassal status to the order or the church, but repeatedly (and unsuccessfully) tried to escape their jurisdictions, as countless number of cities had done in western Europe in past centuries. Periodically, representatives of the main corporations held meetings called *Landtage* to discuss common problems, but the effectiveness of this body depended upon general agreement and it had no legislative authority. In due course three events had a major impact on this constellation of power: in 1494, Walther von Plettenberg became Master of the Livonian Order; in 1517, Martin Luther posted his ninety-five theses on the door of the Wittenberg church, thus launching the Protestant Reformation; and, in 1557, there began a long series of conflicts that came to be known as the Livonian Wars, which brought an end to the confederation as a polity in the Baltic littoral.

When von Plettenberg (1449–1535) assumed the mastership of the order in 1494 he was forty-five years old. During his forty-one years at the helm he faced three major tasks: first, he administered the relationships between the Livonian Order and the Teutonic Order in Prussia, of which the Livonian Order was nominally a branch. Second, he retained control over the increasingly independent-minded layer of *commendatores* in the Livonian Order (the governors of the order's castles and administrators of its territorial districts). Lastly, he staved off the attacks on the confederation by the principality of Muscovy, which began in earnest in 1501. The first of these tasks von Plettenberg dealt with in 1513 by buying from the Teutonic Order the right of the Livonian Order to name its own master, and by persuading the Holy Roman Emperor to recognize this privilege. Approximately a hundred Livonian "brothers" (the celibate knights whose numbers had been somewhat higher in the past century) were free to elect their own leader, which was a major step toward complete independence. But he could do little about the growing independence of the brothers from *his* control except exert his considerable moral authority to keep them together. They hungered for "freedom," that is, the right to enjoy the fruits of the considerable properties they "held," which impulse was fed by exactly the same phenomenon among the Prussian brothers of the Teutonic Order, also in the process of dissolution.

Where von Plettenberg did excel was in marshaling the order, along with an army that included many Latvian and Estonian infantrymen, to protect Livonia against Muscovite attacks that had already begun under Tsar Ivan III in the 1480s without much success. In 1501, another Muscovite–Livonian war began, but it ended in a stalemate and an armistice in 1503. The armistice was renewed periodically for the next fifty years; the Muscovites realized that taking Livonia would not be easy and shifted their attention toward Lithuanian territories, giving the Livonian Confederation a respite to deal with its internal problems. Among these was the arrival of Protestantism from Germany, which proved to be very effective in changing the nature of the confederation.

Launched in Germany, Martin Luther's challenge to the authority of the church and the papacy was initially only a variant of a reform idea that had been discussed most recently in the church councils of the fifteenth century. But what emerged did not satisfy the reform-minded within the church, and the scandalous activities of the Renaissance popes in Italy simply underscored the much more drastic overhaul that was needed. The church had become too worldly, the papacy too centralized, its high officials too concerned with increasing church revenues rather than with saving people's souls. The sale of indulgences was particularly galling to reformers. The changes called for, if implemented thoroughly, could be of major significance to the Livonian Confederation, where the church was an important political and economic power.

Such changes could have an impact as well on the other church-related corporation in the confederation – the Livonian Order. By the end of the fifteenth century it had lost its *raison d'être* because the

6 Walther von Plettenberg. Master of the Livonian Order from
1494 to 1535, he had to become a superb diplomat to defend
the order's littoral territories from a growing list of ambitious
external enemies.

Baltic littoral, even Lithuania, was no longer inhabited by pagans in
any meaningful sense and did not need crusading orders. Also
impacted was the future of the city of Riga, whose secular-minded
patriciate had been looking already for ways to escape the controls of
both the church and the order. Luther maintained that the Roman

church did not have monopoly over personal salvation, that there existed a "priesthood of all believers," and that the relationship between God and the individual believer was "justified" by "faith alone" and did not need to be mediated by elaborate organizational structures and complicated rituals. These teachings were a sharp challenge to the way the church had become institutionalized and to all corporate entities (such as crusading orders and monasteries) that justified their existence by reference to overall church authority.

By the middle of the sixteenth century, the impulse of religious reform had spread much farther than Luther initially had intended, landing in a variety of political contexts and altering a variety of power relations. In the German lands of central Europe, a civil war – the so-called Schmalkaldic War (1546–1547) – ensued and pitted the reformist German states against the Catholic states and the Holy Roman Emperor Charles V, who chose to defend the unity of the church. Elsewhere the reforming impulse became increasingly more extreme, spawning such intellectual radicals as John Calvin in France and such uncompromising movements as the Anabaptists in Switzerland. In France thirty-six years of religious warfare (1562–1598) tore the country apart; in England, a strong-willed monarch – Henry VIII – used his marital difficulties to provoke a complete break with Rome and to establish the Anglican Church. The reformist impulse coming to the Livonian Confederation early in the Protestant period – in the 1520s – was more purely "Lutheran," though Calvinism also received support later in the century in the Polish-Lithuanian lands. As elsewhere, Protestantism in the Livonian Confederation affected much more than the realm of the spirit; the established church – in the form of the archbishopric of Riga and three bishoprics – was deeply involved in secular life and the confederation's internal politics. In Riga, the first public "disputation" between church officials and adherents of the new Protestant doctrines took place in 1522; in a few decades, most members of the Riga patriciate became converts to Lutheranism and the church was on the defensive. The response of the Livonian Order to Lutheran teaching was more complicated. Even though the Teutonic Order in Prussia had already gone over to the Protestant side in 1525, the Livonian Order under the leadership of von Plettenberg initially remained a defender, sometimes reluctantly, of the established church. There were major divisions about the new doctrines in the leadership of the order and among the powerful landholding brothers. The number of converts grew in time, however, but the master of the order (now Heinrich von Gahlen) together with nine high officials did not attend the first evangelical Lutheran service in the Dome Church in Riga until 1551. In 1554, a Livonian *Landtag* proclaimed "religious freedom" in Livonia, which meant, in the short run, that both the Catholic and Lutheran forms of Christianity could exist in the confederation. A year later, in 1555, the Peace of Augsburg ended the religious conflict in the Holy Roman Empire under the principle of *cujus regio, ejus religio*, meaning that a ruler would determine the religion of his subjects. In the confederation, Lutheranism and Catholicism henceforth had equal standing among the ruling orders; a major conflict had been avoided, but neither side truly accepted in perpetuity the truths of the other.

Measuring the depth to which Lutheranism penetrated into the general population of the confederation – the peasantry – is difficult. Rural people had the status of an apolitical social order, and their advice was not sought on matters of religion either; they had to conform to the dictates of their immediate overlords and follow their lead. Nothing resembling the Peasants' War in Germany (1524–1525) occurred in Livonia, though in a few places in the Estonian lands isolated incidents of peasants launching direct attacks on church institutions did occur and probably not for spiritual reasons. More than likely, most of the peasantry of the confederation did not even know who Martin Luther was, even if they understood that the religious discipline imposed on them had become more differentiated from parish to parish. Nonetheless, one aspect of Luther's teachings did begin to change the religious aspects of peasant life, however sporadically: Luther had insisted that Christian congregations receive the word of God in their own language, which meant, at least among the clergy who adhered to the new teachings, that as part of their normal duties they needed to be systematically concerned with the vernacular languages of the littoral. For the first time since the start of christianization, the printed word made its appearance in the Estonian and Latvian languages of the period in the form of translations of catechisms and other incidental religious literature. For the first time also, sources mention the training of a few churchmen, in both the Catholic and Lutheran churches, whose family origins lay in the indigenous populations. (The cultural meaning of the written word in the vernacular languages of the littoral will be examined later in this chapter.)

The adherents of Protestantism and Catholicism in the confederation remained unreconciled to one another during the rest of the sixteenth century, their conflict intensified by the program of the Catholic Church's Counter-Reformation, which was spearheaded by the long (though intermittent) meetings of the Council of Trent from 1545 to 1563. But religious strife was pushed to the background by another set of events – a complicated and drawn-out series of military encounters starting in 1557 and known as the "Livonian Wars." Involved in the fighting were Denmark, Muscovy, Sweden, and Poland-Lithuania, while the rulers of the Livonian Confederation cast about desperately in search of the most useful allies. Military activities in and around the littoral lasted until 1583, relative peace was restored until 1600, but warfare resumed in that year and this time lasted until 1629. The Livonian Wars – as they came to be called – started with the resumption of attacks on confederation territory by Muscovy, which had been pushing against the confederation's (and Lithuania's) eastern borders since the middle of the fifteenth century. With the ascendancy of Ivan IV (the Terrible, tsar from 1553 to 1584) the pushing turned into a continuous campaign when the Russian army, using as pretext the non-payment of tribute by the bishopric of Tartu, invaded Livonia and gained control over the Tartu bishopric's territories.

Muscovy's successes, even though temporary, triggered among the other power-holders of Livonia a desperate search for protectors. The bishops of Courland and Saaremaa sold parts of their territory to the Danish King Frederick II, who thus renewed Denmark's involvement in the littoral as a rival of Sweden. In the meantime, the Livonian Order sought protection for itself and its territories in the arms of Poland-Lithuania in 1561, when the last master of the order, Gotthard Kettler, pledged his loyalty to King Sigismund II Augustus. Sweden had already gained a foothold in Livonian territory in that same year, when the city of Tallinn and adjacent territories sought protection by surrendering to the Swedish King Eric XVI. The triumph of imperial ambition over kinship ties was

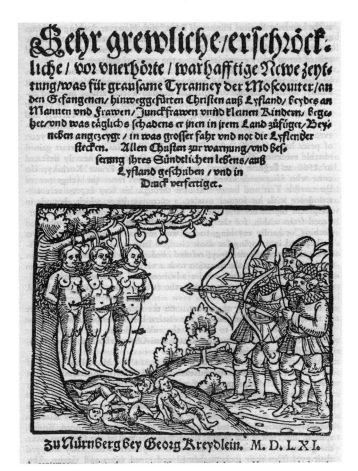

7 Muscovy atrocities. Sixteenth-century propaganda print
warning Europeans of the atrocities perpetrated by
"Muscovite" invaders of Livonia during the warfare of the
second half of the century.

signaled by the ascent to the Polish-Lithuanian throne of Sigismund
III, son of King John of Sweden of the Vasa dynasty. Throughout the
Livonian Wars, Sigismund III (monarch from 1587 to 1632) ably
defended the interests of Poland-Lithuania against the aspirations in
the region of the Swedish homeland of his ancestors. The patriciate of
Riga, as before, sought to preserve the city's independence from all
control but was able to do so only until 1682. By the end of the first

phase of fighting in 1582–1583 (agreed to in a treaty), control over parts of the Livonian territory had been acquired by the monarchs of Denmark, Sweden, and Poland-Lithuania, with Muscovy holding on to a small section of its earlier gains. The armed forces of Muscovy were in the process of withdrawing to their home territory, the tsars having become embroiled in succession conflicts.

The agreement of 1582–1583 created a seven-year period of peace, but acquiring only a part of Livonian lands was not enough for the remaining contestants. In 1600, Swedish armies under the personal leadership of King Karl IX landed in the Estonian territories of the Livonian north and began to drive southward against Polish-Lithuanian territory and what remained of the Russian holdings. This time the conflict (sometimes known as the Swedish–Polish War, but here viewed as a continuation of the Livonian Wars) lasted for about twenty-nine years – an entire human generation – though it was not continuous over the whole period. By 1629, clearly neither Sweden nor Poland-Lithuania could gain complete victory over the other, even though Russia had been expelled (temporarily) from the littoral. The Peace of Altmark in 1629 brought the fighting to an end, and, as a result, Sweden acquired imperial holdings consisting of the northern half of the old Livonian Confederation; these lands would henceforth be called Swedish Livonia. Poland-Lithuania retained control over what had in the meantime become the Duchy of Courland as well as an eastern section of the old Livonian territory that would henceforth be referred to as Polish Livonia (and Latgale by Latvians). Denmark held on to two islands – Saaremaa and Kuresaare – until 1645, when these were surrendered to Sweden. Denmark had already shown diminishing interest in Livonian territory in 1585 when it transferred to Poland-Lithuania (for a payment of money) its rights over the westernmost section of Courland called the Piltene District.

Viewed from below, that is, from the vantage point of the Estonian- and Latvian-speaking peasantries of the confederation, these new territorial arrangements did not bring major structural changes, because their immediate masters – the largely German-speaking landholding vassals of old Livonia who had refashioned themselves into landed aristocracies – remained in place and simply shifted their political loyalties to the new overlords, the monarchs of Sweden and

Poland-Lithuania. Nor was there a clean break with the past in terms of religious and cultural influences. The Duchy of Courland, though now under control of the Polish-Lithuanian monarchs, became increasingly lutheranized, and the Polish-Lithuanian government did not seek to reverse this trend. Polish Livonia (Latv. Latgale), however, where the great majority of the population was a peasantry that spoke a variant of Latvian – Latgalian – experienced continued catholicization, as the Polish-Lithuanian government implemented Counter-Reformation policies. Also, Polish Livonia had a slow but steady infusion of Polish and Lithuanian landowners. The Swedish and Danish parts of old Livonia – already Lutheran and now under the sovereignty of Lutheran monarchs – had no reason to expect changes in their religious life. In sum, if major structural changes were to come in the daily lives of the peasantry, they would have to emerge from royal policy directed at the powerful landholding aristocrats who, in turn, were becoming increasingly self-conscious defenders of their own privileged status.

Though the continuing warfare in and around old Livonia is referred to as the Livonian Wars (or alternately the Livonian War and the Polish–Swedish War – both terms suggesting one or two compact events), the common people of the old confederation of the Baltic littoral experienced the conflict as a long series of intense and destructive battles, interspersed with periods of calm. The movement of armies across Livonian territory brought nothing but misery in the form of ruined crops, requisitioning, the burning of farmsteads, and various acts of violence against civilians. The main belligerents frequently recruited (or impressed) men of peasant standing into the infantry and cartage service. The military experience of these soldiers took them to new territories and sometimes resulted in their settling down in new places. The physical toll of warfare was accompanied by periodic epidemics, sometimes worsened by bad harvests even when the land was at peace. Population statistics for the first half of the seventeenth century are non-existent, but by the beginning of the seventeenth century the rural population of the old Livonian territories was likely to have decreased since the start of the conflict. The population could recover, of course, but the Livonian Confederation had disappeared from the political maps of Europe and the political superstructure of its territories had changed entirely. The upper social orders of old Livonia redefined their loyalties as the land and its residents were allocated by treaty to different sovereigns. When warfare ceased in 1629, the centers of power important to the littoral peoples had moved outside the littoral. Even in the case of Poland-Lithuania, as we will see, power in that joint state had shifted from Vilnius (in the Lithuanian territories) to Cracow (in Poland). The peoples of the littoral had become residents of imperial peripheries.

THE REPUBLIC OF TWO NATIONS: POLAND AND LITHUANIA

While the Livonian Confederation was paying the price for having remained a brittle amalgam, the Grand Duchy of Lithuania moved ever closer to its structural partner – the Kingdom of Poland. The result was a state that veered from the centralizing model that western monarchs such as Elizabeth I of England and Henry IV of France sought to realize, and farther yet from the royal absolutism that later in the seventeenth century in France under Louis XIV would be become much admired and emulated. Unification of territory in the Polish-Lithuanian lands slowed; instead of a strong monarchy, the power of a national diet (parliament) and regional diets, both dominated by landowning nobilities, increased. The "election" of the monarch by the mighty and the powerful competed with the principle of dynastic succession in legitimizing the sovereign. The question of exactly how the two principals of the partnership – the Polish monarchy and the Lithuanian dukedom – should be related to each other remained contentious. A king (Poland) outranked a duke (Lithuania), but how could that prevail in a state that was supposed to be a partnership of two equal entities? If two separate individuals occupied the two offices, from which lineages should each come? By tradition, the two offices should be occupied by the same person of Lithuanian lineage, but it was becoming increasingly clear during the sixteenth century that being a *Polish* king in the full cultural and linguistic sense invested the occupant with more luster and greater standing among the crowned heads of central Europe.

These questions seemed to be moving toward a final settlement by the Union of Lublin of 1569, which ended the formal separation of the Kingdom of Poland and the Grand Duchy of Lithuania and created a new polity designated a commonwealth (in Polish, *rzecz-pospolita*). This agreement between the nobilities of the two lands was the final step of a merging process that began in 1386 with the Union of Krėwe and over two centuries tilted the internal arrangements of the partnership increasingly in favor of the Polish kingdom. After 1569, the residents of the commonwealth thought of themselves as living in a single state with two component parts – a republic of two nations – with each nation retaining many of its traditional ways. Such a double political identity was difficult to maintain, particularly for the Lithuanian side. The magnates and gentry (*boyars*) of the duchy witnessed their ancestral land gradually diminishing in stature, almost to the position of a province in a territorial state dominated by Poles. Numerically the Lithuanians were becoming a minority within a large polity that still bore their name but increasingly was viewed by outsiders as Polish. The commonwealth's monarch soon abandoned the custom of regarding Vilnius as a capital equal to Cracow and conducted the affairs of state from the Polish capital. His visits to Vilnius took on the character of a tour of the provinces.

The situation contained temptations that most of the magnates and gentry of the Lithuanian lands could not resist; they willingly stepped into the process of polonizing themselves and their family lines. This sociolinguistic and cultural process, however, was not unique to the sixteenth century, having been going on in somewhat more restrained ways since the late fourteenth century and the Union of Krėwe. The last Lithuanian grand duke who is known to have spoken Lithuanian was Casimir (1440–1492), the son of Jogaila. The network of institutions created by the Catholic Church after the personal union and the duchy became Christian brought into the Lithuanian lands a host of Polish churchmen who conducted services and did church business in Latin and Polish, not Lithuanian. To receive their higher education, the sons of the Lithuanian magnates and gentry traveled westward to Polish universities, and not surprisingly frequently married into Polish families of equal or higher rank. The growing prestige of Cracow as the center of the commonwealth was a clear signal to the energetic and upwardly mobile in the Lithuanian lands that the Polish linguistic and cultural track was

8 Vilnius in the sixteenth century. Probably founded by Gediminas, by the mid-sixteenth century Vilnius had become the undisputed political and cultural center of the grand duchy.

the right one to follow. The result of these processes was that during the sixteenth century the Lithuanian-language community in the Lithuanian lands continued to lose its most influential members, despite the fact that politically these same persons insisted on maintaining a degree of separateness from the Polish kingdom.

At the apex of Lithuanian society, the cultural and linguistic drift toward Poland continued even as Lithuanian magnates and gentry nurtured institutional separateness in the form of ministries, military contingents, treasuries, codes of law, and control over royal landholdings located in Lithuania. Yet to the outside world, a highly placed noble family of Lithuanian ancestry that bore a Polish-looking and Polish-sounding surname was Polish, regardless of the sentiment of family members. In the commonwealth the process of cultural stratification was being concluded in favor of a "high" culture using an east Slavic language, with the Baltic language – Lithuanian – identified almost exclusively with the peasantry, especially in Žemaitija. In the northern part of the littoral an analogous process, starting earlier and lasting a much shorter time, had turned German into the language of high prestige, and Estonian and Latvian into the languages of the rural hinterlands and of a small urban laboring class.

What in retrospect seems a betrayal was not perceived as such at the time. For the self-polonizing Lithuanian magnates and gentry cultural emulation could coexist with a protectionist attitude toward the ancestral homeland. Emulation of Polish institutions brought to the duchy the practice of meeting regularly in a territory-wide assembly (Pol. *sejm*, Lith. *seimas*), a custom that built on the irregular advisory councils of the duke; and also local and regional assemblies (Lith. *seimiki*). Both groups became increasingly important during the sixteenth century as institutions that the sovereign had to consult in policy matters; in fact, they became centers of opposition when actual or proposed policy was not to their liking. The gentry of the Lithuanian lands began demanding the same rights as their Polish counterparts, and this pressure led to the codification of Lithuanian customary and statutory law in the Lithuanian Statute (1529). It was revised and amended in 1556 (Second Statute) to accommodate the gentry and again in 1588 (Third Statute) to incorporate the principles of the new relationship created by the Union of Lublin. Each of these documents moved relationships between power-wielders and land-owners in Lithuania farther from the realm of custom and unwritten practices into the realm of written law. All three also placed additional constraints on the monarch in his relationships with his Lithuanian subjects.

The proportion of Lithuanians in Poland-Lithuania was reduced still further through the policy of tolerance the government extended toward the populations under its control. This inclusiveness continued attitudes already exhibited by Gediminas two centuries earlier. By 1500, the approximately 7.5 million inhabitants of Poland-Lithuania included (to use the modern terms of reference) Lithuanians, Poles, Belarussians, Ukrainians, Russians, and Jews; some 52 percent of this congeries lived in the lands of the Grand Duchy. Many of these peoples, of course, made up the permanent residents of the eastern territories of the commonwealth and showed no desire to move en masse to other regions. Jews, however, were expelled from other countries and frequently found a home in the commonwealth; the Jewish population is estimated to have risen from about 10,000–15,000 in 1500 to about 80,000–100,000 in 1600. It was the multilingual nature of the duchy and the commonwealth that partially explains the abandonment by the Lithuanian upper orders of the language and culture of their native realm. Being embedded in a polyglot society, they did not perceive language as a particularly important marker of personal or collective identity as long as institutional arrangements could serve that purpose.

In the long run, these developments made the commonwealth more fragile, but in the short term, they did not affect effective state-craft, even expansion, which in the sixteenth century proceeded at a much slower pace because of Muscovy's counter-expansionism on the commonwealth's eastern borders. The prolonged wars in and over the Livonian Confederation, however, benefited the commonwealth. During the wars themselves, the Polish-Lithuanian monarchs followed an opportunistic, though always anti-Muscovy, foreign policy, even allying themselves with the old enemy, the Livonian Order, to fight the foes from the east. The inconclusive fighting between Sweden and Poland-Lithuania, however, was eventually recognized as such by both sides, and the 1629 Altmark treaty was the result. After the hostilities had ended, Poland-Lithuania had to

Courland

governance over

chy's landowners full of

tory peasant labor and install

y of peasants, the two hall-

antry) – the other new territory –

dom of Poland and the Grand

ernment sharing in the appoint-

5. Although, initially, German-

prominent in Polish Livonia, in

ugh the reallocation of their land n

an aristocrats; also, some of the

polonized themselves. The land,

ular interest in collectively defend

of their Courlandic counterpart

ory much more open to influenc-

nteenth century, its peasantry l's

of the rules governing manda of

ent, and thus were no less ensure

ecause Polish Livonia was gov a-

ducal house as in Courland), in

ral influences and population he

mmonwealth generally. The ed

9 Gotthard Kettler. The last of the masters of the Livonian Order, Kettler in 1562 secularized its landed properties in the Baltic littoral, turned the order into a corporation of nobility, and established his family's long-lasting ducal dynasty in Courland.

Latvian peasants, landowning aristocrats of varying ethnic background, and mobile peoples such as Jews became much greater there than in either Courland or Swedish Livonia, and the everyday language of the Latvian peasantry in Polish Livonia developed features that distinguished it from the Latvian spoken in the western Livonian territories.

SWEDISH ADMINISTRATION OF ESTONIA AND LIVONIA

During the late sixteenth and early seventeenth century, all the residents of the eastern Baltic littoral felt the impact of adventurous rulers directly or indirectly. Among the most audacious were the monarchs of the Vasa dynasty in Sweden. From the 1520s onward, they were intent on making Sweden the dominant power in northern Europe and proceeded with that task by ending the trade monopoly of the Hanseatic cities (1530s), becoming involved in the Livonian Wars (1560s), and gaining control over the northern part of the Estonian territories. By the second decade of the seventeenth century they had managed to cut Russia off from access to the Baltic Sea (Treaty of Stolbovo, 1617). Warfare against Poland-Lithuania resulted in Sweden becoming the new master of the rest of Livonia (1620s), but its belligerency did not end there. In the 1630s under Gustavus II Adolphus (1594–1632) Sweden became involved on the Protestant side in the immensely destructive Thirty Years War, which was tearing apart the Holy Roman Empire. The acquisition of Livonia was but one part of the grandiose colonial plans of the Vasas, which also included in the 1630s a short-lived colony in the New World (the present-day state of Delaware). The Baltic littoral became a colonial area, figuratively speaking, with high-level local administrators frequently having to make certain their decisions did not interfere with the grand policies being made in Stockholm and Cracow. Even so, to describe Livonia as having become Swedish is something of an exaggeration. Between the faraway crowned heads and the common people of the littoral there lay a formidable, privilege-conscious and opportunistic stratum of German-speaking landowners and urban patriciates whose loyalty to their current sovereign lord was always in question.

The Swedish-controlled territory north of the Daugava River had come under Stockholm's jurisdiction in a piecemeal fashion: the province of Estonia during the Livonian Wars and the rest of Livonia after the Peace of Altmark (1629). The Estonian-speaking population, largely peasants, was cut into two parts by an administrative border demarcating the provinces of Estonia and Swedish Livonia; the Latvian-speakers, also largely peasants, were divided by borders between Swedish Livonia and Courland to the south and

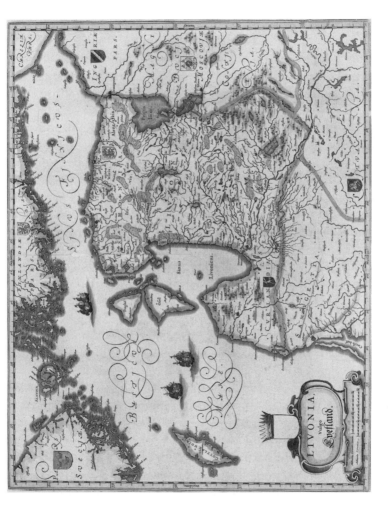

Map 4 Livonia in the seventeenth-century. The name "Livonia" was well known in seventeenth-century Europe, but it was Poland, Sweden, and Russia that dominated the region's politics.

Swedish and Polish Livonia (Inflanty and Latgale) to the east. The
city of Riga had formally submitted to Sweden in 1621 and had
negotiated its status separately. The governmental apparatus differed somewhat in each of the Swedish-controlled lands, but both
Estonia and Swedish Livonia were administered by governors-
general appointed by the Swedish monarch, one residing in
(Tallinn) Reval and the other in Riga. The task of the governors-
general initially was to integrate these "colonies" and "reform"
them in accordance with the values of the Swedish political and
legal culture and economic system. But before this effort made
much headway, the governors-general ran into opposition from
landed aristocracies and urban patriciates. The intent of landowners
(somewhat less than of the city populations) was to maintain the
status quo and to retain absolute control over their properties and
resident peasants (now largely serfs).

The Swedish monarchy had achieved a *modus vivendi* with the
landowning aristocracies on the Swedish mainland. However, the
continuing opposition among the Livonian and Estonian upper orders
to Stockholm's wishes was, to put it mildly, annoying. Yet Swedish
administrators needed to be careful. As recent experience had shown,
the local Baltic power-wielders had no deep-seated loyalty to the
Swedish crown: though both the crown and the littoral colonies
were Protestant, loyalties could shift easily to the Catholic monarch
of Poland-Lithuania or even, in the extreme, to the Orthodox Russian
tsars. Neither of these regional great powers was reconciled with the
long-term presence of Sweden on the Baltic Sea's eastern shore.

Just as royal absolutism was difficult to implement in the Swedish
Livonian holdings, so were the accompanying economic policies.
These policies were illustrative of what has come to be called "mercantilism," even if they differed in the seventeenth century from
country to country and were nowhere applied as a single doctrinal
system. At the core of mercantilism was the notion that central
governments should be deeply engaged in promoting economic
growth, which meant encouragement of commercial activities, government protection for and promotion of economic enterprises
through grants of monopoly rights, the establishment of colonies
whose growing populations could be put to use, and the expansion
of tax revenues flowing to the central government from all sources.

10 Reval, 1625. By the early seventeenth century the city of Reval (later renamed Ta linn) had become an important urban center in the Estonian territories of the Baltic littoral.

None of the seventeenth-century governments of the Baltic littoral – including the Swedish monarchy – however, quite fit the definition of an effective apparatus that could centrally direct such economic activity. Landed aristocracies as well as cities were suspicious of any kind of royal centralization, and the activities of wealthy individuals were aimed more often than not at personal enrichment rather than the enrichment of the state. Mercantilism required a belief in the salutary effects of a strong central government, and the powerful in the littoral easily recognized that hard work on behalf of the governments in Cracow and Stockholm would diminish local and regional control.

Still, the central governments were not dissuaded from making an effort. One member of the ducal dynasty of Kettlers in the Duchy of Courland – Jacob (duke 1638–1658) – for example, sought to make his duchy into a colonial power by obtaining a small territory in West Africa called Gambia, and an island in the Caribbean called Tobago, which he hoped would turn a profit. Jacob was active economically as well in funding various kinds of small-scale manufactories in Courland. He sought with protectionist measures to increase exports over imports, tried his hand at minting his own coinage, and invited expert foreign craftsmen to live in the province. There is some disagreement about whether his activities were meant to enrich the duchy as a state or his own family, but his policies were definitely along mercantilist lines. Unfortunately, they turned out to have little staying power. By the end of his rule, Courland was no more advanced economically than the other lands of the Baltic littoral.

Although Sweden's economic policy in Estonia and Livonia had the same characteristics as Jacob's in Courland, from the Swedish government's point of view theirs had more potential for enrichment of state coffers. Enterprises of all kinds were taxed to increase royal revenues, and a system of licenses and monopolies was devised. Courland was seen as a competitor, and controls over the flow of trade in and through Estonia and Livonia sought to divert trade from Courland to Estonian and Livonian cities. Cities were generally favored as sites of energetic activity that could benefit the Swedish crown. The Daugava River was recognized and protected as the main highway for trade with the Russian lands. There was government-sponsored encouragement of the shipbuilding industry and small-scale manufactories. Weights and measures were standardized throughout Swedish-controlled territory, and the never-ending disputes between guilds over spheres of activity were halted. Maritime trade in the Baltic Sea, from and to Estonian and Livonian ports, was routed through ports on the Swedish mainland. The population growth that was expected to ensue from economic development was pictured as a boon to the state, since a larger population was equated with growing strength. Local reception of these government-led intrusions was mixed, however. The Baltic cities and their merchant elites perceived a close fit between their own interest and state policy, and generally complied with government directives, the landowning aristocracy resented government interference in the affairs of the countryside and also saw the rising fortunes of the urban areas as a threat to their own control. No reliable statistics exist about economic development in the Swedish territories in the seventeenth century, but the likelihood is that through much of that century all the indicators were positive.

The Swedish administration of Estonia and Livonia did accomplish, through pro-urban mercantilist policies, the expansion of the role of cities in littoral life, which could only grow in the future. Commercial activities in Swedish Livonia were centered in Riga, though the port cities in Estonia – Tallinn and Narva, for example – expanded their activities as well during the seventeenth century. The Riga merchants, still organized in guilds, served as middlemen for imports via the Daugava River. Goods arrived from the littoral itself as well as from the Russian states further east and from the Lithuanian Grand Duchy, with which Riga had had good, though frequently interrupted, trade relations ever since the time of Gediminas.

By the mid-seventeenth century, the merchant patriciates of Riga had become impatient with the restrictions placed on them by membership in the Hanseatic League and welcomed Dutch ships to promote trade with western Europe. Walking a fine line between compliance and resistance with respect to the Swedish government in Stockholm, the Riga merchants insisted that all goods meant for export pass through their hands. This policy ran counter to the interests of increasingly market-savvy landowners who had begun to grow crops for export and sought to deal directly with foreign

11 Riga, 1701. The Great Northern War brought an end to Swedish control of Riga. This early eighteenth-century engraving shows the Swedish army moving south across the Daugava River to attack a contingent of soldiers from Saxony (allied with Russia).

merchants. This seeming hypocrisy – resistance against external control of trade together with heightened controls locally – was typical of merchant-dominated cities everywhere, but the urban patriciates portrayed it simply as exercise of their traditional rights. Local control of production by guilds, guild organizations, and brotherhoods was also in full bloom in Riga and the other cities of the Swedish-controlled littoral. Entrepreneurial activities in the city itself and on its adjacent patrimonial territories were declared illegal unless they were specifically permitted through a license or grant of monopoly All such monopoly-granting and monopoly-using urban corporations were, of course, controlled by persons of German ancestry, who nonetheless did permit the entry of "non-Germans" into various kinds of less-organized support occupations (hauling, ship construction, maintenance of urban infrastructure). Though the walled city of Riga looked like a German Hanseatic city architecturally and its language of business was predominantly German, its total population of some 12,000 was of mixed ethnicity, with the Latvian population estimated at 40–50 percent.

Another accomplishment of long-lasting importance under Swedish rule both in Estonia and Livonia was the improved system of major roads. Similar efforts to improve internal communication and transportation in the littoral had begun under Gediminas in the Lithuanian territories; the Livonian Order also had taken steps in this domain primarily for military needs. But these earlier efforts had had uneven results, in part because road-building and upkeep was frequently delegated to the estate owners through whose lands roads ran, who were reluctant to perform such public works (such as assigning peasants to the task) unless pressed; also, the insubstantiality of road-building materials played a role. Moreover, upkeep of roads proved to be a much more labor-intensive activity than anyone realized. Land had to be cleared to make roads straight, drainage ditches had to be dug and kept clear of weeds; bridges had to be built and other water-crossing means devised; established roads had to be rebuilt after spring floods, and again during the rainy seasons. Old and established roads did exist: the Teutonic Order in the fourteenth century, for example, produced maps showing a system of roads that were to be used during a major invasion of the Lithuanian lands and these ran in a west–east direction through Žemaitija into the central

Lithuanian region of Aukštaitija. But a coordinated effort to create an effective and permanent *system* of roads was not undertaken by any government until the Swedes obtained Livonia and Estonia.

The Swedish government sought two things: a road system running east to west and north to south that would speed the movement of goods to Riga and other trading centers and at the same time serve a more effective postal system. The plan was to be implemented through government edict in Swedish-controlled territory. To establish linkages to major centers in the Lithuanian and Russian lands – to Pskov and to Memel, for example – treaties had to be negotiated with a suspicious Poland-Lithuania (which controlled the territory between the eastern border of Swedish Livonia and the Russian principalities) and the Russian states themselves. In a period when military conflict between these powers was always imminent, these agreements were reached surprisingly easily, evidently because the governments in question recognized the benefits that would accrue to all signatories. The Swedish effort remained serious and systematic. Swedish and German engineers drafted elaborate instructions that specified the width of roads and drainage ditches, the hardness of the surface, and the extent of clearing on both sides of the road to prevent fallen trees from blocking the roads after storms. One immediate byproduct of the use of these roads, when they were finished, was the appearance at regular intervals of horse-changing stations and taverns. Once established, the road system remained in place and was extensively used to move military forces when conflict broke out again between Sweden and Russia in the second half of the seventeenth century.

THE MANORIAL REGIME AND SERFDOM

Particularly grating to the Swedish administrators of Livonia and Estonia was the condition of the peasantry, or put more precisely, the control landowners exercised over the rural population, thus placing them beyond the reach of royal will. The contrast with mainland Sweden was stark. In the littoral itself, from the Lithuanian to the Estonian lands, the inviolability of the rights of landowners over the people on their properties had been fought for and largely obtained over the past several centuries. Even though at the bottom of the

social structure, as everywhere else, peasants in Sweden were nonetheless relatively free with a degree of representation at high levels
of government. In the Baltic littoral, peasant customary rights had
been severely abrogated, and those that remained were easily
circumvented. In a single word, there was no *serfdom* in Sweden,
but it flourished in the littoral. The German terms *Leibeigenschaft*
(possession of the body) and *Erbuntertänigkeit* (hereditary servility) describe the essence of Baltic serfdom; the Latvian term –
dzimtbūšana – refers to the heritability of the servile condition,
while the Lithuanian term – *baudžiava* – has reference to labor
requirements. The general vagueness of the indigenous terms is
due to the fact that the whole complex of obligations, rights,
restrictions, privileges, sanctions, and penalties that comprised serfdom did not originate locally but was imported piecemeal to
Livonia and Estonia from central Europe starting in the fourteenth
century. Consequently, in Lithuania, where lord–peasant relations
evolved within the context of a Lithuanian state, serfdom was
comparatively less onerous; in Estonia and Livonia it had already
become constricting on the rural population by the seventeenth
century. In Lithuania during the reign of Sigismund II Augustus
(Grand Duke 1544–1572) wide-ranging agricultural reforms had
been carried out. Among other things, these "volok reforms"
demarcated crown from private estates, introduced the three-
field system, systematized the obligations of the peasantry, and
provided each peasant household with a parcel (Lith. *valakas*) of
land. Though increasing state revenues and demonstrating what a
truly determined monarch could accomplish in his own kingdom,
the volok reforms did not seek to eliminate serfdom, nor could they
have done so without severely damaging the relations between the
grand dukes and the landed upper orders.

By definition, the practices summed up in the word "serfdom" in
the Baltic littoral thus varied from place to place and region to region.
The two main features – obligatory labor and restriction on movement – came into being during the fourteenth and fifteenth centuries
as byproducts of the manorial or estate system through which vassals
held land from sovereigns and sub-vassals from vassals. The precise
number of estates in the littoral territories in the seventeenth century
cannot be known, but about 700 existed at mid-century in the

Courland duchy, with the ducal family controlling about 215. The Latvian-language area of Swedish Livonia contained about 360 estates. Landowners became wealthy by controlling very large estates or many estates, or a combination; the ducal family of Kettlers in Courland was probably one of the wealthiest in the entire Baltic area. In the Lithuanian lands, a somewhat different calculation reports the wealth of the Zamoyski family: the estates which they controlled contained more than two hundred villages and eleven cities. Types of estates were legion: crown, private, hereditary, non-hereditary, leased, rented, fully farmed, partially farmed, and estates owned by cities. Peasant settlement patterns also differed widely throughout the littoral. The typology included, at the one extreme, the individual farmstead in the Livonian and Estonian territories where no village organization stood between the decisions of the estate owner and the peasant family. At the other extreme were villages (of different kinds) in the Lithuanian lands and Latgale, where a peasant community could mediate between its members and the landowner.

The internal working rules and practices of estates were superimposed on peasant customs over a long period of time, sometimes displacing them or merging with them. During the fifteenth and sixteenth centuries, as the estate system stabilized, a variety of lord–peasants relations ensued. In some places peasants remained free to come and go, but rendered rental payment to the landowner with labor. Elsewhere, peasants retained their land free and clear from all obligations. Yet another pattern consisted of a mix of labor obligations, payments in kind, and severe restrictions on mobility. Variations in practice always remained, but when the Swedish administrators confronted the system in the seventeenth century in Estonia and Livonia, the harshest restrictions and labor obligations had moved to the forefront, and the manorial or estate regime had become entrenched. Even if estate owners, in theory, held their estates from some higher lord, in practice they considered their properties as their own. Even if peasant custom, in theory, still protected peasants in some ways, these protections were easily overridden by self-interested decisions by the estate owners. By the seventeenth century, as was said, estate owners in Estonia and Livonia had become somewhat market-oriented. The medieval ideal of manorial self-sufficiency no longer held, and the material interest of the estate owner dictated that an estate's peasants be tied to their holdings as an immobilized labor force. A large part of their working week was spent on the estate's fields with the rest of their labor time going to cultivate the peasants' own holdings. In return, and again in theory, the estate owner had so-called "patriarchal" responsibilities toward "his" peasants: protection against predators and criminals, dispensation of justice (including corporal punishment) at the local level for local disputes, assistance from the estate's granaries in times of famine or bad harvests, and the safeguarding of customary rights and privileges.

The Swedish efforts to change the distribution of power in the countryside revealed the limits of royal absolutism, because the Swedish crown in many ways had to retain the cooperation of the Baltic nobilities. The thin layer of crown-appointed administrators was not deep enough to administer the littoral properly. Not until the reign of Karl XI starting in 1680 did the Swedish crown devise a way to reduce the power of the landed aristocrats – the technique of "estate reduction." A system-wide reexamination of the titles to landed estates was started, and in those cases where the appropriate criteria were not met, the estate "reverted" to the Swedish crown. Through this mechanism, the Swedish crown obtained title to about five-sixths of the landed estates in Livonia and about half in Estonia. The estates were then regranted to the same owners and holders as before, but they now had to pay a considerable sum to the crown for the privilege of holding the land and to modify the rules by which the peasantry had to live. Here and there labor norms were reduced and corporal punishment brought under control. Restrictions were placed on the practice of moving peasants around at will. While this mechanism did increase the revenue flow to Stockholm, the long-term betterment of peasant conditions did not hold. The process that reduced peasant movement and increased labor norms had started before the Swedish arrival and continued after Sweden departed. This was in fact the case for all of the European east and the Russian territories as well; the Baltic littoral was no exception to the rule. Basically, the growing market orientation of landowners meant that greater productivity of the estate would bring greater profits. The only limit to how many days peasants would be required to work for the landowners to produce a marketable surplus was set not by legal norms but by human endurance. There could not be effective long-term legal prohibitions against severe exploitation even under Swedish rule, because landowner control of local law enforcement made evasion easy. It was not in the self-interest of landowners, of course, to create a situation in which peasants had absolutely no time to work their own land, but since the final arbiter of labor norms remained the individual landowner, the quality of peasant life always varied from estate to estate. The main recourse of peasants who felt unjustly treated was flight, as it had been before and remained after the Swedish conquest. Livonian peasants fled across provincial boundaries to Courland or Latgale, but also to the Prussian, Russian, and Lithuanian lands; many fled to cities, especially Riga. Flight was two-directional because many other peasants came to the littoral from neighboring lands in hopes of finding a better life. Rumors, mostly exaggerated or even false, about where labor obligations were less onerous evidently circulated widely. Initially fleeing peasant families might be temporarily rewarded in their new estate of residence by lesser labor norms and seed grain. Also, it was rumored that life on crown or ducal estates was marginally better than on private estates. The phenomenon of serf flight was common enough during the entire seventeen century to become the cause of legal action by landowners against each other and to serve as the subject of numerous condemnatory sermons by the Lutheran clergymen.

Described in abstract terms, the manorial system with its enserfed peasant population creates the impression that peasants were an anonymous and undifferentiated labor force – a dark mass of interchangeable parts – and undoubtedly some landowners thought of their peasants as that. Yet in the seventeenth century Swedish administrative efforts provided real glimpses into the everyday lives of individual peasants. The Swedish attempts to extend their influence into the countryside often started with land surveys called cadasters, which in turn required a census-like procedure of farm-to-farm visits and surveys of peasant and manorial land. The forms filled out for individual peasant farms in the process of cadastration contained the names of the resident peasants and some information about their families.

Similar kinds of information were also contained in the visitation books kept by individual Lutheran clergymen. Generally speaking, neither Estonian nor Latvian peasants in the seventeenth century had surnames, in large part because such identifiers were not needed for people who rarely moved across the boundaries of the estates in which they lived and had few dealings with institutions of government; their farmsteads, however, bore unique names. Personal references in the cadastral and visitation records might be to, say, Jaan of the Ozolian farmstead, which evidently was a sufficient identifier for clergymen and government enumerators. Such records attest to the fact that the peasantry, within the boundaries of their low social rank and local world, was a highly differentiated population with its own hierarchy that ranged from those with customary rights to a full holding, to those with various kinds of partial holdings, to others who were completely landless. The last were not necessarily the most impoverished, because their numbers were dominated by peasants who moved from farmstead to farmstead as laborers, frequently on the basis of annual verbal contracts. The landed peasants lived in family groups that had as their core a married couple (the farmstead head and his wife) with children. Not infrequently, married siblings of the head were also present as well as the aging parents of the head or his wife. The proportion of such complex family groupings was rather high in comparison with western European rural families. The size and composition of the residential group depended in large part on how many people were needed to fulfill labor norms on the manorial fields. Thus, the number of farmhands – male or female – on a particular farmstead was not necessarily a measure of its general wealth but of the size of the labor norm. Comparative research on how peasants across the littoral adapted to the manorial system in different regions remains to be done thoroughly; even now available information warns against any kind of simplification. Although Swedish efforts at peasant protection left in the oral tradition of the Estonian and Latvian peasantry memories of "the good Swedish times," the landed orders remained sufficiently entrenched to try to reverse their losses when the time was ripe.

As military and political conflict continued to roil life in the littoral, another much less noticeable change was happening in the intellectual world of the region: the appearance in printed form of reading materials in the indigenous languages. These materials were the first links in a chain of similar writings that over the next two centuries created Estonian, Latvian and Lithuanian literary languages. In the sixteenth and seventeenth centuries, however, their authors, or more frequently translators, had no such goals for their efforts. The translators were churchmen, both Lutheran and Catholic, the former responding to Martin Luther's contention that the word of God should be available to common worshippers in their own language and the latter following suit within the framework of the Catholic Counter-Reformation. Both were taking advantage of the new printing technology devised and popularized by Gutenberg. Very likely as much of their work was lost as survived, because in the Baltic region there were no repositories in which such writings could be systematically collected and preserved. Even so, in the aggregate these writings were an innovation in the cultural world of the littoral.

In the Livonian Confederation and the Polish-Lithuanian Commonwealth for several centuries, both oral and written communication had been taking place across the boundaries of many language communities. The vernaculars of the region were the least likely to have taken written form, however. The governing orders from the medieval centuries onward used Low German, Latin, Polish, Church Slavic (Ruthenian), or Swedish for official internal communications, and only in the Lithuanian territories are there suggestions that the vernacular – Lithuanian – remained in use for oral communication among the highly placed, perhaps even into the sixteenth century. Estonian, Latvian, and Lithuanian entered the sixteenth century as the principal means of communication among the lower orders of society. Of the three, the Latvian language was still in a formative process during the fifteenth and sixteenth centuries. So indeed were the people designated as "Latvians," as distinctions diminished among Couronians, Livs, Semigallians, Latgalians, and Selonians. The listings of names of peasant tax- and tribute-payers in the medieval centuries clearly show that below the users of the "higher" languages there were vast populations whose names were markedly different from those of officialdom. But collective designations of these subordinated peoples were in flux, and the governing classes apparently had little interest in carefully distinguishing among the language communities below them for scholarly or any other purposes. The translation of sacred writings into the vernaculars by Lutheran and Catholic churchmen did require such distinctions as well as a deeper understanding of the unique character of each language, and it is precisely this that renders the churchmen's efforts noteworthy.

The business of the upper orders and of officialdom was obviously in no way hindered by their ignorance of the region's vernaculars. More than likely, there was a proliferation of pidgins – vulgarized forms of the spoken languages, perhaps amplified by hand gestures, which could be varied to suit the encounters and transactions of high- and low-placed people in these language communities. Doubtless there were also intermediaries – persons who had learned the prevailing languages well enough to serve as translators. Among these intermediaries were the clergy who had been placed in charge of rural congregations. In the medieval centuries they had been instructed by the church that learning the languages of their parishioners was important even if church ritual was performed in Latin. Enforcement of and compliance with these instructions remained uneven, and in the Grand Duchy of Lithuania, it was mainly Polish-speaking clergy who had to deal with their Lithuanian-speaking parishioners. If earlier the church *encouraged* parish priests to learn the vernacular tongues, Lutheranism (and Calvinism in Poland) made this knowledge virtually mandatory. Consequently, most of the early printed matter in Latvian, Estonian, and Lithuanian was religious in nature; purely secular forms of the printed word in the vernaculars were a tangential phenomenon, subordinated to the larger religious purpose.

Translations of sacred texts were part of a much larger corpus of printed works published about or in the Baltic region and written in the principal languages of scholarship of the time, namely, Latin, Low German, or Polish. These reflected the literary thrust of Renaissance humanism in the sixteenth century and took the form of chronicles (such as Balthasar Russow's *Livonian Chronicle*,

1578), history (Michalonus Lituanus, *De moribus Tartarorum, Litunaorum, et Moschorum*, 1615), and poetry (for example, by Mikolajus Husovianus, *c.*1475–1540). Works of this nature became more numerous over time. A wide variety of genres and subjects were used, both secular and religious. In the seventeenth century they included such well-known descriptions of paganism in Livonia as Paul Einhorn's *Die Wiederlegungen der Abgotterey und nichtigen Aberglaubens* (1627) and what became a standard text of contemporary anti-witchcraft literature, Hermann Samson's *Neun Auszerlesenen und Wolgegrundete Hexen Predigt* (1626).

Intellectually inclined young men residing in the Baltic littoral could obtain an excellent education at the University of Vilnius, founded by the Jesuit Order in 1570 and raised to university status by Polish King Stephan Bathory in 1579; Dorpat (Tartu) University established by order of Gustavus II Adolphus in Estonia in 1632; and the university in Königsberg, Prussia, called "Albertina" in honor of its founder, Duke Albert of Prussia, who established it in 1544 as a counterpart to the Jesuit-founded Cracow Academy. The life of the mind in the Baltic littoral could be quite lively in spite of disruptions and warfare, but to make their mark writers had to use the "cultural" languages (Ger. *Kultursprachen*). Some of these authors may have been of Estonian, Latvian, or Lithuanian peasant ancestry, but latinized and polonized proper names render the social origins of many authors unknowable.

Writings in the "cultural languages," however, represented no particular turning point, but rather attested to the littoral's having become the northeastern sector of general European culture, reflecting its trends and interests. What really represented a break with the medieval past were such works as the Lutheran catechisms published in Estonian in 1535 by Johann Koell, and in the South Žemaitian dialect of Lithuanian in 1547 by Martynas Mažvydas in Königsberg. Additionally a Latvian translation of the Lord's Prayer was included in Simon Grunau's *Chronicle* in 1529–1531. These works, following Luther's injunction, testified to all who could read that the vernaculars of the littoral had potential for becoming literary languages. Catholic efforts of a similar sort were not far behind, as shown by the *Catechismus Catholicorum* translated from German into Latvian by the Jesuit Ertman Tolgsdorff in 1585. The work of Mažvydas also illustrated the importance to Lithuanian cultural life of the existence of a Lithuanian language enclave in Prussia, where he was a Lutheran minister. These works were joined by other translations similarly small in scope: some craft guild statutes and the Psalms (*Undeutsche Psalmen*, 1587) into Latvian, and even more ambitious works such as the never-published translation of the entire Bible into Lithuanian by Jonas Bretkunas between 1575 and 1590.

During the seventeenth century, interest in the littoral vernaculars became broader and deeper and eventually included not only translations but also learning aids and original religious prose and poetry. In 1637, Heinrich Stahl published the first Estonian grammar, in which, typical of many of these efforts, the Estonian language was adapted to German grammatical rules; and in 1653, Daniel Klein published the first explanation of Lithuanian grammar, *Grammaticus Litvanica*. There were also dictionaries and grammars: the three-language (Latin–Polish–Lithuanian) dictionary compiled in 1629 by the Jesuit Konstantinas Syrvidas; an Estonian grammar published in Latin in 1639 by Johann Hornung; and the first Latvian dictionary, *Lettus*, published in 1638 by Georgius Mancelius. Mancelius was an exceptional pathbreaker, having learned Latvian so well that his *Langgewünschte Lettsiche Postill*, a collection of his sermons published in 1654, remained favored reading in Livonia for other scholars well into the eighteenth century. Almost of the same importance was Christophorus Fűreccerus (*c*.1615–1685), whose translated and original religious songs could be found in Latvian Lutheran hymnals well into the twentieth century. A clerical intellectual of Latvian extraction, Jānis Reiters (*c*.1631–1695), himself a translator of fragments of the Old and New Testaments, was critical of Mancelius' use of Latvian and evidently paid for his comments by being marginalized in the Livonian Lutheran Church.

These linguistically adept clergymen all realized the importance of Martin Luther's translation of the Bible for the development of the German language. Although they attempted to replicate that feat for the littoral vernaculars, success came relatively late. An early translation of the Bible into Lithuanian by Bretkunas was, as noted, never published; another such abortive effort was made by Samuel Chylinski in 1657–1660, surprisingly, in London. Not until 1710 was a Lithuanian New Testament translation published by Samuel

Bitner. The first entire Bible followed in 1753, again in Königsberg, based on Luther's German translation. Andreas Virginius translated the New Testament into the South Estonian dialect in 1686, but it was the translation of the whole Bible into the North Estonian dialect in 1739 that subsequently became the basis of literary Estonian. The Latvian Bible in its entirety was translated by the Lutheran pastor Ernst Glück (1652–1705) who started the task in 1681, finished it in 1689, and finally saw the printed version, much edited by his clerical colleagues, in 1694. Indeed, the Bible translations in all three cases were to play roughly the same role for the three littoral vernaculars as Luther's translation had for German.

It is not always clear how many of these writings in the vernacular languages were created for the peasantry to read directly and how many were created by the more linguistically adept clergy for their clerical brothers. Reading skills were not widespread among the peasants, nor is it certain that peasants would have recognized in these writings the languages they spoke. Spoken vernaculars were not themselves standardized among those who used them, nor was there any standardization of how their sounds should be transliterated. It is difficult to speak of a demand for religious literature among the peasantry, but the interest among both Catholic and Protestant clergy in learning the vernaculars never abated. Although with each passing generation the amount of printed materials increased, it did not constitute a literacy revolution; very few peasants learned to read or write. At least in the Livonian lands, estate owners frequently voiced opposition to the development of such skills, fearing that "educated" peasants would flee to cities where such skills were in much higher demand.

A complete list of the book-length works produced by the Lutheran and Catholic clergy in the vernacular languages might suggest a veritable outpouring. In fact, however, the pace of their appearance was rather slow, though it did increase noticeably as the seventeenth century wore on. In the Latvian language, for example, about ten works appeared in the first half of the seventeenth century, whereas the second half saw between fifty-seven and sixty. In the period from 1631 to 1710, some forty-five books were published in Estonian. These are impressive numbers compared with the emptiness of earlier centuries, but they are not great enough to have made the printed word commonplace. Most peasants associated written and printed material with the authorities above them, either those in secular administration or those in the church. Reading and writing skills remained largely exceptional and were associated with the kind of upward social mobility that would carry their practitioners out of the language communities of their birth and into those of the over-lords. Printing establishments in the littoral were few in number, and methods of distributing books remained primitive. Authorities could easily prevent the printing of books with suspicious content, and the printing of books and other materials could not be counted to earn anyone a living because the reading public was simply too small. Rural schools remained an exception, and although both the church and secular governments, particularly in Swedish Livonia and Estonia, reiterated their intention to establish elementary schools in all parishes, the implementation of this policy was patchy owing to the scarcity of resources and trained schoolteachers.

By spreading the word of God in the vernaculars, the literary clergy had another quite open element in their agenda: combating what they thought was the pernicious influence of the oral tradition among the peasants. The "superstitious nonsense" of their rural parishioners remained very much alive, and the exasperated clerics sometimes associated elements of the oral tradition such as curses, sayings, and the incantations of folk medicine with witchcraft and devil-worship. Paul Einhorn, for example, in his *Die Wiederlegungen der Abgotterey und nichtigen Aberglaubens* (1627) portrayed Livonia as a land of werewolves and witches. Others, such as Mancelius, who were perhaps more familiar with the oral traditions in the vernacular languages, were less condemnatory but still assumed that the intellectual content of the oral was vastly inferior to that of systematic and organized learning in the languages of the upper orders.

The hope of Catholic and Lutheran clergymen that peasants would readily abandon their beliefs was somewhat naïve. As long as distinct social and occupational groups in the littoral populations were sep-arated from each other by the languages they used, peasants could count on the oral tradition as uniquely theirs and would use it to escape the harsh realities of everyday life. They resisted what the clergy understood to be a civilizing and christianizing effort on their part. Beyond this, however, the clerics engaged in the effort clearly found it intellectually stimulating. They studied the structure of the vernaculars, listened carefully to their sounds, queried native speakers about grammatical rules, experimented with new words the languages did not already contain, and corresponded with each other about their findings. In the process, they developed a new if paternalistic regard for the ways of the peasantry. Even if the social distance between them and their flocks remained, some of them, such as Georgius Mancelius in Livonia, produced sermons that, when collected and published, occupied a place of honor next to the Bible translations in the homes of the peasants who could afford them. Missing from this sympathetic attitude, of course, was any systematic criticism of the socioeconomic conditions of the peasantry. The Lutheran clergy especially held to the notion that social hierarchy was established by God and that those at the bottom, however numerous, needed to bear their burdens with patience and in a submissive, Christian spirit.

COLLIDING AMBITIONS AFTER 1650

As the manorial regime, serfdom, and books in the vernacular languages were quietly becoming fixtures of everyday life in the littoral, geopolitics were coming once again to preoccupy the thoughts of the regional monarchs. The negative aspects of location resumed their destructiveness. The royal dynasts of Poland-Lithuania (of the Vasa family), Sweden (also the Vasas), and Russia (the Romanovs) decided that they were not satisfied with the territorial settlements of the first part of the seventeenth century and began to lay plans for achieving complete hegemony over the entire area. The Polish-Lithuania monarchs were the most cautious; the internal dissensions of their realm no longer enabled them easily to marshal military support from their landed aristocrats for any kind of preemptive expansion. This was not the case with the Swedish rulers, however. Having obtained control over Livonia and Estonia in the Peace of Altmark, Sweden rightly pictured Poland-Lithuania as the weakest of its regional potential opponents, and with the support of the elector of Brandenburg (the former territory of the Teutonic Order), it invaded Poland in 1656, winning a crucial victory at Warsaw. The pretext of this invasion was intra-dynastic: Charles X Gustavus of Sweden (ruled 1654–1660) claimed that John Casimir of Poland (ruled 1648–1668) refused to recognize the Swedish monarch's legitimacy. The Swedish foray into Polish territory was enough, however, to bring Russia into the fray on the side of Poland, and the Swedish venture suffered a final defeat in 1657. This conflict was concluded with the treaties of Oliva and Kardis in 1660 and 1661, in which Sweden managed to solidify its hold over its littoral territories through negotiation.

Russia took the absence of a major triumph by Sweden as a sign of the latter's weakness as an expansionist power, which suggested to the Russians (under Tsar Alexis, the second Romanov, 1645–1676) that better regional alliance-making with Poland-Lithuania would feed off resentments over Sweden's hegemonic plans and possibly expel Sweden from the Baltic littoral. Russia's machinations took a generation to bear fruit. Meanwhile, the Swedish monarchs continued their policy of estate reduction in Livonia and Estonia. Ironically, this policy appeared to be designed to turn the landed aristocracies of these two territories against the Swedish crown. These factors combined to trigger a series of conflicts known as the Great Northern War, lasting from 1700 to 1721. At the conclusion of the fighting, the configuration of power in the eastern Baltic littoral was changed completely: Sweden had been expelled from the region, Russia had added Livonia and Estonia to its western borderland, and Poland-Lithuania revealed itself even more than before a weak and weakening regional great power.

The littoral was the stage on which much if not most of the fighting took place. The first act of the Great Northern War, however, took place both on- and off-stage, as it were, with the 1700 Danish invasion of Schleswig (controlled by Sweden) and the invasion of Livonia by Augustus II of Poland, who was both the elector of the German state of Saxony and the elected king of Poland-Lithuania. In 1699, Denmark, Poland-Lithuania, and Russia had concluded a secret alliance against Sweden, and the two invasions were the fruit of that alliance. These early battles might have remained contained if two very ambitious teenage monarchs had not come to power – fifteen-year-old Charles XII in Sweden (1697) and seventeen-year-old Peter I (the Great) in Russia (1689). Both they and their counselors and advisors nurtured far-reaching plans.

Charles wanted to maintain and even expand Sweden's position in northern Europe; Peter wanted to make Russia into a naval power, for which he needed the seaport cities of the eastern Baltic littoral. Initially, Charles proved to be the more innovative of the two aspirants: he quickly settled the conflict with Denmark and then arrived in Livonia in November 1700 to do battle against the Russians, defeating them in a major battle at Narva on the northern Baltic coast. Turning south in 1701, Charles then relieved Riga of the siege that had been imposed on the city by Poland-Lithuania which had allied itself with Russia and together with Saxon troops had invaded Livonia from the south.

Charles drove the combined Polish-Lithuanian-Saxon forces southward out of Livonia and then invaded Polish-Lithuanian territory, managing to capture both Warsaw and Cracow in 1702. The war had thus been brought to Poland-Lithuania where it played out over the next six years. Peter of Russia withdrew from the fray temporarily, expecting that the continued fighting between Sweden and Poland-Lithuania would drain them both militarily and financially and offer Russia a better opportunity to intervene. In 1706, Augustus II of Poland-Lithuania was forced to abdicate by the estranged magnates and gentry. The Polish parliament (*Sejm*) elected Stanislas Leszcynski – from a prominent Polish magnate family and a pro-Swedish ruler – to the monarchical office. Augustus, however, refused to leave, and plotted with the Russians for his return to office. For the next four years, Poland-Lithuania had both a seated and an unseated monarch: the former in alliance with Sweden, and the latter with Russia. Augustus' abdication, however, brought a brief respite in the fighting on Polish-Lithuanian soil.

Even at this juncture of the Great Northern War clearly the belligerents were growing progressively weaker internally, with Russia poised to benefit. Many gentry and magnates of the Grand Duchy of Lithuania were at daggers drawn with the Polish monarch Augustus II, seeing him pursuing policies in the interests of Saxony rather than those of the commonwealth. The landowning nobility of the Courland duchy (nominally loyal to the Polish-Lithuanian king) increasingly feared that their land was becoming a permanent battleground between externally situated monarchs – the Swedish king, the Polish monarch, and the Russian tsar – in a struggle that could end with the loss of the Courland landholders' "traditional rights." Consequently, the Courlanders tried to practice a kind of neutrality. The landholding nobilities of Swedish Livonia and Estonia were already seething over the estate-reduction policies of the Swedish crown, and some of their number were casting an eye toward the benefits that might accrue from a Russian sovereign. In Polish Livonia – an intermediate territory – landowners recognized their precarious position since they were vulnerable to invasion from all sides. In fact, they were invaded as Swedish forces advanced from Estonia toward Lithuania. Here also attitudes toward the Polish-Saxon Augustus II were less than enthusiastic. The urban patriciates of Riga were exploring which of the powers would defend them against the others, while the vast populations of peasants – Estonians, Latvians, and Lithuanians – were fully preoccupied with trying to stay out of harm's way. Some of the Latvian and Estonian peasantry joined the armed forces of Sweden, and numerous others were dragooned by the invading armies into support units for digging, building, and carting. Among the peasants, survival rather than loyalty was the driving force: there were no obvious polities to which they could attach their loyalty, their immediate lords were themselves ambiguous, and none of the warring monarchs at this juncture looked like a victor.

The fighting resumed in 1707 as Sweden's Charles, emboldened by his victories in Poland-Lithuania, now turned his full attention to Russia. Peter, however, had managed to strengthen his position in the north to the point of founding his new capital city of St. Petersburg at the mouth of the Neva River in 1703, retaking Narva in 1704, and replenishing his army. Active engagements between the Swedish and Russian armies resumed on Estonian territory in 1708, even though Charles' main army was now located in the south and was marching toward Moscow. Here Charles miscalculated: he turned toward Ukraine and met with a crushing defeat in the Battle of Poltava in 1709. The Swedish army broke up, and Charles fled to Turkey to regroup and plan a return. Duplicitous deal-making between Peter and Augustus II of Poland resulted in the latter's return to the Polish-Lithuanian throne with the promise that Augustus' continuing support of Russia in the final expulsion of Sweden from littoral territories would earn him the Swedish Livonian lands. Charles returned to Sweden in 1714 to plan for further military ventures but was assassinated in 1718. His sister Ulrica Eleanora succeeded him to the Swedish throne; she ruled for two years and was in turn succeeded by her husband, Frederick I, in 1720.

Under Ulrica, the Swedish nobility began to reassert powers against the absolutism practiced by the Swedish crown during the seventeenth century. By the time Frederick I came to the throne a large part of the nobility demanded and obtained a less adventurous foreign policy. In two treaties in 1720–1721 Sweden settled its Baltic affairs, first with Poland-Lithuania, then with Saxony, and finally with Russia. The Treaty of Nystad in 1721 ceded Livonia and Estonia (and other territories farther north) to Russia; Riga had already surrendered to the Russians in 1709. Swedish rule in the littoral thus came to an end. Poland-Lithuania, much weakened by its internal political divisions and smarting from Russia's broken promise about Livonia, was able, however, to retain suzerainty over the Duchy of Courland and Polish Livonia. Peter the Great had succeeded in expelling from the littoral his strongest rival. Now that his erstwhile ally Poland-Lithuania was no longer a serious threat, Peter had his Baltic ports.

Judgments differ about whether the Great Northern War was more destructive than the extended Livonian Wars of the late sixteenth and early seventeenth century. The warfare that produced the breakup of the Livonian Confederation lasted longer and had more intervals when fighting ceased, thus providing more opportunities for rebuilding. The Northern War was more compact and involved the presence of larger armies on the soil of the littoral. Both were long enough for non-combatants, particularly the peasantry, to experience them as a seemingly unending series of raids and depredations to the point that sudden waves of destruction must have seemed a part of normal life. In both wars, all the armies that traversed the littoral made great demands on the local populations. In the Northern War the Russian forces particularly used a scorched-earth strategy, especially in the Estonian territories, because the Russians wanted to deny Sweden a haven for its return because the Swedish army in the early phases of the war remained undefeated. The often-cited reports written to Peter by the exceptionally cruel Russian general Boris Sheremetev seemed to delight in describing looting, pillaging, raping, and killing, and the depopulating of Estonian and Livonian districts through the deportation of thousands of inhabitants to the Russian interior (the translator of the Latvian Bible, the pastor Ernst Glück, among them).

As if deaths directly or indirectly due to military movements were not punishment enough from God (as some thought), there were also famines and plagues during the period of the Northern War. A major famine struck the region even before warfare began (1695–1697), while the plague visited the littoral's populations again at the midpoint of the fighting. The famine of 1695–1697 was actually a northern European phenomenon; in some districts of Livonia about one-quarter of the population died before the war started in 1700. One consequence of the famine before and during the war in the affected districts was a sharp rise in criminality: impoverished and hungry individuals and families roamed the countryside, plundering and murdering those who had survived. In 1697, Riga had to cope with the incursion of 2,250 beggars, according to the city records. The plague – the most deadly of the epidemics that struck the littoral populations from time to time in the seventeenth century – was on this occasion an eastern European phenomenon, first affecting Turkey, Hungary, and Poland (1707); then in 1708 Silesia and Lithuania; finally reaching Courland in 1709, and both the Swedish and Polish Livonia lands and Estonia in 1710. In the littoral, the death toll from the plague was far beyond the previous experience of its residents. In Žemaitija, for example, estimates place population losses at about 50 percent for the whole region; in Courland both urban and rural populations lost at least that proportion. One estimate for the Latvian-speaking regions of Livonia suggests the population dropped from 136,000 before the plague hit to 52,000 immediately after. In Estonia, Tallinn lost about three-quarters of its population, and the rural population was reduced by about half. Not all districts were equally affected, of course, and estimates are all approximate. In the countryside, sudden depopulation in the short run worsened the relationships between the remaining peasant-serfs and their lords: the former often fled to seek their fortunes with landowners who promised lighter work loads; the latter sought to bind the remaining peasantry even more tightly and by force to their own estates.

The reduction of the labor force in the affected districts in the littoral delivered a blow to both rural and urban economic productivity that continued to be felt for at least another generation.

As a result of these demographic catastrophies, the populations of the littoral began the eighteenth century with their numbers at an unprecedentedly low level. The estimated population of Estonia (which became part of the Russian Empire after 1721) had fallen from 350,000 in 1695 to about 120,000–140,000 by the time of the Nystad Treaty in 1721. The population of Livonia (both its Latvian and Estonian parts, which also went to Russia in 1721) fell from about 503,000 in 1700 to 333,000; that of Polish Livonia from about 103,000 in 1700 to 70,000; that of Courland, which was somewhat less affected, from 211,000 in 1683 to 209,000; and that of the Grand Duchy of Lithuania from about 4.5 million in 1650 to about 1.7 million after the Northern War. It is highly likely that the littoral had fewer Estonian, Latvian, and Lithuanian inhabitants at the start of the famed century of Enlightenment than when the sixteenth century began.

4

Installing hegemony: the littoral and tsarist Russia, 1710–1800

At the start of the eighteenth century, the Baltic littoral was a battleground for regional powers, but by the end it had become part of the western borderlands of the Russian Empire. Sweden had been expelled from the eastern shore of the Baltic by the 1720s and the Polish-Lithuanian Commonwealth appeared increasingly unable to keep Russia from meddling in its internal affairs. In western and central Europe, competing powers fought a series of wars about questions of succession while seeking to consolidate European colonies in the New World. At the same time, innovative thinkers in France, England, and the German lands launched and presided over the Enlightenment, writing timeless works about the social contract, the perfectibility of man, and the separation of powers.

In Livonia and Estonia, the new Russian ruling elite, having replaced the Swedish overlords, struck deals with regional and local landowning nobilities in order to secure social and political order and to establish effective administration of the enserfed peasant populations – the Estonians, Latvians, and Lithuanians. Old administrative boundaries were reaffirmed and new ones created in a manner that cut through the language communities of old Livonia, dividing the Estonians in two. The Latvian population remained divided between southern Livonia, on the one hand, and the Duchy of Courland and Latgale, on the other, both the latter still under the authority of the Polish-Lithuanian Commonwealth. In dealing with the upper orders of the western territories, Russia played different roles in each of the western territories: permissive in the case of

Estonia and Livonia, intrusive in the case of Poland-Lithuania. Not until the last quarter of the eighteenth century did the St. Petersburg government under Catherine II (the Great) complete the task started by Peter I (the Great) in bringing the Polish-Lithuanian Commonwealth fully into the Russian fold.

In its dealings with the regional power-holders, the Russian government needed to expend little effort to persuade them to fall into line politically. In Livonia and Estonia the loyalties of the dominant orders shifted so easily from the Swedish king to the Russian tsar that the process could be described as as the fulfillment of the agendas of both sides. Estonia and Livonia came to the Romanovs as much as the Romanovs came to them. At the end of the century, after the more complicated absorption of Poland-Lithuania had run its course, the Russian Empire was bordered on the west by two new neighbors: the kingdom of Prussia and the empire of the Austrian Habsburgs. This close proximity to central Europe remained important, if in no other sense than culturally. Even if the local governing orders of the littoral reoriented their political loyalties to the east and rendered service militarily and bureaucratically to the Russian tsar, their cultural and religious connections remained solidly anchored in central and western Europe. To some extent the Romanov rulers themselves remained western-oriented: Catherine was German, for example, and corresponded with such Enlightenment figures as Voltaire and Diderot; the French language was used with increasing frequency in Russian court circles; and thus the obviously "western" culture of the Baltic littoral's upper orders was accorded a begrudging respect, at least for the time being. Appreciation of this relationship in the eighteenth century went along with Russian satisfaction about having brought under their control the old Hanseatic cities of Riga and Reval (Tallinn), from whence western influences were expected to radiate farther into Russia proper, thus aiding the task of westernization.

RUSSIA AS A PERMISSIVE AUTOCRACY

During the year 1710 the Russian army commanders and Tsar Peter I accepted the capitulation of the *Ritterschaften* (corporations of nobility) of Livonia and Estonia, as well as of the residents of Riga,

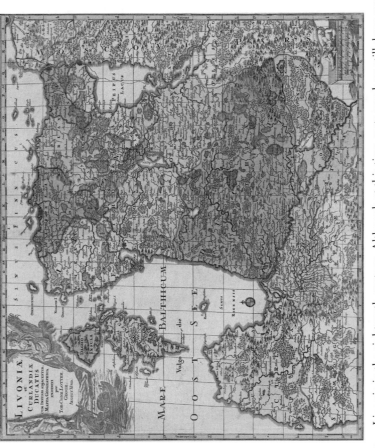

Map 5 Livonia in the eighteenth century. Although at this time cartographers still drew maps of "Livonia," slowly but surely the entire littoral was being absorbed by the Russian Empire.

Kuressaare on the island of Saaremaa (Ger. *Ösel*), Pärnu, Tallinn, and the other principal cities of the littoral north of Courland. The Northern War continued in other venues until the Treaty of Nystadt in 1721, but the power centers of the Baltic littoral, decimated by battlefield losses and the plague, had had enough. The capitulation agreements were designed to preserve maximum freedom of action for the Russian tsar, the nobilities, and the urban patriciates; the peasantries, of course, were not part of the negotiations. Lutheranism was reaffirmed as the principal confession of the two Baltic lands – now to be known officially as the *gubernnias* (provinces) of *Lieflandskaya gubernnia* and *Estlandskaya gubernnia* (from the German *Liefland* and *Estland*). Also reaffirmed were the rights of the governing orders and the use of the German language in provincial administration. Tsar Peter was heard to remark during the negotiations that it was only right that the German language should be used in these provinces since only Germans lived there. The landed aristocracies (and in a limited way the urban patriciates) alone were to be involved in the institutions of governance. The claims of the *Ritterschaften* were grounded in a 1561 document called "privileges of Sigismund Augustus" in which the said Polish monarch was alleged to have granted them a wide variety of rights; the original document, however, had been lost in the course of time. The Swedish government in the seventeenth century had refused to recognize the validity of these so-called "privileges" since there was no documentary proof, but Peter I did not hesitate. The capitulation agreements essentially restored in full the rights and privileges the Swedes had eliminated or restricted, which meant, among other things, that the landed properties the Swedish crown had claimed in the "estate-reduction" process were returned in full to the *Ritterschaften*. The practical affect of all these Russian promises and reassurances was that the *Ritterschaften* and urban patriciates, in theory, were to enjoy greater autonomy than they ever had before.

Seemingly innocuous phrasing in the capitulation agreements, however, reserved to the Russian tsar the real rights and privileges of his high autocratic office, and this meant in practice that the Russian government could intervene in the affairs of the Baltic lands whenever the situation appeared to warrant it. Tactically, this was a clever move on Peter the Great's part: while appearing to be exceptionally permissive, the tsar-autocrat had no intention of limiting his own rights of action. The Russian side needed the full support of the Baltic landed aristocrats, because there was no real guarantee, at least in the short run, that Sweden might not try to regain its lost territories. Peter also recognized the deep hunger for autonomy the Baltic landowners had nursed in reaction to the reforms of the Swedish period. At the same time Peter understood that once the Baltic lands entered the imperial system, he and his successors could repeal whatever noble rights and privileges needed to be removed or restricted when a particular situation demanded, and that the Baltic nobility would have no power, legal or military, with which to oppose such decisions. In practice during most of the eighteenth century, the Russian rulers did not need to invoke their "higher" rights in full, but the fact that the new Russian overlords were no strangers to duplicity was already symbolized by their quick abrogation of some rights granted to the city of Riga and, in another domain, the cavalier manner in which Peter broke his promise to Augustus II of Poland-Lithuania that Livonia would be added to the commonwealth after the Swedes were defeated.

The *Ritterschaften* of Livland and Estland seized the opportunity afforded by Peter's permissiveness to formalize their own standing as a closed noble corporation. In 1728, the Livland nobility received permission from the tsarist government to establish a formal register (*Matrikul*) of its corporate members and to have the exclusive privilege of admitting new ones. The final version of this register was approved by the Livland diet (*Landtag*) in 1747 with a membership consisting of 172 families. The number of registered members would be slowly expanded over the next century, with some of the new members being Russian noble families whom the tsarist government persuaded the German nobility to accept as equals "voluntarily." Similar registers of nobility were established for the province of Estland (127 families) and the island of Ösel (25 families). This formalization of the noble order had two consequences. It restricted to a tiny, Germany-speaking minority the number of persons who had the right to govern, and it produced divisions in the ranks of the Baltic German elites with the *Ritterschaften* on one side and all other powerful people on the other. It is probable that the St. Petersburg government understood that, on the one hand, extensive provincial autonomy would aid the crown in governing the new territories, and that, on the other, it did not harm the crown's cause to have potential rifts in the provincial elites. This strategy was certainly one way of handling the problems that might arise from the accumulation of new territories in which the population was almost entirely non-Russian and retained strong cultural ties with western and central Europe.

In the third decade of the eighteenth century, the authority of the St. Petersburg government was represented in the two Baltic provinces by a pair of governors-general with seats in Tallinn (for Estland) and Riga (for Livland). The tsar, of course, had no formal authority in the territories south of the Livland border – the Duchy of Courland, Inflanty (Latgale), and the Grand Duchy of Lithuania – since they remained constituent parts of the Polish-Lithuanian Commonwealth; St. Petersburg, however, quickly found other ways to make its will felt there. The governors-general of Estland and Livland were appointed by the tsar, but in the eighteenth century most of them actually spent little time in the Baltic region, so that everyday governance was handled by their administrative assistants, who were appointed from among the Baltic German *Ritterschaften*. Initially, the representatives of the crown had two principal practical interests: caretaking of the military units that continued to be stationed in the littoral, and the collection and efficient delivery of taxes to the treasury in St. Petersburg. The apparatus of government in each province was expanded during the century by representatives of various departments (*collegia*) of the central government as it developed an interest in other domains of life such as the administration of justice, mining, forests, industrial development, and administration of crown estates. Frequently these officials were also chosen by St. Petersburg from the Baltic German landed nobility. Religious matters were handled through consistories (*consistoria*), which were boards of Lutheran clerics retained from the Swedish administrative apparatus of the seventeenth century. In many ways, the Russian administrative structures in the two provinces resembled what the Swedes had created, since Tsar Peter was in fact an admirer of his former enemy's centralized government. The main difference was staffing: the Swedish government of Livonia had been staffed mostly by Swedish officials, whereas the Russians relied heavily on the Baltic Germans. Because of the prominence of the German language in provincial administration, of course, this arrangement made sense: the frequently absent Russian administrators were less likely to learn German than the Baltic Germans were to learn the languages of the central government. Of course, the arrangement created the possibility of divided loyalties for the Baltic German administrators, who had to serve the tsar and represent his interests while at the same time protecting the interests of their own social order. The number of ethnic Russians in the provincial governmental apparatus (other than the army) remained considerably less than one percent of the total population throughout the century. To ensure against surprises the *Ritterschaften* eventually developed a kind of permanent "lobby" in St. Petersburg – well-placed and wealthy Baltic German aristocrats who kept an eye on the proceedings of the Russian government and sought to divert or modify decisions that might be inimical to Baltic German control over littoral affairs.

The permissive attitudes of the St. Petersburg government encouraged some in the Livonian and Estonian landowning aristocracy to advance highly inflated definitions of their rights in the region, particularly with respect to the peasants on their estates. The notorious 1739 declaration of *Landrat* O. F. Rosen to the Livland governor-general announced that "just as peasants in their person and body belong to their lord and are subordinated to him, so also such ownership extends to the property of the peasants . . . In accordance with these rights, everything that the peasant makes and grows he makes and grows not for himself but for his lord." Such an attitude lay behind a series of changes that continued on estates throughout the eighteenth century at the expense of the peasants. Peasant labor obligations were increased through the manipulation of vague passages in regulations (what was "a day of work"?); unregulated customary obligations were transformed into fixed obligations; estate lands were resurveyed so as to reduce the proportion allocated for peasant farmsteads and increase the proportion allocated for the estate owner (the demesne); labor obligations were detached from the individual farmstead and attached to the persons living on the farmstead; new obligations were invented in the form of piecemeal labor; obligations that earlier had been transformed into monetary payments were changed back into labor. Because appeals against internal decisions of estate administration almost always were quashed early on within the existing legal system, the peasantry really had no place to go to complain. The Livland *Landtag* remained adamant, declaring in 1765 that "peasants are the slaves (*servi*) of their lords in the full meaning of Roman law; their return can be demanded [if they had fled], they can be given [to others], and they can be sold. Even though [former monarchs] tried to lighten serfdom, the *Ritterschaft* has determined that this is impossible because serfdom is rooted in the natural character of these nations [Estonians and Latvians]." Numerous landowners took literally the notion that they owned the bodies of their peasants. An erudite commentator on Livland affairs, A. W. Hupel, wrote in his 1770 book *Topographische Nachrichten von Lief- und Ehstland*, published in Riga, that "peasants here are not as expensive as negroes are in the American colonies: a farmhand can be purchased for 30 to 50 rubles, while a craftsman, cook, or weaver may cost as much as 100 rubles. A whole family costs just about as much: kitchen maids rarely bring more than 10 rubles, and children are sold for 4 rubles each. The occasional laborer and his children can be bought and sold or can be traded for other things – horses, dogs, smoking pipes, and so forth." Rumors circulated in rural areas that conditions were less harsh on larger estates than on smaller ones, and less on crown than on private estates. Such rumors were at the root of the persistence of serf flight throughout the century. A constant theme of dealings between landowners became the refusal to return runaway serfs. How many of the more than eleven hundred owners and lessees of estates exploited their local power maximally is difficult to say, but the land allocated to peasants on estates did shrink over the century, and labor obligations did increase in amount and intensity. Estates had every incentive to push hard against their captive labor force, because during the second half of the century it was becoming increasingly clear that an external market existed for the grain they produced.

As the eighteenth century wore on, any revanchist move in the region by Sweden seemed unlikely, and the St. Petersburg government allowed the Baltic German *Ritterschaften* wide latitude in running the new territories. The government probably could not have done otherwise, short of flooding the littoral territories with Russian officials. The system was set up to convey orders from the top – from an autocratic monarch and his advisors – which it did without fail. But it lacked effective oversight institutions to ensure that the tsar's decisions were implemented in the intended manner, especially in the interface between the all-encompassing enserfed peasant populations and the owners or renters of landed estates. The justice system in principle allowed peasants to bring complaints, but such grievances had to be in the German language since the lower ranks of the justice system were staffed by Baltic German officials. Though periodically Russian administrators made inspections tours, in the end the accuracy of the information they received about the state of affairs in the new territories depended on the honesty of the same people whose interests would be hurt by unwelcome royal interventions. Estonians and Latvians, because of their low social standing, were by definition excluded from the administrative apparatus; only at the end of the century did some Latvian entrepreneurs in Riga undertake successful court cases to defend their "rights." In most respects during the post-1721 period, the St. Petersburg government remained almost an invisible force in the countryside; and in the few urban areas, especially in Riga and Tallinn, the Russian presence took the form only of soldiers stationed in barracks. Only in the eastern reaches of the littoral, close to the Russian border, did the government try to settle empty land with "imported" Russian peasants, but even there their numbers were minimal.

One prominent reason for a relatively light-handed Russian approach to the region was the visible devastation that had come to it during the period of the Great Northern War. Urban areas – which were of undoubted interest to St. Petersburg as sources of revenue – had been severely impaired. Only a fraction of the populations of the main cities and towns of Estland – Tartu, Tallinn, Narva, and Pärnu – remained. Tartu (Dorpat) did not return to its prewar population of about 2,000 until the last decades of the eighteenth century, and Tallinn did not rebound to its prewar population of about 11,000 until 1782. In Livonia, the population of Riga in 1710 of about 8,800 had been severely impacted by the plague of that year and in 1728 it stood at about 6,100; as the most active city of the new territories economically it rebounded to about 14,000 inhabitants in 1760 and to about 24,500 in 1782, but the rebuilding process took almost two generations. Numerous rural areas had also been depopulated, which of course directly impacted the incomes of the landed nobility. Thus the empire had acquired not an economically booming territory with a brisk urban dimension but a severely damaged one. Recovery could come only from the active efforts of the existing population as it exploited whatever new opportunities the new situation provided.

RUSSIA AS AN INTRUSIVE NEIGHBOR

The 1721 treaty did not directly affect the status of the other littoral territories – the Polish-Lithuanian Commonwealth, the Duchy of Courland and Semigallia, and Inflanty (the former Polish Livonia). The commonwealth remained nominally an independent political entity. The ducal dynasty of Courland and the landed nobility remained in place with the Polish king as their sovereign, and Inflanty continued to be governed by administrators appointed from Cracow and Vilnius. On maps of the period, these lands were shown with borders separating them from each other within the commonwealth and from the former Livonian lands now governed directly by Russia. But this separation belied reality, because during the Northern War and increasingly with each decade thereafter, the Romanovs found small and large ways to intervene in the further development of these lands, sometimes by direct invitation from the Polish monarch and other times surreptitiously. At the very least, the commonwealth and the lands it contained were being viewed by Russia's political leadership as within its sphere of influence. At the same time the existing borders were respected by all, and Governor-General George Browne (1762–1792) of Livland was quoted as describing serfs who fled from Livland into Courland as having taken refuge "abroad."

For decades after the Northern War the considerable amount of border-crossing in the littoral by fleeing serfs, economic migrants of various kinds, traders, and army units was seldom successfully controlled by the governments of the respective territories. Even so, the lands of the southern part of the littoral remained distinguishable from one another in terms of the combined ethnic, linguistic, and religious character of each. By the mid-eighteenth century, the population of the Grand Duchy of Lithuania consisted largely of polonized Lithuanian magnates, somewhat less polonized gentry (Pol. *szlachta*), and Lithuanian-speaking peasants. The Courland duchy had as its governing stratum a Baltic German dynasty and Baltic German landowners, and as its majority population mostly Latvian-speaking peasants. The ruling circles of Inflanty consisted of polonized landowners of Baltic German extraction, other land-owners who were Polish by ancestry, and a peasantry who spoke a dialect of the Latvian language. There were also religious distinc-tions: the Lithuanian lands were primarily Catholic, the Courlandic territories were primarily Lutheran with a substantial subpopulation of Catholics, and Inflanty was a mixture with the Catholic faith predominant. Interspersed among these principal religious groupings were the Russian Orthodox and Jews, both of whom were especially numerous at this time in Inflanty and the Lithuanian duchy, in sharp contrast to their numbers in the Courland duchy, Livonia, and Estonia. Not surprisingly, the number of Jews in Poland-Lithuania was large, given the long history of receptivity toward them, primar-ily for economic reasons, in both the duchy and the commonwealth. By the second half of the century (1764–1766), their number in the commonwealth was estimated to have been about 750,000 (about 5.3 percent of the total population) with about 210,000 in the Lithuanian Grand Duchy (4,000 in Vilnius and about 2,000 in Kaunas). These numbers dwarfed the small totals of Jews in the littoral lands to the north, including Inflanty.

After the Northern War, the monarch of the Polish-Lithuanian Commonwealth continued to bear the titles of King of Poland and Grand Duke of Lithuania, but sharp distinctions between the Polish and Lithuanian territories had already been fading during the latter part of the seventeenth century and continued to do so during the eighteenth. The idea of a fully independent Lithuanian duchy – an equal partner – remained alive in the minds of the magnate and gentry families there and was revived periodically for political pur-poses; the idea was also buttressed by the continued robustness of the Lithuanian codes of law and area-specific governmental institutions. Yet the cultural and linguistic polonization of the landed social orders in Lithuania reduced the visibility of the distinction for every-one else. To other governments in central and eastern Europe, the Polish-Lithuanian Commonwealth had become simply Poland and the Lithuanian language spoken by many of the duchy's commoners was one of the many "peasant languages" of the Polish kingdom. Both partners of the old Lublin union were also feeling the enervating consequences of being decentralized entities – sometimes referred to as gentry republics – in a region of Europe where absolutist monarchies could act swiftly and decisively. Conflicts continued between the Polish king and the magnates and gentry gathered in the national diet (Pol. *Sejm*) and in regional diets (*sejmiki*) over an array of questions about the military adventures of the monarch, royal and regional revenue flows, and administrative appointments. The requirement of a unanimous vote on proposed measures – the infamous *liberum veto* – in these parliamentary bodies easily produced inaction and obstruction to monarchical plans.

These internal conflicts were on display during the Northern War and in the decades after it. The monarch Augustus II "the Strong" – King of Poland and Grand Duke of Lithuania – had invited the Russians into the commonwealth during the war in order to increase his own leverage against the Swedish invaders and his internal opponents. Once there, however, the Russian military forces would not withdraw completely or willingly. Augustus had been promised sovereignty over Swedish Livonia by Peter I of Russia, but this had not happened. Later in his long reign lasting until 1733 Augustus came to regret his decisions, as did his successor Augustus III (the son of Augustus II and also King of Saxony). The latter was "elected" King of Poland by the Polish *Sejm* in 1733, after the so-called War of Polish Succession in which Augustus was backed by the Austrian Habsburgs and the kingdom of Prussia, while France and Russia backed the exiled Polish nobleman Stanislaw Leszczynski, who in the meantime had become the father-in-law of French King Louis XV. At the conclusion of considerable internal skirmishing, Augustus III was indeed chosen by the *Sejm*, but this royal "election" demonstrated to all ambitious external parties how domestically disunited the commonwealth had become. Overall, Augustus III performed creditably, ruling until his death in 1763. He spent much of his time, however, preoccupied with the interests of his other realm – Saxony – and thus remained incapable of exerting absolutist principles against the entrenched nobility of his Polish-Lithuanian kingdom. In 1764, after Augustus

III had died, and again after Russian military intervention, the *Sejm* "elected" to the royal office Stanislaw August Poniatowski, who had been the Polish ambassador to England and Russia and was without a doubt a very influential political leader. Poniatowski was reform minded, and immediately after his election sought to bring order to his Polish-Lithuanian realm and reanimate its standing as a regional power. His proposed reforms were clearly against the long-term interests of many of the commonwealth's magnates as well as neighboring powers. Thus, with the backing of the Russian army, the so-called Warsaw *Sejm* was convened in 1786 with the intention of returning internal arrangements in the commonwealth to the *status quo ante*. In fact, the practical result of the internal and external opposition to reform was the reduction of the commonwealth to a Russian protectorate. Tsarina Catherine II (the Great) of Russia – Poniatowski's former lover in St. Petersburg – assumed the role of guarantor of political order.

The internal divisions evident in the commonwealth during the reigns of Augustus III and Poniatowski were not simply power struggles between ambitious families but truly reflected fundamental disagreements within the political elites about how the commonwealth should be governed. In a state in which magnate and gentry landowners were at least as powerful as the monarch, this was potentially a fatal flaw. By the midpoint of the eighteenth century, the internal divisions were no longer just the predictable ones about how Poland and Lithuania should relate to each other. Instead, they were over basic questions of royal and parliamentary power, the role of the Catholic Church and its relation to the monarchy, the extent to which the commonwealth should be involved in central European conflicts because some Polish monarchs were also kings of Saxony, and the nature of Russian involvement. Admittedly, the internal conflicts did involve powerful magnate families jockeying for position – the Czartoriskys, the Radziwills, and the Potockis, for example – and their various branches and followers. Depending on the issue at hand, they would form temporary alliances with each other and with outsiders, or oppose each other seemingly at a moment's notice. The fact that these warring factions were able to marshal what in effect were private armies made matters even worse. These familial struggles, however, were only a symptom of something much deeper and fateful: the gradual erosion of belief in the commonwealth as a collective entity, a homeland worth defending.

The 1721 Nystadt Treaty did not formally challenge the jurisdiction of Poland-Lithuania over the Duchy of Courland and over Inflanty (Latgale). Both had northern boundaries that were also the northern boundary of the commonwealth; these territories now became increasingly interesting to St. Petersburg. Inflanty (Latgale) – formerly Polish Livonia – was more directly affected by the internal weakening of the commonwealth than was the Duchy of Courland. Inflanty, with a population of about 107,000 in 1700 (190,000 in 1800), was in the northeasternmost corner of commonwealth territories. Despite its somewhat marginal location, Inflanty had been affected by the movement and depredations of armies during the Northern War as much as the other part of the littoral. Under the control of the commonwealth government since the Livonian Wars of the late sixteenth and early seventeenth century, it had gradually developed a character of its own and differed considerably from the old Swedish-controlled Livonian territories, the Lithuanian lands to the south, and the Belorussian and Russian lands to the east.

Divided into four districts and presided over by a governor (*voievod*), Inflanty had its own provincial diet (*seimik*) in Dvinsk (Latv. *Daugavpils*) consisting of local landowning nobles, two from Lithuania and two from Poland. The dominant social order here was the gentry (*szlachta*) which consisted of about sixty landowning families. The thirty-seven who held most of the power reflected the diversity of Inflanty's population: fourteen were polonized Germans, seven Lithuanians, five Poles, five Belorussians, five of mixed ancestry, and only one native to Inflanty. The bulk of the Inflanty population – enserfed peasants – was descended from the Latgalian tribal society of pre-Christian times. The language of the common people was a variant of the Latvian used in Livland and Courland; none of these variants, of course, was standardized. The seventeenth century had witnessed the appearance of a written form of the local vernacular in incidental religious writings, but in Inflanty the scholars who took on this task were Jesuit fathers rather than Lutheran churchmen. The first printed book in Latgalian – a Catholic hymnal – was published in Vilnius in 1730; the next (to our knowledge) – an evangelium meant for the clergy – appeared in 1753, also in Vilnius. Just as the Lutheran churchmen transliterated the spoken Latvian vernacular through the prism of German, the Jesuit fathers used the prism of Polish, adding, for example, the letter "y" which did not appear in the western Latvian transcriptions. The Jesuits had been an active force in peasant education in Inflanty since the early seventeenth century; before that, the Dominican Order had carried out minimal scholarly endeavors from the thirteenth century onward. In contrast to church-related efforts, the landed aristocracy of Inflanty showed little regard for peasant education of any kind; their interest in the province was principally economic. Consequently, as in Lithuania, the governing order had been receptive to Jewish in-migration, and Inflanty then had the largest Jewish population of all of the former Livonian lands, approximately 3,800 by 1784. There was only one city of notable size – Dvinsk (Daugavpils) – with about 3,000 inhabitants in the 1780s; other population concentrations were no larger than hamlets. In her correspondence with the governor-general of Livland, Catherine the Great of Russia described Inflanty dismissively as a territory the Russian army could cross without opposition if the army were needed in Livland and suggested that the military live off the land if a crossing were made.

Contemporary descriptions suggest that Inflanty remained something of a *terra incognita* to all outsiders, whether Poles, Russians, or Baltic Germans in Livland. For reasons of economy, no Polish-Lithuanian military force was posted there, which explained Catherine's attitude toward Inflanty. Nonetheless, during the eighteenth century, the Russian government in its dealings with Poland-Lithuania continued to advance the notion that Russia had historic rights to Inflanty and maintained that most of its population was really Belorussian and therefore a natural part of the Russian cultural sphere. Inflanty had been separated from Russia, so the argument went, by the Polish conquest of the territory and it should be rejoined to its original territory. This argument about Inflanty, of course, was later subsumed by St. Petersburg into the larger claim that the Russian Empire was entitled to all the Slavic-language eastern territories of the Polish-Lithuanian Commonwealth since they, too, had been seized by conquest.

No such claims could be made by St. Petersburg about the Duchy of Courland and Semigallia, however. Still, because of the careless- ness with which the Courland dukes governed it, the duchy also came under increasing Russian influence in the course of the eighteenth century. The rule of the original ducal family – the Kettlers, who had assumed that role in the sixteenth century when the last master of the Livonian Order, Gotthard Kettler, secularized the order – ended in 1737 with the death of Duke Ferdinand aged eighty-two. The diet (*Landtag*) of Courland, under Russian pressure in the form of an army contingent that had occupied Mitau (Jelgava), elected Ernst Biron (changed form of the last name *Bühren*). He was the son of a low-ranking official in the ducal administration who had managed to become a favorite of Tsarina Anna of Russia.

The later Kettlers and then the Biron dukes distinguished them- selves largely in finding reasons not to spend much time in their Courland capital – Mitau – preferring more interesting places, such as St. Petersburg. Fortunately, a relatively well-functioning adminis- trative structure had been established in the province in the seven- teenth century so these absences did not leave the duchy rudderless. But it did mean that after the Northern War the influence of the landed aristocracy – especially the oldest families – remained paramount. Unlike Livonia, where the aristocratic register (*matrikul*) was not formalized until after 1721, Courland's register of nobility (*Ritterschaft*) had been established in the early seventeenth century and contained an admissions clause that said new entrants could be registered only after three generations of "public service." To a sub- stantial degree, power in the duchy thus resided in an elite of about 110 long-lived families of landed aristocrats, such as the Fircks, Hahns, Korffs, Medems, Tiesenhausens, Noldes, and Vietinghoffs. Ducal power rested on their assent, and it was they who had to bring into balance the pressures on the duchy from the Polish king, the Russian government, and the near-absent Courland dukes, while they sought to protect their own privileges as landowners.

The Russian government revealed its adeptness in exploiting this situation even as the Polish monarchs seemed to be increasingly oblivious to their loss of control over what was frequently referred to in Russian diplomatic correspondence as a "plum" territory. From Peter the Great to Catherine the Great, a succession of Russian rulers

MITAU.

12 In the eighteenth century, the residential structures of the Courland dukes featured prominently in Mitau (later Jelgava), the capital city of the Duchy of Courland; this engraving shows the old castle, which later in the century was replaced by an entirely new building.

used bribery, sought to arrange dynastic marriages, lavished hospitality at the St. Petersburg court on luxury-loving dukes, and made sure that Russian "advisors" were always present in the Mitau court to steer decisions in the direction of separating Courland from its Polish sovereign. Somewhat more ominously, Russia kept an armed force – sometimes several – stationed in the duchy, justifying their presence by vague references to potential Swedish resurgence. At one juncture in the absence of the duke, even the management of the duchy's treasury was placed in the hands of the Russian governor-general of Livonia (which had been under Russian control since 1721). Although the Polish kings at times protested the more obvious Russian interventions, they were themselves too preoccupied with internal threats to be taken seriously by the Russian government in planning its long-term Courland strategy.

Not surprisingly, during the tenure of the Biron dukes, a political faction began to form within the Courland nobility that welcomed the growing Russian role in the duchy's affairs. As in the provinces of Livland and Estland, the landowning aristocrats basically wanted a sovereign who could provide stability and ensure the continuation of noble privilege. The Polish monarchs were growing increasingly weaker as protectors of their own territories, while the influence of the St. Petersburg government was clearly ascendant. In 1772, after the death of Ernst Biron, the ducal office fell vacant and the Polish-Lithuanian king considered a Catholic successor. Catherine the Great, who had become tsarina of Russia in 1760, instructed her diplomats to inform the Polish government that Russia would not accept a Catholic and fully expected a Lutheran duke to be named to the office. Thus the sovereign of one country instructed the sovereign of another about what appointments would or would not be permitted in a territory ostensibly controlled by the latter. This incident revealed fully the extent to which the duchy had come under Russian sway as well as how much the Polish-Lithuanian monarch had lost control over the flow of events in the northern reaches of the commonwealth.

ENLIGHTENMENT ECHOES AND PEASANT MAJORITIES

The Great Northern War and the plague epidemics of the war years reduced both the urban and rural population of the Baltic littoral, but the institutional makeup of the cities and the countryside scarcely changed. In the cities, merchant guilds continued to dominate affairs and craft guilds to defend their second place in the power hierarchy, while all other urban residents were excluded from decisionmaking. In rural areas, the manorial system continued in place, managed by the landed aristocracies who either owned or leased estates. The concentration of power and influence in the hands of numerically small elites was justified by the centuries-old idea that society consisted of social orders with different functions and that the prestigious orders at the top were entitled to the power they possessed. This notion had been eroding in the writing of some western European intellectuals since the seventeenth century, but in the Baltic littoral it continued to have a powerful hold both intellectually and institutionally. Even so, among the Baltic-area *literati* during the second half of the eighteenth century, a small number of writers – far fewer than those who fully accepted the status quo – had begun to reevaluate the inherited ideas of social hierarchy. Initially, they focused on the conditions of the rural majorities, namely, the peasants. These writers were echoing the central sociopolitical ideas of the Enlightenment and, in the critical spirit of that intellectual movement, were homing in on what they considered to be unreasonable and unjust in the society around them.

The intellectual Enlightenment of the eighteenth century was a complicated set of attitudes among prominent writers and philosophers of western and central Europe, particularly in France, Great Britain, and the German lands. These attitudes owed much to the so-called scientific revolution of the seventeenth century, which proposed that the world could be understood by the human mind through the uncovering of its laws – the laws of nature – and that such laws were present not only in the realm of physical nature but also in human society and political life. Reason was the investigative tool and scientific method the procedure by which truths would be laid bare. Carried forward by this confident spirit, Enlightenment intellectuals directed their frequently angry writings at religion and religious institutions, calling them a relic of the superstitious medieval period of European history; at absolutist monarchies wherever they existed; and at all social and political arrangements that kept human beings "in chains," to use Jean-Jacques Rousseau's phrase.

Reason showed that human beings were created equal, that they had certain natural rights, and that republican forms of government were the most likely to ensure that these rights would be respected. Before the French Revolution of 1789, the sociopolitical criticism of the Enlightenment tended to be melioristic, that is, it urged reform. Few of these critics advocated revolution or nurtured the belief that society could be torn down and then rebuilt according to a rational plan. Taken together, the Enlightenment involved too many intellectuals in too many lands to have what might be called an organized program and to remain internally consistent in its preachments.

The Baltic littoral was far removed from the main centers of Enlightenment and the Baltic critics of littoral society were writing in a derivative mode. They included such "enlightened despots" as Catherine the Great of Russia, who carried on a brisk correspondence with such French luminaries as Voltaire and Diderot. She and other crowned heads – Fredrick II of Prussia and Maria Theresa of the Habsburg monarchy – portrayed themselves as frustrated reformers who were doing their best against the accumulated irrationalities of the societies over which they presided. In the littoral, Enlightenment ideas found resonance in the university at Königsberg across the Lithuanian border in East Prussia (the university at Dorpat was closed by the Russian government in 1710). Most of the sons of the upper orders of Baltic society went abroad for their higher education to Erlangen, Strasburg, Göttingen, Rostock, Halle, Leipzig, or Jena in the German lands, and to Leiden in Holland. University-educated persons, of course, were few in number, and those who were inspired by the new ideas and returned to the littoral to assume positions in the church or governmental administration were immediately confronted with recalcitrant socioeconomic realities in the form of organized landed nobilities who were ready to protect vehemently their rights to run their estates as they saw fit. University-bred idealism usually gave way before these realities, but the contrast between such philosophical notions as "humanity" and "natural rights" and the condition of the majority of the population in the littoral remained very much alive and grew increasingly vivid as the century wore on.

Facing determined opposition to reform of any kind, those who felt angry or even uneasy about the status quo in the littoral – particularly about the conditions of the peasantry – remained uncertain about how to proceed. There were some isolated attempts by relatively highly placed persons to improve peasant conditions. Thus the Lutheran clergyman Johann George Eisen (educated in Jena) in the Estonian-language region in Livland in 1764 worked out a plan that even attracted the attention of St. Petersburg. Also in Livland, Baron Karl Friedrich Schoultz, who was familiar with the works of Voltaire and Montesquieu, created a new "peasant law" for the peasants of his own estate, and with the help of the reform-inclined governor-general, George Browne, managed in 1765 to have some parts of it accepted as general regulations by a very reluctant Livonian *Landtag*. The brothers Karl Reinhold and Christian Nikolay Wilcken, both barons and landowners in Livland, followed Schoultz's example for their own estates but modified his regulations. Most such experiments that concerned the norming of peasant labor and restrictions on corporal punishment turned out to be easy to ignore or evade by the opponents of change. In the Lithuanian lands in the period 1762–1774, Canon Paul Brzostowski, archdeacon of the diocese of Vilnius, graduate of the Collegium Clementinum in Rome, and owner of a nearby estate, freed his peasants from serf status, placed their tenures on the basis of money rents, and even worked out a kind of peasant self-administration on the estate. These were all isolated instances of the reformist impulse at work. Intended to create models for other landowners to follow, these idiosyncratic reforms fell far short of their purpose precisely because they were individualized and had little more behind them than the conscience of the well-meaning reformer.

Toward the end of the eighteenth century, educated people in the littoral, including the critics of the status quo, were frequently referred to as the *Gelehrtenstand* (the learned estate) – a term more often heard in Livland and Estland than in the Lithuanian lands. In the theory of social orders there was, of course, no such *Stand*, but in the *ständische* thinking of the times all people had to be incorporated into a group and that group into a hierarchy of groups. The *Gelehrtenstand* was an inchoate collectivity with no such register of members as the *Adelstand* (nobility) possessed; its membership included those with some degree of higher education who were employed as teachers, tutors, journalists, and administrators of various kinds; many were associated with the Lutheran and Catholic churches, but others were free-floating among such well-established corporate organizations as the nobilities and the urban guilds; another term – *Literaten* – was sometimes applied to them collectively. They shared with western European Enlightenment *philosophes* an interest in exotic lands and peoples, which in the case of the Baltic *Literatenstand* manifested itself as a probing interest in the peasant majorities among whom they frequently lived and moved – Estonians, Latvians, and Lithuanians. Their writings, however, differed from those of their seventeenth-century predecessors by being as much prescriptive and didactic as descriptive and critical. They were a new type of person in the littoral, and they resembled what in the late twentieth century, at least in western countries, came to be called "public intellectuals." The terms "middle class" or "bourgeois" do not describe them precisely, because too often they were in fact "incorporated" into one or another of the traditional groupings. Their writings were varied in focus and approach; at times they published outside the littoral to avoid regional censors; and some wrote but never published in their own lifetimes. In Livland and Estland they wrote in German, in the Lithuanian lands, in German, Polish, and Latin. The peasants about whom they wrote were in no position to appreciate the fact that they had come to the attention of the *Literaten*.

An early example of the *Literaten* was Heinrich J. Jannau, a clergyman educated in Göttingen and serving in an Estonian parish in Livland. In 1786, he published a work called *Geschichte der Sklaverey, und Charakter der Bauern in Lief- und Ehstland*, the main themes of which flowed overtly from Enlightenment premises. Jannau started with the supposition that all men were born equal and drew the conclusion that *Sklaverey* (by which he meant serfdom) was the product of the historical development of the Baltic littoral rather than the outcome of the "nature" of the peasant population, as defenders of the status quo claimed. The crude and barbarous peasants of Livonia were serfs not because that status suited their natures; rather they had become serfs through the machinations of landowners in times past, as they increased mandatory labor requirements and tightened the rules against geographical mobility in order to guarantee for themselves a captive labor force. The use of the

German term *Sklaverey* (literally, "slavery") indicated that even though Jannau took a historical approach to the topic, he was no historian, as his critics pointed out. Critics also disliked his praise of the Swedish administration of Livonia in the seventeenth century, during which, Jannau argued, the lot of the Livonian peasant had been improving until the Great Northern War and the triumph of Russian administration wiped out all earlier gains. The conditions of serfdom dictated the character of serfs: this was also an Enlightenment premise. If the circumstances in which peasants grew up were reformed, they had every capability of becoming fine citizens. This approach enabled Jannau to spend many pages describing what he disliked about peasant behavior – their crudeness, their earthy humor, their stealth – and oftentimes the description reads as though he were an early believer in the idea of "national character." His descriptions waver between the categories of "peasant" and "Estonian" or "Latvian," suggesting that membership in the nationality categories was a filter though which the personality-warping influences of serfdom had to move. It was clear, however, that Jannau had ceased to think about the peasantry as an undifferentiated gray mass of laborers; the evidence of his eyes and ears in a Livland that contained a northern Estonian-speaking and a southern Latvian-speaking section had taught him that. His analysis separated, however imprecisely, the two peasant peoples (*Völker*) from each other, and these in turn from the German-speakers who governed both of them.

On balance, Jannau was on the side of agrarian reform, but his suggestions were typically mild. "Freedom" could not be granted to serfs immediately because they were too "uncultured" not to misuse it. He thought proper reform entailed the gradual reduction of the constraints that marked the daily life of serfs: labor had to be normed, movable property had to be guaranteed, and laws pertaining to peasants had to be translated into the vernaculars so that their subjects could become familiar with the duties of their station in life. In spite of his Enlightenment premise of human equality, Jannau was unwilling to attack directly the society of social orders: there had to be a peasant order (*Bauernstand*) but its hardships could be ameliorated. Jannau looked to the landowners themselves to be the initiators of amelioration, appealing to their rationality.

The angriest of the *Literaten* was without doubt Garlieb Merkel, born in 1769, the son of a clergyman in the Latvian-speaking region of Livland. His father had been educated in Strasburg and was an admirer of Voltaire and other Enlightenment critics of French society. Merkel himself remained a lifelong resident of Livland, working in various posts as a teacher and private tutor, but entry into the higher reaches of Livland society remained closed to him because, though not a bohemian, he showed every sign of wanting to be a free spirit. In 1797, at the age of twenty-seven, he published in Leipzig a work entitled *Die Letten, vorzüglich in Liefland, am Ende des philosophischen Jahrhunderts* filled with his disgust over the condition of the Latvian and Estonian peasantry, particularly the institution of serfdom. His material came from personal observations and from stories he had heard, which often served as the starting point for flights of fancy and invention. Though he tried to maintain a tone of evenhandedness by repeating that not all landowners mistreated their serfs, his imagination was seized by accounts of cruelty and sadism. His criticism of serfdom was rooted in a view of littoral history in which the present-day overlords appeared as invaders and colonizers who subjugated the native peoples (*Völker*) of the region. In other words, for Merkel, the story was less about stratified social orders each fulfilling its God-appointed duty and much more the tale of a stronger people oppressing the weaker. Untypical of much of Enlightenment writing was Merkel's invocation of the possibility of revolution if change did not happen ("the oppressed peoples will reclaim their rights with fire and sword and the blood of their oppressors"). But conditions *could* be changed if only the landowners would use their "reason" to understand that the status quo could not be preserved. Somewhat more typical was Merkel's belief that the ultimate sovereign of the Baltic area – the Russian tsar – could improve matters if only he were to use his power adroitly and push for reform. The *Aufklärer* of the German lands admired *Die Letten* and the book had a few admirers in the Baltic littoral as well, but their praise was drowned out by condemnation. Toward the end of his life, Merkel estimated that some 250 polemical writings had been directed against his book, some accusing him of exaggeration and others simply calling him a liar. The more temperate critics of his work, though not denying his examples, argued that they were exceptions to the rule. But this missed Merkel's larger point: condemnation of a system of agrarian labor that permitted such treatment, exceptional or not.

A *Literat* of more philosophical bent was Johann Gottfried Herder (1744–1803) who was not a native but lived and worked in Riga during the 1760s as an assistant teacher in the Riga Dom School and in similar teaching jobs in other parts of the region. He was among the handful of intellectuals who not only echoed Enlightenment concerns but eventually, after his death, became a major force in the nationalist movements of the later nineteenth century, in the littoral itself and far beyond it. His interest in the Baltic-area peasantry had a broad philosophical framework, and in that sense he was less a "provincial" writer than the others. Herder was concerned with the nature of culture: its origins, its organization, and its differentiation. His thinking revolved around the twin concepts of *Humanität* and *Völker* – humanity and the peoples who comprised it – and his general philosophy of culture was much less rooted in the configuration of states and political boundaries than in the configuration of languages and the products of the imagination expressed in these languages. These concerns predated his residence in the Baltic littoral, but in Riga and its environs Herder appeared to have found a laboratory in which to work out the implications of his ideas. Human culture comprised culture-carrying *Völker* (peoples), each of these rooted in particular natural environments and settings and each having its own unique history. Each *Volk* produced in time a spirit or soul – a collective cultural identity that manifested itself in a wide array of cultural products: songs, habits, sayings, customs, and folkways; it was the responsibility of the investigator of cultures to collect, explicate, and bring them to the attention of a wider public. These manifestations of collective identity were at least as important as the sophisticated writings of cosmopolitan intellectuals; in any event, they were not less important than the latter even if they were produced by untutored and frequently illiterate people. Together, the *Völker* comprised *Humanität*, which spoke not with a single voice in a single language but in a chorus of voices in many languages.

Musical metaphors are appropriate here because Herder spent much of his time in the littoral gathering and transcribing Latvian and Estonian folksongs (*dainas*). He also asked friends to send him examples of Lithuanian folk singing (*dainos*), which became part of

13 Bust of J. G. Herder, Riga. The German Enlightenment philosopher lived and taught in Riga in the 1760s, and the influence of his cultural ideas on the formation of Baltic-area nationalism is undeniable.

larger collections that were published separately, as well as later in his collected works, under such titles as *Stimmen der Völker in Lieder* (1787). His enthusiasm for what later would be called "the oral tradition" was unbounded, and he contrasted this kind of cultural expression positively with what he had observed in court circles and higher society: "You must know that I myself have had the opportunity of observing among living peoples the living remnants of these primitive songs, rhythms, and dances; among peoples whom our virtue has not yet deprived of their languages, songs, and customs, only to replace them with something crippled or nothing at all." It is ironic that in collecting materials about the oral culture of Latvian peasants, Herder relied upon the work of Baltic German clergymen who laced their own commentaries on the Latvian oral tradition with didactic observations, urging the peasantry, as good Christians, to distance themselves from such primitivisms.

Criticism of existing agrarian conditions was minimal in Inflanty (or Latgale) in this period. Intellectual endeavors there were almost entirely in the hands of Catholic churchmen, whose primary concern was the salvation of souls in harsh circumstances rather than sociopolitical critiques. The Lithuanian lands were similar in this respect; even though literary culture expanded quantitatively and qualitatively in all of Poland-Lithuania during the second half of the eighteenth century, few critical assessments of agrarian relations, particularly with respect to Lithuania, made their way into print. There was, however, one unusual writer who addressed the situation of the Lithuanian peasantry indirectly – Kristijonas Donelaitis (1714–1780), a Lutheran minister who grew up and worked in the Lithuanian-language district of Gumbinė in East Prussia. Although the district had a large German population, Donelaitis knew Lithuanian well and used it in his pastoral work. Having received his education at the University of Königsberg, Donelaitis was proficient in the classical languages as well as French. He himself had resisted polonization and germanization while retaining a close connection to his Lithuanian ancestry and his Lithuanian parishioners. Poetry was an avocation for him: he wrote some poems in German but, more importantly, also in Lithuanian, including a long poem of some three thousand lines which, when published posthumously, was given the title *Metai* (*The Seasons*). The poem did not appear in print until the nineteenth century, but then it quickly achieved the stature of the first lengthy literary work in the language written by a Lithuanian of peasant origins. The poem was *sui generis*, since Lithuanian was widely believed at the time to be the language of peasants (a belief shared even by the polonized Lithuanian gentry), and incapable of serving as a medium for poetic composition. In describing the annual cycle of Lithuanian peasant life, Donelaitis did not idealize his subjects, but described them and their activities so realistically that his nineteenth-century editors felt compelled to edit out some of the harsher descriptions. Although Donelaitis seemed resigned to existing rural conditions, displaying a kind of fatalism about life, he did criticize severely the landowning class of his region for living dissolute lives and setting a bad moral example for the peasantry. Other didactic lines of the poem suggested that the Lithuanian peasantry preserve their language, dress, customs, and folkways against the influences of the German in-migration to the area, which was at a high point when the poem was written. The underlying sentiments in Donelaitis' work resembled those of Herder, even if the Lithuanian wrote for his own edification only while the German was conscious of having an international audience.

COMPLETION OF HEGEMONY AND GOVERNMENTAL INNOVATIONS

Even as the *Literaten* of the Baltic littoral announced their unhappiness with the status quo, the rulers of the regional powers continued to demonstrate their abiding interest in territorial expansion. The "enlightened monarch" image projected about themselves by Catherine II "the Great" of Russia (empress 1762–1796), Frederick "the Great" of Prussia (king 1740–1786), and Maria Theresa of the Habsburg lands (empress 1740–1780) did not preclude opportunism. During the last three decades of the eighteenth century, for Catherine that meant maintaining and enlarging Russia's influence in the Polish-Lithuanian Commonwealth, and for Frederick and Maria Theresa, resisting the same. In the eyes of contemporaries the commonwealth had become a tempting target: the "sick man" of the European east (to use the phrase that was to be applied to the Ottoman Empire at end of the nineteenth century). Multiple interventions by Russia in the commonwealth's internal affairs had become so commonplace that the other two powers worried about the annexation by their rival of this vast and seemingly defenseless territory. To prevent a large-scale war between the three, Frederick proposed a three-way annexation of Polish-Lithuanian territory in 1772 that was meant to satisfy all three powers. A second "partition" of sections of remaining commonwealth territory followed in 1793, at the conclusion of invasions by both Russian and Prussian forces, and a third in 1795, following an unsuccessful national uprising in the remaining Polish territory, led by Tadeusz Kosciuszko (1746–1817). The process of partition was a drawn-out affair that understandably involved opposition from the commonwealth's ruling orders, but this resistance was weak and ultimately inconsequential. Indeed, the *Sejm* voted to accept the 1772 partition for a loss of about 30 percent of territory and some 35 percent of the population. In the interval between the first and second partitions, Stanislav II Augustus (Poniatowski), who had been elected to the Polish throne in 1763, continued to rule his reduced kingdom. He assented to internal reforms of various kinds, and even to a new constitution in 1791, which, among other changes, ended the formal distinction between the Kingdom of Poland and the Grand Duchy of Lithuania. By the end of 1795, however, Poland-Lithuania had disappeared from the map of Europe: the once-great power that had dominated affairs in east-central Europe from the fifteenth century was no more.

The partitions, of course, affected the eastern Baltic littoral by changing the status of Inflanty (Latgale; formerly Polish Livonia), which came under Russian rule in 1772; the Duchy of Courland, which had a similar fate by 1795; and the former Grand Duchy of Lithuania, which lost its ancestral lands piecemeal in all three partitions. By 1795, all Latvians had become subjects of the Russian tsars, as had the bulk of the Lithuanian population. A small number (est. 200,000) of Lithuanians continued to live in the territory of East Prussia (referred to by Lithuanians as Lithuania Minor) which projected northward from the main Prussian lands along the Baltic seacoast and included the important city of Königsberg with its famous university.

To many residents of Inflanty (Latgale) the change of sovereigns in 1772 may have seemed a non-event since very little changed in the short run, in terms of either administrative structures or population composition. The region had become used to the presence of Russian troops even before the partitions; its culturally and linguistically Polish or polonized landowning families were not organized enough to offer resistance; the institutions of the Catholic Church remained undisturbed for the moment, and the peasantry enserfed. In the 1772 partition, Russia claimed some of the commonwealth's eastern territories that, as Catherine the Great argued, had been "tradition-ally Russian," in other words, which the Grand Duchy of Lithuania had absorbed in its expansion during the fifteenth and sixteenth centuries and which were now populated by a mixture of eastern Slavic peoples referred to as Belorussians or Ruthenians. In truth, the Slavic populations differed among regions, and in Inflanty were very much diluted by the presence of Latgalian-speaking Latvians, Poles, and Lithuanians. In terms of religious faiths, the population of Inflanty, estimated in 1784 at 190,000, was divided between Roman Catholics (62%), Uniates (31%), Lutherans (4%), Jews (2%), Reformed (0.5%), and Old Believers (0.2%). Catherine the Great and her immediate successor, her son Paul I (tsar 1796–1801), tried a series of schemes of administrative reorganization in which different parts of Inflanty territories were attached to, detached from, and reattached to other sectors of the newly acquired Polish-Lithuanian lands and renamed in the process. Inflanty dis-appeared as a distinct territory, but the new province of Vitebsk, which did not become established until 1802, had a Latgalian population until 1917.

The Duchy of Courland and Semigallia was added to the Russian Empire in 1795 in the third partition of the commonwealth, the final act of the process of absorption having started long before the partitions. Both the ducal family and large segments of the Courlandic nobility were complicit in the absorption, first by accept-ing and so obviously enjoying the blandishment offered to them by a succession of Russian rulers and the St. Petersburg court, and second by concluding from the Livland example that loyalty to the Russian sovereign might just provide more security and better protection of privilege than a continuing connection to the weakening Polish monarch.

After several years of high-level political intrigue and negotiation between Prussia, the Habsburgs, and Russia, during which the divi-sion of spoils of a third partition were arranged, it was concluded that Russia would "get" Courland among other territories. A smooth transfer was marred only by the negative reaction to this partition in the Duchy of Lithuania. The objections there led to a brief military conflict between Russian and Polish-Lithuanian mili-tary contingents. In fact, the latter briefly invaded Courland and almost reached the duchy's capital of Mitau (Jelgava). But this did not forestall the inevitable. In April 1795, Catherine the Great issued an act, printed in both Russian and German, "accepting" the submission of Courland's political leaders. In the act Catherine explained that Courland was becoming a part of the Russian state through "the providence of the Almighty" and assured the Courlandic governing elite that "We declare upon Our imperial word that not only will you retain in full the right to exercise freely the religion that you have inherited from your forefathers, the rights, privileges, and legally owned property of all, but also that henceforth [you] shall enjoy the rights, privileges, and advantages which all Russian subjects have enjoyed by grace of Our ancestors and of Ourselves." The properties of the ducal family passed to the Russian throne in exchange for a one-time payment of two million rubles and an annuity of 86,250 rubles to Peter Biron, the last of the Courland dukes, who then retired to Silesia.

These assurances to Courland were quickly forgotten by Catherine even in the short run. A governor-general was appointed for the new province and given the task of dealing with those members (not a large number) of the Courlandic *Ritterschaft* who had opposed the act of submission. Their landed properties were confiscated by the crown and they themselves were exiled to Siberia. The Russian-appointed governor presided over a *Ritterschaft* Council, the rights of which were circumscribed by Russian law. The powerful Courland *Landtag*, which for a century or more had opposed various absolutist moves by the ducal family and the Polish king, initially lost any control over how the province would be governed. On balance, though, the distribution of power below the top layer remained roughly the same. The lord–serf relationships in landed estates did not change; the Lutheran Church and other religious organizations remained intact; and the proportion of Russians – both military and non-military – in the province remained small, no more than about 2 percent of the total population. Customary law dating back to the seventeenth century remained in force, and except for a few minor adjustments, the borders of the province did not change either. In the thinking of the Russian government and on the ground as well, the old territories (Estland and Livland) and the new (the former Inflanty and Courland) remained distinguishable, with Courland now referred to officially as *Kurlyandskaya gubern-nia*. In Estland, Livland, and Kurland, the German language remained the official language of state affairs and of record-keeping, with an overlay of Russian when the local officials had to deal with the Russian crown. In terms of primary language, the Kurlandic population of about 390,000 at the end of the eighteenth century contained an estimated 82.6% Latvians, 9.0% Germans, 2.0% Russians, 1.2% Jews, 0.6% Livonians, and about 1.0% all others (Poles, Swedes, Lithuanians). Virtually all Latvian speakers were enserfed peasants living on private or crown estates; the Kurland cities were small (compared with Riga in Livland) and thus offered peasants few opportunities to pursue non-agricultural occupations.

After the partitions ended, the Grand Duchy of Lithuania – *Magnus Ducatus Lithuaniae* – disappeared as a distinct political entity, though not necessarily from the consciousness of its residents. That the *idea* of the grand duchy remained alive is not surprising, since of all the Baltic littoral territories its history had been the most illustrious. Over the centuries it had retained institutional features – such as the Lithuanian Code – that provided a mooring for the notion of an independent Lithuania. Yet the designation of the Lithuanian territories as the *Magnus Ducatus* in official documents had become increasingly rare during the eighteenth century; the Lithuanian upper orders – landowning magnates and many of the gentry – were thoroughly polonized linguistically and oriented themselves culturally to the Kingdom of Poland. The peasantries of the Lithuanian territories – most of whom were serfs – remained Lithuanian speaking, but those among them who managed to leave the peasant order to take up grander occupations faced the same prospect as peasants in Estland, Livland, and Kurland: assimilation to another linguistic and cultural world, but in their case Polish rather than German.

The partitions were also the last phase of the duchy's territorial losses. Under Vytautas the Great, the duchy had reached the apogee of its expansion to about 930,000 square kilometers, as territory after territory was included within eastward- and southward-moving borders. After the Union of Lublin in 1569, the duchy's territory began to contract; the 1569 settlement included the transfer of about half of its territory to Polish control. After the disastrous Northern

War and the serious weakening of the commonwealth during the subsequent decades, the first partition in 1772 reduced the Lithuanian territories to about 250,000 square kilometers. In the second partition (1793) the Lithuanian territory was reduced to approximately 130,000 square kilometers, and in the third (1795) all Lithuanian lands came under the sovereignty of the Russian tsar. The two-hundred-year period during which the Lithuanian upper orders had sought to preserve co-equal status with Poland within the commonwealth, then some kind of autonomy, and then perhaps no more than a symbolic recognition from its Polish "partner" of Lithuanian separateness, was now over. After 1795, the Russian government experimented with several different administrative schemes for the Lithuanian territories, and finally by the mid-nineteenth century settled on four adjacent provinces (*gubernnias*) of Vilnius, Kaunas, Gardinas, and Suvalkai, whose total population was 2.5 million, including 1.6 million Lithuanians. About 200,000 Lithuanians remained residents of the eastern districts of East Prussia – so-called Lithuania Minor – and were therefore outside the borders and control of the Russian Empire.

In thinking about newly acquired territories like Livland and Estland and others in the empire's south, Catherine the Great was concerned about their incorporation. She did not want these lands to consider leaving again – to be "like a wolf looking at the forest," to use her phrase. Although it would be foolish to rescind the rights and privileges guaranteed to the power-holders in the new lands, the territories "should be russified with gentle methods . . ." This was a somewhat different attitude than Peter the Great had had after 1710, and her efforts began in 1767 with a large meeting in St. Petersburg of representatives of aristocratic landowners and urban patriciates intended to launch the codification and standardization of imperial law. In the prolonged discussions, which lasted for two years, it was pointed out "that it is an honor to be an equal with us in a single community. Livland and Estland are not foreign countries. Neither in climate nor in agricultural pursuits nor in other undertakings do they differ from Russians. They are capable of living by the same laws as we, and they should do so."

The meeting failed to produce the desired results, but it did provide Catherine with sufficient information to promulgate a new law about provincial governance, which was then applied in a stepwise fashion to individual provinces over a period of time. Because the littoral territories entered the empire piecemeal (1710, 1772, 1792, 1795), the law was first introduced into Inflanty (Latgale) in 1778, in Livland and Estland in 1783, in Courland only after 1795, and in the Lithuanian lands progressively after the first Polish partition. The essence of the law was centralization through the following measures: representation of royal power in the provinces was increased through additional administrators reporting to St. Petersburg ministries; urban governments and the *Ritterschaften* were reorganized to expand participation; a new system of royal taxation (the head tax) was introduced; some principles of estate ownership were changed, and the court system was renovated. Provincial power-holders in the littoral, especially the landed aristocracies, resisted most of these changes as best they could without displaying overt opposition, but what ended the reforms was not resistance but Catherine's death in 1796. These administrative reforms were aimed not just at the littoral but also at one specific subpopulation in the western borderland – the Jews – whose numbers in the empire had skyrocketed after the absorption of Russia's share of Poland-Lithuania. With the creation of the so-called "pale of settlement" (Russ. *cherta osedlosti*) in 1794–1795, together with the requirement that Jews in the empire live only there, the imperial government sought to concentrate and control the Russian Jewish population in the western provinces, even though the "pale," lasting as a legal structure to World War I, became increasingly porous during the nineteenth century. The "Baltic provinces" of Kurland and Livland, and somewhat less so Estland, all three of which lay just north of the "pale," received considerable numbers of north-to-south migrants after the Napoleonic Wars.

Catherine's son, Paul I, succeeded her, and, disliking his mother, proceeded to rescind many of her reforms (though not the "pale of settlement"), returning most of the littoral territories to almost a *status quo ante*. A few changes remained – the head tax, the allodification of some landed properties, some alterations in the court system. In return, Paul demanded that the Baltic territories be more helpful in housing the Russian army and in providing recruits from the peasantry. Even though Catherine's experiment failed, it gave the Baltic-area elites a taste of what the St. Petersburg government could do if it chose. It was more than a gentle hint that if reforms desired by the crown did not come from the bottom up, they could be imposed from the top down by ukase.

SOCIAL ORDERS AND LANGUAGE COMMUNITIES

The prolonged shifting of sovereign power to Russian monarchs might have initiated an integration process among the disparate littoral territories had Peter followed a different policy and had Catherine's centralization experiment worked. But that was not the case. By the end of the eighteenth century, the various parts of the region remained as particularistic as before. To the old administrative boundaries that had always cut across language communities, new ones had been added, while the old boundaries had become more fixed. In the northern part of the region, the old social order had perhaps become slightly more open, but the dominant orders – the *Ritterschaften* – retained their power and the social distance between them and the others continued as before. In the Lithuanian territories, the magnates and the gentry were in disarray and continued to nurse grievances against Russian rule in a more profound way than did the Baltic German elites. New grids of power relationships were superimposed upon old ones, but these changes did not reach very far into the lives of the littoral's peasant populations where enserfment remained the dominant condition and movement out of the peasant order remained minimal.

The old interfaces between language communities also remained in place, though some of them were generating more cultural material than before. Writing in the vernacular languages of the littoral comprised a world seemingly untouched by the momentous political changes: Lutheran and Catholic clergymen continued to learn the littoral languages and to publish in them, seemingly oblivious to the change in sovereigns. Even though the written word in German incorporated new themes – as illustrated by the works of Jannau, Merkel, and Herder – writing in Estonian, Latvian, and Lithuanian mostly retained its previous characteristics. It originated in the minds of *Literaten* for whom these languages were their second or third; it retained many features of the writer's first language (grammatical forms and orthography); and it was produced to instruct fellow *Literaten* as much as to create reading material for the peasantry.

Donelaitis' *Metai* – the lengthy poem written by a Lithuanian in Lithuanian – had silently broken the mold, but no one knew about that until the early nineteenth century. The statistics concerning published materials in the littoral vernaculars suggest continuing growth: the sixteenth century produced 34 known works in Lithuanian, the seventeenth produced 58 and the eighteenth 304. Before the eighteenth century, known publications in Estonian were fewer than 10; in the eighteenth century altogether 220 are known. If the period 1701–1721 saw 5 publications in Latvian, there were 55 in the period 1721–1755, and about 700 in the period 1755–1835.

Alongside the social world of the littoral, stratified by corporate order, an intellectual world had emerged in which one component – writing in the vernaculars – was anchored in seemingly the wrong place, among the German speakers rather than among the speakers of these same vernaculars, the Estonians, Latvians, and Lithuanians – the peasantries. The existence of this component and its seemingly unstoppable expansion was testimony to those who used these writings that the vernacular languages were not fated to remain "peasant" tongues suitable only for communications about the everyday concerns of rural life. The *Literaten*, who were themselves an anomaly in a world of corporate social orders, were enlarging the intellectual life of the littoral with a cultural component that disturbed existing mental models of how much value attached to each of the littoral languages and where each belonged in a culturally stratified society.

At the end of the eighteenth century, the littoral continued to be a region without a single dominant language, and even in its various linguistic components, diversity ruled. It was a society in which distinct language communities lived side by side and where language boundaries were broached only when there was felt a need to do so. No process of merging was evident. The diversity of language communities increased as one moved from Estland south across the Latvian-language areas of Livland into the Lithuanian lands. The Estonian-language region was the least differentiated: its languages were Estonian, German, and Russian, with the last two being used by only a small (but powerful) portion of the population. At about the geographical mid-point of Livland province, the language of the majority became Latvian, with German and Russian remaining in commanding positions. In Courland, which entered the Russian Empire only in 1795, the same array obtained – Latvian, German, Russian, with an admixture of Polish. In Inflanty (Latgale), by the second half of the eighteenth century, Latvian (Latgalian) speakers were a bare majority, and there were substantial Polish, Russian, and Jewish subpopulations, with the number of German speakers being much reduced from that in the sixteenth century. In the lands of the former Lithuanian Grand Duchy the array of language communities was the greatest: Lithuanian was still the largest numerically, but Polish was not far behind, while the subpopulations using Russian, Yiddish, and Ruthenian (Belorussian, Ukrainian) were sizeable. Practical needs prevented these language communities from being heremetically sealed against outside influences, yet most of them (except for the very smallest) had internal cultural lives that in a variety of ways could be protected against such influences. Linguistic penetration tended to be unidirectional: thus, for example, Estonians and Latvians, because of their socioeconomic position, could not penetrate the German-speaking world without becoming Germans; Germans, by contrast, because of their position, could penetrate the Estonian-, Latvian-, and Lithuanian-language communities without loss of linguistic identity by learning their languages and writing. A similar relationship obtained between Polish and Lithuanian users in the duchy. The only non-elite language community that could, in a sense, protect itself and choose the manner of its interface with others was the Yiddish/Hebrew-using population of the grand duchy; it had a thriving, long-standing, and book-based interior culture of its own that it could readily maintain. The sole publisher of Jewish books in the commonwealth – Uri ben Aaron Halevi in Żołkiew – produced a total of 259 books between 1692 and 1762; after that date, more presses were founded and 781 Jewish titles were published between 1763 and 1791.

During the 1730s the development of reading and writing skills among enserfed peasants received a major boost with the appearance of pietism within German Lutheranism. This development manifested itself primarily in Livland and Estland, less in the Duchy of Courland, and, for understandable reasons, not at all in Inflanty

(Latgale) and the Lithuanian lands. In the latter two areas where Counter-Reformation Catholicism had been particularly strong, pietism had no institutional base and no theology in which it could be embedded. In Livland (particularly in the Wolmar [Valmiera] district), and in Estland (particularly on the island of Saaremaa), pietism arrived in the form of missionaries from the Herrnhut community in Bohemia (Moravia), where Count Nicolaus Ludwig von Zinzendorf had established a kind of headquarters for its adherents. The Latvian name for the movement – *brāḷu draudze*, or congregation of brethren – came from the term "Moravian Brethren." Zinzendorf himself visited the Baltic littoral once, in 1737; otherwise, he left the work of disseminating Herrnhutism to missionaries whose presence was initially welcomed by the Lutheran establishment but eventually came under suspicion. The brethren preached a heartfelt and allegedly purer form of Christianity with little formal theology and much-simplified forms of worship. The doctrine centered on spiritual egalitarianism that sounded attractive to many peasants in so far as it deemphasized the value of and need for social orders and other forms of formal separation among believers. The faithful came together in meeting houses that, by comparison with the spired stone churches of the Lutherans, were just slightly larger than peasant homes. By 1740 the movement appears to have attracted some four thousand members among the Latvian peasantry in Livland and at least as many Estonians. But as its popularity grew, the Lutheran Church became alarmed. In due course it complained about the movement to St. Petersburg, which resulted in a decree of prohibition by Tsarina Elizabeth in 1743. Missionary work among the peasantry, however, was not deterred, but continued during what the brethren called the "quiet period." The prohibition was lifted in 1763 by Empress Catherine and from that time until the end of the nineteenth century, the brethren remained an active and influential form of Christian worship paralleling official Lutheranism.

The Moravians were far from being as subversive as the official Lutheran Church pictured them; in fact, to the extent that they had an explicit sociopolitical philosophy at all, it encouraged submission to constituted authority. Whatever role it may have had in the reinvigoration of Lutheran doctrine (part of pietism's larger history), the attractiveness of Moravian preachings to the enserfed peasants

14 The capacious meeting houses of the eighteenth-century
Moravian Brethren movement in Livland could still be seen in
the countryside a hundred years later, as in this 1925
photograph of a nineteenth-century meeting house in Kauguri
near the city of Valmiera (Ger. *Wolmar)* in Latvia.

lay in a different direction. Herrnhutism insisted that each person –
regardless of social rank and economic standing – was valuable and
capable of becoming a true servant of God. By extension everyone
needed to be able to read and write; also, the brethren urged that all
adult converts write out in their native languages the story of their
path to God in the form of a biographical account. Such writings,
though remaining unpublished, were certainly the first request for
literary self-portrayal peasants had ever faced, and the biographies
underscored the value that pietism attached to each and every
Christian soul.

Moreover, the movement offered intellectual and spiritual connections to the outside world: a number of the more active Latvian
and Estonian members of the movement traveled to Herrnhut,
Moravia (some remained there), and news accounts of missionary
activity in other parts of the world (especially in the American colony
of Pennsylvania) were sent out to congregations everywhere. This

was analogous, in a lesser manner, to the international connections that the Roman Catholics of the littoral had developed through the organization of their church and its head in Rome. The importance pietism placed on the perceptions of the individual believer, of course, could be pushed to extremes: thus, among Latvians some of the brethren sang of the coming of the "Latvian Savior," and in Estonia a preacher named Tallima Paap advocated the ignoring of landowners because by their very nature they were evil. Other excesses of the movement included the forming of personal relationships ("of the heart") that were almost childlike in their simplicity and lack of nuance, as well as a continual dwelling on – almost worshiping of – the blood, wounds, and physical suffering of Jesus. Nonetheless, in the larger context of eighteenth-century conditions among the littoral peasants, the Moravian emphasis on the need for education, literacy, self-expression in writing, and spiritual connections with the outside world was a significant, if unintended, counterpoint to the fatalistic preachments of official Lutheranism concerning acceptance of one's station in life and the onerous duties of serfdom.

The incentives pietism provided for Lutheran peasants to become literate remained informal and outside the framework of the rural school system, which during the eighteenth century seemed to be making little forward movement when compared with the Swedish period of the seventeenth century. Among Estonians, the Forselius Teachers Seminary, in its four-year existence (1684–1688), managed to train some 160 rural schoolteachers. A century later (by 1786–1787) some 275 village schools had been established in northern Livland and 223 in Estland province. Yet the number in Estland had dropped to 29 by 1800. Peasant education in Inflanty (Latgale) and the Lithuanian lands was struck a serious blow when in 1773 Pope Clement XIV suppressed the Jesuit Order in whose hands peasant schooling had made notable gains for more than a century. The Polish-Lithuanian state confiscated the schools and property of the order. The Education Commission, set up in 1773 by the commonwealth government, developed grandiose plans for public education, which remained unimplemented because of the objections of many magnates and the gentry to the whole idea of educated peasants. Thanks to the energetic activities of Governor-General George Browne in the matter of public schooling, Livland ended the eighteenth century with more peasant schools (at the parish and township level) than it had at the century's midpoint. By contrast, in the province of Kurland, which had a *Ritterschaft* that opposed peasant schooling and no activist governors, the actual number of peasant schools remained low and perhaps even decreased. One estimate, possibly useful for the entire littoral during the second half of the eighteenth century, is that only about 4 percent of pupils in the two-, three-, or four-year rural elementary schools received additional schooling at a higher level. Many peasant children learned literacy skills at home from parents (mostly mothers) while preparing for church membership; they then supplemented these skills with formalized instruction in the rural schools. Literacy statistics for the period are of dubious quality, but generally in the Lutheran areas somewhat more than half of the littoral's children reached young adulthood with some basic skills in reading and writing, whereas in the Catholic areas the proportion was less than half. Nowhere in the littoral, however, was there a school system that regularly, routinely, and continuously produced a critical mass of persons from the peasantry with excellent reading and writing skills in the vernacular languages and with aspirations to create a literature in them.

This was the larger context in which the variegated German *Gelehrtenstand* and Jesuit fathers worked. The composition of the *Gelehrtenstand* – a *faux* social order since it had no special rights or privileges – was mixed, with theologically educated, church-related persons dominating. Included as well were minor government officials, private secretaries of prominent individuals, tutors working in landowning families, schoolteachers, estate officials, and recent immigrants without permanent institutional connections. The few who actually came from the local peasant populations pursued the same literary efforts as their fellows who came from German or Polish backgrounds. They had received their university educations in Königsberg, the Jesuit universities in Vilnius and Cracow (before 1773), or in central Europe, since Dorpat (Tartu) University in Livland had been closed in 1710 during the Northern War. Thus they continued to translate Latin, German, and Polish texts into Estonian, Latvian, and Lithuanian. They corresponded extensively with each other about the vernaculars and frequently used informants from their congregations in ways that resembled the methods of modern-day fieldwork anthropologists probing the mysteries of exotic cultures. Since the grammar books of the indigenous languages had been written either by them or by their predecessors, new knowledge could come only by careful listening, transcription analysis, and the compilation of dictionaries. Their continual probing into the vernacular languages and the lives of the peasants also meant that they heard and recorded (and oftentimes published) songs and proverbs, sayings and legends, and words only in vogue in the eighteenth century. The writings meant for the peasantry tended to be didactic, continually juxtaposing the "nonsense" of the peasant oral tradition with Christian beliefs to the detriment of the former. Yet the care with which the *Literaten* collected elements of the oral tradition suggests the strong presence of a scientific interest, if not fascination, in spite of the prevailing conviction that the content was wrongheaded.

In some cases a kind of identification with parishioners developed: the most prominent of the Livland *Literaten*, Gotthard Friedrich Stender (1714–1796), went so far as to request that his gravestone be inscribed with the term *Latvis* (Latvian). The didacticism was frequently accompanied by patronizing attitudes characteristic of patriarchalism, as though the objects of their attention were children. Yet none of these attitudes was uniform throughout the *Stand*: Stender, who considered himself a rational Christian with a heartfelt dedication to educating the peasantry, urged that his parishioners abandon the oral tradition; while Herder, no less a rational investigator of that tradition, thought that it manifested the very soul of the *Volk* that produced it and valued it highly.

The end product of these literary endeavors was a diverse corpus of translations and writings in the vernacular languages that is difficult to categorize precisely. It was not organically linked to the peoples in whose languages it was written. Yet much of it – especially the translations of central Christian documents such as the Old and New Testaments, collected sermons of well-known clergymen, and church hymns – became revered in peasant homes for generations, regardless of how much the "literary" language in it contrasted with the spoken version. The conversion of spoken languages into written forms was accompanied by the intent to modernize them by introducing grammatical forms and vocabulary from the presumably more "advanced" *Kultursprachen* (German, Polish, Latin). At the same time, the most challenging documents (such as the Bible) forced the translators to stretch the vernacular languages so they could describe phenomena and express thoughts and concepts for which these languages had never before been used. They became innovators as well.

The need not only to translate but to find ways of communicating facts about the external world to peasant readers became particularly important during the second half of the eighteenth century when the *Literaten* began to introduce into the written materials entirely secular themes and descriptions of everyday life. Examples were calendars and several kinds of periodicals. The calendars acquainted peasant readers with a different kind of time framework meant to replace the traditional names for months, seasons, and the changes of seasons, but also offered geographical descriptions of lands near and far and their exotic flora and fauna. Because they were costly to produce, periodicals had very short runs and dealt with the practical matters of rural life.

In the Estonian territory of Estland and Livland, the so-called "Estophile" branch of the *Literaten* included people with broadly based interests as well as lesser lights. August Wilhelm Hupel (1737–1804), educated at Jena, was well known for his descriptive accounts – in German – of the Baltic littoral, but he also prepared in Estonian works on medicine and agriculture and tried his hand at founding an Estonian-language newspaper. Otto Wilhelm Masing (1763–1832), a Lutheran minister educated in Halle and eventually Bishop of Tartu, produced the first elementary school reader in Estonian in 1795 and continued his efforts in the Estonian language, including the founding of the first Estonian weekly newspaper (1821–1825). In 1782, Friedrich Gustav Arvelius compiled a typical peasant almanac – called "A Nice Book of Tales and Instructions" – promoting obedience and praising peasant humility. Among the Latvian peasantry, the prolific works in Latvian of Gotthard Friedrich Stender (mentioned above) and his son, Alexander Johann Stender (1744–1819), both Lutheran pastors, straddled almost the entire century, continuing religious-didactic themes but also introducing secular motifs in the form of invented fairy tales, plays, and commentary about the problems of everyday rural life. In a similar vein, Karl Gotthard Elverfeldt (1756–1819), another Lutheran pastor, wrote the first original play in Latvian, called "The Birthday." It dealt with inoculation against smallpox.

In Inflanty (Latgale), the Jesuit fathers produced the first printed book in Latgalian – a popular hymnal – first published in Vilnius in 1730 and reprinted in 1733 and 1765; typically, the lengthy Latgalian title of the book used Polish orthography (for example, the letters "y" and "w" which Latvian does not use). The well-known Jesuit Michael Rota (1721–1785), born in Kurland, worked at developing a system of peasant schools and produced writings in Latgalian meant for classroom instruction. In the Lithuanian lands, writing in the Lithuanian language in the eighteenth century continued in the patterns of the earlier period. Among other religious publications, a major book of Lithuanian grammar (author unknown) appeared in 1737, and the works of two Lutheran ministers in "Lithuania Minor" (East Prussia) – Christian Gottlieb Mielke (*c.*1736–?) and Adam Friedrich Schimmelpfennig (1699–1763) – underlined again the importance of this Lithuanian enclave for the development of Lithuanian writing. Schimmelpfennig, educated at Königsberg, participated in the Lithuanian translation of the Old Testament (published in 1735) and compiled a popular hymnal in Lithuanian (published in 1751). Among the approximately 500 hymns, 200 had been created or adapted by him. Mielke's main contribution was in the form of a Lithuanian–German/German–Lithuanian dictionary published in 1751. A major problem faced by the *Literaten* in the Lithuanian-language area was resisting the powerful and persistent influence exerted on written Lithuanian by written Polish – a task more easily accomplished in the German-language enclave of East Prussia than in the lands of the Grand Duchy, where a substantial proportion of the magnates and gentry were culturally and linguistically polonized and the Catholic clergy either polonized or Polish.

Though the peasant-friendly *Literaten* believed themselves to be doing their best with a difficult assignment, by the end of the century their collective efforts to educate the peasantry came under a cloud: the anti-monarchical and anti-aristocratic French and American revolutions intensified the suspicions among the landed Baltic aristocrats that peasant literacy encouraged sedition. Censorship became more intense, pressures on private and institutional publishers much more overt, and increasingly this type of literature had to be printed "abroad" and then smuggled into the littoral. This mood also diminished the willingness of local authorities to subsidize peasant schools in spite of repeated calls from "enlightened" governmental bodies that popular education should be promoted. By the end of the century, opinion among the governing elites of the littoral remained as divided on the subject of peasant education as it did on the question of peasant enserfment.

5

Reforming and controlling
the Baltic littoral, 1800–1855

The peoples of the Baltic littoral entered the nineteenth century in a fragmented state. The governing social orders of Estland, Livland, Kurland, Latgale (Inflanty), and the Lithuanian lands had to deal with the unpredictability of monarchs in St. Petersburg, the backwash of the French Revolution and the Napoleonic invasion of the Russian Empire, the lagging incomes of their own landed properties, and the collective resentments of the enserfed peasantries. Liberally inclined intellectuals – the *Gelehrtenstand* – provisioned Baltic cultural space with increasingly precise descriptions of the littoral and with writings in the vernacular languages, while many among them worried that the restless peasantry were insufficiently civilized (germanized or polonized) to handle any new freedoms they might be granted. In this autocratic political system, however, the chief reference points were always the personality and governance style of the tsar-emperor, and the main themes of the littoral's history in the first half of the nineteenth century were indeed set in many ways by the concerns and policies of two tsars – Catherine the Great's grandsons Alexander I (1801–1825) and his younger brother, Nicholas I (1825–1855). Alexander I prided himself on being a westernizer, ruling in the style of European absolutist monarchs, which in his view meant the encouragement of reform, particularly in the area of agrarian relations. His brother Nicholas was far more conservative, and sought to diminish regional autonomy by emphasizing the military character of his rule and heightening controls over wayward provinces. Since neither of them, however, wanted to share

Map 6 The Russian western borderlands in the nineteenth century. During the nineteenth century, the littoral became a collection of adjacent provinces, the borders of which corresponded badly with the ethnic distribution of the indigenous populations.

power, a national parliament or diet remained unknown to the Russian system throughout the nineteenth century.

An autocratic political system turned out to be both beneficial and threatening to the peoples of the Baltic littoral. Initially, the St. Petersburg government continued to deal warily with the littoral, seeing in its peculiarities something of a model for westernization but also experiencing frustration over the success of its regional over-lords – the Baltic German nobilities – in resisting the changes desired by a reforming tsar, such as Alexander I. In the 1816–1819 period, Alexander had to cajole and pressure the Baltic German nobles of Estland, Livland, and Kurland to emancipate their serfs, a major reform that proved to be impossible for the rest of Russia (and the rest of the littoral) until forty years later. Yet these so-called Baltic provinces – Estonia, Livonia, Kurland – exhibited no revolutionary tendencies. The polonized magnates and gentry of the Lithuanian lands, on the other hand, after the Polish partitions were viewed by the central government with mistrust. From the government's point of view, this turned out to be the correct attitude in light of a major revolt against tsarist authority in the Polish and Lithuanian territories in 1830. The revolt was a serious challenge of a kind that the Baltic German *Ritterschaften* would have no truck with. They preferred to use stealth and influence at court to get their way. The St. Petersburg government's response in the Lithuanian lands (and Latgale), resulting in increased and harsh control from the center, meant that the history of the littoral after 1830–1831 was differentiated on a north/south axis. In the north (Estland, Livland, and Kurland), the peasant majorities adjusted to their new-found personal freedom and their new juridical status as subjects of the tsar, while in the south (Latgale and the Lithuanian lands) the old order continued under the watchful eye of tsarist officials and military commanders.

RESEARCHING THE LITTORAL

Judging from the offhand comments by officials, the St. Petersburg government had at best only a general notion of the human composition of the littoral territories the empire had acquired. Its ignorance was no obstacle to administration, however, since the government was interested primarily in the land and its productivity, borders, efficient flow of tax revenues, military-strategic utilization of the territory, and cooperation of the elites already in place. All these matters could be dealt with even in the absence of any information about the lower layers of Baltic society, their languages, and their folkways. Similar willful ignorance existed among the littoral's landowning aristocracies and urban patriciates; but it was less evident among the *Gelehrten*, who had accumulated a considerable amount of information about the peasants by the beginning of the nineteenth century. Still, such information came to their governors filtered through a series of traditional categories: the common people

15 Jews in Riga in the nineteenth century. The Baltic German artist Theodor Heinrich Rickmann was well known for his engravings of the ethnically diverse Riga population, as in this portrayal of Polish Jews in the Riga market square.

belonged to one or another social order; peasants were free or unfree; they belonged to this lord or that one; people were Lutherans, Catholics, Jews, or foreigners; they headed farmsteads or served as farmhands. Though the governing classes thought in terms of categories, the on-the-ground population of the littoral evidenced considerable geographic mobility that was sometimes captured by the artist's eye (see Figure 15).

Collective terms referring to languages, ethnicity, and nationality were rare in conceptualizations or in documents; angry critics such as Garlieb Merkel, who in fact referred in his writings to "Latvians" and "Estonians," were pioneering new usages since even peasants themselves rarely talked about each other with these words. Information about them as individuals was contained in parish registers that recorded births, deaths, and marriages; but even in these documents, personal identity remained vague. Enserfed peasants – the vast majority of rural residents – had no surnames; the first names of both men and women were drawn from a relatively small pool; the first name was accompanied by the name of the place (farmstead) where the person resided; and above all people were always identified using terms that placed them in a particular niche within the peasant order – farmstead head, farmhand, relative of head or farmhand, stranger, old man or old woman. These socioeconomic categories were of greatest significance to the estate owners, since numerical aggregations under these headings provided information about the labor force.

During the last decades of the eighteenth century and increasingly with each decade of the nineteenth, information about the littoral became more readily available as the central government mandated the gathering of information for tax purposes, the churches began to improve their internal record-keeping methods, and a segment of the *Gelehrten* began to publish lengthy descriptive accounts of these new provinces. This new hunger for precise information had many causes. Even if the century of Enlightenment was now over, the scientific thrust of Enlightenment thinkers remained in full force, demanding precise and comprehensive information on every subject. In 1782, the St. Petersburg government applied the law that required a precise inventory of "souls" living in the provinces of Estland and Livland so that calculations could be made for the payment of a head tax. The management of landed estates was also becoming more systematic, in part because income from estates was diminishing and landowners sought to correct deficits through better internal accounting. Church officials visited rural congregations more frequently and required parish clergy to keep better records of the number of communicants and more precise vital statistics. All such information, flowing upwards from localities in the form of reports, statistical summaries, and numerical charts, was grist for the mill of the *Gelehrten*. August Wilhelm Hupel, a prolific contributor to this genre of descriptive writing, had already published such works as *Topographische Nachrichten von Lief- und Ehstland* (Riga, 1774–1781) and *Statistisch-Topographische Nachrichten von den Herzogthumern Kurland und Semgallen* (Riga, 1785). Peter Ernst von Keyserling and Ernst von Derschau, government officials in Kurland, published a 375-page work named *Beschreibung der Provinz Kurland* (Mitau [Jelgava], 1805), dedicated to Alexander I, and H. von Bienenstamm published the *Neue geograpisch-statistische Beschreibung des kaiserlichen-russischen Gouvernements Kurland, oder der ehemaligen Herzothümer Kurland und Semgallen mit den Stifte Pilten* somewhat later, in 1841. Initially, these books tended to be more descriptive than statistical, even presenting in narrative form population statistics about towns, estates, and provincial subdivisions culled from the results of the soul revisions. In time, they took on the character of handbooks or reference works, using statistical tables and long lists of administrative subdivisions and places together with relevant numbers intended not to entertain but to inform. Eventually these investigations branched out and became specialized, turning their attention to different aspects of the littoral. Thus, for example, Joachim Lelewel (1786–1861), a Polish historian who taught at the University of Vilnius after it reopened in 1803, wrote an extensive history of Poland-Lithuania in Polish (*Dzieje Litwy i Rusi*, 1839). Also at the Vilnius University Simonas Daukantas (1793–1864) and Theodor Narbutt (1784–1862) wrote voluminously about the history of the Lithuanian region, the latter authoring, also in Polish, a nine-volume history called *Dzieje narodu litewskiego* (1833–1841).

Such individualized efforts were paralleled by the founding of scholarly societies dedicated to a better understanding of the Baltic littoral: in 1817 the *Kurländische Gesellschaft für Literatur und Kunst*; in 1824 the *Lettisch-literärische Gesellschaft*, in 1834 the *Gesellschaft für Geshichte und Altertumskunde der Osteseeprovinzen*, and in 1838 the *Gelehrte Estnische Gesellschaft*. Although the Lithuanian equivalent, the *Litauische Literärische Gesellschaft*, was founded much later, in 1879 in East Prussia (Lithuania Minor), a similar organizing role was played by the University of Vilnius until it was closed by Russian authorities. The intention of the descriptive publications and scholarly associations was not, in the first instance, to educate the peasantry, but to inform the educated public: hence the language of publication and of business in the scholarly societies was either German or Polish. Technically, Estonians, Latvians, and Lithuanians were not excluded from the ranks of these writers or from the organizations, but it was assumed that the few who did participate would understand that they had to do so via the prevailing *Kultursprachen*.

One question on which there was disagreement among the learned of the learned societies had to do with germanization and

AÚSSICHT VON DER STADT RIGA

L . *Das Kayserliche Palais*	Q . *Die Reformirte Kirche*	V . *Die Sunder Pforte*
M . *Das Rathhaus*	R . *Die Neu Pforte*	X . *Die Schwimm Pforte*
N . *Die Petri Kirche*	S . *Das Capponier*	Y . *Diverse russische Buden*
O . *Die Wasser Kunst*	T . *Das Haus für ertrunckene zu retten*	Z . *Die floss Brucke oder Schiffs Brucke*
P . *Die Johannis Kirche*	U . *Die Schaal Pforte*	a . *Batterien — b . Duna Fluss*

16 During the first half of the nineteenth century, Riga was
developing into one of the most important seaports of the
Russian Empire, as this contemporary engraving suggests.

polonization: whether, that is, the few individuals of peasant background who had received sufficient education to count among the
Gelehrten needed to change their basic identity. This was hotly
debated especially among the German-using intellectuals (particularly clergymen) of the Baltic provinces proper (Estland, Livland,
Kurland), but no consensus was possible. The larger *Zeitgeist*,
informed by attitudes launched by Herder as well as such intellectual notables as J. G. Fichte in Germany, had already absorbed the
view that national identity was basic to human culture; but in the
Baltic region, this view collided with the prospect of hundreds of
thousands of Estonians, Latvians, and Lithuanians – peasant peoples – demanding cultural equality while rejecting tutelage of the
upper orders. Such a prospect could be warded off by the instrument
of systematic germanization of those who rose above the peasant
ranks.

By the beginning of the nineteenth century, the governing social orders of the Baltic littoral were becoming increasingly aware of the hazards presented to their position by both the revolutionary events in France after 1789 and the reformist impulses of the royal government in Russia. Yet they fully expected that long experience in negotiating with new sovereigns would once again result in averting major changes. Retaining full control over their landed properties and the people on them was essential for their way of life. How expansive their sense of entitlement had grown was illustrated well by the 1739 declaration of principle by the Livonian *Landrat* O. F. von Rosen in which it was claimed that "the peasant belongs to the estate owner in his body and person."

Such claims resonated well, even if not literally, with most of von Rosen's peers, though critics of serfdom such as Merkel and Jannau in the late eighteenth century were able to use this and similar statements to focus their attacks. The Swedish government in the seventeenth century, no stranger to brutal policies when it suited state interests, was nonetheless appalled by the uncontrolled license with which Livonian and Estonian estate owners dealt with their peasant population, but their efforts to reduce arbitrariness had come to naught in the Northern War, after which Peter the Great reassured the Baltic landowners that their dealings with the peasant population would not be interfered with. Although Catherine the Great had also been appalled, her son Paul chose to pacify landowner sentiment.

The emphasis placed by the vocal critics on the exploitative nature of the serf system had the effect of disguising the complexity and diversity of the landed estates on which serfdom existed. Because the system rested on the individualized implementation of its core principles, variations were to be expected. In fact, it is somewhat misleading to speak of serfdom as though it were a "system" implemented according to some generic blueprint. Abstracted from all implementations, a landed estate in which the peasant population was enserfed rested on a kind of unwritten compact between the person (or family) who held (owned, rented, leased) the estate and the peasant population that comprised the estate's more or less permanent residents. The estate holder, on his side, was obliged to provide protection to his peasants against outside malevolent forces, maintain internal law and order, dispense justice and settle disputes, offer material assistance in times of need, and observe peasant customs. On their side, the peasants were to pay to the estate holder rents in the form of labor, money, or kind; strictly observe the rules against movement away from the estate without the permission of the lord; and submit to corporal punishment when the estate judged it necessary. This abstract version of the "serf estate" was analogous to the medieval manor, but much had changed since that time. By the eighteenth century, the landed estates of the littoral had become fully oriented toward both external and internal markets and no longer strove for self-sufficiency; in principle, the estate was to be a profit-making enterprise. That meant, among other things, that agricultural work on the estate had become, in a sense, open-ended rather than restricted to the need of the estate's own population: greater productivity meant a larger income for the estate holder. In turn, the estate holder had every incentive, first, to expand the estate's arable land that was allocated by custom to the estate farm and reduce the land allocated to peasant use; and, second, to extract as much labor time from the enserfed peasants as could be obtained without significantly impairing their ability to produce sufficient crops for their own use. Logically, estate holders did not seek to render peasants too weak to work, since there was no other labor force available. Over time, estate holders had accumulated other rights, depending on the region in question: the right to sell parts of their property together with the peasants on them, to sell peasant families by themselves, to appoint the local clergymen, to restrict peasants' hunting and fishing privileges, to interfere in peasant marriages, to assign peasants the task of repairing roads and bridges, and periodically to introduce temporary extraordinary labor services. Once asserted and exercised, such rights tended to become permanent, and by the eighteenth century, no external authority existed to constrain brutality and arbitrariness in their enactment. Visitors to the Baltic littoral were aghast at the omnipotence of the landowning orders, but negative comments of any kind tended to fall on deaf ears: the provincial diets (*Landtage* in the Baltic provinces proper, and *sejmiki* in the Lithuanian lands) normally sided with the landowning orders where privileges were concerned.

By the end of the eighteenth century there were an estimated 4,700 landed estates in the Baltic provinces (Estland, Livland, Kurland), Latgale (Inflanty), and the Lithuanian lands. This number included estates now owned by the Russian crown, by individuals outside the *Ritterschaften*, by cities, by members of the noble corporations, by pastors, by judicial personnel, and by philanthropic foundations. Ownership was distinguished from holdership, and holdership was further differentiated by reference to the terms on which estates were held. The variety was enormous: there were the knightly estates (*Rittergüter*) which had been the heritable property of a single family for generations; estates held by non-noble private individuals and officials of the crown; estates with the holder/owner in residence and those that were managed for absentee owners; estates that were owned, leased, and rented; estate fragments allocated to the needs of the resident clergy and attached to the parish house; allodial estates and those that could not be bought and sold; fragments of land (half-estates), which were either the remnants of an old estate or a new estate in the making, but which in either case had a resident peasant population; estates that had been gifted, granted, deeded for a time or in perpetuity. Estland, Livland, and Kurland estates tended to be of moderate size – comprising on average 100–200 peasant families – though throughout the eighteenth century, there was a marked tendency for mean estate size (measured in terms of peasant "souls") to grow. Truly large estates, with thousands of "souls," were exceptional and were found more frequently in the Lithuanian lands and in Latgale (Inflanty) than elsewhere in the littoral. Estates of a size comparable to those in the interior of Russia, some of which had tens of thousands of serfs, were non-existent in the littoral. Of course, some magnate families owned or held many estates and were therefore in charge of truly substantial peasant populations. The proportion of usable land allocated to the estate itself and to peasant holdings varied immensely as well, having been set over time by dozens of individual decisions and the working of custom. During the eighteenth century there was also a marked tendency, especially in private estates, for the demesne (the estate land) to be expanded at the expense of peasant holdings, which correspondingly expanded the estate's need to increase labor norms of peasant families.

Each of these landed properties also had variety in their human population. Not all people residing in rural areas were peasants, nor were all peasants serfs. The quasi-censuses of the late eighteenth century – the newly introduced soul revisions – normally started the list of inhabitants with a category designated as "free," a sub-population that normally comprised 4–5 percent of total estate residents. The free people included, of course, the owner (or holder) and his family, estate officials such as the bailiff, peasants who had been hired to work in the manor house or on the estate farm and who may have been granted free status, and non-peasant artisans of various kinds (if the estate were large). Others who had taken up residence on the estate for various reasons could come and go as they pleased.

Most peasants, however, were listed under the rubric of *Erbuntertänig* (servile by heredity) in the German-language documents. The critics of serfdom were most horrified by the condition of this population. These were the real serfs, bound to the estate and to the person of the estate holder and responsible for delivering a certain amount of labor each week to the estate's lands as well as various payments annually (mostly in kind) to the manor house. But the enserfed population was also stratified, the most important lines being drawn between the serfs who had a holding, such as farmstead heads and their families, and those who had no holding of their own but circulated among the farmsteads as hired labor – the farmhands, married or unmarried. Then there were those who were too young, old, or infirm to be included in the labor force and had been allocated to one or another farmstead in the absence of poorhouses, orphanages, or facilities for the partially or fully disabled. For enserfed peasants, upward social mobility meant, in the first instance, acquiring free status, or, while remaining unfree, acquiring the headship of a holding; downward social mobility meant entering the ranks of the landless laborers who circulated among the farmsteads of the estate.

Another feature that contributed to the diversity of rural conditions in the littoral was varying settlement patterns. In determining how much labor time was owed to the estate, owners throughout the region had to reckon with the fact that an estate's serfs sometimes lived in farmsteads isolated from each other, sometimes in small farmstead clusters, and sometimes in villages. Consequently, how a particular labor requirement was actually fulfilled and by whom depended on the unit of the population to which it was attached. In the main, in Estland, Livland, and Kurland the dominant rural settlement pattern was the individualized farmstead or small cluster of farmsteads, and here the owner dealt with each peasant family separately. In Latgale (Inflanty) and the Lithuanian lands, the village pattern was the norm, so that estate managers did not deal with individual peasant families but rather with collectivities. How the "team" of laborers sent to the estate was recruited was frequently up to the peasants themselves, as long as the norm was met. With individual farmsteads, the labor team inescapably was composed of the residents of a particular farm; in the case of collectivities, more options were available in forming it. The final configuration of the labor force depended on the kind of work the estate lands needed in a particular week, whether the work required man-and-horse teams or just "foot-labor," and who was sending labor to the team. Thus, individual peasant families or farmsteads experienced a set labor norm not in a uniform fashion but as one that differed from week to week. The requirement was never zero, and at the other extreme, it could involve all seven days of the week, especially at planting and harvesting time. Ultimately, however, the number of workdays a peasant family had to divert to the needs of the estate land was an omnipresent factor and normally ranged from three to five. The winter months, when agricultural work was minimal, did not provide a respite; the estate required peasants to supply the manor house with wood from nearby forests.

The prevailing tendency in the second half of the eighteenth century was for estate owners arbitrarily to increase labor norms, which predictably increased the flight of serfs from their natal estates and also occasionally sparked violent though localized collective opposition. Complaints against one another by landowners over serfs who had fled one jurisdiction and were welcomed into another became more frequent. Some landowners were receptive to the idea of a free labor market that benefited them: they simultaneously opposed lightening the punishment for flight and favored lightening the punishment for receiving fled serfs. One perfectly legal way to escape obligatory labor was for a peasant family to convert the norm into a cash payment, but this option was only rarely exercised in Estland, Livland, and Kurland. It appears to have been fairly widespread in the Lithuanian lands, however, where such conversions (resulting in a payment called *činšas*) had proliferated from the sixteenth century onward. The conversion was disadvantageous from the point of view of the estate owner: the littoral was under-monetized, which made regular payments unpredictable, and it was generally easier to increase labor requirements than to increase monetary payments.

Whether enserfed peasants were able to absorb the estate's compulsory labor norms into their working week and still adequately farm their own fields for a steady supply of food remains incertain. All numerical evidence suggests that labor requirements were increasing during the eighteenth century. Yet continuing population growth also suggests that a larger portion of the rural population in each generation survived into old age – in-migration to the littoral was low – which in turn hints at least at a stable quality of life if not an improving one. The demographic recovery from the deadly decades of the Northern War (1700–1721) was rapid; as it entered the Russian Empire at the end of the eighteenth century the littoral had a larger population than ever before. This demographic outcome could have been due, of course, to peasants' survival skills as they coped with their powerless status. The alleged shiftiness, slyness, and untrustworthiness of the littoral's peasants, which landowners frequently complained about and visitors remarked upon, may have been precisely what was needed in the situation.

However varied the experience of being enserfed had been for many generations, it continued to be the lot of most (though emphatically not all) of the littoral's peasant populations. By the beginning of the nineteenth century, many in the ruling orders agreed that the *Agrarfrage* (agrarian question) needed to be addressed and that reform of some kind was needed, but there was no consensus about what should be done. Indeed, among the *Ritterschaften* there was not even much of a debate and opinions expressed in the regional diets took the form of defensive speeches. It was pointed out that external criticism of serfdom by "enlightened" thinkers in the west was hypocritical, given the existence there of slavery and the Atlantic slave trade. But as long as the autocracies of the European east depended for their power on the consent of the landed aristocracies, the elimination of serfdom by fiat seemed impossible, as Catherine the Great commented in her private correspondence.

REFORMING SERFDOM

As soon as Alexander I ascended to the Russian throne in 1801 at age twenty-four, he proposed several projects for reforming serfdom in Russia, but these proved to be of minor significance. Nevertheless, he did not give up on the idea of reform of some kind, and continued to experiment, having decided that some elements in the landowner– peasant relationship could be changed more easily than others. Serfdom could not simply be declared null and void: the Russian serf-owners opposed that as did the various landowning aristocracies of the Baltic littoral on whom the tsarist government depended for good governance in the western borderlands. But piecemeal reform could be introduced, and thus for almost the entire duration of his reign (1801–1825), Alexander devoted some of his attention to the matter. The question involved more than simply quieting peasant unrest; almost continuous negotiation with the power-holders of the littoral was essential, together with a not inconsiderable amount of pressure from St. Petersburg through the representatives of the tsar appointed by him to govern the borderlands.

What were the issues reformers had to address? There was, to begin with, imperial taxation: if the Baltic-area peasantry were heavily burdened with exactions in the form of labor, money, or kind, should the crown provide some relief from these at least on the crown estates? Was it possible to establish norms for the maximal amount of obligatory labor that estate owners could require? How could landowners be prevented from exceeding the norms by divising new categories of labor obligation not covered in the existing rules? In fact, in Livonia the category of "extraordinary labor" had become as demanding on the peasantry as the category of formally required labor.

The division of estate land between that allocated for peasant farmsteads and that being used directly by the owner also raised questions. How could the demonstrable encroachments on peasant land be prevented? What were the rights of peasant-serfs over the farmsteads where they worked? Could they bequeath the land itself to their heirs or only the *right* to be on a farmstead? Did the rights of the estate owner trump all customary arrangements, leaving a peasant-serf entirely at the mercy of the landowner's will? Did serfs have any rights to the movable property that they had acquired through hard work, or did all movables on the farmsteads of an estate belong ultimately to the estate? What about corporal punishment: could landowners exercise it freely, or were there limits? And did the status of hereditary servility mean that a serf-owner could "sell" serfs as though they were chattel, prevent or force marriages between them, and deal with them as if they were no different from the estate's livestock? Finally, there was the question of a landowner's right to prevent his serfs from moving elsewhere: was this right absolute, or could it be restricted by a clause that said, for example, that a serf could move except when he was indebted to the estate?

These and similar questions swung into view whenever reform of the lord–serf relationship was placed on the agenda. The administrators who dealt on the tsar's behalf understood how complex the matter was, as did the landowners themselves, and therefore the process of reforming serfdom in the littoral became protracted. Predictably, the landed aristocracies were masters at foot-dragging, understanding correctly that Alexander I was quick to propose fine-sounding reform schemes and just as quick to back away from them. At the same time, reform-minded administrators realized that if Alexander's attention was not completely diverted from reform projects, that on his behalf and in his name, they could keep the pressure on until some kind of recognizable result occurred. The slowness of reform revealed the limits of royal absolutism, and, what is more, during the entire period of his rule (including the Napoleonic Wars), Alexander was constantly faced with the temptations of devoting all his time to great-power politics on a continent-wide scale.

Nonetheless, from 1802 onward, a series of orders and edicts issued by the St. Petersburg government did place some limits on the omnipotence of the landowning orders; abolition of serfdom, however, took place only in the littoral in the years 1816–1819 (Estland, Livland, Kurland) and not until 1861 in the rest of the empire when Latgale (Inflanty) and the Lithuanian territories were also included. Measures specifically addressing agrarian relations were interspersed with events that spurred on the process or slowed it down, and the staggered manner in which "freedom" arrived among the peasants underlined once again that the St. Petersburg government did not think of the littoral as a single entity and that it trusted some areas in it more than others. The differentiated timing of reform and emancipation in the littoral's regions also contributed to the further differentiation of the regions in terms of the pace of socioeconomic development.

As mentioned earlier, a handful of individual landowners in the littoral, motivated by Enlightenment ideas or by conscience, had implemented reforms on their own estates, but these had virtually no wider ramifications. The first measure to affect the entire peasantry of a province was the new peasant law proposed by the *Landtag* of Estland and accepted by Alexander I in 1802. The measure came into being in part following a series of peasant disturbances in both Estland and Livland, and was actually an attempt by the landowner aristocracy to preempt wider-reaching reforms. The 1802 law dealt mainly with the heritability of peasant land and provided that if a peasant had fulfilled his duties (labor, taxes) to the estate, he was entitled to bequeath to his heirs the right of occupancy to the holding. Although this was a formalization of a customary right that had been widely practiced before this time, it had the potential of reducing to some extent the arbitrariness of estate owners. In practice, however, such a peasant right was exceedingly difficult to monitor, especially if it entailed proceedings in a legal system that was heavily tilted to favor the aristocracy and required proof concerning the fulfillment of peasant duties. The imprecise, and sometimes unwritten, nature of such duties was itself an object of peasant ire because estate owners over the years had been easily able to increase obligations by inventing one-time tasks that then became permanent. For a farmstead head to demonstrate that all duties and obligations had been fulfilled was a daunting task, subject to judgments by officials who were likely to give the benefit of the doubt to the landowner.

Nonetheless, the 1802 law was a first step, and it intensified discussion in the Livland *Landtag* about whether it also should adopt a similar measure. When the formalization of the right of heritability among half of the Estonian peasant population (those in Estland) came quickly to be known among the other half of the Estonian peasants who lived in Livland, some sort of equalization seemed inevitable. Also, in Livland, in the Latvian-language area around Cēsis (Wenden) in the Kauguri district, in October of 1802 peasant unrest of considerable proportions underlined how distrustful the peasantry had become. In this region, serfs began to insist that they were entitled to deal directly with the crown's representatives in matters of imperial taxation; the local landowners saw this demand as intolerable; some three thousand peasants gathered, armed with hunting rifles, scythes, and wooden stakes; the army had to be called, and twenty-two peasants died from gunshot wounds then and later. An investigation of the incident showed that the more literate peasant leaders had been reading newspaper accounts about the French Revolution; moreover, for decades this area had been a center of the Moravian Brethren (Herrnhut), who were suspected of instilling in their followers a spirit of disobedience. The Baltic German landowners had to rely on units of the Russian army to quell the peasant unrest; the need for such intervention carried with it another kind of threat since it brought into question the extent to which the landed aristocracies could be relied upon for "good governance."

After much continuous discussion the Livland *Landtag* finally proposed a new law in 1804 that seemed needed under the circumstances. Conversations outside and during the meetings, however, suggested strongly that in the minds of serf-owning aristocrats a law to assuage the tsar and its implementation were two different things altogether. In any event, the Livland law incorporating the heritability principle of the 1802 Estland measure affected about 2,600 estate owners and some 500,000 serfs, half of them Estonian and half Latvian. The new law retreated from the long-held principle that a peasant-serf was legally bound to the person of the estate owner; he was now to be considered bound to the county of his birth. A serf and his family could not be sold or bequeathed to someone else. In addition to heritability of the farmstead and the serf's locational tie, the law also set rules about how the owner could deal with the serf's person, about the dispensation of local justice, and about norming of labor requirements. With respect to justice, a county court was created as the first instance for peasants and their complaints: it consisted of three members, one chosen by the estate owner, one elected by farmstead heads, and one elected by farmhands. Peasants could appeal cases to a parish court (the term "parish" having a secular rather than a religious meaning in this context), which consisted of four members: the estate owner as the presiding officer and three chosen peasant representatives. The next level was the land court (*Landesgericht*) consisting of three estate owners and two peasants (one representing the crown and the others, private estates of the region). The next higher level was the *Hofgericht* in Riga, which was to create a special department for cases involving peasants. After three grievances against a landowner, the complaining peasant was to suffer corporal punishment if the courts held the grievance to be unjustified.

Thus, the new law did create a legal structure more receptive to peasant grievances, and it also recognized the important status distinction between farmstead heads and farmhands, though it did not seek to regulate their relationship. The peasant-serf population of any district consisted of these two major categories with a proportional breakdown sometimes as high as 50–50. The life-chances of farmstead heads and their family members in this system, now to be regulated by law, were much better than those of the farmhands; the latter, married or unmarried, served a farmstead head on the basis of a verbal agreement, normally for a year. The heads and their families mostly stayed put; the farmhands circulated among the farmsteads of an estate. Strictly speaking, an eternal divide did not separate "landed" and "landless" peasants, because a farmstead head still could be removed from a holding for incompetence fairly easily, and thus have to enter the farmhand population; and able farmhands, especially if they were married, could be placed into the headships of a holding by the estate owner. Both groupings could therefore experience upward or downward social mobility, and heritability of a holding was not absolute. Because these two subpopulations were so large and their relationships governed by an unwritten "contract," friction between them was inevitable, and the new court system did recognize that the interests of people from the two groupings could clash.

The sticky question of labor norms became a stumbling block from the beginning because the norming of labor requirements in Livland was to be based on the relative size and fertility of peasant land and estate land (the demesne): who held how much in an array of size and quality categories would determine how many workdays a given farmstead owed to the estate, whether the serf-laborer would have to bring a horse to the labor team, and how the required labor would be distributed over a working year. All these determinations presupposed the existence of accurate empirical information about holding size and quality and about existing labor norms. Such information was not readily available, because, even though by 1804 Livland had been under Russian control for some eighty years, the agricultural labor system and the allocation of peasant land still rested on the seventeenth-century surveys and measurements of the Swedish period. Now, however, both estate owners and peasants wanted a new numerical basis for the 1804 law – peasants because they believed correctly that over the past three generations the owners had skewed numbers in their own favor, and the estate owners probably hoping that the tasks of resurveying and recalculating would be so costly and prolonged that the reforming impulse from St. Petersburg would dissipate in the meantime. In any event, the new numbers were to be contained in an account book (*Wackenbuch*) for each peasant holding, which would record the kinds and quality of land involved and the nature and amounts of the farmstead's labor and other obligations. Now written down, these norms would, in principle, remain inviolable.

The 1804 measure favored the peasantry but it was also a complicated law, involving a mixture of definitions and mechanisms of conflict resolution. It was in fact so multifaceted that the Russian administrators who were to oversee its application frequently had to rely on the estate owners, who understood local conditions, for assurance that implementation was proceeding properly. As a measure of whether the job was being done, they tended to use the number of peasant grievances as an indicator, although this standard was not necessarily the most accurate since peasants complained about many things unrelated to the new law itself. In any event, the law could not be implemented quickly because one part of it – the norming of labor – depended on the resurveying of estate and peasant land. In the case of individual estates, this prerequisite prolonged implementation by a decade or more, which provided opportunity for the landowners to maneuver. They persuaded Russian administrators that the implementation process had created, as it were, four different 1804 laws – one for each major district of Livonia – and that supplementary measures were necessary for the entire law to be applied evenly. This resulted in the 1809 Supplementary Points, which also addressed the question of labor norms and created a definition of laborers that permitted estate owners to claim more weekly peasant labor than had the 1804 measure. After 1804, however, most farmsteads did receive *Wackenbücher*, allowing the estate owners to claim that the question of labor norms had been settled. Since neither the 1804 law nor the 1809 supplements dealt systematically with the question of "extraordinary" or "supplemental labor," these categories were left to the discretion of estate owners. Many peasants felt cheated, but the landed aristocracy's hope that the prolongation of implementation would diminish the tsar's interest in the issue was not fulfilled either.

In the meantime, the landed aristocracies of the provinces of Estland and Kurland sought to follow the Livonian example. The 1802 law had to be brought into line with the 1804 Livland measure in Estland, where landowners pleaded poverty with respect to implementation: they could not carry, they said, the costs of resurveying and remeasuring their properties; instead, they would use the Swedish-period measures and would resurvey in specific instances when individual peasants complained about the numbers being used. The plan seemed acceptable to the St. Petersburg government, and the *Wackenbücher* in Estonia were readied at record speed. In Kurland, the situation was more complicated because that province, having been under the control of the Polish-Lithuanian Commonwealth until 1795, had no Swedish-period measurements. There lord–serf relations remained largely unchanged and unregulated until nearly the end of the Napoleonic period.

After 1804, Tsar Alexander became increasingly worried about agrarian relations in the Baltic littoral because, on the western horizon, loomed the figure of Napoleon Bonaparte and his relentless and victorious drive across central Europe toward Russia. Among the reforms of the Napoleonic empire was serf emancipation in the lands its army defeated. Serfdom had been abolished in Schleswig-Holstein (1805), Pomerania (1806), and Prussia (1807); by contrast, in Livland even by 1810 the debate continued about rules within the serf system rather than about the serf system itself. The Baltic littoral was drawn into the Napoleonic episode after the defeat of Prussia in 1807, which led to the creation of a Polish territory, the so-called

Duchy of Warsaw: this now became a dependency of France and immediately initiated a general emancipation of serfs.

In 1812, Napoleon invaded Russia and a part of his army briefly occupied the province of Kurland and threatened to take Riga. After Napoleon's defeat and during the Congress of Vienna (1815), Alexander wanted to continue to play the role of a progressive European ruler. Yet on the one point that seemed increasingly to separate progressive from reactionary states – the existence of serfdom – he had made little headway in his own realm. In the Baltic littoral, only a small segment of the Lithuanian population had experienced emancipation. Still, after 1815, what Alexander really wanted – abolition – was now perceived by the Baltic German landowners not as the pipe dream of an unpredictable tsar but as a reform that was inevitable. Therefore the administrators assigned to implement the 1804 and 1809 measures increasingly turned their attention to the larger question. Admitting that the *Zeitgeist* and the tsar wanted measures cast in terms of liberation rather than just reform, the *Landtage* of Estland, Livland, and Kurland began to work on projects that would result in the "emancipation of serfs" (*Bauernbefreiung*), expecting that with some skillful maneuvering they could create new laws that would not do wholesale damage to their material interests. The projects were finalized at different times for the three provinces – Estland in 1816, Kurland in 1817, and Livland in 1819. By the end of the second decade of the nineteenth century "freedom" had come to a large portion of the littoral peasantries. The peasant-serfs of Latgale and most of the Lithuanian territories at this juncture were not recipients of any liberating measures; their time would not come until 1861 with the general emancipation of Russian serfs under Alexander II.

THE ABOLITION OF SERFDOM IN THE BALTIC PROVINCES

Reform of Baltic-area serfdom would not have turned into emancipation had it not been for the goading created by external pressures – the Napoleonic ascendancy and Tsar Alexander's anxieties. The history of the 1802, 1804 and 1809 measures in Estland and Livland suggests that the landed aristocrats saw reform and emancipation as separate categories of change: reforms need not lead to emancipation. The micro-history of the 1816–1819 emancipation measures is the story of triangulated negotiations between the *Landtage*, the Russian administrative officials stationed in the littoral, and the St. Petersburg government; again these revealed the power of inertia. A number of "liberal" landowners thought emancipation was overdue, but theirs were not the commanding voices. The conservatives recognized that emancipation was becoming inevitable and finally voted in favor, extracting from the reform as much as they could that favored their own socioeconomic interests. The conservatives also understood that the tsarist government shared with them two thoughts: that formal proclamation of personal freedom for peasant-serfs could trigger massive population dislocations and that it would be best if emancipation were stretched out over time.

The emancipation laws of 1816 (Estland), 1817 (Kurland), and 1819 (Livland) were massive documents of some 600–800 paragraphs

17 Abolition of serfdom in Livland, 1819. The Baltic German painter Johann Lebrecht Eggink (1784–1867) in 1824 portrayed serf emancipation in Livland as involving nearly classical figures – robed and grateful Estonian and Latvian peasants and a beneficent Tsar Alexander I.

each. The new laws were not entirely original because all three incorporated elements of the earlier reform measures, especially the
Estonian reforms of 1802. Though they had rather inglorious origins –
the negotiations and lobbying efforts of the reform period – the
proclamations that accompanied them resounded with language
announcing the birth of freedom and liberty for the peasants. Seen
against the agrarian history of the littoral, such language was perhaps
not entirely inappropriate because the emancipation laws finally
ended an institution that had been an essential part of the littoral's
history for about 250 years. Yet the manner in which this message of
freedom arrived among the peasantry is difficult to comprehend,
because only a few sections of the new laws were translated into the
vernacular languages – Estonian and Latvian. Translations were made
mostly by the Lutheran clergy who understood only imperfectly the
complex legal ideas of the emancipation documents. The exact meaning of the "freedom" that had now arrived was resolved in hundreds
of thousands of concrete situations and over time, until all the peasants
understood the scope of the liberation and also the constraints that
continued to exist. For the next decade and a half – in fact until the
mid-1830s – the constraints were far more significant in everyday
rural life than were the new freedoms.

The emancipation laws directly addressed and immediately
affected almost every aspect of the lives of enserfed peasants. In the
three provinces about 84–85 percent of the population was involved:
in Estland an estimated 188,000, in Livland 530,000, and in Kurland
250,000. The laws dealt with the distribution of the ownership of
land and how holdings were to be rented, the question of labor
norms now that they could no longer be mandatory, the geographical movements of the peasantry and the personal identity of peasants, local institutions of self-government, and the adjudication of
disputes and criminal activity. The three laws varied in terms of date
of initiation and contents, but since the speed of implementation
differed in each province, it was not until the end of the 1820s that
the peasantries of the three provinces were living in roughly the same
circumstances. Differences remained, but these now lay primarily
in the manner in which the landed aristocracies, who retained
their monopoly over political power at the provincial level, interpreted the new situation. The most notable disparities, it needs

repeating, would now develop between those Latvian-speaking peasants who lived in the Latgale region of the adjoining Vitebsk province and the Latvian peasants in Livland and Kurland, and between the Estonian and Latvian peasants and the peasantry in the Lithuanian lands. Two generations separated the emancipations in these regions of the Baltic littoral.

The three new laws made emancipation a process rather than an overnight occurrence. Farmstead heads and their families, farmhands and theirs, and the peasants attached directly to estate farms were to be emancipated as separate groupings at six-year intervals, starting with the farmstead heads. This staggering of the process meant, of course, that the peasantries contained "free" and "unfree" subpopulations for a time after the new laws were promulgated, with the unfree nurturing resentment over the disparate treatment. Behind this procedure stood the fear that thousands of newly freed peasants would immediately seek to abandon the estates on which they were living and seek their fortunes elsewhere. Special measures were introduced in some places to prevent this phenomenon, after some farmstead heads interpreted their new freedom to mean that they were entitled to give up their headships immediately, together with the accompanying responsibilities. The new laws were unclear on exactly when and in what manner peasants could claim their freedom. Repeated incidents involving differing understanding of the letter of the laws required ad hoc interpretations, which inevitably favored the landowners. The tsarist government, having accomplished its main goal of emancipation, was clearly pulling back from the oversight of its implementation, permitting the landowners of the littoral to adjust the new laws to suit their interests. Continued low-level peasant unrest in all three provinces during the 1820s, 1830s, and 1840s signaled that the landowning aristocracies did not interpret their acquiescence in the emancipation process as a surrender of their powerful sociopolitical status.

Whatever their inadequacies, the emancipation laws, targeting as they did the vast majority of the rural population (and therefore of the entire population) of Estland, Livland, and Kurland, created a larger context for and lay behind most of the changes that took place over the next generation. They transformed the personal standing of all peasants and shaped the socioeconomic environment of what peasants could do with their new status and what they could aspire to do, both the opportunities and limitations. One major limitation was the shifting of formal ownership of all land to the landowner. For example, the Livland law formulated the principle that "the Livland and Ösel (Saaremaa) landowners renounce all the rights that heretofore, as hereditary landowners, they have had over the hereditarily servile people on the land. But the landowners retain the land as their property with which they can do as they wish ..." With a stroke of the pen, such provisions cancelled whatever customary rights to holdings peasants believed themselves to be entitled to. Commentators on the new laws explained this as a *quid pro quo*: serfs received personal freedom, estates received title to all land. Lost in this transaction were not only customary rights but also the security that had been created in the 1804 peasant law: if peasant-serfs rendered their obligations to the estate without fail, they could not be put off their holdings. Now, however, circumstances had changed: in principle, estate owners could now legally expel peasants from their holdings at will, if, for example, the estate wanted to add a farmstead's fields to the estate fields. Such expulsions did happen, but their frequency remains debated. Empirical studies of headship transmission between generations of peasants in the 1816–1850 period show that in the vast majority of cases the farmstead remained in the hands of the same peasant family as headships were transmitted from father to son. Still, the expectation of fair treatment was not the same thing as absolute possession of the land, and the emancipation laws precluded the latter option unless the peasant purchased the holding outright from the estate. In the first half of the nineteenth century, such purchases remained rare.

The economic theory embedded in the emancipation laws was unabashedly a version of the economic liberalism of Adam Smith, whom better-read aristocrats and government officials frequently cited by name in their discussions about the new laws. The central notion was that, once freed, the peasant became an autonomous agent, capable of selling his labor to the highest bidder and establishing an independent contract with the buyer of that labor. As the Kurland law stated, "henceforth, the freed peasants ... and the lords who own the estates shall conduct themselves in a manner arrived at by means of a contract agreed to by both sides." Peasants brought to the transaction their labor and estates their land, the result being an agreement fair to all.

The new arrangements in the Baltic provinces were thus to embody the most progressive economic ideas of the time. To some extent the idea was cynical, yet England's burgeoning industrialists believed the same thing with respect to industrial enterprise and the workers in it. Some liberally inclined landed aristocrats immediately identified the flaws in this proposition: the notion of a fair contract between a traditional omnipotent landowner and a deferential and newly "freed" peasant seemed to make little sense. But their objections changed no minds. Moreover, the presumed equality that the laws had created was further eroded by the claim that estate owners also possessed the value peasants had added to the holding through their earlier work. The concept of the "iron inventory" of a holding specified that not only land but also movable goods – livestock, farm equipment, vehicles – were the property of the estate owner. Furthermore, the idealized circumstance in which peasants were to enter contractual agreements with landowners in an alleged free marketplace of labor was contradicted by the fact that the new laws forbade movement of peasants across estate boundaries: in practice, therefore, the free marketplace was something of a fiction. For the most part, the freed peasant and the landowner were the same actors as before emancipation, except that now labor service by the peasant for the foreseeable future was to be rendered not as a customary obligation but as rent in exchange for a less secure tenure.

The discussions preceding the emancipation laws projected substantial economic improvements for the peasantry as a result of freedom, but this did not occur in the short run. The period from 1820 to 1850 remained comparatively bleak in terms of agricultural productivity, punctuated by bad harvests, continuing incidents of peasant unrest, and only spotty improvements in agricultural practice on estates willing to experiment with new crops and new methods of increasing output. In addition, the traditional landowning aristocracies of the Baltic provinces were demonstrating their weaknesses as managers of their estates – their principal source of income. The number of heavily mortgaged estates rose with every decade of the nineteenth century as did the sale of estates at auction. Financially hard-pressed landowners sought permission from their peers and from the government to sell their estates outright to non-aristocratic well-to-do burghers and, in a few instances, even to sell small estates to ambitious peasants. By 1818, the Livland aristocratic landowners had mortgaged about one-third of their estates and had received 7.5 million rubles in loans from the St. Petersburg government. Sixteen percent of the Livland estates had been sold for non-payment of debt and almost half of all estates were being operated by persons who were not of the noble order (*Adelstand*). The emancipation laws had done little to resolve the conflict between the frequently lavish lifestyles among the landed aristocracy and the diminishing incomes they received from their landed properties.

The labor-rent system created by the emancipation laws perpetuated negative pressures on peasant self-improvement, but the same laws rendered permanent an earlier reform, namely, local and regional courts in which after a fashion peasants shared power with representatives of the estate owner or the estate owner himself. These courts were something of a compromise for the landowners: on the one hand, estate owners were freed of the "patriarchal" burden for rendering local justice and resolving peasant disputes, but, on the other, they now had to suffer the indignities of sitting around the same table with people of lower social rank and having to consider their opinions seriously.

In some districts, the old habits of deference died hard, and peasants were forced to choose representatives to these institutions. Nonetheless, the peasant courts were the first component in the gradual but very real development of local self-government, which became obligatory. The emancipation laws required the election of local elders whose job it was to distribute equally the tasks of public works (such as road and bridge repair) and to call public meetings periodically to consider all manner of local problems – orphans, the aged, community granaries – that heretofore had been handled by the estate. These new institutions and the practices they entailed became everyday realities only as the process of emancipation worked toward a conclusion. If in the pre-emancipation period the mental geography of peasants had had only three reference points – the farmsteads and their lands, the estate and its requirements, and the local religious congregation and its formalities – after emancipation a fourth reference point was added – the local peasant community functioning as a collectivity. This innovation was particularly difficult to establish in those areas of the littoral that had a centuries-long settlement pattern of scattered isolated farmsteads and no village communities. Here the habit of each farmstead head dealing directly with the estate owner or his agents now had to be changed to incorporate cooperation and collaboration with the heads of other farmsteads and in some circumstances with the farm-hand population.

Emancipation laws indirectly affected the peasant's conception of self-worth. Though the old notion of a peasant social order (*Bauernstand*) did not disappear altogether, the meaning of belonging to it began to lose many of the earlier connotations of total subordination. The new laws required that each individual who was emancipated be identifiable publicly as a unique person, a separate entity in the eyes of the law, capable of signing legal documents and entering into agreements without mediation by his or her "owner." This enhanced the standing of males – they were no longer in any sense property; females, however, no matter what recognition was extended to them by formal law, continued to be represented in the public sphere by fathers, husband, brothers, or other male relatives. But both sexes were required to have a unique identity symbolized by their names, and thus hundreds of thousands of peasants in Estland, Livland, and Kurland had to adopt surnames. Some peasants already had them, but most did not. As with other provisions of the emancipation laws, implementation lasted well into the early 1830s, in part because the Kurland law neglected to include the requirement, while elsewhere a surname-adoption procedure had to be invented. During the transition period – about 1816–1835 – many peasants kept their old names while others received new ones. Confusion persisted in the public records because not everyone remembered later what surname they had chosen or had been given: these peasants continued to use their old names, while in official documents they would be referred to as something else. In fact, some local-level listings (for example, soul revisions) for a time continued to use both the old and new names for people until they became familiar with their new identities. The renaming procedures varied widely, but in most cases the new surname was required at the moment when the person was officially emancipated. At that juncture, peasants either were asked to provide a new surname or were assigned one by the local authorities. Under the old dispensation, most people were known by a first (Christian) name and the name of the farmstead in which they were currently living; in the new system, they acquired a new surname to add to the first name with which they had been baptized, while the locational designator fell away. In fact, most peasants, if allowed to make a choice, chose as their surnames the farmstead name in which they were living at the time. If a surname were assigned to them, it could be quite arbitrarily chosen. In the Latvian-language areas, clergymen urged their parishioners to avoid German-sounding names, evidently expecting a mass emulation of the names of social superiors. If estate owners became involved in the process, the resulting name could depend on their whims. This aspect of emancipation nonetheless intensified for many peasants the feeling that a new age had dawned, for not only were they now free, in the eyes of the law they were also different persons. The generation of Latvians and Estonians who were born during the emancipation period adjusted to their new identities easily in most cases, yet throughout the nineteenth century, many petitioned for the right to change their surnames to something they thought more suitable.

THE UPRISING OF 1830–1831
IN THE LITHUANIAN LANDS

Although in the decades after formal emancipation localized rural disturbances in Estland, Livland, and Kurland remained commonplace, control of these provinces by the St. Petersburg government was never at risk. The unrest had the character of chance incidents, strong reactions to some perceived wrong, and they were easily put down by a show of force or minimal use of it. Ideological claims were not involved, though in many such occurrences a simmering resentment against the lack of more profound changes was detectable. Most certainly they did not involve questions of political separation or statehood by any definition. Such radicalism was far from the thinking of Estonian and Latvian peasants. The Baltic German landed aristocracy – the only social estate in a position to consider such lofty questions – was also increasingly less inclined to do so, particularly under Alexander I's conservative brother Nicholas I, who ascended to the Russian throne in 1825.

The main goal of the governing orders in the Baltic provinces was preservation of the privileges granted to them earlier; moreover, in the course of the nineteenth century, an increasing number of Baltic Germans of middling and high standing were quite willing to enter Russian state service for career reasons and because the St. Petersburg government needed such educated "westerners." The government was intent on expanding bureaucratic institutions;

18 Emilija Plātere. A young leader of the abortive 1830–1831 uprising against tsarist authority, Plātere (1806–1831) finds a heroic role in the military history of Lithuania (where she was born), Poland (which spearheaded the revolt), and Latgale (where she lived and conducted her guerilla operations).

even in the absence of a national parliament, the Russian autocracy still had the problem of administering effectively a sprawling multinational empire, and educated and talented persons were needed at every level. The first tsar to concern himself seriously with questions of internal governance was Nicholas I (1825–1855), and his son Alexander II continued centralization and coordination efforts. Ironically, just like numerous Baltic Germans, during the 1840s many Estonian and Latvian peasants also made their peace with Russian hegemony, but not for career reasons. They wanted to escape labor rents. In the hope of obtaining land, peasants converted to Russian Orthodoxy in large numbers. By 1848, in Livland some 65,600 Estonians and 40,400 Latvians had converted (an estimated 16–17 percent of all Christian congregants in the Baltic provinces). The conversion movement did not affect Kurland; there Orthodox prelates were unreceptive to converts of any kind.

In many respects – emancipation, reform, conversion – the Lithuanian lands of the littoral during the post-Napoleonic decades contrasted sharply with the territories to the north. The peasantry who used the Lithuanian language, of course, now resided in three or four adjacent government-defined provinces (as well as Lithuania Minor in Prussia) and their everyday lives were shaped by somewhat differing administrative practices and rules. Most Lithuanian peasants remained enserfed until 1861; the entire territory of the old Grand Duchy had fewer and smaller cities and towns than the Baltic provinces; the Roman Catholic Church remained a powerful influence throughout; and the pronounced ethnic and linguistic diversity characteristic of the duchy before the partitions of the commonwealth continued and perhaps even increased through the expansion of the non-Lithuanian population. By contrast with Estland, Livland, and Kurland, one prominent socioeconomic group in the region – the landed gentry – remained restive under Russian rule. Its character was complex: most of the gentry were polonized linguistically and even culturally, and it was difficult to draw a line between a distinct Lithuanian and a distinct Polish consciousness within the gentry population. The ties that had developed among the Polish and Lithuanian landed orders of the territories of the old commonwealth were deep and extended into the domains of genealogy, language, and general culture. To outsiders, and particularly to Russian administrators of these territories, the differences were unrecognizable and in the final analysis unimportant. But the gentry, as well as some of the magnate families, did have a strong historical memory, and the year 1795, when the commonwealth finally disappeared, was only a generation in the past. Among many of them residual loyalty to independent statehood existed, however much it had been compromised during the last decades. Moreover, the offspring of the last generation who had experienced independent statehood had been growing up in a Europe in which the idea of revolution, Napoleonic transformations of central Europe, and political liberalism were living realities. The brief Napoleonic presence in the Baltic region in fact had ended in 1815 in the creation of something like a revived Poland – the so-called Congress Poland – so that the reemergence of earlier political forms was by no means in the realm of fantasy. There were very good reasons, in other words, for the St. Petersburg government to mistrust the political elites of the Polish and Lithuanian borderlands, and this mistrust extended well into the third decade of the nineteenth century.

Alexander I viewed the former commonwealth territories somewhat more benignly, however, seeing an opportunity to experiment there with constitutionalism as he had experimented with agrarian reform in the Baltic provinces. Overriding the suspicions of his top administrators, Alexander was tolerant of Congress Poland and refrained from seeking to russify its courts and educational system. Several highly placed Polish aristocrats had Alexander's ear in formulating policy toward these borderlands. Liberalism, however, did little to pacify sentiment among the gentry, and during the first two decades of Alexander's reign, anti-imperial opinion continued to grow, especially in the minds of younger people who were studying or had studied at Vilnius University. Alleged conspirators, such as the group called Philomaths, were discovered and dealt with harshly, which in turn stoked the perception of Russian oppressiveness. These governmental intrusions were the Russian version of the antinationalist drive created and spearheaded in central Europe by the Habsburg foreign minister Klemens von Metternich, who saw all varieties of nationalism in the post-Napoleonic period as dangerous to the established order created by the Congress of Vienna in 1815. The "Metternich system" especially targeted institutions of higher learning in the German and Austrian lands.

19 Adam Miczkiewicz statue, Cracow, Poland. The great nineteenth-century poet Miczkiewicz (1799–1855) eventually became a cultural hero of both the Poles and Lithuanians, as happened to many creative people from the culturally layered and complicated territory of the old Polish-Lithuanian Commonwealth.

In the Polish and Lithuanian territories anti-Russian nationalism attracted such future luminaries as the poet Adam Miczkiewicz (one of the founders of the Philomaths), prominent members of the professoriate, and even some highly placed clerics in the Catholic hierarchy. Opposition tsarist authority became especially strong during the 1820s, particularly after the tolerant regime of Alexander I was replaced in 1825 by the conservative reign of Nicholas I. Ultimately, the simmering opposition was inspired by events in France in 1830, where the restored Bourbon dynasty was overthrown and replaced by the so-called bourgeois monarchy of Louis Phillippe. Polish political refugees in France communicated to their brethren at home that oppressive regimes were once again on the defensive. In November 1830, an outright struggle began in Congress Poland against the Russian political and military presence; by March 1831 the confrontations had spread to Lithuanian territory. In both places, however, the fighting had ended by October 1831 and "the revolution" was defeated.

Although for some four to five months the "revolutionaries" in the Lithuanian lands claimed to be in control of the situation, their successes were illusory; first, they were militarily unprepared for a drawn-out struggle, and, second, their stated goals had little clarity. The revolutionaries entered the battle phase as divided among themselves as they had been in the preceding years. Some of the insurrectionists thought they were fighting to restore the unified commonwealth, some believed that the freed territory would respect the old boundaries between Poland and Lithuania, and some envisaged that a new form of Polish-dominated state was in the offing. A few in the Lithuanian area appear to have believed that they were fighting to free the Lithuanian lands from both Russians and Poles. The aims of the insurrection in the Lithuanian provinces were particularly hazy, in so far as it involved activists who – though bilingual in Polish and Lithuanian – were culturally and socially more linked to the Polish world than to the Lithuanian peasantry.

Also, in the Lithuanian districts, a base for a continuous organized military opposition to Russian forces was absent, and ammunition was in short supply. Moreover, such support as was shown by the Lithuanian peasantry dissipated quickly when it became clear that the gentry were uninterested in any kind of agrarian reform, let alone the abolition of serfdom. Thus, by autumn 1831, the insurrection had petered out in both the Polish and Lithuanian territories, its leaders had been arrested or had fled abroad (mostly to France), and none of the goals of the insurrectionists had been reached. In Vilnius province, 3,880 insurrectionists were tried and 150 gentry estates were confiscated. The Russian government then proceeded with a wholly predictable series of repressive measures. New taxes were imposed, the scope of censorship was expanded, the Polish monarchy was abolished as an institution, and what remained of the Polish army was dissolved. In the Lithuanian region, in 1832 Vilnius University was closed, and in 1840 the sixteenth-century Third Lithuanian Statute was revoked and replaced by Russian law. Russian became the official language of all institutions, and soon most senior-level administrative positions in the Lithuanian-area provinces were filled only by Russians. Censorship reached into the Catholic Church, requiring sermons to be vetted, and convents were closed. In 1840 Nicholas ordered that such terms as "Lithuania" and "Belorussia" were not to be used in official discussions of and correspondence about the western borderlands. Repetition of the names of the nine provinces into which the Polish and Lithuanian lands were now divided – Grodno, Kiev, Kovno, Minsk, Mohylew, Podolia, Volhynia, Vilno, and Vitebsk – was to erase former territorial identities from official consciousness, and to eliminate the possibility that the residents of these provinces would retain ties across the new administrative boundaries. To the north, the Baltic provinces of Estland, Livland, and Kurland had been permitted to retain their historic pre-Russian territorial names, but the post-1830 territorial nomenclature of the Lithuanian lands was meant to destroy historical memory.

One of the new administrative entities into which the lands of the Grand Duchy had been divided – Vitebsk – assumed, population-wise, the same position for the Latvian population as Lithuania Minor in East Prussia had for the Lithuanians. The old Polish Livonia – Inflanty (Latgale) – had been added to Vitebsk province to form its westernmost districts (about one-third of the province's territory), and about 190,000 peasants who spoke a variant of Latvian lived in these districts. It is not likely that Russian administrators understood or cared about the linguistic and ethnic makeup of the peasant population in these districts, since they dealt primarily with the approximately 280 landed estates in the region, which were owned or rented by a mixture of polonized German families, late-arrival Russian gentry, and a few Polish magnates. Inspired by serf emancipation next door in Estland, Livland, and Kurland in 1817–1819, a handful of the Latgale landowners launched a project for emancipation and gained approval from Alexander I for the idea, but it came to naught owing to profound disagreements in their own ranks about how emancipation should be implemented. Consequently, the Latgale countryside remained "unreformed," and, under Nicholas I's Russian administrators, was treated similarly to the Lithuanian lands, namely, as a suspect region because of Polish influences. Although the 1830–1831 uprising had little resonance in Latgale among landowners or peasants, because it had belonged to the old commonwealth territories, it was easily conceived of as a possible source of separatism.

In addition to keeping an eye on Latgale's landowners, tsarist administrators had to deal with the institution of the Roman Catholic Church, which over the past two centuries had become an inextricable part of the lives of Latgale's common people. Estimates of denominational membership in Latgale in the 1840s offer the following numbers: about 65% Roman Catholic, 12% Old Believer, 11% Russian Orthodox, 7% Jewish, and 4% Lutheran. The russification policy applied to the Lithuanian lands after the 1830–1831 uprising was extended to the Latgale territory, where it focused mainly on reducing the influence of Roman Catholicism and generally used careful measures. Forced conversion of hundreds of thousands of Catholic peasants to Russian Orthodoxy could not be implemented, but in-migration into the region of Russian Orthodox peasants could be encouraged, with the expectation that intermarriage would occur and offspring would be raised in the Orthodox faith. Peasant schools could not simply be closed to eliminate the baleful influences of Polishness and Catholicism, but the language of instruction could be Russian and a parallel Russian-language rural school system funded by the government could be created. Church property could not be totally "nationalized" with the stroke of the pen, but the church could be gradually deprived of many of its properties through a selective closing down of convents and monasteries. Catholic churchmen could not simply be expelled from the empire, but their continued work within it could be narrowed, for example, by the imposition of limits on how frequently they could correspond with Rome and how frequently they could travel outside their own immediate districts. While sermons could not be easily forbidden, they could be censored, and clergy could be required to pray from the pulpit for the success of government policy, such as the repression of the 1831 insurrection.

These regulations, coming fast one after another, forced the papacy to work out special secret instructions after 1831 about how the church should perform its mission, especially when government pressures became increasingly heavy-handed during the 1840s and began to include punishment of landowners who were perceived to be helping the church. In 1847, Pope Gregory XVI and Nicholas I signed a concordat about the treatment of the church in the empire but this did not significantly change government policy, since some of the components of the concordat were completely ignored by tsarist officials. The cultural, economic, and social cleavages between the Latvian-language populations in Livland and Kurland and those in Latgale continued to widen, so that a generation later Latvian nationalist activists in the Baltic provinces proper had to rediscover the linguistic kinship between themselves and the peasantry beyond the Vitebsk provincial border.

CULTURAL PATRONAGE AND CULTURAL CLIENTAGE

The conservative reign of Nicholas I from 1825 on was increasingly characterized by the themes of "autocracy, Orthodoxy, and nationality" and the russification policy the regime followed in the Lithuanian lands looked to be an expression of them. Nonetheless, Russia remained a particularistic country in which the history of regions remained quite varied. A simple imposition of cultural uniformity everywhere was impossible. In the Baltic littoral, what the mid-century decades in fact contained, alongside all else, were some interesting changes in the ongoing relationships between its cultural elites – the Baltic Germans and the Poles – and their cultural clients – the Estonians, Latvians, and Lithuanians. These relationships were of no particular interest to Russian administrators as long as civic peace was maintained and the larger policy goal of control was met. Yet the non-Russians of the region were tied to each other in many ways other than socioeconomic, and the loosening of those ties through serf emancipation in Estland, Livland, and Kurland could not help but have a spillover effect in other domains of life.

Thus the generation of Estonians and Latvians born just before or around the enactment of emancipation measures (1816–1819) matured in a society where age-old habits of deference and gratitude no longer worked as they once did. The Baltic German *Gelehrtenstand* understood this: the issue of germanization of the peasantry continued to be a source of debate, with some insisting that a large-scale program be implemented while others (thinking in the Herderian mode) saw the continued cultivation of Estonian and Latvian language and folklore to be almost a religious obligation. Now nearing old age, Garlieb Merkel, the fiery anti-serfdom writer of the late eighteenth century, observed in 1820 that the education of peasants was a threat: it would lead to unwelcome "separatist" tendencies among educated rural youths, and he wanted no part of it. The period from about 1820 to 1855 did not see a change in the main *dramatis personae* in the cultural life of the Baltic provinces, but in small but increasing numbers the extras on stage were becoming different. More persons of Estonian and Latvian (and therefore of peasant) backgrounds received higher education; more of them wrote and published in the languages of their birth; more joined with colleagues among the Baltic German *literati* in their concerns for the education of peasants and the production of entertaining literatures in the vernacular; and more believed that the life of the mind needed no further justification. They played little part in the larger power skirmishes between Russian administrators and the Baltic German *Ritterschaften*; their struggle was conducted at a lower level.

When the Baltic German press surveyed annually the state of "our Latvian" or "our Estonian" literature, their use of the collective personal pronoun continued to emphasize a sense of ownership – the Baltic Germans had created it, continued to nurture it, and therefore in that sense "owned" it as well. The first generation of Estonian and Latvian literary aspirants reflected this mindset fairly faithfully, and there was nothing in the numbers of persons involved that suggested a different understanding. But the situation involved a new psychology. For most Baltic German *literati*, continued writing about Latvian or Estonian subjects in Latvian or Estonian was an avocation. For the Latvians and Estonians, however, whose numbers could grow if the rural education system were able to school all those who wanted schooling, creating literary works in their own languages contained elements of a mission (*Sendung*). No one of their background had ever been involved in such a task and no one could predict what the outcome of such a development would be.

In the Baltic provinces of Estland, Livland, and Kurland the patron–client relationship of course favored the Baltic German side: it was they who in 1822 began publishing the first Latvian-language newspaper, *Latviešu avīzes* (the initiator of this enterprise was a Lutheran pastor, K. F. Watson). As members of the *Lettisch-literärische Gesellschaft* (founded in 1824), Baltic Germans wrote extended essays on Latvian language and folklore; and as participants in the so-called "Estophile" grouping in the Estonian-language section of Livland and in Estland, they argued for the preservation and nurturance of Estonian language and folklore. As owners of sometimes impressively large personal libraries and as teachers in peasant schools they lent books to the brightest of their pupils to prepare them for higher education. A training institute for rural elementary schoolteachers was established in the university town of Dorpat in 1828; a similar establishment, directed by the Latvian-born Jānis Cimze (1814–1881), was founded in Valka in 1839; both were funded by the Livland aristocracy and private monies, and both over time graduated literally hundreds of rural schoolteachers for service in parish-level schools. The leading educational institution of the Baltic provinces – the university – was also in Dorpat (Tartu); it was reopened by Alexander I in 1802 after a century of inactivity following its closure during the Great Northern War. Under the rectorship of the estimable Georg Friedrich Parrott, who was a personal friend of Alexander, Dorpat remained well funded for most of the nineteenth century and gathered into its faculty many prominent Baltic German scholars, also recruiting outstanding academics from other parts of Europe. It was precisely toward Dorpat University that the eyes of young Latvians and Estonians turned during the 1830s and 1840s as they dreamt about pursuing their

20 Dorpat in the nineteenth century. Dorpat (later Tartu) was
the second largest city in the Estonian part of the province of
Livland, with a thriving economy that dated back to the city's
membership in the Hanseatic League.

education beyond the certificates obtained from the teachers' institutes. Their numbers in these decades, however, remained low –
perhaps several dozen in each case – but by comparison with the
recent and distant past even the small numbers were impressive.

Whatever their numbers, the phenomenon of *university-educated*
Estonians and Latvians was unprecedented but hardly imaginable as
a threat to Baltic German cultural hegemony with its close ties to the
general culture of central Europe. The "rules" of local upward socioeconomic mobility remained unchanged: at a certain juncture in
one's education and development one was expected to leave behind
one's personal past and enter – socially, linguistically, and culturally –
the higher level of civilization represented by the dominant institutions of Baltic life. Thereafter, a scholarly interest in the local
cultures could be pursued from an entirely new vantage point.
The adult careers of such young Latvians as Ansis Līventāls (1803–
1877), Ansis Leitāns (1815–1874), Jānis Ruģēns (1817–1876), and
Ernests Dinsberģis (1816–1902) all suggest the same pattern: exceptional intelligence detected early by a schoolteacher; encouragement

by that teacher not to cease education too quickly (always a temptation in peasant families); further education with the financial assistance of parents, relatives, or patrons; an occupational history in a
practical field (medicine, teaching, law, local government officialdom); a lifetime of writing in Latvian and publication in such outlets
as *Latviešu avīzes*; marriage to women from families of similarly
striving Latvians or from among Baltic Germans. Such seemingly
unremarkable biographies, however, could produce momentous
achievement: thus in the Estonian-language area, Friedrich
Reinhold Kreutzwald (1803–1882), an Estonian born when his
parents were still serfs and a medical doctor with a degree from
Dorpat (1826), pieced together and published during the period
1853 to 1862 the Estonian folksongs that eventually would comprise
the Estonian national epic poem *Kalevipoeg* (Son of Kalev). His
friend and colleague Friedrich Robert Faehlmann (1788–1850),
who received his medical degree from Dorpat in 1824 and was an
Estonian born into an estate overseer's family, developed the field of
cardiology, yet spent most of his life writing about Estonian folklore,
language, and epic poetry.

One other feature was notable in this generation: few of its members in the littoral could be associated with only one literary accomplishment. When writing in their native tongues, they were
frequently polymaths, trying their hand at many genres of creative
expression – poetry, prose, translation, popular science – and they
sometimes continued to do so over long lifetimes. Their relationships
to their Baltic German colleagues, who were also writing in the
vernacular languages and continuing to fund scholarly societies to
bring their efforts before the public, remained friendly, but with the
most talented of them it became clear that overt patronage in the old
style was no longer necessary.

The decades between 1820 and 1850 in the Lithuanian lands
cannot be referred to as "post-emancipation" because there was no
serf emancipation in these territories and, as mentioned, the Russian
government kept particularly tight controls there in response to the
1830–1831 uprising. A different socioeconomic context notwith-
standing, cultural life in the Lithuanian territories during Nicholas
I's reign continued in the old tracks and contained considerable
accomplishments that marked the similarities and differences

21 Friedrich Reinhold Kreutzwald (1803–1882) was born into a family of serfs but eventually earned his medical degree and compiled the poem *Kalevipoeg*, which almost immediately was seen as the national epic of the Estonian people.

between these territories and the Baltic provinces. The closing of the University of Vilnius was clearly a setback for higher education in the Lithuanian borderlands; at the same time, many who aspired to high education seem not to have been hampered. Lithuanian literary activity after 1820 became concentrated in the Žemaitija region, where the language unquestionably remained the patois of the peasantry as well as of the lower gentry (elsewhere in the old territory of the Grand Duchy, Lithuanians were likely to speak a mixture of Lithuanian, Belarussian, Russian, Polish – depending on the region).

Some twenty individuals wrote and published primarily in Lithuanian during the 1820–1850 period. The intellectual biographies of the three most prominent illustrate well the challenging context in which they conducted their work. Dionizas Poška (1757–1830), for example, coming from a family of Žemaitijan lesser nobles, tried his hand at several occupations but finally settled on being a court clerk and a notary public for most of his life. He never finished his university education, but remained in correspondence with the professoriate at the University of Vilnius (before its closure) about a wide range of scholarly questions involving linguistics, poetry, archeology and other similar fields. Simonas Daukantas (1793–1864), from a peasant family in Žemaitija, took his master's degree at Vilnius in 1825 and for the next fifteen years worked as a translator in the governor-general's office in Riga and in similar bureaucratic occupations in St. Petersburg. His career as a man of letters was marked by self-limitation: he categorically refused to write in Polish but in spite of this decision became the first Lithuanian to publish in his own language a source-based history of Lithuania (1822) and of his own region of Žemaitija (1838). His fields of activity included also the collection of Lithuanian folktales and folksongs. Motejus Valančius (1801–1875) accommodated more readily the dominant Polish intellectual culture of the Lithuanian lands. Early on he polonized his surname to Wołonczewski and entered the service of the Roman Catholic Church, served as rector of several theological seminaries and eventually was consecrated as Bishop of Žemaitija in 1850. Displaying a dynamic and readable Lithuanian writing style (he wrote in numerous languages), he continued throughout his life to produce books and shorter writings in Lithuanian, covering a host of subjects and themes including the history of his diocese and religious works dealing with the lives of Jesus and the saints, particularly the life of Thomas à Kempis. He also wrote fiction aimed at a peasant audience, children's books, and realistic portrayals of Lithuanian village life. He steered away entirely from writings of a political nature – a useful survival strategy for prominent Catholic churchmen during Nicholas I's reign. Nevertheless, he must have understood that his prolific literary endeavors in Lithuanian had a political-cultural meaning, with respect to both the domination of the Lithuanian church by the Polish-language clergy, and to the tsarist authorities' efforts to render the old Polish-Lithuanian territories culturally innocuous.

The twin phenomena of cultural patronage and cultural clientage – two sides of the same coin – could not be eliminated by edicts: they were mindsets kept alive by the established imbalance of political and economic power in the littoral for many decades. Cultural self-confidence and self-assurance were detectable in the lives of individual Estonian, Latvian, and Lithuanian writers working during the decades after 1820, and their persistence also signaled the makings of an audience for the writings they produced. But there was no critical mass of such writers, no Estonian, Latvian, or Lithuanian *Gelehrtenstände*. To be properly appreciated for their work, they still had to function within the existing circles of German- and Polish-language intellectuals. The latter in turn were themselves becoming more conscious of their role as defenders of western culture within an increasingly assertive Russian-language political context, a censorship system that affected all published work but was perhaps heaviest in the Lithuanian-Polish lands, and also growing worries among imperial administrators that the western borderlands of the empire were too vulnerable to separatist impulses.

In addition, the lure of the practical world was very strong in the thinking of the educated offspring of peasants: the empire needed specialists of all kinds at all levels, employment could be found, if not in the littoral, than certainly in expanding metropolitan centers elsewhere, and self-russification in the cultural sense was no more difficult than self-germanization and self-polonization. The commitment to the language of one's ancestry, the steady production of writings in it over decades, the readiness to assume the role of cultural client to those who thought of themselves as one's social superiors – all these required a special dedication that was difficult to engender and sustain. The general situation had already produced anomalies: a Donelaitis who on his own had already written (but not published) what later was to be judged one of the cornerstones of modern Lithuanian literature; an Indriķis Hartmanis (1783–1828; aka "Blind Indriķis"), an enserfed artisan who had lost his eyesight early in life but composed Latvian-language poetry of sufficient literary quality to attract the attention of his Baltic German pastor-patron (Gustav Elverfeldt) who transcribed and published it; an F. R. Kreutzwald, an excellent physician who, however, was to be remembered as the "discoverer" of the Estonian national epic. The work of such men demonstrated clearly that in the realm of literary culture important accomplishments were not directly correlated with the chronology of political and socioeconomic history and could not be explained simply with reference to context; the psychology of individual creativity has to be understood as well.

6

Five decades of transformations, 1855–1905

The 1850s contained two internal events of great significance for the Russian Empire: the arrival on the imperial throne of Alexander II, another "reforming" tsar, in 1855; and the lack of accomplishment in the Crimean War (1853–1856). The latter set off in imperial circles discussion about fundamental reforms to bring Russia to the level of what was perceived to be the advanced western European countries. In the Baltic littoral, these developments coincided with certain local dissatisfactions: the emancipation of serfs in Estland, Livland, and Kurland and the introduction of labor rents had not produced endless agricultural progress. The rural populations continued to be restive, liberalism of different kinds seemed to taking firmer root even in the minds of some members of the *Ritterschaften* and certainly among the *Gelehrten*; and the urban patriciates were becoming more resentful over their inability to seize growing economic opportunities in trade and commerce. In the administratively fragmented Lithuanian lands, the harsh russification measures of Nicholas I had not succeeded in eroding memories of statehood and of the failures of the 1830–1831 uprising. Other events, originating outside the empire, also found resonance in the western borderlands: the 1848 revolutions in central Europe, though viewed as unsuccessful, nonetheless toppled the "Metternich system" of intellectual control and left a generation of central European nationalists with a deep craving for another "spring-time of peoples." The national unification of Italy (1860) and Germany (1870–1871) created models for those in Europe who were living in multinational empires under elites of a different nationality and language. The phenomenon of change was supplied with a new and positive cachet by the interaction of all these developments, even if those who wanted change were inspired by the vaguest ideals and had no real conception of where change might lead.

Over the next five decades, the pro-change, pro-reform, and pro-modernity *Zeitgeist* produced transformations of a fundamental, mostly irreversible sort, for the peoples of the Baltic littoral. Moreover, change not only became commonplace, but its pace increased in an unprecedented fashion, spurred on by the arrival of new technologies of transportation and communication, the spread of new means of production in the form of the factory system, the diffusion of a hunger for education in every layer of society, the elimination of barriers to internal migration within the empire, and the appearance of new and more intensively experienced forms of national consciousness. Causality became more complex, as changes in all sectors of socioeconomic life interacted with and fed others. The one area of everyday life, in the empire generally and in the Baltic littoral in particular, in which modernizing change did not penetrate very deeply was governance: the empire continued as an autocracy, political power in the Baltic provinces (Estland, Livland, Kurland) remained a monopoly of the traditional Baltic German upper orders, and in the Lithuanian lands, another unsuccessful insurrection (1863) resulted in the further extrusion of the Polish governing orders from positions of power and their replacement by Russian administrators. The overall situation in the Baltic littoral became more anomalous with each decade, as a rapidly changing society took on the features of modern life while confronting a political system that appeared determined to resist all efforts to modify the hegemony of narrow elites. The continuing confrontation and the frustrations it produced eventually led to an ongoing loss of human capital, as thousands from the Baltic provinces sought greener pastures in the interior provinces of the empire, while other thousands from the Lithuanian provinces departed to the promised lands of North America.

UNFINISHED BUSINESS: LABOR RENTS AND SERFDOM

The serf emancipation laws of 1816–1819 in Estonia, Livonia, and Kurland and their free-contract core had resulted in agrarian relationships that left few of the involved parties entirely satisfied. Legal ownership of all farmland had been shifted to estate owners, the peasantry had obtained personal freedom as well as local institutions of self-government, and the vast majority of peasant residents of estates now rented the land they worked with their labor, though in principle they could have paid money rents. From the 1820s onward, however, labor rents increased, reducing the time peasant families had to devote to their own fields. By the 1830s, resistance to labor rents had become widespread, being passive most often but occasionally breaking out in violent opposition. Such was the case of the 1858 "Mahtra War" in the Estonian area where it affected ten estates, involved a thousand peasants and several units of the Russian army, and left several dead on both sides.

In fact, both sides of this free-contract agricultural economy were increasingly dissatisfied with it. Peasants were unhappy about rising labor rents, short rental contracts that foreclosed the growth of any sense of landownership, and the deliberate policy of some estate owners to expand the arable land directly farmed by the estate itself at the expense of peasant land. Estate owners were dismayed by the complicated enforcement responsibilities that came with labor rents, the inability of peasants to shift in any appreciable numbers to money rents (let alone buy their properties outright), and the growing numbers of landless peasants whose status could not be transformed into that of paid agricultural laborers. Regardless of the favored status ownership of landed estates conferred, profit margins from agricultural properties decreased while bankruptcies increased. Meanwhile the new court system introduced by the emancipation laws allowed for the proliferation of grievances by peasants against each other and against landowners, who were involved ex officio in the adjudication. The result was constant discussion in the *Landtage* about how "the system" should be reformed further, with no single reform being obvious. From the estate owners' viewpoint, the ideal landed estate would be one in which estate fields were cleanly separated from those of the peasants. Only a cash nexus in the form of rental or mortgage would exist between the estate owner and individual peasants. The labor force would consist of agricultural laborers working for a wage either for the peasant-proprietor/renter or for the estate farm. This ideal was also much closer to the free-market

philosophy behind the earlier reforms: free and independent agents –
estate owners, peasant landowners, agricultural laborers – relating to
each other through written contractual agreements. By the 1840s it
became clear to the St. Petersburg government that the rapid agricultural flowering the Baltic nobility had promised in return for control of
all land had been a pipe dream, and that the Estonian, Kurlandic, and
Livonian landed nobilities should make haste to move their peasants
toward greater independence and landownership.

The pressure from St. Peterburg resonated well with the more
liberally inclined members of the landowning nobility in the
Livland *Landtag*, especially Hamilkar von Fölkersahm, who became
the driving force behind new reforms and carried more than half of
the Livland *Landtag* with him. A new peasant law was adopted in
1849 for Livland and a similar one by the Estonian Diet in 1856. This
new legislation mandated the allocation of land attached to an estate
into three categories: estate land, peasant land, and the so-called
quota land. The first of these categories contained arable land that
remained entirely the property of the landowner (or renter), who was
expected to continue to farm it using a paid labor force. The second
contained land made available for peasants to rent or buy by means
of long-term mortgages or money rents. The quota land was an
indeterminate category at the disposal of the estate owner, normally
intended for the use of paid farmhands working on the estate.
Predictably, opposition to these measures arose among more
conservative landowners, who saw the emergence of peasant
smallholders as a threat to their traditional authority over all rural
people on their lands. But equally predictably, they understood the
pressures coming from St. Petersburg and assented to the reforms to
forestall even more intrusive actions. The actual implementation of
these reform laws, as with the earlier emancipation laws, was again
protracted, although their opponents had less opportunity to sabotage them because of the accession to the Russian throne of
Alexander II (1855), who was just as unequivocally a reform-minded
ruler as his grandfather had been. It was not until later in Alexander's
reign, in 1863, after general serf emancipation was proclaimed in
Russia in 1861, that the Kurlandic nobility, also driven by pressures
from the crown, finally accepted the principle that peasants had the
right to purchase in perpetuity the land they worked.

Verlag a. W. F. Häcker in Riga   *Nach einem Gemälde von J. Siegmund*   *Stich u. Druck v. Weger in Leipzig*

Hamilkar von Fölkersahm.

22 Hamilkar von Fölkersahm (1811–1856) was a liberal Baltic German landowner whose work in the Livonian diet on behalf of agrarian reform laid the groundwork for the later expansion of peasant landownership among Latvians and Estonians.

During the 1830s and 1840s, an appreciable number of peasants in Estland, Livland, and Kurland did convert to money rents, but it was the purchase of farmland that in the long run was the most decisive break with the past. The exact mechanisms through which title of land was transferred differed among locations and provinces, but once the process started in the mid-1850s, it continued for the next half-century. By the early 1870s, 20% of the peasant land on private estates in Kurland had been sold, and about 25% in Livonia. By the late 1880s, the percentages were 77% and 75% for the two provinces, respectively; by 1902, 95% and 85%; and by 1910, 99% and 89%, respectively. The pace of sales on crown estates was similar. It was slower in Estland, however, where by 1897 only about 50% of peasant farms had been sold. The absolute numbers were also impressive: by 1885, some 9,000 farmsteads in Kurland were now owned by peasants, and by 1905 about 22,000 in Livland. Because the total population was overwhelmingly rural, the impact of these sales (as earlier the effect of emancipation) was widespread. During the second half of the century, the effects were felt by upward of 70–80% of all rural families, and perhaps in some 60% of all families in each province. For the first time in living memory peasants became owner-occupiers of the land they were working. The insecurities of occupancy of the serf past and the more recent labor-rent past fell away; proprietorship changed incentives since now farmers had a very high probability of bequeathing improved farms to the next generation. A palpable return could be expected on expansion, improvement, and the adaptation of "scientific" farming.

The effects extended far beyond the material domain into the psychosocial domain of peasant life. The situation should not be idealized, however, since no utopia had been achieved. During the drawn-out sales process, estate owners quickly learned that through various half-legal and legal means they could diminish the proportion of land on their estates that had to be sold; consequently, the absolute number of proprietors grew along with the absolute number of landless agricultural laborers, whose life situations scarcely improved. The peasants who bought land were implicated in purchase agreements of twenty-five to thirty years and in loans from the estate owners or credit facilities (created by the estate owners) usually at a 5 percent annual rate of interest. Few of the new proprietors could start their lives as property owners debt free. The number of foreclosures also grew, and not until the end of the century was there an appreciable number of farmers who were not financially encumbered in one way or another. Being on their own, peasant-farmers were also now subject to market changes in prices and in demand, and mere self-sufficiency could no longer be the high road to expanding wealth. Since capital-rich landowners learned quickly that it was expedient to have hundreds of local peasants indebted to them in the long run, they took full advantage of the situation through quick foreclosures and quick resale. In short, peasants learned that farming for profit was no easy thing, and favorable outcomes were not guaranteed. The turnover of peasant-proprietors remained high. Yet with each decade after the mid-century a new peasant subpopulation established itself in the Estland, Livland, and Kurland countrysides – successful and relatively well-off farmers who by the century's end were being referred to as the "gray barons." At the same time, the existence of the permanently landless rural population remained an intractable problem. Some of them left the countryside to search for work in urban industry (also expanding at this time) in the Baltic region and in the interior of Russia; a relatively small number from the Baltic provinces were attracted to opportunities offered by migration to North America; but most remained in the countryside hoping to find a way out of their permanently low incomes and low social standing. By the end of the century, the proportion of estate land that would ever be sold had been; large landowners (still for the most part Baltic Germans) employed paid agricultural laborers to work their own estates, but this labor market did not expand; and as long as the estates continued to own about 50 percent of arable land in the countryside, no obvious solution to the remaining problem of landlessness was in the offing.

In 1860, the 260,000 Latvians who lived in Vitebsk province – just to the east of Livland and Kurland in the Latgale region – and the approximately 1.5 million inhabitants of the Lithuanian provinces to the south had remained largely unaffected by the serf emancipation edicts and further reforms that by mid-century had changed the status, contractual obligations, and future prospects of the farming populations of the Baltic provinces proper. The musings of some landowners in Latgale that the reforms of the Baltic provinces should be emulated there had come to nothing, and in the Lithuanian territories, the insurrection of 1830–1831 turned imperial authority toward control rather than reform. To reduce the hold of Polish landowners in these regions, Tsar Nicholas I experimented with various forms of peasant protectionism: a ukaz of 1846 forbade the eviction of peasants from their holdings, mandated inventories of landed properties that would fix holding sizes and obligatory labor amounts, and ordered that if circumstances dictated the addition of peasant to estate land, peasant families were not to be left entirely without land.

The coming to the Russian throne of Alexander II pointed to additional action along such lines. In fact, the general 1861 edict emancipating serfs in imperial Russia differentiated the needed reforms by region, with Latgale and the Lithuanian territories being included in the new regulations for the northwestern provinces. The first step in handling the process of emancipation was to be the creation of local administrative bodies that would adjudicate lord–peasant relationships. The second involved preparation of thorough written documentation of agrarian relations within an estate: holding sizes, labor and other obligations, and an inventory of the human population by status (farmheads, laborers, non-working residents). Since Alexander II was determined not to free serfs without rights to land, the third step involved the transfer of rights to land from the landowner to the individual farmer or to a village (depending on location). Landowners were obliged immediately to offer individual peasant families the land they had worked; in compensation, the government guaranteed to the landowner 80 percent of the value of the land, with the peasant paying 20 percent of this amount directly and borrowing the rest from the government to be repaid over fifty years. In Estland, Livland, and Kurland, thirty years separated the arrival of personal freedom from the right to buy land; in Latgale and the Lithuanian lands both freedom and land arrived at the same time. This fact structured the "agrarian problem" differently than in the Baltic provinces for decades to come: in the Baltic provinces rural stratification (landed/landless) became more pronounced, whereas in Latgale and the Lithuanian lands it was the negligible size of the holding received by peasants (on average six to seven hectares) that created difficulties. The proliferation of smallholderships of the most extreme kind generated more out-migration than did the proliferation of absolute landlessness.

The smooth implementation of reforms in Latgale and the Lithuanian lands became impossible because of the Polish-Lithuanian insurrection of 1863; also, the emancipation law ensured that the process would last for some time in any event. By the 1870s, when some degree of stability had arrived, the emancipation of 1861 was shown to have created as many problems as it had resolved. Peasants were now free, but, as in the Baltic provinces, they were still burdened by financial obligations (more to the government than to landowners) that could not be dismissed. With smaller average holdings and smaller incomes, no rapid economic development of the rural sector could be expected. Moreover, the landowning elite was in disarray (in Latgale it was, in fact, immiserated), severely reducing available capital for the modernization of farming methods. In Latgale, customary inheritance practices dictated that landholdings be divided equally between sons upon the father's death, and this practice reduced further the size of the already absurdly small and economically unsustainable farms. A new passport law of 1863 – part of Alexander II's larger reform program – permitted migration to any part of the empire and served for some time as a safety valve for a potentially explosive situation in the Lithuanian lands. Development of the rural economy, however, remained very uneven; agricultural production and incomes in some parts of the Lithuanian territories gained momentum much more quickly than in others. Statistics at the end of the nineteenth century revealed that forty years after the abolition of serfdom, about 40 percent of all arable land in the Lithuanian territories still belonged to landed estates, the vast majority of which were owned by Polish or polonized gentry and retired Russian military officers and government servitors. These groups tended toward lifestyles that in effect made them into absentee landowners rather than hands-on and business-savvy managers of their landed properties. Though high living was by no means absent from the *Ritterschaften* in the Baltic provinces, the estate-as-a-business viewpoint there had penetrated much more deeply – especially in the generation now in their forties and fifties – than among their high-status colleagues in the southern littoral.

AWAKENING THE NATIONS: THE BALTIC PROVINCES

The spate of reforms that changed the nature of agrarian relations in the Baltic provinces had differentiated effects on their rural populations, including generational ones. In a handful of young people of Estonian and Latvian backgrounds they produced a strong desire to expand the options for personal development, that is, to challenge publicly the widely held proposition that education beyond primary schooling inevitably meant assimilation to the German-language-dominated world of the Baltic littoral. Their goal was to demonstrate that occupational choice did not require the abandonment of identity as Estonians or Latvians, and that the culture in which they were raised was respectable and portable as they moved up in the socioeconomic hierarchy of Baltic littoral society. These highly individualized strivings, when aggregated, produced what the participants themselves soon (and thereafter later generations) began to refer to as "national awakenings" or "national revivals." Within several decades after the mid-century, these unprecedented phenomena had introduced into the world of the littoral new cultural dimensions to be reckoned with. By the mid-1870s, the national awakenings of the Latvians and Estonians had gained sufficient momentum for the Baltic German elites – conservative and liberal alike – to charge that they were dangerous, though repeated efforts to quash them by appeals to the St. Petersburg government proved largely unsuccessful. Understanding the intolerance of the tsarist government toward any kind of political challenge to central authority, the "national awakeners" were careful and chose their polemical battles – when they sought any confrontation at all – only in the realm of Baltic German cultural hegemony and socioeconomic privilege. They expected in these causes a certain degree of sympathy at least from Russian Slavophile journalists, who for their own reasons were championing cultural uniformity in the western borderlands.

However individualized their quests, the awakeners followed well-trod paths, but always sought to evade what seemed to them unnecessary Baltic German control and tutelage. Thus, for example, the Baltic German clergy had initiated translations of cultural and religious materials into the vernacular languages centuries ago; now, however, translations sought to demonstrate that the job could be done without distorting the Latvian language in the direction of German grammar and vocabulary. For example, the 1856 book of translated poems by a young Latvian student at Dorpat, Juris Alunāns (1832–1864), is normally cited as the start of the Latvian national awakening. Latvian-language newspapers had also originated with the German-language clergy – most notably

Latviešu avīzes (1822), published in Kurland. In 1862, it faced a competing paper, *Pēterburgas avīzes*, published in the Russian capital by three young Latvians, Alunāns, Krišjānis Barons (1835–1923), and Krišjānis Valdemārs (1825–1891). The Kurland paper was reverential toward the superiority of German-language culture and took very seriously its self-assigned task of enlightening the Latvian-language peasantry. By contrast, the St. Petersburg paper was irreverent toward all things Baltic German, deliberately caricaturing Baltic German cultural efforts. It was closed by the Russian authorities in 1865. Among Estonians, Friedrich Reinhold Kreutzwald, the compiler of the Estonian epic poem *Kalevipoeg*, was not the first to gather and transcribe elements of the Estonian oral tradition; that task had already been started by Baltic German scholars. But whereas the latter were motivated primarily by scholarly interest, for Kreutzwald and other Estonians the task had a deeper meaning: they were resuscitating the spiritual record of their own people.

Numerically few, the truly engaged activists among the national awakeners were riding a wave not of their own creation. They did not invent the central organizing ideas of their efforts, and they had no real control over the trajectory of events. National awakenings in the Baltic littoral did not take place in a vacuum. Throughout Europe after the Napoleonic era, heretofore subordinated and fragmented peoples were launching many different "nationalistic" challenges against a variety of traditional arrangements they now found unacceptable and oppressive. In the German and Italian lands, for example, unification movements spearheaded by young people sought to consolidate those who spoke these languages into national states. During the revolutions of 1848, Czechs, Magyars, and other nationality groups lashed out against the Habsburg dynasty that controlled their fates from Vienna. Each situation was different, and no single variant of militant nationalism could be useful everywhere. Among the Estonian and Latvian awakeners, philosophical writings were rare, but behind their activities was a set of ideas that could translate into common goals. They believed that each individual person had a fundamental "national" identity; each person was born into a "people" (Ger. *Volk*; Latv. *tauta*; Est. *rahvas*) which was at the same time a "nation" even if it currently had no such group identity.

Most people, such thinking went, had to be "awakened" to the fact of their membership, and this task could be carried out by teaching them about the characteristics their grouping had developed over time: a heroic past, a distinguished record of having been a state, perhaps a history of civilizing others, distinctive institution, and great wealth.

The Estonians and Latvians possessed none of these accomplishments, but they did have one characteristic that made them unique: they spoke languages that distinguished them from the other residents of the littoral, and they had an oral tradition expressed in those languages. From the outset, therefore, the Latvian and Estonian nationalistic efforts were language- and folklore-centered and remained for a long time within the domain of cultural claims. Clearly, such ideas originated in the cultural and political philosophies of Johann Gottfried Herder and Johann Gottlieb Fichte in the late eighteenth and early nineteenth century. Garlieb Merkel, about whose writings the Latvian and Estonian awakeners were only now learning, had applied them to the Baltic situation. Their immediate assignment was to demonstrate through their writings and organizational efforts that Latvians and Estonians were perfectly capable of the stewardship of their own language and of further cultural development. The Baltic German *Gelehrtenstand*, having initiated these tasks, could now stand aside. But for this demonstration to succeed, much more was needed than a handful of dedicated proponents. There also had to be a broader public whose financial and institutional strength could attest to their own awakening to the new ideas. Persuading thousands of people who lived in different *gubernnias* that their state of fragmentation was not important, that they were a single entity with language as the principal evidence of that basic unity, was not easy. Also, since neither the Latvian nor the Estonian awakeners had a single prominent leader or even a well-organized leadership group, exactly how the "national struggle" was to be translated into action caused from the outset considerable disagreement. The awakener generation had to pay homage to their direct Latvian and Estonian predecessors who had worked along similar lines; but they also had to reject the quietism these predecessors had demonstrated toward Baltic German patronage. The correct stance toward the Baltic German past and present cultural efforts thus became a point of division, as did the relationship between further economic and cultural development. Should scarce resources be directed more toward cultural endeavors (the written word in the vernacular languages this time produced by the native users of those languages)? Or should they go toward establishing an organizational base (self-help societies and educational institutions) for cultural growth? There were no road maps for the best way to proceed, and thus the Latvian and Estonian national movements were much less single-minded than was implied by the term *fanatischen Nationalisten* frequently used about them by the Baltic Germans.

The attitudes of the Baltic German population toward this new phenomenon remained mixed, ranging from the desire for persecution (such as that of the complainants who succeeded in having the *Pēterburgas avīzes* quashed) to disquiet and even receptivity. Perhaps much more widespread was the feeling that Estonian and Latvian national awakeners were ungrateful: in his memoirs the long-term president of the *Lettisch-literärische Gesellschaft*, the pastor August Bielenstein (1826–1907), described it thus: "Latvians were always complaining about the subjugation in which German overlordship had held them, but they have not noticed all the benefits that German overlordship has brought to Latvian culture ... The kind of education and the understanding their current cultural endeavors presuppose could not have been reached by the Latvian nation by its own efforts alone." Many of the *Gelehrtenstand* felt surrounded by clamoring barbarians. Bielenstein in his correspondence with a Finnish colleague observed that "we Germans possess too rich a spiritual, literary and scientific inheritance in our own language for us to put it aside to form a new cultural entity together with the Latvians ... The Latvians, regardless of how much their living standards and education grow, are still under the control of the Russians and have no possibility of forming their own *gymnasia* or universities or of experiencing the full flowering of their uniqueness. The Latvian nation is too small to live up to such high requirements." Intellectuals such as Bielenstein tended to view the Estonian and Latvian national awakenings as premature because the two peoples were insufficiently "developed": they needed the help and guidance of a more mature people who had already reached a higher stage of development (such as, for example, the Germans). All peoples and societies have to pass through developmental stages to become "civilized" or "cultured" and to take their place among already fully developed *Kulturnationen*.

On the other side of these polemics, Estonian and Latvian activists viewed the developmental argument, no matter how rationally stated, as patronizing in the extreme. To the most fervent of them, it seemed nothing more than a cover for continuing Baltic German privilege and control. The most outspoken persons in these public disputes were unlikely to persuade each other, because their disagreements on basic issues were fundamental. The polemics sharpened with efforts by some in the Baltic German *Gelehrtenstand* to highlight the political dangers of the Estonian and Latvian awakeners by labeling them *Junglettland* and *Jungestland*, thereby suggesting kinship with the various revolutionary and quasi-revolutionary movements (such as "Young Italy," "Young Germany") that had appeared in central Europe around the revolutionary year of 1848. Such charges did not seem plausible to Russian authorities, particularly since the same authorities had granted permission for the formation of such nationally inclined organizations as the Riga Latvian Association (1868), the Estonian Alexander School (1871), and the Society of Estonian Literati (1871). Once founded, such institutions became central organizational expressions of the national movements, and they provided a kind of headquarters for such activists among the Estonians as Johann Voldemar Jannsen (1819–1890), Jakob Hurt (1839–1906), Johann Köler (1826–1899), Carl Robert Jakobson (1841–1882), Friedrich Reinhold Kreutzwald (1803–1882), and Lydia Koidula (1843–1886). Among the Latvians the activists included Krišjānis Barons, Krišjānis Valdemārs, Atis Kronvalds (1837–1875), and Mikus Krogzems [pseudo. Auseklis] (1850–1879). The organizations, however, never did succeed in imposing a single agenda upon the nationally inclined activists, who entered the fray from a variety of circumstances, tried their hand at various literary endeavors, disagreed with each other in the extent of their animosity toward the Baltic German past and ongoing contributions of the Baltic Germans to the linguistic and cultural development of their respective peoples, and also had differing attitudes toward the Russian government.

Because no single agenda could be imposed on the activists, the goals of the national awakeners in both the Estonian and the Latvian

23 Lydia Koidula (1843–1886) was a poet during the Estonian national awakening, best known for her patriotic verse, who later became probably the most widely read Estonian poet of all time.

territories remained differentiated. Such agreement as existed was the result of nationalistic ideas of German origin being adapted to the context of the littoral. The Estonian activists agreed that the two Estonian-using populations – in Estland and in Livland – comprised one nation and that the boundary that separated them was epiphenomenal: it did not create two different kinds of Estonians. The Latvian activists had a three-part division to reconceptualize: namely, the Latvians living in the southern districts of Livland, those in Kurland, and the Latgalians living across the border in Vitebsk province. While the Latgalians were never directly excluded from the definition of who comprised the Latvian *tauta*, their unique characteristics set them apart from "western" Latvians much more than did any regional peculiarities of Latvians living in Livland and Kurland. Spoken and written Latgalian retained substantial

24 In the Latvian "national awakening," Atis Kronvalds
(1837–1875) registered a strong presence as something of a
firebrand and did more than most to develop and legitimize
Latvian as a versatile language deserving status equal to the
Baltic region's "large" languages.

influences from Polish and Lithuanian; Catholicism there appeared
to be much more deeply rooted than in the subpopulations of Latvian
Catholics in the western regions. Because of the late emancipation of
serfs there (not until 1861), life in Latgale seemed to have a slower, or
at least a very different, tempo than among the Latvians in Livland
and Kurland. The writings of the respected Baltic German pastor-
ethnographer August Bielenstein were unequivocal about this

question – Latgalians were Latvians – but many of the awakeners were much more tentative and remained so until the turn of the twentieth century. As regards the purpose for which the Latvians and Estonians were being awakened, there was considerable agreement: greater self-consciousness would enable them to assert their right of independent cultural development without the help of Baltic Germans.

There was, however, disagreement among the Estonian and Latvian activists about how national self-consciousness should be brought to a full flowering. Among Latvians, Krišjānis Valdemārs, for one, stressed the need for Latvians to achieve economic independence, while others, such as Atis Kronvalds, believed that cultivation of language, collection of the oral tradition, and production of a written literature and a written history were paramount. Among Estonians the principal fault line was somewhat different: Johann Voldemar Jannsen and Jakob Hurt shied away from direct confrontations with the Baltic Germans and believed in reconciliation, while Johann Köler and Carl Robert Jakobson thought Estonian national consciousness would be aided more by friendliness toward the Russian government and a harder stance against Baltic German hegemony. Köler's and Jakobson's attitudes toward Russian cooperation were also present in the thinking of the Latvians Krišjānis Valdemārs and Fricis Brīvzemnieks (1846–1907), the latter an assiduous collector of the Latvian oral tradition, especially the folksong (*daina*). Though such disagreements were indeed "internecine" in every sense of the word, they were more than squabbles and reflected deeply held differing views about how Estonians and Latvians should orient themselves in the world of the littoral in which they were playing an increasingly significant role.

All printed material in Latvian and Estonian published in the Baltic provinces had to be submitted to censorship, but this requirement did not hamper the development of *belles lettres* in these languages. Most literary genres were represented among the works that appeared: the lyric poetry of Juris Alunāns among the Latvians and of Lydia Koidula among the Estonians was markedly popular in the "awakener" generation. In Estonian prose writing, Juhan Liiv (1864–1913) and Jakob Pärn (1843–1916) were successful pioneers, and, on the Latvian side, the brothers Reinis and Matīss Kaudzīte (1839–1920 and 1848–1926, respectively) authored in 1879 the first Latvian novel, which contained, among other things, a biting parody of the windbag nationalism of rural schoolteachers. Friedrich Reinhold Kreutzwald had already compiled and published what became the Estonian national epic, *Kalevipoeg* (Son of Kalev), in 1860. Among Latvians, the absence in their oral tradition of epic poetry led Andrejs Pumpurs (1841–1902) to publish in 1888 a similar epic, *Lāčplēsis* (The Bear-Slayer), which readers quickly folklorized and treated as if it were an authentic component of traditional culture. Even though it was impossible for anyone to earn a living by writing, the temptation was great to contribute to the national cause by writing in Estonian and Latvian, and many of the educated succumbed to it even if their talents were minimal. Outlets for creative products in various literary genres were plentiful, first in the form of Latvian and Estonian newspapers, and then, starting in the late 1880s, literary periodicals as well.

The success of so open-ended an enterprise as an "awakening of nations" remained uncertain, and proponents appeared unsure about how to make such judgments. The numbers of people attending cultural events and those who were reached through Estonian- and Latvian-language publications, were crude measures, but judging by them with each year the interest in such national undertakings was growing. The slow, steady enlargement of a relatively well-to-do stratum of peasants continued, creating with each decade more parents willing and able to finance education for their offspring. Rural to urban migration continued as well, increasing in the major cities and towns of the littoral the proportion of Estonians and Latvians in the total population, thus enlarging the potential membership base of cultural organizations. Attendance at and participation in song festivals was a barometer of at least a persisting interest in the national cause after they became regular events from the later 1860s onward. The first all-Estonian song festival took place in 1869 in Tartu (subsequent festivals were in 1879, 1880, 1891, 1894, and 1896); by 1896, participations through choirs from all the Estonian territories had grown to about 5,500 and attendance by 1894 was estimated to be around 50,000. The first all-Latvian festival took place in 1873 in Riga with a joint choir of 1,003; subsequent festivals occurred in 1880, 1888, and 1895, by which time the joint choir numbered about 4,000 voices and the audience an estimated 25,000. Notably, all these events received permission from the tsarist government, being "cultural" in nature; for the Estonians and Latvians themselves, however, they had political meaning as well. Other cultural statistics corroborated the enlargement of the Estonian and Latvian cultural presence. A potential reading audience expanded: the imperial census of 1897 reported that among Estonians the ability to read was 78.2% overall (77.6% for men, 78.9% for women); remarkably, the number of *adult* Estonians (ages thirty to thirty-nine years) who could read was 96.1 percent. Among Latvians, the ability to read stood in 1897 at 70.4% overall (69.6% for men, 77.0% for women) and 89.2% for adults (ages thirty to thirty-nine). The continuing development of this skill had not been hampered much by the tribulations of elementary schools as a result of russification efforts by the central government (discussed below). By contrast, the same proportions for the Russian population of the empire in 1897 stood at 22.7% overall (34.3% for men, 11.6% for women), and 28.8% for adults. Correlatively, the number of publications in Estonian and Latvian over the period increased as well: in the Estonian regions during 1860–1900, the annual output of Estonian titles increased from 55 at the start to 312 at the end of these decades; a different kind of calculation placed the total number of new titles in Latvian at 2,300 during 1867–1885, rising to an astonishing 35,000 in the period 1886–1900.

In both cases of these rapidly expanding literatures (in the broad sense), the content of publications was becoming increasingly secular, leaving an estimated 15 percent of religious works in Latvian and 28 percent in Estonian. The rocky history of the periodical press published in Estonian and Latvian makes estimates of the number of subscribers virtually impossible, but most certainly the totals for the main newspapers (the short-lived *Pēterburgas avīzes* and the long-lived *Baltijas vēstnesis* for the Latvians; *Pärno Postimees* for Estonians) grew from several thousand initially to twice or thrice that number by the mid-1880s. These statistics do not capture the numbers of people among whom both books and newspapers were circulated locally; the phenomenon of a book or periodical being passed around from farmstead to farmstead was noted by all who

25 Masthead of *Pēterburgas avīzes*. The continued broadsides
aimed by this weekly Latvian newspaper against Baltic German
privilege in the decades of the Latvian national awakening led to
the paper's closure after a three-year run (1862–1865).

grew up during these decades. In any event, the statistics more than
suggest that gone forever was the cultural configuration of the past
centuries – the written word in the vernacular languages being produced by non-native speakers and forming a small subcategory of all
publications in the littoral. The cultural spaces in which Estonian and
Latvian had become the principal languages of discourse were now
firmly established and demarcated, and a return to the earlier pattern
was as impossible as returning all Estonians and Latvians to the serf
status they had in the early decades of the nineteenth century.

SEARCHING FOR THE NATION: THE LITHUANIAN
LANDS AND LATGALE

In Estland, Kurland, and Livland cultural nationalism entered the
public arena relatively quietly in the 1850s and 1860s, having
received permission for many of its main manifestations from the
Russian government. By contrast, in the Lithuanian lands and in
Latgale the same decades were marked by violence that resulted in
repressive government policies the likes of which Estonian and
Latvian nationalists did not have to contend with. After coming to
the Russian throne in 1855, Alexander II sought for a time to return

to his grandfather's liberalism in dealing with the Polish and Lithuanian borderlands, but this softened attitude (as compared with that of Nicholas I) led many residents of the former Polish-Lithuanian Commonwealth to believe that the time had (again) arrived to throw off "the Russian yoke." The insurrection of 1863–1864 conventionally referred to as "Polish" did indeed begin in the Polish territories in 1862 in the form of localized disorders, which were countered by the government by the drafting of perpetrators into the Russian army. This measure triggered more overt opposition, and by January 1863, guerilla-style attacks against symbols of Russian authority had become widespread throughout the Polish, Lithuanian, and Belorussian provinces. The St. Petersburg government's reaction, not unexpectedly, was a military one which occasioned protests from western governments, and in turn nationalistic reactions in the Russian press. The insurrectionists were suppressed with great severity in May 1864, and the measures taken by the government were not unlike those used after the 1830–1831 uprising, although more severe in terms of cultural impact. The 1863 revolt drew supporters from all walks of life, including the landed aristocracy and the peasantry, even though the numbers of militants were perhaps somewhat fewer than in 1830–1831, the pitched battles more scattered, and the military equipment available to the revolutionaries less battleworthy than before. There was, however, better organization than in the earlier revolt, and temporary successes spurred on the insurrectionists. But just as in the 1830–1831 revolt, the goals of the Polish insurrectionists were diffuse. When their Lithuanian counterparts joined the revolt, activities became even less focused: some joined in to throw off the "double yoke" – Polish and Russian; the Polish participants in the Lithuanian territories appeared disdainful of Lithuanian aspirations; and many of the peasants lashed out against landowner privilege regardless of the landowners' nationality, thus adding a class-war element to the events. In the Lithuanian territories there were an estimated 15,000 rebels, whereas the Russian military had about 90,000 troops at its disposal. By spring 1864, there had been 119 confrontations with rebels in the region around Kaunas, 38 in the Vilnius region, and 17 in the area of Šuvalkija. Ironically, the Latgale districts of Vitebsk, with their roughly 200,000 Latvian-speaking peasants, were drawn into this momentous event of Polish-Lithuanian history through the participation of prominent Polish and polonized Lithuanian gentry – clearly a consequence of the region's historic identity as "Polish Livonia." Here the peasants who participated in the insurrection did so for even more mixed reasons.

Following the insurrection, General Mikhail Muraviev (who was already known as "the Hangman" among Lithuanians) was appointed governor-general of Vilnius province. Muraviev was not hesitant about applying maximal punishment: in the Lithuanian districts, at least 129 persons were executed, 972 were condemned to forced labor, 2,956 were exiled to the Siberian regions of the empire, 345 were drafted into the army, 864 were imprisoned, and 4,096 were exiled administratively to other parts of Russia and were required to live out their lives far away from their homeland. Some 1,740 private estates of participants and reputed participants were confiscated, and an estimated 6,000 residents of the Lithuanian lands died in battles against the Russian army. Institutionally, the price that was paid for rebellion was widespread russification which became the centerpiece of Russian administrative activities generally and in the educational system specifically. The government also placed major restrictions on the participation of the Catholic Church in primary education and on its contact with other church institutions, including the papacy, beyond the borders of Russia. The very name "Lithuania" ceased to exist officially: the region was referred to in official documents as the Northwest Territory (*severo-zapadny krai*). A remarkable measure affected the realm of the printed word: for forty years after 1864 the publication of printed materials in the Lithuanian language using the Latin alphabet was forbidden, and the only Lithuanian-language texts permitted were those that used the Cyrillic alphabet. Displaying their disdain for ethnic and linguistic differences among the peasants, administrators also prohibited publications in Latgalian, which also used the Latin alphabet; thus Latvian-language-using Latgalians were conceptualized as interchangeable with Lithuanians. Such strictures targeting cultural activity and the life of the mind were not as injurious to the long-term sustenance of Polish-language culture, of course: because of the partitions of Poland at the end of the eighteenth century, there were large Polish populations in the German and Habsburg empires whose writings could sustain Polish cultural activity relatively freely. But virtually all Lithuanian speakers lived in the Russian Empire, and any effort to suppress language and literary development by means of fiats could prove disastrous unless special measures were taken to counter them.

These special measures created a name for the next forty years of Lithuanian cultural history: the period of book smuggling. This entirely entrepreneurial effort was organized by private individuals: contrabandists (*knygnešiai*) created suppliers in the Lithuanian communities in East Prussia ("Lithuania Minor"), brought their illegal goods across the Prussian–Russian border by various means, and dispersed books throughout the Lithuanian-using populations in the Russian provinces. Existing statistics (by definition unreliable) suggest that the operations started slowly, with only 214 different titles being brought in during the first ten years, but with the total number of titles for the whole period (1864 to 1904) being around 4,100. Most of these came from printers and publishers in East Prussia, but in the later decades about 780 were printed by Lithuanian émigré presses in the United States. The Russian government managed to confiscate about 200,000 illegal books, which probably meant that a multiple of that number managed to get through. The size of the network of smugglers remains unknown, but Russian police records show that 2,854 people were detained for possession of this contraband: 86 percent were peasants, 6 percent townspeople, 6 percent gentry, and 2 percent undetermined. The government sponsored the printing of about fifty different Lithuanian titles using the Cyrillic alphabet, but they failed to circulate to any extent and in some instances were burned in protest. The Russian government made a few exceptions to the ban, resulting in the publication in Roman script of several collections of Lithuanian folksongs. Thus, the term "national awakening" was not much used among Lithuanians, in contrast to its frequent use in the Baltic provinces, since the most concrete forms of such an awakening rested on an entirely illegal base.

What the development of writing in Lithuanian would have been without the press ban is difficult to surmise, especially since the obstacles the ban created appeared not to have slowed very much the proliferation of works in the Lithuanian language. Historians of

Lithuanian writing cite about forty authors as the notables of the press ban period, some of whom, such as Bishop Motejus Valančius, were already active writers before 1864. Patriotic poetry continued to be written during the ban period, with authors such as Vincas Kudirka (1858–1899) coming to the fore in the 1880s. Kudirka had received a medical degree from the University of Warsaw, but then turned to writing for the Lithuanian newspapers such as *Aušra* and *Varpas*. One of his deeply felt poetic celebrations of Lithuania, *Lietuva, Tėvyne Mūsu* (Lithuania, Our Homeland), eventually became the Lithuanian national anthem. Jonas Mačiulis (1862–1932), whose doctoral degree was from the Theological Academy of St. Petersburg, turned to history and poetry and, though an active member in what was largely a polonized Catholic clergy, supported and participated in the expansion of Lithuanian-language literature under the pen name of Maironis. Among prose writers, Jonas Biliunas (1879–1907) launched his literary work as a Lithuanian nationalist while attending secondary school in Liepaja (Libau) in Kurland; his skills as a short-story writer produced notable results only after the turn of the twentieth century, but the maturation of his talents in the last two decades of the nineteenth century took place in a rich Lithuanian literary context.

Firing the national imagination of the younger intellectuals from the early 1880s onward were the Lithuanian newspapers *Aušra* (The Dawn, 1883–1886), *Varpas* (The Bell, 1889–1906), and *Šviesa* (The Light, 1887–1890). All three were published in Tilsit, East Prussia, and had to be smuggled into Lithuania. Under the editorship of Jonas Basanavičius (1851–1927), an émigré Lithuanian physician who had lived in Prague and Bulgaria, *Aušra* became a particularly important literary outlet, even if its mild tone toward the Russian government sometimes disturbed its more fiery readers. Basanavičius himself was intensely interested in Lithuanian history and folklore and published extensively in those fields, contributing to the romanticization of the Lithuanian past and hypothesizing that Lithuanians as a people were descendants of the Thraco-Phrygians who once had lived on the shores of the Black Sea. *Varpas* tended to favor secular topics, but always stressed the basic unity of the Lithuanian people and the need to perfect the Lithuanian language. The short-lived *Šviesa*, a newspaper of the Catholic intellectuals, opposed russification but carefully avoided accusations of fomenting anti-tsarist sentiment.

26 Jonas Basanavičius (1851–1927), described by foreign publications as the "grand old man of Lithuania" because of his persistent efforts on behalf of Lithuanian independence before and during World War I.

Even though in the writings of Lithuanian activists over the period of the ban language was assuming a central position in the answer to the question of who was a Lithuanian, the question itself was much thornier than for Estonians and Latvians. The Estonian population was more compact, with only one political border between the Estonians who lived in the north (Estland) and those who lived in the south (Livland). In addition, the recent historical experience and memory of all the

Estonians, as residents of the Baltic provinces, was roughly identical. Latvians had three such political borders: between those who lived in Livland, those in Kurland, and those in Latgale – the western districts of the province of Vitebsk. While recent historical experience and memory of the Livland and Kurland Latvians was nearly the same, those of Latgale by comparison had been distinctive for a very long time. There was also the question of the Livs or Livonians, whose communities, mostly in Kurland, in the second half of the nineteenth century still numbered several thousand. Among Lithuanians, however, at least five such political borders existed as well as a history that barely justified claims of Lithuanianness among sociopolitical groupings – such as the gentry – who spoke hardly any Lithuanian and whose cultural orientation was entirely to Polish-language culture. The erstwhile existence of a Grand Duchy of Lithuania was useful for nationalistic purposes by obviating the need to *invent* a glorious past, but it played havoc with current efforts to define the Lithuanian nation. If the historic borders of the Grand Duchy were used and the Russian-introduced internal borders ignored, then the Lithuanian nation included many people who did not fit according to strict linguistic criteria. If the linguistic criterion alone were used, thousands of polonized residents of the region would have to be excluded as non-nationals, along with most of the populations of such major cities as Vilnius and Kaunas and many pro-Lithuanian activists. In fact, all of the typical differentiating criteria of nineteenth-century nationalism – blood, soil, language, history, culture – were in some way inadequate and none of them could easily override the cultural and linguistic legacy of the old composite Polish-Lithuanian Commonwealth and the after-effects of earlier population movements within its borders.

Within the realm of the written word in the Lithuanian lands, the question of national membership was moot for the time being, as the growth of Lithuanian-language literature was contributed to by writers with Lithuanian names and Polish names, as well as some who by force of circumstances had both. Russian political authorities remained largely oblivious to these ethnic/national distinctions; they continued to think in terms of territory, used the terminology of the society of social orders (*soslovie*), and concerned themselves with preventing civil strife and integrating the western borderlands with the rest of the empire. Much to the chagrin and frustration of the nationalist activists in the littoral, there were tens of thousands of people – all potentially members of the Estonian, Latvian, or Lithuanian nations as now defined by the activists – for whom collective abstractions were not as important as economic survival, and who read publications in their own languages as mere entertainment and not as an act of commitment.

THE TRANSFORMATION OF CITY LIFE

As the spotlight turns to changes in the littoral's cities and towns, and the economic activities associated with them, care must be taken not to be dazzled by implications of such terms as modernization, urbanization, and industrialization. Although these processes were present during the second half of the nineteenth century, none describes a transformation so far-reaching that it neutralized the overwhelming agricultural and rural aspects of littoral life. The population of most urban centers increased, and non-agricultural economic activity expanded; the progressive loosening of laws regulating internal migration made rural to urban movement common; the inclusion of the littoral in an imperial network of railroads connecting Baltic ports to the Russian hinterland increased the flow and volume of goods. At the end of the 1870s, a new imperial law changing city governance enlarged somewhat the number of urban residents with access to power; and many agricultural practices were mechanized.

Yet the momentum of all this change was slow. By the end of the century, the urban share of the Baltic populations had grown from about 10 percent to 20 percent; urban property ownership by Estonians, Latvians, and Lithuanians had increased, but the total weight of other nationality groups (Baltic Germans, Poles, Russians, and Jews) remained impressively high; and the domestic product of the littoral's provinces continued to be primarily agricultural, as did trade. Even though the celebrities of the national movements were normally university-educated and carried out their mission while residing in cities, they retained close family ties to the countryside; moreover, the foot soldiers of the nationalist movement were predominantly rural schoolteachers. As nationalistic philosophy tightened into ideology, it placed peasanthood, rural ways, and rural virtues at the center of the national identity of Estonians,

Latvians, and Lithuanians, even while the instruments of disseminating that ideology – newspapers, literary magazines, and books – emanated mostly from urban centers. The desire to find "pure" forms of the indigenous languages led inevitably to the countryside, as did the gathering, transcribing, and publishing of the oral – now considered the national – tradition. For those inclined to think nationalistically, rural areas were repositories of national virtues, and peasants – farmers, agricultural laborers, and rural artisans – were much more than simply crude tillers of the soil; they were all potential members of the Estonian, Latvian, and Lithuanian "nations." Were it not for them, there would be no nation to awaken.

In the thinking of the littoral's rural people, cities and towns were admirable places, and songs in the oral tradition reflected that admiration. Peasants within the market networks of sizable towns had for centuries been hauling products to and from them; they had always served as magnets for fleeing serfs; peasant grievances against their overlords usually ended up in urban legal institutions that handled peasant affairs; and the largest cities – such as Riga, Tallinn, Vilnius, and Kaunas – as part of their permanent populations had a sizeable percentage of the indigenous peoples working at what later would be called service occupations. Therefore, urban ways were by no means alien to the total cultural experience of the peasant populations, and that relationship remained unchanged as long as the cities and towns themselves did not change appreciably. After the mid-century point, however, suspicions about urban areas were increasingly confirmed. While cities and towns offered great economic opportunity, they were also unforgiving places, impatient with failure and with the inability to compete. They were highly stratified and filled with corporate entities closed to outsiders, except as servitors. The stratification was economic and linguistic, as seen in the existence of neighborhoods that bordered on one another but did not intermingle. Styles of dress and places to eat, sleep, work, and relax (such as city parks) all underlined differences rather than commonalities and discouraged integration.

Thus, growing urban areas were for national awakeners a base of operations even as they praised the virtues of rural life. Yet peasant-born nationalists were not the only littoral subpopulation that placed a high value on the countryside. Amidst hundreds of thousands of Estonian, Latvian, and Lithuanian rural people, the traditional estate-owning aristocrats – primarily Baltic German in Estland, Livland, and Kurland, primarily Polish and Russian in Latgale and the Lithuanian lands – had successfully protected their way of life against serf emancipation, land purchase reforms, and other restrictions on their old privileges. Though their estates now operated with a different kind of labor force, the estate-based lifestyle had not lost its attractions. The estate owners were a distinct minority everywhere: only about one-fifth of the Baltic German population of Estland, Livland, and Kurland lived in the countryside; the occupation survey included in the 1897 imperial census showed only about 35 percent of the total Baltic German population in these provinces to be "working" at agriculture as estate owners and managers, at specialized ancillary occupations on estates as craftsmen, and as Lutheran clergy and church officials. Though small in number, the rural Baltic Germans – especially the nobilities (*Ritterschaften*) – remained immensely powerful, since they had a near-monopoly over such political institutions as the provincial assemblies (*Landtage*). That influence extended into urban life in numerous ways: they were wealthy, had money to invest, and many were clearly entrepreneurial and knew how to diversify their incomes. Influence was not difficult to wield: the seat of the powerful Livland nobility was in Riga, just blocks away from the dominating institutions of the urban patriciate, the Great Guild (long-distance merchants) and the Small Guild (locally oriented merchants and craftspeople). Moreover, the *Ritterschaften* knew how to create and manipulate friendships with high Russian officials – one elite speaking to another – and therefore had substantial influence at the St. Petersburg court. But in their rural estates, they stood out: there were virtually no peasants of German origin in the Baltic populations, which magnified the social cleavage through the superimposition of a linguistic cleavage. Such clear distinctions were more difficult to observe in Latgale and the Lithuanian lands, where the estate owners were predominantly Polish with an admixture of Russians. Yet still in the second half of the nineteenth century an appreciable number of Polish-speaking landowners – largely those with small estates and small incomes – continued to claim Lithuanian nationality by virtue of their ancestors having been citizens in good standing of the Grand Duchy of Lithuania. Also, because of the insurrections of 1830–1831 and 1863–1864, the Polish landowners were suspect in the St. Petersburg court, and their influence was minimal in comparison with that of the Baltic Germans. But here also a manner of living based on the country estate was enjoyed and thought proper for persons of high standing. The concept of *Stilleben* (life without change), as used by Baltic German writers, was applicable to both the northern and southern parts of the littoral: the status quo in perpetuity, a deeply rooted social conservatism to which the landed estate was central, the belief that the hustle and bustle of modernity was an unwelcome intrusion, and that strife was the creation of outside agitators.

Nonetheless, the relative significance of towns and cities continued to expand during the second half of the nineteenth century, in a pattern that was to be broken only by the momentous changes brought about by World War I. Of all the urban areas in the Baltic littoral, the largest by far was the city of Riga, which by 1867 already had almost four times as many people as it had at the beginning of the nineteenth century (1800: 27,894; 1867: 102,590). This high rate of growth continued until 1914 when the city's population stood at 517,500. The Russian government treated Riga as the littoral's metropolis and located many of its regional administrative offices there. The city had long striven for an identity separate from the territories that surrounded it, and in the seventeenth and eighteenth centuries its wish had come true: the new masters of the littoral (Swedes and Russians) saw it as advantageous to make separate peace treaties with the city and to reaffirm the economic "privileges" it claimed as a port city and as the main location of mercantile activity in the region. By the mid-nineteenth century, however, Riga had become one of a network of large urban centers in the empire, exceeded in size by St. Petersburg, Moscow, Warsaw, and Odessa; by 1910, Kiev and Łodz as well had pushed Riga to seventh position in terms of population. The city's governing Baltic German patriciate accommodated population growth: during the 1860s the confining medieval wall of the city was torn down, suburbs were annexed, and serious urban planning began. Many of the small summer estates built by the wealthy outside the city walls became part of city territory.

Also in the 1860s, a network of railroad lines began to connect Riga to other large cities – St. Petersburg, Warsaw, Moscow – and to the Russian interior, and within the littoral, to Dvinsk (Daugavpils) in Latgale, Mitau (Jelgava) in Kurland, and Valka in Livland. These main lines were followed by secondary connections between other littoral cities, and the entire network expanded Riga's role as a hub. Modern industrial enterprises – steam-driven, machine-using factories – proliferated in number and size, with the pace of growth exceeding the average pace of industrial growth in the empire as a whole. In the period 1879–1914 the annual average growth rate in terms of the number of factories and workers and the value of production in 103 of Russia's largest industrial centers was 0.9, 3.3, and 4.8, respectively, while in Riga growth rates in these categories were 2.0, 5.2, and 7.3. In terms of absolute numbers, if in 1864 the number of wage-workers in Riga's industrial establishments was 6,114, by 1905 it was 43,252, with this expanded labor force living in working-class neighborhoods in the so-called Moscow suburb, St. Petersburg suburb, or on the left bank of the Daugava River (in Latvian *Pārdaugava*). The "medieval" part of the city (*Vecrīga*) on the right bank of the Daugava remained separated from the newer neighborhoods by a chain of parks and a canal. Beyond this divide, long semi circular streets of grand apartment buildings were erected to house the expanding middle- and upper middle-class population; along with the close-knit medieval structures, these edifices remained the territory of the Baltic Germans, a handful of successful Latvian businessmen, and members of the so-called free professions (medicine, law, and architecture). Riga's population growth reflected the increasing "weight" of the Latvian population in the affairs of the city and in both Livland and Kurland: the proportion of Baltic Germans in Riga fell from 42.8 percent in 1867 to 25.5 percent in 1897 as Latvians increased from 23.5 percent in 1867 to 41.6 percent in 1897; meanwhile, Russians decreased from 25.1 percent in 1867 to 16.9 percent in 1897. The other growing subpopulation in Riga was that of the Jews, whose proportions increased from 5.1 percent in 1867 to 6.5 percent in 1897. The German population, though decreasing in absolute numbers and proportions, revealed its ability to maintain its economic power: in 1912 (when the proportion of the Baltic German population had dropped to 16.4 percent), 38.5 percent of the 2,829 urban properties in Riga valued at more than 10,000 rubles were owned by Baltic Germans while 36.9 percent were owned by Latvians.

27 The 1861 opening of a railway line between Riga and
Dünaburg (Russ. *Dvinsk*; Latv. *Daugavpils*) in the adjoining
Vitebsk province was of great significance for the economic
development of the Baltic littoral.

A similar long-term pattern of growth – limited expansion before
1850, much more rapid growth afterwards – that involved many
fewer people took place in the other prominent cities and towns of
the Latvian-language areas of the Baltic provinces. Several of these
cities were now less important than in the past: Jelgava (Mitau), for
example, had for centuries been the capital city of the Kurland duchy
and the seat of the ducal dynasties; now it was a relatively small
town (population 28,531 in 1881) in a relatively small Russian
province. Cēsis (Wenden) had at one time been the headquarters of
the Livonian Order, but now (population 4,300 in 1881) its central-
ity had disappeared. As other lesser cities increased not only in
population but in importance in the course of the nineteenth century,
their role in the littoral's economy became more significant: Liepāja
(Libau) and Ventspils (Windau), both port cities on the western
Baltic coast of Kurland, took advantage of their location to enter a
period of growing prosperity. Still, when the population is divided
into rural and urban categories, the numbers in the former continued

to dominate, so that by the end of the century the proportion living in urban areas had just reached about 30 percent in the Latvian regions of the littoral. Livland was the most "urban," Kurland somewhat less so, and in Latgale urban growth was negligible; there, the largest, and at century's end the most important, city was Daugavpils (Dvinsk), which owed its growth primarily to its significance to the Russian military. Daugavpils was also one of the least Latvian of cities: in 1897 its population was primarily Jewish (46 percent), Russian (30 percent), and Polish (16 percent).

In spite of the impressive proportion of Latvians in the growing urban population, it was very difficult for all Latvian awakeners to fit cities into portrayals of the Latvian people as a future *Kulturnation*. Most urban areas continued to maintain a German atmosphere and Baltic Germans entirely dominated city governments. Though the Latvian oral tradition frequently referred to cities and towns with the adjective "our" (*mūsu*), this term suggested shared provincial residency rather than a growing sense of cultural ownership. Moreover, all the urban areas not only retained German political dominance, but linguistically the Russian and Yiddish languages were frequently at least as prominent as German or Latvian. Cultural and linguistic merging due to intermarriage was marginal and never exceeded 3–4 percent even among small-town Latvians and Germans. Each language community in the cities expanded on its own without the inescapable daily economic interactions producing a common urban culture. Cultural historians of the period, for example, describe the burgeoning population of Riga in the 1850–1900 period as producing many Rigas, a distinct and separate one for each linguistic-cultural community. This could as well be applied to other larger cities and towns, unless for idiosyncratic reasons one language group had come to dominate an urban entity. This type of multiculturalism was double-edged: while it generated an interesting variety, cohabitation was based on convenience and self-interest rather than on a common communal spirit. Some of the Latvian *literati* in the 1880s – Jēkabs Apsītis (1858–1929) is a prime example – were already portraying cities as venues of insidious values likely to corrupt the job- and adventure-seeking young men and women arriving from the "purer" Latvian countryside.

Such literary reactions did nothing to stop rural to urban migration, which was primarily economic, but they did insert into the new and growing Latvian-language literary culture a nostalgia for the countryside, the implication being that modernity should not be pursued with the fervor that prominent members of the awakener generation (such as Valdemārs) advocated. Nonetheless, even writers such as Apsītis took full advantage of urban and economic growth, which offered a larger readership – Latvian newspapers and the periodical press – and an increasingly well-to-do Latvian audience in the countryside and in the urban locales. In spite of such ironies, from the beginning Latvian-language nationalism had as its principal characteristics a language- and rural-centeredness: Latvians were a people who spoke the Latvian language and had a close attachment to the countryside, specifically to that part of the littoral that had been the land of their ancestors. The socioeconomic developments of the second half of the nineteenth century that were engendering Latvians with very different values were suspect.

In Estland and the Estonian part of Livland, urban growth was also present in the second half of the nineteenth century, but it did not produce such large metropolitan areas as Riga. The two largest and most prominent cities at the start of the nineteenth century – Tallinn and Tartu (Dorpat) – remained so at the end. Both had once been members of the Hanseatic League, and both had sought, like Riga, to maintain a quasi-independent status in dealing with the *Ritterschaften*. In the nineteenth century, however, their Baltic German populations continued to dominate both cities. In Tallinn they controlled the guilds and both long- and short-distance trade as well as the early factories built in its environs. The primarily German professoriate of Tartu (Dorpat) invested the city with its deserved reputation as the principal university center of the littoral.

As the main city of Estland province, Tallinn had also become the center of Russian administrative officialdom after 1710 and experienced rapid population growth from the mid-nineteenth century: from 27,000 inhabitants in 1850 to about 160,000 by 1913. To much of the rural Estonian population in Estland and the northern part of Livland, Tallinn was becoming one of the industrial magnets of the north, a role it shared with the city of Narva; rural to urban migration tended to flow to these two places. In Narva the textile industry was dominant, and in Tallinn the production of metals and machines. By 1900, 41 percent of all industrial workers in the Estonian territories were located in Narva and 33 percent in Tallinn. Though the dynamics of economic and demographic change were the same, in terms of absolute numbers the Estonian lands were clearly second to the Latvian parts of the littoral. The number of industrial workers in the former grew from 6,500 in 1860 to 24,000 in 1900, while the population of the Estonian-area cities tripled, their proportion of the total population increasing from 8.7 percent in the 1860s to 19.2 percent by the end of the century. As in the Latvian territories, most of the Estonian population (and the Baltic German landowners) remained rural and depended on agricultural incomes; for this reason also, the philosophy of Estonian nationalism in this period linked Estonianness to peasanthood or at least peasant origins, located virtue in rural areas, and viewed the oral tradition as the essence of the *Volksgeist* (spirit of the people). Thanks to the relatively smaller urban populations in the Estonian areas, however, the Estonian literary imagination drew the urban/rural distinction less sharply than did its Latvian counterpart. Also, by the end of the century there were more Estonians living in the cities and towns of the area than in the Latvian region; in twelve of thirteen urban locations in the Estonian lands by that time, the Baltic Germans comprised less than 20 percent of the total population.

As the sole university town in the Baltic provinces, Tartu (Dorpat) played a unique role that was unaligned with its moderate size (13,000 persons in 1854; 40,000 in 1900). It had already achieved considerable fame in the seventeenth century when the Swedish government, in control of Livland, founded the Academia Gustaviana in 1631. The town was also the site of the first printing house in the Estonian lands (established 1631) as well as the Forselius Seminary, the first teachers college in Estonia, founded in the eighteenth century. The association of the town with institutions of higher learning was well established, and even the closing of the university by the Russian government during much of the eighteenth century (it reopened in 1802) did not dilute the connection. The "town" population remained relatively small but the "gown" population gave Tartu (Dorpat) its prominence. The Baltic German population of the littoral portrayed the university as theirs, with

28 The buildings of Dorpat University. In the second half of the nineteenth century, the University of Dorpat (Tartu) was the most significant institution of higher learning in the Russian Empire's western borderlands and the site of the beginning of both the Estonian and Latvian national awakening movements.

considerable justification. Latvian students from Livland and Kurland, as their matriculation numbers rose during the nineteenth century, had their own names for the town – "Tērbata" or more colloquially "Mētraine" – while the Russians alternated between "Dorpat" and "Jurjew," the latter being the name of the town in the ancient Rus' chronicles and also the name given to it after russification of the Baltic provinces began in earnest after 1883 (see below). A large portion of the Baltic German youth coming of age in the littoral received their university educations there, as did many of the active Latvian awakeners. It was in Dorpat that Latvian students founded the first Latvian student fraternity (*Lettonia*) on the model of Dorpat's German *Burschenshaften*. To the small but growing population of university-educated Latvians in the second half of the century, Dorpat (Tartu) seemed as much a natural part of their mental landscape as did for different reasons Riga and Jelgava (Mitau) in Kurland. Many of the important events in the Estonian national awakening – the first song festival in 1869, the establishment of the first national theatre in 1870, the founding of the Society of Estonian Literati in 1871 – took place in Tartu (Dorpat). At the same time, the Latvian students of the university were laying the groundwork for a Latvian awakening and the Baltic German students had their sense of cultural superiority confirmed by the Germanness of the place. A new educational magnet in the littoral appeared in 1862, however, with the establishment of the Riga Polytechnic Institute, which planned to stress technical and practical sciences in contrast to the humanistic leanings of Dorpat. Traditional enrollment patterns at Dorpat were substantially changed with the onset of russification in 1883, when the university was renamed (as Jurjew) and Russian became the obligatory language of instruction.

The region of the littoral inhabited by Lithuanians was the most agricultural at the mid-century point and remained so during the rest of the century. Some 90 percent of the population were peasants; the emancipation of serfs in 1861 had given them land but had also bound them to long-term payments to the government for that land. Nonetheless, the Lithuanian area had two prominent cities – Vilnius and Kaunas – both of which grew in size from 1850 onward, reaching 154,000 inhabitants in Vilnius and 86,500 in Kaunas by 1897. Both cities had had their heyday in earlier centuries; now, in the nineteenth, they were simply large urban places in the Russian western borderlands. Neither had the economic advantage of being a port city (as Riga and Tallinn were), and like other larger Lithuanian cities neither was marked by rapid industrial growth. By 1912, the Lithuanian *provinces* of Vilnius, Kaunas, and Šuvalkija had only 21,800 industrial workers who were concentrated in the *cities* of Vilnius, Kaunas, and Šiauliai. Throughout the Lithuanian territories by 1912, only 7 of the total of 3,143 industrial establishments employed more than a hundred workers. These workers were the product of rural to urban migration, as elsewhere in the littoral, but, unlike in the Estonian and Latvian territories, the trajectory of the migrants did not noticeably increase the proportion of Lithuanians in the larger cities. In both Vilnius and Kaunas, the proportion of Lithuanians hovered between 2 percent and 6 percent; in these cities, the populations consisted primarily of Jews, Poles, and Russians, and in both by 1897 Jews formed a plurality of about 40 percent of the

total. During the last decades of the nineteenth century, the nationality composition of the largest cities stood in sharp contrast to city
populations of the northern littoral, where Estonians and Latvians
were approaching absolute (though politically ineffective) majorities. The north–south contrast did provide one similarity: hamlets,
villages, and other small settlements in both regions were peopled
primarily by the "indigenous" populations. In addition to the hin-
drances created by the Russian government to the expansion of a
Lithuanian-language culture, the awakeners in the Lithuanian
lands could not count on city dwellers; they had to persuade a
largely rural audience.

Even though relatively small, almost entirely non-Lithuanian, and
decidedly under-industrialized, both Kaunas and Vilnius still played
a powerful role in the collective memory of Lithuanians because they
had once been prominent places in a Lithuanian state – the grand
duchy. Both had suffered over the centuries because of their location:
during the existence of the Polish-Lithuanian Commonwealth, both
cities were located, as it were, on the highway of marauding armies –
Polish, Swedish, and Russian – and as a result of their relative wealth
were primary targets of besiegement and capture. Several times
Vilnius was razed almost to the ground; by the beginning of
Russian rule at the end of the eighteenth century, its population
had declined to about 20,000.

The population of Kaunas had been and remained smaller –
about 5,000 persons – until the mid-nineteenth century, when the
town became the administrative center of the *gubernnia* of Kaunas,
triggering an influx of rural to urban migrants and quadrupling the
population by the end of the century. Also, because of its proximity
to the Russian–Prussian border (especially with a considerable
Lithuanian population in Lithuania Minor just across the border),
the Russian government began to enlarge Kaunas as a military
center. With the disappearance of the commonwealth and the
grand duchy during the partitions of the eighteenth and the early
nineteenth century, both cities had lost the larger political context
that had invested them with stature; now, they were moderately
sized urban centers with populations that were barely Lithuanian.
Yet some of the Lithuanian nationalists of the awakening period
imagined a reawakened Lithuania – restored, refurbished, and

autonomous – in which both cities were included because the restoration would be – so the belief went – of an entity closely resembling the old grand duchy.

The rural to urban migration wave in which the littoral nationalist movements were embedded, and which at the same time provided these movements with much of their audience, had another feature not as favorable to the nationalist cause: the wave carried many people out of the Baltic littoral and placed them in contexts in which loss of language and cultural identity were even more of a threat than in the Baltic littoral itself. With each decade after the 1860s, the proportion of Estonians, Latvians, and Lithuanians who lived outside the littoral increased as migrants sought better careers, land, or simply a life that promised greater opportunity elsewhere. Exact numbers describing the process of out-migration are not available, but the 1897 imperial census provides an insight into this diaspora at the end of the nineteenth century and some hints about motives. By 1897, about 23,200 Lithuanians had left the Lithuanian provinces and were living in Estland, Livland, and Kurland, most of them (53%) in the countryside; about 5,000 Latvians had moved from the Latvian-language part of Livland into the Estonian-language part of that province. The provinces of central Russia contained 1,300 Lithuanians (27% rural; 72% urban), 6,079 Latvians (83% rural; 17% urban), and 2,537 Estonians (77% rural; 22% urban). Even the Siberian provinces of the empire had people who spoke one of the three littoral vernaculars: 1,900 Lithuanians (83% rural; 16% urban), 6,700 Latvians (93% rural; 6% urban), and 4,200 Estonians (93% urban; 6% rural). Many of Russia's largest cities contained enough ex-littoral residents for them to be able to form clubs, associations, and cultural programs: in Moscow there were 435 Lithuanians, 710 Latvians, and 318 Estonians; St. Petersburg had 3,763 Lithuanians, 6,277 Latvians, and 12,238 Estonians; but in Warsaw the numbers were smaller – 116 Lithuanians, 649 Estonians, and 624 Latvians. The largest cities of the Baltic littoral also received people from elsewhere in the region: in Riga, there were 6,362 Lithuanians and 3,702 Estonians; in Vilnius 164 Latvians and 19 Estonians. One estimate places the number of Estonians in Russia outside the littoral at 120,000 and the number of Latvians at about 112,322. The comparative numbers who had left the littoral but stayed within the empire are roughly comparable and suggest no greater or lesser attachment to native soil on the part of any of the language communities. Yet the Lithuanians stand out as truly adventurous as far as very long-distance migration was concerned. Using figures for only the United States, it is estimated that in the period from the 1860s to 1914, around 300,000 Lithuanians arrived there – mostly in the steel and coal towns of Pennsylvania and the stockyards of Chicago – and immediately began to form parishes, fraternal organizations, and mutual aid societies. The number of Estonians and Latvians who were willing to make that voyage was meager by comparison: an estimated 5,100 Estonians and 4,309 Latvians by 1900, most of these ending up in eastern seaboard cities. These numbers for Estonians and Latvians increased immediately after the revolution of 1905 (see chapter 7), but at no time did they reach the impressive numbers of the Lithuanian émigrés. The meaning implicit in all these numbers is clear: by the end of the century, littoral residents by the thousands, when confronted by the choice of staying in their homelands or seeking betterment in their lives, chose the latter, even if that choice meant placing themselves in social and cultural local environments that required adaptation to new languages and customs, and perhaps, ultimately, led to assimilation. While some return migration occurred (numbers unknown), when the émigré communities were large enough in their host cities or countries, they organized activities in which their native language was used. It was also true that the continuation of such migration patterns introduced a certain fragility in the accomplishments of the awakener generation: they recognized that, however much had been accomplished to create Estonian-, Latvian-, and Lithuanian-language cultural institutions in the littoral, their existence and future promise were not sufficiently binding for thousands of compatriots. The work of constructing national cultures continued, but the certainty that it would ultimately succeed was becoming increasingly less predictable.

TESTING NATIONAL IDENTITY: RUSSIFICATION AND SOCIALISM

Among the longer-lived participants of the littoral's national awakenings the question of how successful their efforts had been at any given moment was always an open one. In how many of their compatriots had they caused consciousness of linguistic differentiation to transmute into a consciousness of national differentiation? How deep was this new sense of national identity, and what were the outward signs that a conversion had taken place? Answers to these questions were always ambiguous. One could point to the rising attendance at national song festivals, the subscriptions lists of newspapers, and the rising number of books published in Estonian, Latvian, and Lithuanian as positive answers. But one could just as easily point to the continued survival of the belief, especially among upwardly mobile sons and daughters of peasants, that German- and Polish-language usage and participation in German and Polish cultural activities was inevitable for personal success, or to the equally strong belief that Estonian, Latvian, and Lithuanian cultural efforts would forever remain linked to their peasant origins and could never rival the accomplishments of the larger *Kulturnationen*. The latter notion was very much alive even in liberal publications such as the Baltic German monthly *Baltische Monatschrift*, which, in 1881, opined that "the assignment of Estonians and Latvians at the moment is not to force into existence an independence in the realm of intellectual matters . . . Their cultural mission is to be fulfilled in the realm of practical affairs. Over the course of centuries, they have matured as honorable peasant peoples, and it is on this that Estonians and Latvians who care about their people's welfare should concentrate." This reiteration of the position held by many in the Baltic German *Gelehrtenstand* had been articulated for decades: thus in 1864 the Riga newspaper *Rigasche Zeitung* told its readers that "nature has decreed that in a territory in which fate has placed two peoples, the people with the highest cultural level is obliged to assimilate the people which has not reached such a level."

Similar attitudes were expressed by Polish-using intellectuals toward the cultural strivings of Lithuanians. What was troubling to the first generation of awakeners was the suspicion that many in the Estonian, Latvian, and Lithuanian language communities shared some variant of these notions. What was not considered by any side in these continuing polemics over the "national" question was the unlikelihood that 5–6 percent of the littoral's population (Baltic Germans and Poles) could readily assimilate the other 94–95 percent

(Estonians, Latvians, and Lithuanians) into their allegedly superior language and culture. The numbers were against such an outcome, and because of that, the argument sounded like sheer cultural arrogance. Even so, among the national activists there continued a nagging worry that their own efforts at national-culture building were not enough in a socioeconomic context that tempted many thousands to leave the littoral, brought to urban areas other thousands with minimal interest in cultural matters, and promised material rewards for efforts expended in sociocultural domains (government employment, the church) in which the daily use of the Polish, German, or Russian language was mandatory.

A double test of the sustainability of the new national cultures arrived in the last two decades of the nineteenth century: russification, or the extension to the whole littoral of policies that the Russian government had implemented in the Lithuanian lands after the insurrection of 1863–1864; and, in the 1890s, attraction to socialist doctrines among a new generation of Estonian, Latvian, and Lithuanian intellectuals. Russification policy was seeking to bring to heel the troublesome western borderlands, and behind it stood a coterie of Slavophile journalists and policymakers for whom it was unacceptable that any part of the empire should remain non-Russian linguistically and culturally. Socialism preached the international solidarity of the proletariat; for its adherents the true loyalty of the "masses" should be not national culture but the interests of the working class. Russification policy had behind it the power of the state, and socialism was made attractive to a new generation because it was "western" and "modern" and to its adherents appeared to address problems that the nationalist movements were ignoring. Both, however, would put to the test the new idea of national identity that the awakeners had worked so hard to instill in their audiences.

In 1881 Tsar Alexander II was assassinated, an event that caused his son and successor, Alexander III, to reconsider the liberal policies of his father toward the troublesome western borderlands. Eventually, this conservative turn in St. Petersburg led to the conviction that the policy of systematic russification being practiced in the Lithuanian and Polish lands since 1864 should be applied to the entire Baltic littoral, including the heretofore seemingly sacrosanct Baltic provinces of Estland, Livland, and Kurland. Cultural, religious, and linguistic transformation would also be imposed from the top down. The anticipated result was a smoothly functioning empire in which all component parts would be Russian (or be controlled by Russians) and would progress along lines approved by the tsar and his advisors. The policy of russification in the Baltic provinces and Finland from the mid-1880s onward was not, however, predicated on any empirically verifiable success in the Polish and Lithuanian areas, except perhaps on the recognition that no serious uprising had occurred there since 1864. Most members of the Polish-speaking landowning elite seemed to have accepted the status quo. The ban on Lithuanian publications did not affect them directly, and they and the Russian government seemed unconcerned that the thousands of Lithuanian books being smuggled into the Lithuanian areas from East Prussia might be a harbinger of attitudinal changes among the lower orders. That systematic attempts to russify entire provinces just might have long-term counterproductive effects as far as governance was concerned evidently was not considered, in part because the imperial government was not particularly far-sighted and in part because the reaction of those who actually encountered russification – in the court system, in schools, in marriage decisions, in religious observance – did not really matter. Engendered resentments had no way of communicating themselves to St. Petersburg through the existing political system. The reports by a few perceptive Russian administrators in the littoral were more likely than not to ascribe negative feelings as being directed against the local Polish and Baltic German elites rather than against tsarist policy as such. That in the Lithuanian lands and in the Baltic provinces russification policies would inevitably be filtered through an expanding consciousness of nationality and national separateness was not seen as a barrier to their success, if the existence of such a filter were perceived at all.

Russian administrators understood that in the Baltic provinces the main opposition would come from the Baltic German elites – the landowners in the countryside, the patriciates in the urban areas, and the intellectuals who could express their opposition through a wide variety of outlets, including the German-language press in the now-unified (since 1871) Germany. On the other hand, there was also the belief that non-German majority populations – primarily Estonians and Latvians – could be manipulated to side with the government because the thrust of their culture-building events and institutions was also to erode the monopoly of power exercised by the Baltic Germans. In this respect, many Latvian and some Estonian activists had sent the imperial government signals. Among the Latvians, Krišjānis Valdemārs, for example, had made it clear repeatedly in his publications that if sides were to be taken, self-interest among Latvians would dictate standing with the Russian government against the Baltic Germans. When, in 1881, Senator N. A. Manasein visited the Baltic provinces to inspect conditions there, thousands of Latvian peasants petitioned him to urge the government to bring justice to the land question and to solve the problem of landlessness; Latvian activists helped to organize and gather the petitions. Such flirtation with Russian administrators appeared to be a useful tactic, and many believed that with Baltic German power broken and the land question settled the imperial government would permit the indigenous populations to have a high degree of cultural autonomy. What remained invisible to them, however, was the strong desire in imperial government circles to eliminate cultural, linguistic, and religious enclaves of any kind. In the implementation of this desire the attitudes of Estonian, Latvian, and Lithuanian activists, divided as they were, did not really matter.

The division of opinion among the Estonian and Latvian intelligentsia on how russification measures should be received continued well into the 1890s; no united front (as among the Baltic Germans) opposed them. (Such opposition would have had to be very guarded in any case.) Among the Latvians, moreover, the arrival of russification coincided with a generational change among the nationalist activists: a few of the old guard were still prominent (Krišjānis Valdemārs, who died in 1894, Krišjānis Barons, who died in 1923), but the fervor of the 1856–1880 period was gone and many in the younger generation of university-attending Latvians claimed that the entire national movement had become a commercial venture to benefit the wealthy members of the Riga Latvian Association.

Russification policy began to be implemented in Estland, Livland, and Kurland during the mid-1880s in a stepwise fashion. Russian governors-general were appointed in all three provinces; police and judicial institutions were placed under the Ministry of Interior; the education system was relocated piecemeal to the Ministry of Education; and active propagation of Russian Orthodoxy began in order to diminish peasant loyalties to the Lutheran Church. Over the next decade, as the number of Russian administrators in the Baltic provinces grew substantially, russification policies were implemented unsystematically and sometimes haphazardly. But they were felt widely in almost every domain of life. The required use of the Russian language in schools and the court system inevitably led to the dismissal of teachers and government employees who did not know Russian well; they were replaced by Russian speakers who seldom knew the provincial languages – German, Estonian, Latvian, Lithuanian. The St. Petersburg government also funded special schools in which all instruction was in Russian. The offspring of mixed marriages involving a Russian Orthodox partner were required to be brought up in the Orthodox Church, and conversion from orthodoxy to other faiths was strictly controlled, and in the end forbidden. An increasingly large number of Orthodox churches were built throughout the Baltic littoral, especially in those areas that already had sizable Russian and Russian Orthodox populations.

Protestations by Baltic German political leaders and by the Evangelical Lutheran Church, appealing to historic liberties, went unheeded or were brushed aside. Although government measures in the Baltic provinces did not go as far as to forbid the publication of books in the Latin alphabet – a prevailing prohibition in the Lithuanian areas since the 1860s – the printing of books in the Latvian and Estonian languages using the Cyrillic alphabet was encouraged. Some Russian officials in their pronouncements began to refer to Estonian and Latvian as dialects rather than languages. Dorpat University was renamed Jurjew, and its language of instruction was changed from German to Russian. From the mid-1880s onward, ongoing tasks on the agenda of the cultural nationalists – the creation of Estonian- and Latvian-language literatures that included books, newspapers, periodicals, and educating a new generation by means of a Latvian- and Estonian-language school system – became much more difficult. The Estonian and Latvian intelligentsia now had to contend with controls that activists in the Lithuanian lands had already reckoned with for twenty years.

To many, the Russian supporters of russification measures were sounding very much like those among the Baltic German *Gelehrtenstand* who had urged germanization of Estonians and Latvians. In commenting on the 1888 Latvian song festival, which involved 110 choirs, 1,600 singers, and an audience of about 58,000, the newspaper *Novoje vremja* wrote: "The smaller the nation, the greater its pretension. The song festival of the Latvians in its desires and aspirations clearly overstepped acceptable boundaries." Yet the government did not forbid these largest of all manifestations of national feeling in the Estonian or Latvian territories. The organizers of the song festivals usually depicted them as celebrations of some beneficent edicts of earlier tsars, and therefore officials were reluctant to stand in the way. In the Estonian territories, the attendance at song festivals in the 1890s continued to grow, and their musical repertoire became increasingly more Estonian.

The book ban in Lithuania was lifted in 1904 after the Russian senate judged the original order to be illegal; Nicholas II supported an ending of the ban. Russification measures in Estland, Livland, and Kurland, however, lasted until the eve of World War I, by which time some had been modified and others were being enforced laxly. The notion that the western borderlands could be pacified and integrated into the rest of the empire by measures forbidding certain kinds of publications, dictating language use in the educational and legal system, regulating interreligious marriage, and flooding the region with officials ignorant of the local languages and conditions turned out in the end to have been an illusion. Although many of the cultural monopolies of the Baltic Germans and Polish landowners were broken, no evidence exists that this made Estonians, Latvians, and Lithuanians think more kindly about tsarist autocracy and its intentions. Much more impressive for them was the arbitrariness of the entire experiment, the hundreds of schoolteachers whose lives had been interrupted at mid-career, the frustrations of needing interpreters to use the court system: all these made the Russian government seem to be no more friendly to the cause of cultural autonomy in the borderlands than the Baltic German and Polish elites had been all along. In the memoirs of those who grew up in the russification decades, one reads of these measures as making life more complicated but not as an obstacle to realizing life's goals or as persuading people to cease being Estonian, Latvian, and Lithuanian and to become Russian. Another language could be learned, officialdom could be circumvented, and the literary cultures that had come into existence during the earlier decades showed themselves now to be impregnable.

A second challenge to the durability of the idea of national culture came in the preoccupation with "modern" ideas in the thinking of young Estonian, Latvian, and Lithuanian intelligentsia, especially those who were attending universities but also those who thought of themselves as aspiring artists and writers. For them, modernity meant realism, Darwinism, socialism, feminism, democracy, individualism, cosmopolitanism, internationalism, and science. It also meant a sweeping claim that the central concerns of the previous generations – challenging Baltic German and Polish cultural hegemony, creating and sustaining a vernacular-language culture, as well as institutions in which the non-Germans and non-Poles would feel at home, and urging loyalty to the language of one's birth – were no longer of major import. In fact, these efforts had been corrupted – so the younger generation claimed – and become slogans of the new moneyed classes in the littoral's urban areas. Western socialism, especially its Marxist variant, was understood to unmask the workings of industrial capitalism, the reason why different social classes existed, and what the relationship between such classes should be. Marxism fed the vanity of many of the younger intelligentsia by allowing them to think of themselves as a vanguard, as a minority which truly understood the trajectory of history, and as being favorably situated to assist wage-slaves (factory workers, agricultural laborers) to fulfill their historic role of "overthrowing" capitalism. Marxism especially was believed to have uncovered the "scientific" laws of historical development, as Darwin had in the natural world; hence, cleaving to socialism allowed one to believe oneself to be on the cutting edge of scientific modernity. There was a considerable amount of utopianism in such thinking: the same impatience with existing reality that occupied the minds of russifying officials and the same belief that the world could be refashioned quickly by an omniscient minority. The russifiers yearned for an efficient, consolidated, modern, and uniform empire that the recalcitrance and stubbornness of provincial and cultural separatism was preventing; the socialists, for a problem-free world that was being blocked by the preoccupation of the older generation with "national" questions, by the autocracy of the tsarist government, and by the material self-interest of entrepreneurs and landowners.

The generational break in the Estonian, Latvian, and Lithuanian intelligentsias was not equally sharp or marked, being perhaps most self-conscious among the Latvians where from the mid-1890s the "modernists" earned the nickname *Jaunā Strāva* (the New Current). A similarly self-conscious movement among Estonians – called *Noor-Eesti* (Young Estonia) – arose after the revolution of 1905, by which time the critiques it delivered were directed against both nationalism and Marxism. The situation in Lithuania was far more complicated. There socialist organization was initiated by Lithuanian Jews, who founded the General Jewish Worker's Union (known as the *Bund*) in 1897, and by Poles, who established the Polish Socialist Party in 1892, which was active in the Lithuanian provinces as well. The origins of the specifically Lithuanian socialist movement were to be found in the activities of individuals such as Belarussian Evgenii Sponti (1866–1931), and two Lithuanians, Leonas Mikalauskas (1870–1899) and Bronislovas Urbonavičius (1868–1903). The Lithuanian Social Democratic Party was founded in 1895 by two Lithuanian students – Alfonsas Moravskis (1868–1941) and Andrius Domasevičius (1865–1935) – whose personal genealogies led back into the nobility of the Grand Duchy, but who themselves knew hardly any Lithuanian. (The equivalent Latvian and Estonian parties were not founded until 1904 and 1905, respectively.)

Before there were parties or organized movements in the littoral, however, there were study groups and other informal clusters of sympathizers who cautiously avoided the attention of the authorities. Information about Marxism was not difficult to obtain; it came to Lithuania through the usual East Prussian connection; in Latvia, a youthful Jānis Pliekšāns (1865–1929), who was later to become the Latvian "national poet" Rainis, is said to have smuggled a suitcase-full of Marxist classics into Riga from Germany. The left-oriented youth in all three national groups also had Russian connections, since circulation of illegal literature within the empire had become almost normal. In addition, in all three areas well-regarded and well-edited periodical publications of a literary bent, such as *Austrums* (1895–1906) among Latvians, *Teataja* (The Herald) and *Uudised* (The News) (1901–1905) among Estonians, and *Varpas* (The Bell) (1889–1905) in the Lithuanian lands, were willing to print articles about the new ideas as long as they were stated very abstractly and in a philosophical manner. In Lithuania, of course, publications using the Latin alphabet were illegal by definition, regardless of what they dealt with. In *Austrums*, articles about Marxism were disguised by philosophical titles such as "Historical Materialism."

Those of the younger generation whose interest in things modern included Marxist doctrine discovered that "the proletariat" that was to take charge after "the revolution" was described as "international." The "working classes" of all lands had common economic interests and a common role in history, both of which were far more important, according to the creed, than the languages, cultures, and nationalities that separated them. In a sense, Marxist doctrine instructed adherents that the job of continuing to build national cultures based on the Estonian, Latvian, and Lithuanian languages and directed against German, Polish, and Russian cultural hegemony was superseded by the task of organizing all the "working masses" regardless of language and nationality into a single force directed against "the bourgeoisie."

Efforts to resolve this conflict of ultimate goals came to naught in the littoral, producing, on the one hand, more or less dogmatic Marxists who insisted that "class conflict" was primary and "the national question" quite secondary, and, on the other, a large collection of left-oriented young people who retained a strong interest in helping the condition of "working people" but did not believe a revolution was inevitable or that national culture-building should take a back seat to other endeavors. In other words, the brush with Marxist socialism produced in the Estonian, Latvian, and Lithuanian intelligentsias a left wing, but not the single-minded vanguard that orthodox Marxists would have liked. Many more members of the young literary intelligentsia of the three littoral peoples formulated a vision in which cultural autonomy, and not the proletariat, had primacy. The intellectual battles on the left about the relative importance of the national question would continue until the early years of the twentieth century, but left-oriented younger people did not march along a single track.

Although the concepts of modernist, Marxist, and socialist were in the process of differentiation within the generation that came of age in the 1890s, the authorities thought they looked the same. Agitation, speeches, some participation in strikes, illegal publications, and pamphlets – all the byproducts of socialist activism – appeared to be "against the tsar," and in 1897 the government closed *Dienas Lapa* (Daily Paper), the principal publication of the Latvian new current in Riga, searched the homes of 138 suspected participants in illegal activities, and initiated criminal proceedings against 87 of them. The sentences, handed down in 1899, varied from jail terms to exile to Siberia; about ten activists fled abroad during the preceding investigative period. The Lithuanian Social Democratic Party suffered a similar crackdown in 1899, when forty of its most prominent members were arrested and exiled to the interior of Russia; Alfonsas Moravskis, however, fled abroad to engage in organizational activity among industrial workers in both England and the United States. No crackdowns of similar size occurred against the Estonian left at the end of the 1890s, even though there the influence of socialist radicalism was also strong, a result of the proximity of the largest industrial cities (Narva and Tallinn) to St. Petersburg. The actions by the authorities of course were a setback to activist circles, but they did not end the influence of socialism in the littoral.

One consequence of these "new currents" among the Estonian, Latvian, and Lithuanian intelligentsias was to redefine the "right wing" of the embryonic political spectrum. Reacting to the socialist dimensions of the 1890s generation, many heretofore moderate nationalists became greater defenders of the status quo than they normally would have been; they now looked to the tsarist government to maintain order. In the eyes of their more radical compatriots, these conservatives became a new kind of establishment alongside those of the Baltic Germans and the defenders of autocracy. For the conservative nationalists, compromise with the forces of order became preferable to the collectivist philosophies being propounded by socialist agitators. A much larger middle sector of the politically active intelligentsia retained a strong interest in the further development of national cultures but also believed their goal could be reached within a new liberalized constitutional order in Russia.

A third variant sought to achieve an intellectual merger between socioeconomic radicalism and national-cultural aspirations. For the time being, political discussion among the three peoples was more impressive for its mutual recrimination and mutual accusations of backsliding, betrayal, and utopianism than for a clear political program with realistically reachable goals. At the same time, the political discourse of the period – combative and uncompromising as it was – was being conducted largely in Estonian, Latvian, and Lithuanian, a fact that underlined one of the permanent changes introduced by five decades of transformation.

7

Statehood in troubled times, 1905–1940

The eastern Baltic littoral entered the twentieth century quietly, but in 1901 the city of Riga marked the seven hundredth anniversary of its founding with very elaborate celebrations. The multifaceted history of the city, in some sense representing the whole littoral, was symbolized by the existence in Riga of statues dedicated to Bishop Albert, the founder; Peter the Great, the tsar of Russia who brought Livland into the empire; and Johann Gottfried Herder, the philosopher, who had insisted that the *Volksgeist* (spirit of the people) was a supremely important element in human affairs. Also in 1901 the Riga City Council elected as mayor George Armistead, a wealthy merchant with progressive ideas and the scion of a germanized English family that had resided in Riga since 1812 and had become part of its dominant German-speaking patriciate. Since by 1897 the city's population had become mostly Latvian (41.6 percent), with Germans (25.5 percent) and Russians (16.9 percent) comprising most of the rest, it was therefore not clear, in Herderian terms, which of the *Volksgeister* was representative. Armistead's tenure until 1912 was a period of uninterrupted economic growth and urban modernization; at the same time, he and his social class treated the events during the revolutionary years 1905–1906 as unwelcome interruptions to progress and not as the signals of deep-seated socioeconomic and national divisions in the littoral that they undoubtedly were. A similar dismissive attitude toward divisions, cleavages, and rivalries existed in the international arena; it was widely believed that clever diplomacy and material progress would continue to resolve all disputes and gradually enrich all peoples. The Triple Entente and the Triple Alliance – treaty agreements that included all the great powers – were bound to keep skirmishes between states within acceptable limits; peace conferences would reveal to all the folly of war; and continuing industrialization and technological innovation would bind western civilization together so that war and conflict would appear increasingly atavistic.

Too much had happened in the Baltic littoral during the 1880s and 1890s for all residents to view the future as benign. The enlargement of Estonian, Latvian, and Lithuanian cultural spaces continued, as did various forms of opposition to Baltic German and Polish economic and political hegemony; above all, continuing russification measures – in place in the Lithuanian areas since the 1860s and in the Baltic provinces of Estland, Livland, and Kurland since the 1880s – continued to generate dislike, even deep hatred in some cases, of Russian tsarist autocracy, though tens of thousands of educated people from the Baltic learned Russian and left for the Russian cities and hinterlands in search of employment. The 1905–1906 revolutionary events in the empire took a special form in the littoral, where they were at least as much rural as urban as they struck out against symbols of Baltic German and Polish landowner-ship and against autocratic Russian rule. Though the century started quietly, just the first decade of it revealed that the history of the littoral was becoming more dense: few areas escaped nearly annual major changes. The years between 1906 and 1914 remained turbu-lent, containing tsarist flirtation with parliamentarism at the imperial level (the elected *Duma*), loosening of censorship (including the lifting of the press ban in the Lithuanian area in 1904), the sharpen-ing of urban electoral competition in the littoral cities, and the continuing expansion of the urban industrial labor force.

In August 1914, in spite and because of mutual treaty obligations, the European great powers went to war, with smaller countries and stateless peoples becoming unwilling participants and suffering inva-sions, occupations, and depredations of various kinds. In the first months of World War I, there was widespread belief that the fighting would be "over by Christmas" 1914, but as the conflict continued that expectation had to be revised repeatedly. On both the western and eastern fronts, military encounters became trench warfare, with small areas of contested territory costing the opposing sides thousands of lives. The use of poison gas showed how modern technology had contributed to making warfare less humane than ever. As 1915 passed and then 1916 and 1917, belligerents were drained of manpower and resources with no conclusive victory in sight. Popular support for established governments was waning on the home front, particularly in the old monarchies of Germany, Russia, and Austria-Hungary. The entry of the United States in the war tilted the conflict to favor the Allies – England, France, and Russia, among others – and in November of 1918, after the abdication of the Hohenzollern dynasty in Germany, an armistice ended the fighting.

By that time, the Habsburg dynasty was gone from the Austro-Hungarian throne as well, and the Romanovs of Russia, with Nicholas II having abdicated in March 1917, were replaced by a provisional government. In November 1917, an entirely new kind of government, based on the ideas of Marxism-Leninism, toppled the provisional government through a coup and during the next several years struggled to maintain its position in a fierce civil war. During these final years of World War I, the formerly subordinated peoples of the western borderlands of the Russian Empire were presented with the opportunity of separating themselves entirely from their former rulers and of claiming independence as sovereign nations. The birth of these nations in northeastern Europe was paralleled by the emergence in central and southeastern Europe of other new states, successors to the dissolved Habsburg dominions and the old Ottoman Empire to the south. By 1920, some fifteen new countries had emerged on the European map, most of them founded on the principle that each European population with a distinct nationality should have a state of its own. The actual borders of the new states, agreed upon during three years of postwar negotiations, could not reflect this principle cleanly because many borders were based on political compromises rather than on the surgical separation of one people from another.

THE YEAR 1905 IN THE BALTIC LITTORAL

As had happened many times before, external events turned the flow of history in the littoral in unexpected directions. This time the triggers were the Russo-Japanese War of 1904–1905 in the Far East and then the unprecedented challenges to imperial authority across the whole empire during 1905. The defeat of the imperial armed forces by what was presumed to be an inferior Japanese military revealed weaknesses in the empire that could be exploited by critics of autocracy, and not only by the most extreme ones. In November 1904, a large congress of *zemstvo* organizations – the equivalent of local and regional governments – met in St. Petersburg and demanded a representative assembly and civil liberties, a call widely echoed throughout other sociopolitical classes. On "Bloody Sunday" – January 22, 1905 – the demonstration of workers marching to the tsar's palace was met with deadly force by the imperial army (70 killed and 240 wounded) and this supplied critics with clear ammunition to portray the government as corrupt, incompetent, and incapable of responding to the "wishes of the people" except with violence. The newspapers of the Baltic littoral reported on the violence immediately, though in restrained terms, but the reports were sufficiently disturbing for the radically inclined socialists to initiate a series of meetings, strikes, and work stoppages that over the course of the year snowballed into what later Baltic German commentators were to term the "Baltic Revolution."

Though the events of 1905 in the Baltic littoral were necessarily framed by the actions and reactions to the general situation of the St. Petersburg government, they were something more than a reduced regional variant of the larger Russian rising. Of course, many similarities existed between what transpired in the Russian urban centers and in the littoral. Strikes and labor unrest of other kinds, mostly initiated by socialists (social democrats), occurred everywhere in towns and cities – Vilnius, Kaunas, Riga, Tallinn, Narva, and Pärnu. The socialists, whose ranks had been thinned considerably by arrests in earlier years, were still the most organized and therefore the most potent force in the littoral that could take advantage of the ongoing situation. Yet they were riven with disagreements about the ultimate goals of direct action: the more moderate wanted to focus on improving labor conditions, the more extreme to transform all of society, while others took positions in between. University students also were prominent throughout all the year's events, as they organized protest marches and supported workers' actions.

The organized activity in the Estonian lands in 1905 was spear-headed by the *Russian* Social Democratic Workers Party; its Estonian counterpart was formed only in August, in Tartu. In the Latvian regions, the early initiatives were taken by the Latvian Social Democratic Workers Party (founded in 1904), and the Riga branch of the General Jewish Workers Union (commonly known as "the Bund"), founded in 1897. These groupings remained the most active throughout the year. In the Lithuanian lands, the radical vanguard was more complicated, with differing (and sometimes conflicting) initiatives being taken by the Bund (Vilnius being its birthplace and Lithuania its main venue), the Russian Social Democratic Workers Party, the Polish Socialist Party, and the Lithuanian Social Democratic Party (founded in 1896). The hallmark of the "1905 revolution" in the Baltic littoral was its lack of centralized organization: there was no single leader or even a committee, no headquarters from which orders were issued to cadres, and no overall coordination except in the cases of strikes and work stoppages in certain industrial establishments at specific times. Much of the violence associated with radical activity – both urban and rural – involved local radicals settling local scores or striking out in an unorganized fashion against symbols of tsarist authority, Russian cultural policy, and Baltic German landowners.

The spread of the revolutionary impulse to rural areas gave the 1905 events their particular Baltic coloration, involving some of the rural intelligentsia (most frequently, rural schoolteachers) and in many cases peasants themselves. For Estonian, Latvian, and Lithuanian peasants, the larger political framework – discussions of a national parliament and civil liberties – had created the opportunity to articulate their particular grievances – the maldistribution of land, the continued interference of landowners in local decisions especially concerning rural schools, the low wages of agricultural laborers. The target of these complaints was as much the imperial government as the immediate overlords – the Baltic German estate owners and the German-dominated Lutheran clergy in Estland, Livland, and Kurland; Russian-language schools and Russian local officials in the Lithuanian provinces.

An obvious symbol of continuing Baltic German power in the countryside was the manor house, center of work and authority of the landed estate. Correspondingly, in Estland and northern Livland (the Estonian territory) 120 and 47 manor houses, respectively, were put to the torch; in southern Livland and Kurland (the Latvian territory) the numbers were 183 and 229. One estimate is that about 40 percent of manorial properties in the Baltic provinces were destroyed or seriously damaged in the course of 1905. In the Lithuanian provinces, the main target consisted of Russian-language rural schools (a hated presence for some forty years now), Russian local administrators, and symbols of Russian authority in general. For a while peasants ceased paying taxes and stopped redemption payments owed to the Russian government for the property granted to them by the 1861 serf emancipation. Demands were issued for primary and secondary education in the Lithuanian language and for the hiring of Lithuanian Catholics in the institutions of local government. Russian textbooks were destroyed, there were attacks on Orthodox churches and monasteries and even on small contingents of the Russian army. The region most affected by such violence in the Lithuanian territories was Šuvalkija, where the Russian governor reported in November that the land under his authority was "in complete anarchy."

In different ways and to different degrees, by the last months of 1905 the events in the littoral – at least in the countryside – had taken on a national appearance – Latvians and Estonians against Germans and Russians in the Baltic provinces, Lithuanians against Russians and sometimes Poles in the Lithuanian area. The "national" element in the continuing confrontations was anything but clear-cut, and politicoeconomic motives for direct action on balance remained most prominent everywhere. To the distress of the socialists for whom "class" was always paramount, the "national question" was becoming unavoidable and dragged into the mix its inevitable partner, the language question. While the socialists trafficked in rhetoric expressing solidarity with the "working classes" in Russia and elsewhere, the real battle for many of the littoral activists had to do with primary education in the Estonian, Latvian, and Lithuanian languages, the freedom to have an uncensored literary culture in these languages, and the power sharing with the traditional political elites.

During the course of the year, the autocracy seemed to be giving way: in March, Tsar Nicholas announced his intention to convene a consultative assembly, and in April a manifesto announced the creation of an imperial *Duma*. In May Russian liberal activists created a union of unions which was to bring together all liberal organizations seeking reform. In the littoral, as mentioned, hundreds of meetings of a diverse nature and size took place in urban and rural localities, and, since the St. Petersburg government did not opt for massive repression of them, the idea grew that a new and more permissive age had dawned. The October Manifesto (October 30), in which Nicholas II laid out promises for a national parliament and for removal of restrictions on free speech and a free press, also contributed to this somewhat illusory notion. Periodically, however, the regime revealed that it was still willing to use brute force: on October 16, for example, sixty people were killed and about two hundred wounded when soldiers fired on peaceful demonstrators in Tallinn.

In this somewhat ambiguous atmosphere four major gatherings took place in the littoral: the All-Estonian Congress in Tartu on November 27–29, the Great Assembly of Vilnius on December 4–5, and two Latvian meetings in Riga at the end of November, one of schoolteachers and another ostensibly to advance reform proposals for rural areas (the Rural Delegates Congress). These meetings were the culmination of the popular momentum built up during the earlier part of the year, and they seemed to provide a good platform for announcing to the authorities the specific wishes of the littoral activists.

At the same time, the meetings laid bare the stresses and strains of the "opposition," the weaknesses in its organization, and the differing concerns of the activists of the three littoral regions. Although various resolutions were passed, the meetings showed that among politically active Estonians, Latvians, and Lithuanians, opinions ranged widely on most of the important questions, conceivably creating unbridgeable divides. The Estonian Congress split into two factions at the outset: moderates and radicals; the Great Assembly in Vilnius ultimately passed a compromise resolution that was far more political in nature than the organizers of the assembly and its chair, the patriarchal Jonas Basanavičius, had intended; while in Riga, both the schoolteachers' and rural delegates' meetings were generally guided by Latvian social democrats, who successfully sidetracked objections to their leadership and any extensive debate and presided over the passage of resolutions that they had previously prepared. In all these meetings, the language of business was the regional language – Estonian, Latvian, or Lithuanian – but the disagreements before, during, and after the meetings left open the questions as to what exactly the resolutions passed in them represented – the voice of the people? the agendas of left-leaning activists? – and how they should be prioritized and carried out, and, most importantly, who should be delegated to implement them. One issue was prominent among all the concerns expressed in these meetings: the delegates wanted cultural autonomy in the Baltic littoral based on the geographic distribution of the three principal language communities, and institutions embodying that autonomy. In a sense, the meetings were the concluding phase of the national awakening begun earlier: the three "peasant peoples" – now socially and economic differentiated and having demonstrably enduring print cultures in the three languages – were laying serious ownership claims to the cultural space of the Baltic littoral, and those who were not Estonians, Latvians, and Lithuanians were cast in these scenarios as tenants.

In early December the St. Petersburg government began to react with force to what it described as "revolutionary excesses" in the Baltic littoral and elsewhere. By that it meant just about any challenge to authority, whether national or local, by socialists, moderates, and even people who had simply spoken out in ways the authorities did not like. Martial law was proclaimed, and armed units of the Russian army and local militias (Baltic Germans in the Baltic provinces) began to scour cities and the countryside for "participants" in the 1905 events. These actions lasted well into 1906 and trials of real and alleged perpetrators well into 1907. The net was cast very widely, and it included drumhead trials and immediate executions as well as more prolonged court proceedings. Those targeted included persons who had actually committed acts of violence, those who were suspected of supporting them, and many who had simply begun to talk, publish, and act more openly, especially after the October Manifesto. In Estland, Livland, and Kurland, the local Baltic German militias (*Selbstschutz* [self-protection] squads) took the opportunity to settle scores with the rural people whom they suspected of harboring nationalist sentiments; an estimated three to four hundred farmsteads were burned to the ground.

The final count of people caught up in this long sweep remains imprecise, but one estimate is that in the Estonian areas approximately 300 persons were executed, 600 received some form of corporal punishment, and 500 were sentenced to hard labor. Another estimate for the three Baltic provinces has about 2,500 executed, 700 sentenced to prison or hard labor, 2,600 deported to the interior of Russia, and 1,800 expelled from the Baltic provinces. An estimated 5,000 went into voluntary exile, most of them fleeing westward with about 4,000 ending up in North America. The numbers in these categories were somewhat smaller in the Lithuanian area, but even there they numbered in the many hundreds. In the popular memory of the littoral peoples, these bloody "punitive expeditions" remained a more vivid element much longer than did all the meetings and resolutions of the entire year. In the Lithuanian areas such crackdowns had been seen after 1831 and especially after 1863, but in Estland, Livland, and Kurland, their severity was unprecedented; there had been localized incidents of violence before but these had flared up quickly and had been promptly dealt with.

To many the systematic reaction of the central and provincial authorities laid to rest the notion that change could be brought about slowly and peacefully. To the most extreme of the 1905 activists, the violent end to what in the final analysis was an unsuccessful "revolution" simply confirmed what they had believed already: namely, that the upper orders would not surrender any of their power unless forced to do so. The thinking of more moderate activists was perhaps more transformed than that of the "revolutionaries," because the idea of some kind of regional autonomy for the Baltic littoral, broached repeatedly during the discussions and meetings of 1905, remained alive among them during the subsequent decade, even if it could not be discussed openly and publicly. The years 1906 and 1907 – the immediate post-revolutionary period – witnessed something like a revival of press censorship in the littoral, as specific periodicals were closed down, sometimes even for a single unacceptable article, and editors and journalists imprisoned. Two persons who went into exile because of their suspect journalistic activities were Konstantin Päts and Kārlis Ulmanis. Päts, a future president of Estonia, fled to Finland in 1906 and then went to Switzerland; Ulmanis, a future president of Latvia, fled in

1907 to the United States and did not return to the littoral until 1913. Both were reform-minded rather than fire-breathing, but both had good reasons to fear for their freedom, and, in Päts case, for his life since he had been sentenced to death in 1906 in absentia.

The violent reactions of which the imperial and provincial authorities showed themselves to be capable in 1906–1907 diminished over the next several years, as the St. Petersburg government found that it could not return to the *status quo ante*. A *Duma* (national legislature) had been promised and expanded freedoms of various kinds – including of speech and of the press – and these promises now had to be kept. From 1906 to 1917, altogether four *Dumas* were elected with a handful of representatives from the littoral in each. Starting in the immediate post-1905 years and in spite of the renewed militancy of provincial authorities, there was a veritable explosion of press activism in the littoral territories, as newspapers and periodicals were founded, only to be closed down by the authorities or because of lack of readership, and then to be reopened under different names but with the same editors and correspondents. They spanned the spectrum of opinion from monarchism to liberal reform; publications advocating socialism and revolution of any kind had to be (and were) published illegally. There was plenty of evidence to support those who believed that the autocratic system had entered a period of evolutionary reform. But equally convincing was the evidence, pointed to by more radical observers, that nothing had really changed. In fact, the indecisiveness of Tsar Nicholas II and his government continued to send mixed signals during the post-1905 decade on the large questions of the nature of central authority and of governance in the provinces. Although the national *Dumas* provided an opportunity for liberals to air their ideas of reform, the tsar could ignore them. Maldistribution of rural land in the Baltic littoral remained a fact of life, but the tsarist government seemed intent on other kinds of rural reform. The Baltic German elite still controlled most of political life in Estland, Livland, and Kurland; in the Lithuanian areas, the 1905 Great Assembly of Vilnius had not been able to implement its vision of an autonomous Lithuania; change was as much in the air as before 1905, but it remained just as directionless.

One area of the littoral that was less marked by revolutionary excesses (such as the burning of manors) was Latgale (the Latvian district of Vitebsk province), though even that region did not remain entirely unaffected. There were some strikes, peasants began to cut wood in forests belonging to private estates, some smaller towns were for a while controlled by "revolutionary committees," martial law was proclaimed in December, and the punitive expeditions were organized and remained active there throughout 1906. Given the ethnic composition of the region, however, the most active revolutionaries in most places in Latgale were Russian socialists and the Jewish Bund, with only an admixture of Latvians. Permanent structural change was not brought about in Latgale any more than elsewhere in the littoral, and the region retained its general characteristics even after the revolutionary year. Nonetheless, the Latgalian-speaking Latvian population of the region began to show signs of experiencing what later historians of the region described as its "national awakening." The ban on publications using the Latin alphabet was lifted in 1904 (it had affected Latgale as well as the Lithuanian areas), and from that year onward a remarkable generation of activists (Francis Trasuns [1864–1926], Pēteris Smelteris [1868–1952], Francis Kemps [1876–1952]) began to write extensively about who Latgalians were and what Latgale was, arguing that Latgalian-speakers and the districts in which they lived had historically been a part of the Latvian cultural zone and should be so considered now and in the future. This national awakening had several characteristics that distinguished it from what had taken place in Livland and Kurland in the 1850–1880 period. Most of the small but active Latgalian intelligentsia lived and worked in St. Petersburg rather than in Latgale itself; many of the main intellectual activists were Catholic churchmen or were associated with the Catholic Church; the foreign cultural and linguistic influences they sought to diminish were primarily Polish; and the suspicions they had to overcome regarding the soundness of their arguments frequently came from the now well-established Latvian intelligentsia in Kurland and Livland, who were often referred to in Latgalian writings as "the Balts." The western Latvians, having accepted as their literary language the so-called middle dialect of the Latvian language (used in Kurland, Semigallia, and the western parts of Livland), were suspicious of claims of "national" membership by writers who unapologetically used the *augšzemnieku dialekts* (Latgalian dialect) in their

publications. Attitudes toward the Latgalian case remained ambiguous. Western Latvians voiced no principled opposition to the
Latgalian position; in fact, during the decades after 1860, numerous
articles appeared in western Latvian periodicals making the same
argument – that Latgalians were Latvians and should be considered
part of the Latvian *tauta*. Still, another viewpoint found some
resonance: Latgale was "backward" and "different" because serf
emancipation there had come some forty years after serfs were
freed in Kurland and Livland; the Latgalian peasants tended to live
in hamlets rather than in isolated farmsteads; the peasantry did not
have a well-entrenched stratum of relatively wealthy landholders,
which was now the case among western Latvians; Latgale generally
was ethnically too diverse, having not only a large population of
Jews, but Russians, Belorussians, and Lithuanians (non-Latvian
populations comprising an estimated 45–48 percent); Roman
Catholicism and Russian Orthodoxy were the dominant religious
faiths (some 80 percent of the population in both). Counterarguments meant to overcome such suspicions and stereotypes were part
of the Latgalian national awakening from the beginning and continued after the founding of the Latvian state in 1918 (which did include
Latgale as a constituent part).

CLEAVAGES AND COMMONALITIES AFTER 1905

The events of 1905–1906 in the Baltic littoral were perceived by its
inhabitants as a watershed, but the following decade revealed that
the meaning of these portentous years for the future remained
cloudy. On the one hand, the punishment meted out by tsarist
officials and, in the Baltic provinces, the Baltic German elite, against
suspected revolutionaries, sympathizers, and sometimes bystanders
had shocked many and quickly became a permanent fixture of the
political memory of Estonians, Latvians, and Lithuanians. For the
younger generation it was a formative memory; for the older, more
evidence about how the tsarist government and the provincial political leaders were not to be trusted. Yet such deepened distrust did not
prevent the vast majority of the littoral population from continuing
to live as subjects of the tsar and to plan their futures along established pre-1905 lines. Farmers planted crops in the expectation that

there would be a market for them; entrepreneurs started new businesses counting on local and regional sales as well as the continued growth of both a Russian and European market. Students matriculated at universities – Jurjew (Tartu), the Riga Polytechnic, St. Petersburg, Moscow – anticipating degrees at the end of their studies and improved job prospects thereafter. Marital and childbearing rates remained steady, which meant that at the level of individual decisions about the founding of families, the bloody events of 1905 did not play much of a role. Although russification of the borderlands remained official policy, the momentum of cultural expansion among Estonians, Latvians, and Lithuanians continued to be strong and marginalized the threat of cultural extinction; those who received elementary and secondary education in the post-1905 decade would later view the need to learn and use Russian as a nuisance at worst or as a necessary step for personal advancement at best. The notion that learning the language of state required suppression of one's non-Russian national identity had receded substantially.

In the Estonian lands – Estland and northern Livland – relationships between Estonians and the Baltic German elite were more than ever marked by distrust and suspicion: the Baltic Germans looked at imperial Germany for moral support, actively recruited settlers from there to their estates, and viewed all Estonians as potential revolutionaries; Estonian political activity, with the radicals silenced, was dominated by Jaan Tõnnison (1868–?1941) and his Estonian Progressive People's Party (founded in November 1905), which talked about the future of the Estonian lands freed from Baltic German dominance by non-revolutionary means. Radicalism – the overthrow of all current sociopolitical arrangements – continued to have a surreptitious presence but lacked a significant following. The quite public debates about the future showed that fear of an imperial backlash had subsided, even though arrests could still come at a moment's notice. In the debates another position emerged – that of the Young Estonia (Noor-Eesti) movement, led by Gustav Suits (1883–1956). Although it sought a middle ground between nationalism and Marxism, for the time being its proponents focused mostly on cultural matters. All discernible political positions in the post-1905 decade retained the call for cultural autonomy, but since no position had the slightest opportunity of being transformed into reality, all such political debates had an academic quality about them in spite of the gravity of the issues being debated, the profound disagreements they represented, and the threats to personal freedom they carried with them.

Social and economic development proceeded apace along pre-1905 lines. The Estonian peasantry continued its search for land, and by 1913, was using about 75 percent of the arable land in Estland and northern Livland (a much higher proportion than in the Latvian sections of Livland, Kurland, and Latgale). Output and productivity improved, and mechanization and agricultural education expanded. A new form of agricultural association – cooperatives – gained in favor: the Estonian lands had 153 milk cooperatives, 138 consumer cooperatives, and 153 machinery cooperatives by 1914. Credit associations also grew in number: by 1914, there were 129 Estonian credit unions, about 60 percent of them in rural areas. Industrial expansion had not been hampered by the events of 1905–1906, and the number of industrial workers in Estonia (including Narva) had nearly doubled between 1900 and 1914 (from 24,000 to 46,000): Tallinn became the leading industrial center, with Narva in second place. The class composition of the Estonian lands also continued to change. While Baltic Germans and some Russian officials retained their standing as the dominant social order, just below them Estonians were rapidly climbing the social ladder, as measured by property ownership, especially in Tallinn. At the beginning of the Estonian national awakening period (1871) Estonians had owned only 18.3 percent of the real estate in the city, but possessed 68.8 percent by 1912. The expansion of the economic base for urban Estonians was accompanied by growth in their numbers: by 1913, Estonians comprised 69.2 percent of the major nationalities of all Estonian cities, with Russians (11.9 percent) and Germans (11.2 percent) having been left far behind. While Estonian thinking about the future of their nation could make few realistic claims about "ownership" of political space and relatively weak claims about economic space, it could with some justice articulate such claims not only of urban space, but without any question of the cultural space of the territories in which most Estonians lived.

However uncertain the political future, undoubtedly it would have to be anchored in a culturally confident Estonian population:

germanization and russification efforts had had no appreciable results, and the earlier predictions of some of the Baltic German *Gelehrten* that a "peasant people" could not create and sustain active cultural life based on its own language now seemed almost laughable. The activists of the Young Estonian movement – most of them in their twenties – were perhaps even more culturally self-confident than their pre-1905 predecessors, and such confidence was visible throughout the entire population. Intellectuals of a literary bent eagerly sought western European, Scandinavian, and even Russian models of modernity, with no fear that the Estonian language – which was perhaps the most difficult of the littoral languages to adapt to Indo-European literary expressions – could not sustain the effort. The Estonian language itself became standardized through the efforts of linguists, and the first dictionaries of correct usage appeared. Professional literary journals were founded, local cultural organizations were rejuvenated, and the printed word in Estonian reached a peak in 1913 when 702 books and brochures were published in the language – more than twice as many as in 1900 (312). The number of Estonian children in secondary schools doubled, and the number of students attending Tartu University quadrupled. For most of the poets, novelists, and essayists who began to publish in the post-1905 decade these years were just the beginning of longer literary careers that in some cases would extend into the second half of the twentieth century.

Continued cleavages and common efforts also characterized the story of the Latvian sections of the littoral in the post-1905 decade, and there were many similarities with the Estonian situation. As in Estland and northern Livland, relationships between Latvians and Baltic Germans remained strained; the effort by Baltic German landowners to populate their estates with German settlers from imperial Germany (about 20,000 in all) was widely commented on and interpreted negatively in the Latvian press, especially because the problem of landlessness among Latvian peasants was far from being resolved. As in the Estonian lands, the Baltic German press continued to view Latvians as ungrateful revolutionaries; Latvians reciprocated by repeatedly casting German speakers in the role of past and present "colonizers" who were now seeking to reassert "ownership" of the Baltic provinces. Among the post-1905 Latvian intelligentsia, with a few exceptions, the earlier illusion (of the late awakening period) that Russian officialdom could be useful in countering German hegemony had disappeared; St. Petersburg had revealed its preference for order over regional rearrangements; and the expectation that the imperial *Dumas* (each of which had a few Latvian deputies) could lead to regional reform was not yielding any results.

The most politically active of the 1905 participants – the socialists – were splintered, a large number having emigrated (many, as it turned out, permanently), and the Latvian Social Democratic Workers Party (founded in 1905) had to lead a shadowy and mostly illegal existence. Most of the other politically active persons who were not socialistically inclined – the so-called bourgeois politicians – now correctly interpreted politics as potentially dangerous and invested their time in other organizational activities. Except for the shared view that Latvians should have some sort of cultural autonomy within the empire, socialist and bourgeois commentators expressed radically different visions of the Latvian future in their publications. Given the contrasting language of these two discourses – Marxist and quasi-Marxist categories on the one hand and liberal constitutionalism on the other – a likely middle ground was not immediately apparent. Latvian political opinion was complicated by the existence of an outspoken and articulate defender of the Russian monarchy – the publisher Friedrichs Veinbergs (1844–1924) and his daily *Rīgas Avīze* (Riga News); Veinbergs was not only a deadly enemy of the socialist movement who had welcomed the post-1905 punitive expeditions, but in the following decade he continued to voice the opinion that the Latvians' most important task was to gain and maintain the confidence of the St. Petersburg government. All the different political viewpoints welcomed and celebrated the continued growth of factory industry and the continuing emergence of Riga (population in 1913: 517,000) as one of the leading cities of the empire. Yet how the relatively low wages and inadequate housing of the rapidly increasing industrial labor force should be dealt with served as another source of major division.

This fragmented public opinion, however, had a common starting point: it was expressed in the Latvian language. In the 1905–1907 period there were already 107 periodicals in Latvian (some short lived), 63 of which were daily or weekly newspapers; by 1910, 45 publishing firms in Riga catered to a Latvian-language reading public and 79 in the Latvian-language territories of the Baltic provinces. The Latvian written word had achieved a permanent presence in the littoral, and against this background, questions about cultural extinction – germanization, russification – appeared to have become irrelevant. Widely read authors were laying the groundwork for Latvian twentieth-century literature with canonical work: the poet and playwright Jānis Pliekšāns (pseud. Rainis) (1865–1929), his wife the poet and playwright Elza Rosenberga (pseud. Aspāzija) (1865–1943), the playwright and short-story master Rūdolfs Blaumanis (1863–1908), and the poet Jānis Poruks (1871–1911). Organizational momentum beyond politics, evidencing considerable common effort, was also succeeding; speaking only of agriculture, the Latvian-run Central Agricultural Society, founded in Riga in 1906, opened 106 local chapters over the next decade; and *Konsums* – the largest union of cooperative organizations – had 74 local societies as constituent members. By 1914, the Latvian territories had 860 different agricultural societies with an estimated 60,000 members; these societies were fully legitimate and registered with the government. Their quest for legalization was normally cast in practical terms – the further modernization of agriculture, in this instance – and such goals were perfectly acceptable and even desirable in the eyes of the Russian government. It must have occurred to some Russian administrators, however, that these organizational efforts were a kind of political school for Latvians; but if officials recognized the political implications, they did not react. The centuries-old estrangement between the Latvians in Latgale and the so-called Baltic Latvians continued; neither subpopulation was antagonistic toward the other, but there was little common consciousness.

Many features that characterized the Estonian and Latvian regions of the littoral in the post-1905 decade were also present in the Lithuanian lands: strong anti-Russian sentiment; socialists of various kinds as the most dynamic political force (in the form of the Lithuanian Social Democratic Party, which operated only half-legally); extended internal disputes about the future that encapsulated seemingly irreconcilable scenarios; participation in but growing disillusionment with the imperial *Dumas*; continuing growth of factory industry (starting from a lower base than in the Baltic provinces); the emergence of an effective cooperative movement in the countryside; a sharp increase of writings in Lithuanian after the press ban was lifted in 1904; a flowering of Lithuanian literary culture (some 3,200 titles published between 1905 and 1914); and an oft-repeated desire for Lithuanian cultural autonomy. But the similarities paralleled substantial differences. Perhaps the most significant was the continual skirmishing in the Lithuanian provinces between those who envisaged a future Lithuania without any Polish influence and those who insisted that some form of Polishness was inescapably a part of the Lithuanian national ethos. The latter thinking, of course, was anchored in the historic existence of the Polish-Lithuanian Commonwealth. In these discussions, the distant and more recent past collided.

Population statistics concerning the Lithuanian provinces are extremely imprecise, both in the 1897 imperial census and for the decades thereafter, primarily because enumerators had no clear rules to follow about who was Lithuanian or Polish; the coexistence of these two language communities in the Lithuanian provinces and the differing extent to which each used Polish and Lithuanian for various purposes provided few clues to enumerators about the category of nationality. One estimate is that in the post-1905 decades the total population of the lands that had an ethnic Lithuanian component was about 4.2 million. Possibly half were Lithuanian by some definition, while the rest consisted of Polish, Jewish, Belorussian, and people of other nationalities; of these conceivably about 400,000 were Polish by some definition, living in landed estates and cities. But it was not absolute numbers of Polish speakers that mattered as much as the historic influence of Polish language and culture on the region, and it was precisely this that became the bone of contention.

One extreme position in the debate was occupied by those who insisted that present and future Lithuanian institutions, including the Catholic Church, use the Lithuanian language primarily if not exclusively – that they be recognizable internally and externally as Lithuanian. This viewpoint was of relatively recent vintage, born of the Lithuanian national awakening during the last decades of the nineteenth century. At the other extreme, many Polish political activists argued that "Lithuania" was merely a province of the old commonwealth, and that Poland's size, its well-established

European reputation as a "culture nation," and the centuries-long polonization of Lithuanian upper social orders could have only one viable outcome: the complete polonization of the Lithuanian population and the inclusion of the Lithuanian lands in some kind of reborn Poland. Between these extremes lay a host of personal identities that individuals had worked out while living in a multiethnic environment: people who spoke only Polish but insisted they were Lithuanians; people who envisaged themselves as Polish speakers living comfortably in some kind of autonomous Lithuanian entity; people who envisaged a multicultural autonomous Lithuania that would encompass all the different nationality groups of the old duchy; and people who were affronted by the claim that they could be identified with only one nationality. In these matters, the Russian government and its provincial representatives were of no help; for them, the maintenance of good order was paramount, and, as much as possible, the expansion of the Russian language and influence. By the end of the post-1905 decade, however, both of these Russophile aspirations were clearly in retreat in the Lithuanian lands.

Two other cleavages were of major significance in the Lithuanian lands: that which distinguished the Jewish population in the Lithuanian provinces from all others, and that which separated the Lithuanians in Russia and East Prussia and those living in North America. The number of Jews in the Lithuanian provinces in 1913 is estimated to have been around 560,000, the figure having increased steadily during the nineteenth century; the Lithuanian lands had been the northern part of the pale of settlement for over a century now. In the Lithuanian region, Jews dwelt in cities and small towns for the most part; the informal capital of Lithuanian Jewish culture was Vilnius where about 40 percent of the population were Jews. Because of the influential cultural leaders living there – such as Elijah Ben Solomon, the Gaon of Vilnius – the city had acquired the reputation of being "the Jerusalem of the North." As elsewhere, Jews quickly learned enough Lithuanian to carry on their professions and trades; culturally, however, to the extent that they oriented themselves toward any other population than their own intensely religious and thus book- and learning-based culture, it was to the Russian and Polish speakers. Secularist themes emerged at the end of the nineteenth century – Zionism and the formation of the socialist

Bund – the latter cooperating with other socialistically inclined political Polish and Lithuanian (and Latvian) organizations for the common goal of ending the tsarist autocracy.

The other cleavage of significance was that between Lithuanians in the Lithuanian provinces of Russia and those living in North America, primarily in the United States. Thousands had left Lithuania each year between 1869 and 1898; their aggregate numbers by 1914 had reached about 250,000 (the 1930 US census listed 439,000 Lithuanians, less than half of whom were foreign-born). These numbers far exceeded the North American communities of Latvians and Estonians (no more than 5,000 in either case by 1914). In 1913, Jonas Basanavičius and Martynas Yčas – the former a prominent senior nationalist activist, the latter younger but equally active and an elected member of the fourth imperial *Duma* – toured eight-four Lithuanian colonies in North America to raise money for a cultural center – a "National House" – in Vilnius, and did indeed raise the equivalent of about 43,000 rubles. But they also found that the North American colonies were riven by conflict – principally socialistically oriented Lithuanians versus those whose maintenance of Lithuanianness in the new land centered on the Catholic Church. Even though the North American Lithuanians were no longer threatened by polonization or russification, they were becoming "americanized." Basanavičius in his speeches to the Lithuanian Americans stressed the need for them to contribute money to support the growth of Lithuanian culture in the homeland; even more, he hoped that many of them would return with new knowledge and accumulated wealth. There was, however, little return migration from among the American Lithuanians, and their role in the future of "the Lithuanian nation" remained in doubt.

THE GREAT WAR IN THE LITTORAL

It is impossible to say how the history of the Baltic littoral might have unfolded after August 1914, if the regional dispute between Austria-Hungary and Serbia over Bosnia had not erupted and quickly expanded into a state of war among Europe's major powers. The drawn-out conflict initially called the "Great War," and much later "World War I," had started; the prewar alliance system that was

Map 7 The littoral before the "Great War" (World War I). The seemingly frozen provincial boundaries in the littoral belied major changes in the consciousness of nationality among the indigenous populations.

supposed to prevent or contain warfare between European states had had the opposite effect. Austria-Hungary declared war on Serbia on July 28, Germany on Russia on August 1, and Austria-Hungary on Russia on August 6. By July 31, the Russian Empire had begun to mobilize its army. Thousands of young men from the littoral (an estimated 120,000–140,000 Latvians and about 100,000 Estonians) were conscripted to serve the tsar. They entered the army largely because they felt it was their duty to do so even though their feelings in many cases were conflicted. For Estonians and Latvians, the fight was against foes – the German Empire and Austria-Hungary – to which it was easy to transfer the enmity they felt toward the local representatives of the German-speaking cultural world, the Baltic Germans; however, the Baltic German leadership also announced its support for Russia. Feelings of divided loyalty were present but remained latent; russification policies, though weakened, were still in force, and the resentment they had created had to be balanced by the possibility that the littoral peoples might be able to establish culturally autonomous territories within a democratized empire; the entities of which they were a part and which might be changing were therefore worth defending. Lithuanian participation was naturally more complicated. Some 60,000 men had been quickly drafted into the Russian army, but insofar as neither Poles nor Lithuanians within the Russian Empire felt any particular liking for the German Empire they entered the conflict against it willingly enough. Moreover, Lithuanian political leaders had issued a demand that in return for participation the Lithuanians wanted unification of their homeland; the demand was met with silence, but the hope was that St. Petersburg would eventually listen to the aspirations of residents of a borderland that had quickly become the site of important fighting. Anticipation of a quick victory probably made the decision easier throughout the littoral; the propaganda the Russian government had begun to disseminate portrayed an invincible army, and the press in St. Petersburg and Moscow praised the population of the Baltic littoral for their "patriotism." In the littoral, seemingly the only uncompromising opponents of the war were the socialists, but their efforts to provoke labor unrest of various kinds met with little success; the governor of Livland even praised the factory labor force for its "admirable expression of loyalty toward the tsar and toward the homeland." Also, wartime censorship of newspapers meant that those who expressed enthusiastic support for the war effort were given almost free rein, while those who took a standoffish attitude or showed any signs of opposition were censored heavily. Though on the eastern front the Russian army experienced some initial successes, there were also numerous inglorious defeats and failures; by summer 1915, the German forces driving east and north had occupied not only all of the territory of the old Polish-Lithuanian Commonwealth but also the entire province of Kurland. The Daugava River – the boundary between Kurland to the south, and Livland and Latgale to the north – became the front and retained that status for most of the war. Thus from 1915 to 1917, the Baltic littoral was cut in half, with the Russian army holding the territory north of the Daugava while the German military and civilian occupation forces established an integrated system of wartime governance – the so-called *Oberost* – over the territories south of the river, including the Latvian-populated Kurland and the Lithuanian lands. The Estonian areas of Estland and northern Livland, the Latvian area of Livland, and Latgale remained under Russian control. This new partition of the littoral – albeit temporary – permitted only the Estonian political leaders to continue thinking realistically about integration; the new boundaries placed Latvians on two sides of a front between warring great powers and Lithuanians entirely under the control of one of them – the military and civilian authorities of imperial Germany. By anyone's reckoning, Latvian and Lithuanian hopes for integration and autonomy had faded for the foreseeable future.

The immediate goal of the German Reich was to defeat the Russian enemy in the field, of course, but general long-term planning, somewhat vague at that moment, also called for the eventual colonization of the littoral with German farmers after the non-German residents were expelled to the interior of Russia. In view of that, the German occupation forces in the littoral were determined to exploit to the maximum the territories they now controlled, sequestering housing and horses, imposing levies of grain and other supplies, creating wartime taxes, and appointing current landowners of high rank to the occupation government. By summer 1915, however, the resource base the Germans had counted on had diminished considerably.

Anticipating occupation, the Russian government during the first half of the year had issued orders that the industrial infrastructure of the threatened territories (including Riga) be dismantled and transported to the interior of Russia, and that the local rural population be evacuated from the affected regions. Some 500 industrial establishments (about 160 from the Lithuanian region) were in fact disassembled and taken eastward; more importantly, an estimated 700,000 refugees (no precise statistics were kept) left the German-occupied territories. Some crossed the Daugava River and sought temporary residence in Livonia, Latgale, and Estonia, others fled directly to the Russian interior. The overall number included about 300,000 Lithuanians, for most of whom salvation lay in fleeing directly eastward. The rest of the refugees came from the Latvian areas, mostly Kurland; there was some flight even from areas of Livland that for the moment were considered safe. Evacuation of the population of Estland was considered and rejected by the authorities; most Estonians stayed put. In the long history of the region, the littoral peoples had experienced the need to flee before, but never in such large numbers. Hundreds of farms were emptied of their residents; city and town populations were severely reduced in a matter of weeks; livestock was slaughtered or left behind; families were separated, and return was uncertain. The Lithuanian lands and Kurland were by no means depopulated, but the plight of the farming population who did not flee became even more onerous; the refugees were not quickly replaced by anyone, their fields lay fallow and could not contribute to the supplies demanded by the German occupiers, and those who stayed had to make up the difference. A new grid had been imposed on the wartime experiences of the littoral populations: some were still free in the territories not occupied by the Germans; some, in the occupied territories, were subject to German military and civilian rule; thousands were refugees now dislocated from their homes; and thousands more were still serving in the Russian army.

By the end of summer 1915, the "refugee problem" had brought about an organizational response both from the government (mostly in the form of money) and from the Latvians and Estonians in the unaffected territories in the form of refugee committees in the unoccupied parts of the littoral and in St. Petersburg and Moscow; similar committees were created by Lithuanians in the Russian interior.

At the end of August 1915, a congress of 128 representatives of Latvian refugee committees met in St. Petersburg (by this time Petrograd) and formed an umbrella organization: a Central Committee for Latvian Refugees, with its leadership consisting of Latvians with political experience in the imperial *Duma*, began quickly to implement assistance programs to help refugees with housing, food, work, and information. In due course, the committee spoke for 260 Latvian refugee organizations in the littoral and the Russian interior; a newspaper, *Dzimtenes Atbalss* (Echo of the Homeland), was established for communications between these far-flung self-help groups in such places as Petrograd, Moscow, Kostroma, Nizhni-Novgorod, Samara, Saratov, Kharkov, Kiev, Omsk, Krasnoyarsk, and Novosibirsk. By the end of 1916, some ten thousand children were attending refugee schools, and, significantly, were receiving their primary schooling in the Latvian language. Ironically, the networking required by the "refugee problem" and the efforts needed to maintain a steady flow of resources to local committees provided for Latvians an invaluable organizational experience of subordinating ideological and personal concerns to work for a common goal. The refugees required ingenuity, cooperation, organization, and countless hours of strategic planning – all this within the greater context of a large empire that by 1916 was starting to show signs of its inability to sustain a prolonged military involvement and which had little time to spare for the day-to-day problems of its scattered borderland populations.

By mid-1915, the militarization of life in the littoral and the apparent stagnation of the front on the Daugava River led some prominent Latvians to recommend to the Russian high command that the army form several "national" units recruited from the surrounding areas. Such soldiers, the argument went, would be better motivated insofar as they would be defending home territory; scattering conscripted Latvians throughout units far away from their homeland reduced their effectiveness. The Russian government had resisted such ideas all along, believing that national army units would encourage separatist tendencies, but finally in early August 1915, the order came that two units of Latvian riflemen (Russ. *streltsi*; Latv. *strēlnieki*) should be created. A recruitment committee was formed that included several former Latvian members of the

Duma and other political activists; the recruitment call published in Latvian newspapers mixed phrases about "defending the Russian double eagle" with "defending the Latvian homeland under Latvian flags." In short order, about 8,000 volunteers (ages seventeen to twenty-five) were ready to be trained; Latvian soldiers already in other army units stationed elsewhere asked to be transferred to these "national" units. Some 1,246 entered action right away, and their numbers were replenished and enlarged from reserves as the war continued. The Latvian units remained intact as they were merged with larger formations of non-Latvians along the Daugava front as part of the Russian Twelfth Army. From the outset, the Latvians exhibited a discipline and verve that could only come from service under officers who spoke the soldiers' language, from wearing special insignia, and from having distinctive flags for their units. About nine-tenths of the original two battalions – as they came to be called – were Latvian; the other tenth consisted of Estonians, Russians, Lithuanians, and Poles who had been residing in Livland and understood Latvian. Only about 3.5 percent were illiterate, a remarkably low proportion for elements of the Russian army.

Though the Russian high command found these Latvian battalions highly dependable and good fighters, suspicions about them remained alive, especially among highly placed Baltic Germans in the Russian military; to them, armed Latvians brought echoes of 1905. Repeated requests to break up these national units failed. The critics and doubters were not altogether wrong; the Latvian wartime press and the Latvian population at large soon portrayed the two battalions as "our boys" defending "our homeland." Poems were written about them, artists produced paintings about their heroic deeds; they were accorded a kind of fictive autonomy that did not exist, since their placement and movements remained entirely in the hands of the Russian high command. In the Estonian part of the littoral, efforts to create national units came to naught: the Estonian activists themselves were divided on the issue, and the Estonian districts were already saturated with the Russian army – some 100,000 men – because of plans to fortify the seacoast. Therefore no special measures for additional defense were needed. The question of national military units in the Lithuanian lands was mooted by the German occupation, and the Lithuanians who had entered the Russian army in 1914 remained scattered along different parts of the eastern front.

In contrast, the Latvian rifle units continued to expand, and during the course of 1916, the number of units had increased to eight and the number of soldiers in them to about 40,000 (25,000 in the active army and 15,000 in the reserves). By 1916, the command had also begun to use some of the Latvian units where needed outside the littoral. Regardless of where they were stationed, however, the Latvian units (or regiments, as they were designated by 1916) remained something of an anomaly in the Russian army. Their officers – mostly Latvians – communicated with their superiors in Russian, but within each regiment the language of everyday business remained Latvian (though most of the ordinary soldiers could also speak Russian). Younger officers came from the Latvian intelligentsia, and for the sake of morale they worked hard to create in each regiment a kind of Latvian-language subculture consisting of regimental newspapers in Latvian, lectures of various kinds, and theatre performances. Relationships between officers and enlisted men did not involve the kind of deliberate vilification and brutalization of lower ranks that so frequently characterized the Russian army.

The Latvian riflemen continued to fight alongside their Russian comrades at different places on the Daugava front through the rest of 1915 and throughout 1916. Particularly brutal encounters with the German enemy took place in the so-called Christmas battles in 1916 and in January of 1917, when the Twelfth Army experienced 45,000 casualties and the Latvian units had 9,000 (37.5 percent of current forces), including 2,000 killed. These were only the latest encounters in a string of earlier equally disastrous engagements that, in the thinking of the Latvian riflemen, demonstrated Russian leadership at its most inept; the thought also grew that Russian generals were using the Latvian contingents like cannon-fodder. The critics of nationally defined contingents had been right to one extent: resentment and rumor in such units were bound to take on an us versus them mode (Latvians versus Russians). By the end of 1916, considerable discontent had emerged among the Latvian riflemen, and, at this juncture, it could flow only in one direction: toward acceptance of the arguments of left-oriented soldiers, who at the behest of the Latvian Social Democratic Party had formed secret cells in the

Latvian regiments with the task of producing "revolutionary" sentiment. For them, unfocused discontent in the ranks was fertile
ground, and by early 1917 a great many of the Latvian riflemen
had become persuaded they should be fighting not only against the
German enemy but also against the autocratic tsarist regime. The
discontent was articulated not only by those with ideological interests in fomenting revolt but also by many with no political axe to
grind. In March 1917, when Tsar Nicholas abdicated and the
Romanov dynasty exited the political stage, the new provisional
government inherited, along with a riven Russian society, a Baltic
littoral in which political activists and Latvian riflemen were determined to find their way toward better social, political, and cultural
arrangements.

CARPE DIEM

The occupation of Polish and Lithuanian territories by the German
army by summer 1915 had directly affected everyday lives in numerous ways, and it had also introduced among Lithuanians a large dose
of uncertainty about what was to come next. Most of the prewar
discussion had concerned itself, first, with the formation of a
Lithuanian-language cultural zone through elimination of the provincial boundaries that separated Lithuanians from each other; and
second, with the transformation of this zone into a culturally autonomous unit within the Russian Empire. What seemed simple and just
to many Lithuanian activists, however, did not appear so to the
St. Petersburg government, which saw such proposals as just another
form of separatism endemic to this section of the western borderlands. Now, with imperial Germany in control of the territory and
with the Russian military having withdrawn, the time seemed ripe for
increased efforts. Yet the residents of the Lithuanian territories were
themselves divided about their political future: most on the political
left used internationalist language about the solidarity of the "working class" regardless of nationality; the Poles, Belarussians, and
Russians in the Lithuanian territory – especially the Poles – had
their alternative visions, which did not necessarily presuppose a
unified Lithuania; and it was not at all clear that the Lithuanian
residents of East Prussia ("Lithuania Minor," German territory)

would become a part of the new Lithuanian-language zone, whatever its final political shape might be. Besides, an outcome, if it were to arrive soon, would need the assent of the German government, which was not of one mind about the newly occupied territories. It was willing to countenance various Lithuanian proposals and permit some meetings by Lithuanians to discuss such questions; but it took the same approach to the occupied Polish territories and seemed at times to look toward a renewed Polish state without considering the fact that to many Poles such a state would need to include Lithuania. Moreover, highly placed German officials periodically made public plans to colonize the eastern territories, which seemed to preclude any new state arising there. In any event, the war was not over, the Lithuanian lands were still formally part of the Russian Empire, and even by 1916 it was hardly a foregone conclusion that Germany would play a determinative role in the future of the region. All these complicating factors, however, did not appear to many Lithuanian activists as reasons why they should not seize the day and work out an agenda to their own liking. Several meetings, involving both the Lithuanian right and left, took place in spring 1916, the most imme- diate result of which was a public declaration (aimed at the German authorities and the other belligerents in the war) that Lithuanians wanted unification and were also prepared to establish a state. A similar declaration was put forward at another meeting in June 1916 in Switzerland; at that time, Lithuanians also announced the forma- tion of a *Taryba* (national council), consisting of representatives of all Lithuanians, including those in the United States. The desire for political independence was also reasserted.

This sequence of events was interrupted – in a sense – first, by the change of government in Petrograd in March 1917 when Nicholas II abdicated and a Russian provisional government took the reins of power; and, second, when in April the United States entered the war, bringing into the discussion (as far as Lithuanians were concerned) the Wilsonian idea of "self-determination of nations." A series of meetings by Lithuanian political leaders during the rest of 1917 and early 1918 – that is, before and after the Bolshevik coup in Russia in November 1917 – produced impermanent results, largely because of political divisions. Finally, on February 16, 1918, the *Taryba* issued a statement of independence declaring itself the sole representative of the Lithuanian nation and "restoring" an independent Lithuanian state with its capital in Vilnius. Future relations between this new state and other states would be decided by a *Seimas* (parliament) to be elected in the near future. The wording of the declaration made clear that the state that was being "restored" would be a continuation of the Grand Duchy of Lithuania that had disappeared from European maps at the end of the eighteenth century. The Lithuanian nation would once again have a state, but this time with a democratically elected parliament.

Unlike the Lithuanians, who had been dealing with a German occupation government since 1915, Estonian political leaders kept an eye on the turmoil developing in Petrograd, as the ability of the tsarist government to control events waned. By the end of 1916, Estonian political thinking had come to focus on achieving the administrative unification of all Estonians (Estland and northern Livland) and enhancing Estonian control over the institutions of local government. Such aspirations tended to be clothed in the idea of cultural and political autonomy within a reformed Russia. Although implicit in the discussions on the Estonian side, the idea of outright political independence for tactical reasons remained unarticulated. Besides, Estonian political activists were factionalized, and it is doubtful that a general agreement could have been reached on what an independent Estonia would be. The first opportunity to realize the more moderate goals came in March 1917, when Nicholas II abdicated and the provisional government assumed control. The new government's main task was the continuation of Russia's involvement in the war; secondary tasks involved coping with the stresses and strains the war had produced in the Russian economy and society. Using the moment, the Estonian political activists, including the moderate Jaan Tõnnison, lobbied the provisional government to allow changes in the northern Baltic littoral, organized a large demonstration in Petrograd on behalf of Estonian requests, and achieved their goal on March 30, when the new government assented to reorganize the boundaries of the Estonian lands and to eliminate there the Baltic German-dominated political system. When fully implemented, the new arrangements would involve all Estonian speakers living in a political entity called "Estonia" (or something similar), with a provincial assembly elected by all the residents of the new entity and an appointed official – a commissar – the contact person between the central government and the province. In April the Petrograd government appointed the Estonian mayor of Tallinn, Jaan Poška (1866–1920), as the first commissar; elections to the *Maapäev* (provincial assembly) followed in May. Those elected to the sixty-two-member assembly probably reflected accurately the divison of Estonian opinion: the largest blocs were the Agrarian League and the Labor Party, each with eleven seats, and the other seats were divided among Bolsheviks (five), Estonian Social Democrats (nine), Estonian Socialist Revolutionaries (eight), Democrats (seven), Radical Democrats (four), German and Swedish minorities (two each), and non-party representatives (three).

This configuration of party groupings proved to be unstable, because during the following nine months (including the Bolshevik coup in November), continuous friction ensued among and within the left, center, and right parties; municipal elections in late July 1917 showed the political spectrum still fragmented. The general drift of power, however, seemed to be to the left, so that the successful Bolshevik coup in Petrograd brought in its wake an Estonian Bolshevik government in Tallinn as well. The Bolsheviks dismissed Poška, the provisional government's commissar, but in the following months were unable to consolidate their power, in part because of the dearth of loyal Bolshevik officials who could quickly replace those already in office; the latter refused to cooperate, launched strikes, and generally prevented a total remaking of Estonian institutions in line with Bolshevik ideology. Moreover, the Bolsheviks sought to repress all their rivals: they persecuted the non-Bolshevik press, sought to exclude other Estonian parties from power, hesitated about agrarian reform, and refused to discuss the question of political independence. By the end of January 1918, the Estonian Bolsheviks had lost much of their earlier popular support. Understanding this, they canceled the rest of the elections for the Estonian Constituent Assembly. Afterwards, political opinion in Estonia looked increasingly less to the left for solutions and began to talk about other political arrangements, including political independence. All these deliberations came to a halt in February 1918, when the German army, from its southern base in the Lithuanian lands and Kurland, crossed the Daugava, took the city of Riga, proceeded into southern and then northern Livland, and reached Tallinn on February 25. But at this moment of extreme uncertainty about how the future would unfold, with the Bolshevik government fleeing into Soviet Russia and the Germans quickly advancing north, the leadership of the *Maapäev* decided to proclaim Estonian independence on February 24, announcing to the world that Estonia would be an "independent and democratic republic" within its "historic and ethnographic borders." It also announced the existence of a new Estonian provisional government headed by Konstantin Päts. To the German forces, this must have seemed a curious and amusing incident, assuming they knew about it.

The flow of events in the Latvian region of the littoral paralleled those in the Estonian sectors, since both were affected by decisions of the Russian provisional government about the Baltic provinces. During 1916, Latvian political activists had also been looking for opportunities to push their case for regional control, even though, as among Estonians, political opinion was divided on the most basic questions. The divisions tended to fall between conservative, moderate, and leftist camps: conservatives believed that Latvian political activity should operate within the framework of decisions made by the Russian provisional government; moderates, that there should be a continuing push for the unification of all Latvians within a single set of borders and for the creation of institutions of provincial autonomy; and the left (by now divided into Bolsheviks and moderate socialists) tended to downplay all aspirations rooted in the idea of the nation and instead emphasized the "unity of the working masses" across national lines. Such positions were unstable and shifts took place in the minds of individuals and the positions of groups, depending upon circumstances. Formulating clear positions in the Latvian case was perhaps somewhat more difficult than for the Lithuanians or Estonians: about half of the Latvian territories (Kurland) were controlled by the German occupation government, and the other half by the Russian government (northern Livland). In addition, the Latvians considered the three westernmost districts of Vitebsk province – Latgale – part of their "ethnographic region," and perhaps a quarter of the Latvian-language population were refugees, temporarily far from their homes.

Nonetheless, the March 1917 decision by the Russian government to reorganize the Baltic provinces was perceived by most Latvian

political activists as a step forward, as was the appointment of
Andrejs Krastkalns (1868–1939) – a Latvian and a former member
of the imperial *Duma* – as the commissar of Livland. But the unification question had to be shelved for the time being: the provisional
government could not reorganize what it did not fully control
(Kurland), and there was also considerable hesitancy about the
question of Latgale. Redrawing boundaries to produce an Estonia
was one thing, but dismembering Vitebsk province to bring together
all Latvians quite another.

During the summer of 1917, politically active Latvians began to
prepare for the late summer municipal elections in Livland. Clearly,
opinion within the politically active part of the population had begun
to shift leftward, since the Bolsheviks appeared to have a clear program of action: withdrawal from the war, power handed to a host of
locally elected councils (soviets), and land reform. These motifs
appeared even in the thinking of those who had no wish to introduce
any kind of "dictatorship of the proletariat." The activists who
supported some combined form of political liberalization and
national unification, by contrast, were far more divided about what
precisely a future provincial Latvian government should be. Political
organizations formed around the ideas of a national democracy, a
radical national democracy, republicanism, independence, agrarian-
ism; some splinter party formations sought to use minority nationalities (such as Jews and Germans) as their base. At this stage, the
non-left party formation with the largest following was the Latvian
Agrarian Union (founded on May 12). The election results in August
revealed that the social democrats (moderate socialists) had obtained
49 of 120 council seats in Riga, leaving the German list and the more
radical leftists far behind in second place with 19 and 18 seats,
respectively. The so-called middle-class or bourgeois parties were
far behind these three numbers, although they did have representation. In other cities the social democrats were less successful. When
the German army began its northward drive in August 1917, first
taking Riga and then, after a period of quiet, occupying the rest of the
littoral by early March 1918, the political formations among
Latvians were once again thrown into turmoil. By that time, also,
the Bolsheviks had seized power in Petrograd (November 1917) and
seemed to many Latvians, especially large contingents of the Latvian

Rifle regiments, to be the only organized force that could bring about thoroughgoing change. The non-Bolshevik political activists in the Latvian region, however, during the summer of 1918 underwent their own kind of radicalization away from vague notions of cultural autonomy toward the idea of full independence. After a series of congresses meant to build consensus, the major Latvian party groupings (except the Bolsheviks) met in German-occupied Riga on November 18 and proclaimed the founding of a "democratic republic" of Latvia, with a provisional government headed by Kārlis Ulmanis, a leader of the Agrarian Union. Thus by the end of 1918, the three largest nationality groups of the littoral had announced, in inauspicious circumstances, the birth of three new nation-states; the question now was whether they could make these imagined nation-states politically viable.

Isolated from all other events in the littoral and from the larger continental context, the three independence declarations during 1918 seemed to be the final realization of long-held national aspirations among Estonians, Latvians, and Lithuanians. Placed in context, however, they were expressions of hope that further developments would prove beneficial to the national cause. The German army was still ubiquitous in the littoral, and the signing of the Brest-Litovsk Peace Treaty between the Central Powers and Russia in March 1918 did not change that fact. Even though the Bolshevik government in Petrograd appeared to be releasing the western borderlands, Bolshevism was by no means a spent force. Its loyalists continued to harbor the hope that they might yet rejoin a Bolshevized Russia. While the western Allies signed an armistice with the Central Powers in November 1918, it was not at all clear what this meant for the Baltic littoral; the western powers appeared to be willing to allow contingents of the German army to remain in the littoral as a buffer against the western spread of Bolshevism. The political groups proposing Estonian, Latvian, and Lithuanian independence were on their own; their failure would not change the outcome of the war. Moreover, the proponents of independence would have been hard pressed to prove at this juncture that their actions were riding a wave of popular sentiment, that, in others words, the Estonian, Latvian, and Lithuanian populations were unequivocally behind them. At the same time, the independence declarations were not merely the product of the overheated hopes of tiny minorities of political activists; those who joined in the declarations were enacting what they believed were the aspirations – perhaps unarticulated, perhaps latent – of their "constituents." Understanding the "will of the people" correctly during 1918 was difficult if not impossible, and whether the declarers of independence had read it correctly would depend on whether "the people" would rally around the idea as its proponents sought to embody it in institutions of government.

INDEPENDENCE WARS

After the armistice of November 11, 1918 ended hostilities on the western front and a peace conference began in Paris on January 18, 1919, most Europeans could breathe a sigh of relief, but not the peoples of the Baltic littoral. The Hohenzollern dynasty had left the German throne in November, a German republic had been proclaimed, and the western allies agreed that although most German troops would withdraw from the Baltic littoral, some would stay behind to continue fighting against the spread of Bolshevism. Lenin and the Bolshevik regime were not trusted by the western allies, who now included the United States; German plans for colonization of the Baltic appeared to have disappeared along with imperial Germany; and during 1918, emissaries to the west from the embryonic "governments" of the Estonians, Latvians, and Lithuanians had impressed western powers with their seriousness of purpose. But nothing in the Baltic littoral had been resolved with any finality. No ultimate resolution appeared likely in the near future, and no outcomes predicted. The region entered a three-year period that in the national histories of the three Baltic states came to be known as the "wars of independence." The activists who had proclaimed independence began the process of creating institutions to carry out the functions of real states: appropriate elections had to be held, cabinet officials had to be found, ministries had to be created, revenues had to be raised, borders had to be secured, and international recognition had to be sought. Above all, the territories over which the new governments claimed to have jurisdiction had to be protected against those to whom the idea of three independent countries on littoral territory was inimical.

In the Estonian lands, the principal "enemy" was the Estonian Bolsheviks, who had withdrawn to Soviet Russia but now saw a new opportunity in a weak Estonian government and a weakened Germany. With support from the Soviet Russian government, Bolshevik troops (overwhelmingly non-Estonians, chiefly Russians) began an offensive in the second half of November 1918, took the city of Narva by the end of November, and proclaimed there an Estonian workers commune. The Estonian government had to act quickly: by the end of December, it had appointed Colonel Johan Laidoner (1884–1953) as commander-in-chief of the Estonian national army, and by January 1919 it had raised an army of about 4,800 men, mostly Estonians. Assistance came from Great Britain in the form of a fleet of twelve ships, which delivered arms and ammunitions to the Estonian army and prevented a coastal invasion by the Bolshevik forces. Finland, for its part, provided a loan of 20 million Finnish marks to buy weapons and sent some volunteers. The Bolshevik offensive succeeded in occupying about half of Estonian territory, but by early February, the Estonian counteroffensive had managed to drive the Bolshevik forces back into Soviet Russian territory. By that time, the Estonian national army had grown to 74,500 men, and desertions were taking place from the Bolshevik units to the Estonian national forces. Fighting continued on the Estonian eastern front throughout spring and summer 1919, and during these months the Estonian national army was large enough to provide major assistance to the Latvian national army in its battles – going on simultaneously – against Latvian Bolsheviks, independent units of the German army, and some elements of the Russian "White" army. (Soviet Russia was in the throes of a civil war at the same time, with the "Red" army fighting the "Whites.") This assistance was rendered in part because the Estonian government wanted to secure its southern border (with Latvia). Peace talks began between the Estonian and the Soviet forces in September, but even during these negotiations the Bolsheviks launched smaller-scale offensives against Estonian territory. An armistice was agreed early in January 1920, and a peace treaty was signed between the Estonian government and Soviet Russia on February 2. By that time elections had been held in Estonia for a constituent assembly (April 1919), which began to enact significant legislation for Estonia even while the "independence wars" were continuing. What the events of 1919 demonstrated was that a significant minority of Estonians did support the idea of a Soviet Estonia, but that this sentiment did not reach very far into the general population. The constituent assembly election had an 80 percent participation rate among voting-age Estonians, and during 1920 the national government proved its ability to legislate effectively and to defend it borders with the increasing support of the general Estonian population.

The situation in the Latvian lands after November 1918 was complicated first by the continuing German occupation, then also by the Bolshevization of a large number of soldiers in the Latvian Rifle regiments, and finally by the uncertainties surrounding the future of Latgale. The Latvian Bolsheviks were a stronger factor than the Estonian Bolsheviks had been in the northern littoral, and with help from among the Latvian Rifles, they succeeded in setting up a short-lived (December 1918–May 1919) Latvian Soviet Socialist Republic, headed by Pēteris Stučka, in that part of Livland that was not occupied by German forces. The embryonic "national" government of Latvia, headed by Kārlis Ulmanis, fled to the western Latvian port city of Liepāja (Ger. *Libau*) in Kurland, thus in a sense placing itself under the protection of the Germans. Adding to the mix, a counter-government to that of Ulmanis suddenly appeared in the person of the popular novelist and clergyman Andrievs Niedra, who with a small coterie of followers had concluded that Latvian survival depended on close cooperation with the German forces, especially with the Baltic German population. In Latgale, where in spring 1917 a congress of political activists had voted overwhelmingly to join the "western" Latvians in a new state, the Bolshevik cause nonetheless had significant support (as elsewhere in the Latvian lands). Some influential voices (for example, Francis Kemps) called for a separate, autonomous Latgale. The commander of the German contingents, Rüdiger von der Goltz, continued to play an insidious triple game, seeming at times to support the Ulmanis government, then the Niedra government, and then the Baltic German cause. If this were not enough, several contingents of the Russian "White" army joined the fray, led by an adventurer named Pavel Bermont-Avalov who imagined himself to be a Russian count and appeared to have as a goal the restoration of Russia's boundaries of the imperial period. Von der Goltz and Bermont-Avalov were decidedly anti-Bolshevik and therefore potentially helpful to the Latvian "national" government; on the other hand, neither of these political-military leaders had any commitment to the idea of an independent Latvia, and in fact, during the second half of 1919 became as much enemies of the Latvian national cause as the Bolshevik army continued to be.

Given this set of actors, the entire year of 1919 was full of intrigue, alliances of convenience and backstabbing, temporary victories and temporary defeats. During the summer, however, the persistence of the Ulmanis government began to pay off. The brief and relatively bloody tenure of the Stučka Bolshevik government persuaded many Latvians that the Bolsheviks were more concerned with adding Latvian territory to Soviet Russia than with the Latvian cause; the Niedra counter-government proved to be stillborn, having no support whatever in the general population; large contingents of the Latvian Rifles and their officers opted to support the "national" side of the struggle; Latgalian separatism turned out to be of marginal influence; and by October 1919, the Ulmanis government had managed to create a fighting force of about 11,500 soldiers who in fact had very strong support in the general Latvian population. By this time also the western powers, having become convinced of the seriousness of Latvian "national" endeavors, intervened with advice and support on the Latvian side. By the final months of 1919, the German army units had been ordered by the western powers to withdraw from the littoral; the *bermontists* had been defeated decisively; and the only remaining threat to the new state was from the Bolshevik forces in Latgale. To deliver a final blow to the *bermontists*, the Latvian national army received substantial on-the-ground assistance from the Estonian army; to drive the remaining Bolsheviks out of Latgale, Ulmanis negotiated military assistance from Poland and a force of 20,000 Poles under the leadership of Edvard Smigly-Ridz joined the effort. By this time, the Bolshevik government in Petrograd decided not to prolong the effort in the Baltic littoral. Thus, facing a larger force in the field and finding Lenin's support fading, the Latvian Bolsheviks pulled out of Latgale. In the army units that withdrew to the interior of Soviet Russia were thousands of Latvian Riflemen who remained loyal to the Bolshevik cause. The

latter with Bermont-Avalov at its head – invaded Lithuanian territory from the north (from Latvia). Throughout the year the Lithuanian national army demonstrated that it could at least repulse enemy incursions, if not always gain final victory in the field, which encouraged volunteers to join it (along with those conscripted). By August, the struggle against the Bolsheviks was over; they withdrew to Soviet Russia. The Poles, however, chose to refocus their military efforts away from Lithuania and toward Ukraine (bringing about military conflict between Soviet Russia and Poland), thus, for the time being, allowing the Lithuanian government to reestablish its authority fully in Lithuanian territory. This, however, was not the end of the story, because in October 1920, when an armistice between Poland and Soviet Russia had been announced and negotiations had started, a Polish force under the leadership of Lucjan Zeligowski entered the Lithuanian capital, Vilnius, on its way toward Kaunas. Taken by surprise at this violation of the agreement that had ended conflict between the Poles and Lithuanians, the Lithuanian government and army rallied but was able only to stabilize the front south of Kaunas. Polish forces now occupied about a fifth of Lithuania, and for the next three years, negotiations involving the League of Nations continued over the location of the Lithuanian–Polish border. An agreement in February 1923 placed it between Kaunas and Vilnius; thus at the end of the independence wars, Poland continued to control about a fifth of Lithuania's territory, as well as its ancient capital, Vilnius.

The independence wars eventually resulted in the victory of the national armies and the expulsion from the region of all armed forces inimical to the idea of Estonian, Latvian, and Lithuanian statehood. But public attitudes were just as important as military success, and, as pitched battles continued throughout 1919 and into 1920, it was evident that public support for the idea of statehood had taken hold among the general populations. Support for the national efforts was demonstrated in numerous direct and indirect ways in all three cases: increased enlistment in the national armed forces; switching of sides by soldiers from the Bolshevik to the national army; increased public contributions for the national military effort; celebration of national success in poems, paintings, and newspaper articles; engaging of the enemy by the national forces without proper weaponry or clothing; the recurring designation of opponents of the national armies as the "foreign" enemy; and the use in publications of the idea that "our" land and "our" nation were being fought for. Identification with Estonia, Latvia, and Lithuania as national states was diffusing throughout the general populations, at least among those who spoke one of the three languages. These shifts in attitude did not go unnoticed by western powers for whom the future of the Baltic littoral was merged with the worry over the further spread of Bolshevism westward. The formal recognition by the western powers of the three independent Baltic states – arriving disjointedly between 1918 and the 1920s – came after the determination that the new national governments were in fact viable in the long run, and capable of governing three countries as part of a *cordon sanitaire* against Soviet Russia. But the victories of the three national armies did not necessarily mean the pacification of all those who had fought against them. The German army contingents that withdrew from the littoral in 1920 to return to Germany contained many who shortly thereafter entered the fledgling National Socialist German Workers (Nazi) party; the Bolshevik forces contained many littoral soldiers and officers, especially from the Latvian areas, and, after withdrawing from the Baltic area they participated in the consolidation of the Soviet Russian state and formed lively Estonian, Latvian, and Lithuanian subcultures in the USSR without surrendering their dedication to the Bolshevik cause. The only belligerents of the independence wars who would not be heard from again in the region were the White Russian contingents, who after their defeat in the Russian Civil War totally lost their base of further action.

STATE-BUILDING AND PARLIAMENTARISM

The independence wars were being fought at the same time as the new governments of Estonia, Latvia, and Lithuania sought to establish their authority over the territories they had defined as belonging to each country, which was a formidable task by any measure. The Lithuanian government, as mentioned earlier, did not succeed in this; the 1920 Polish seizure of Vilnius and the lands to the south of the city kept them under Polish control for the next two decades, remaining a bone of contention not only in Lithuanian–Polish relations but in the relationships between Lithuania and the other two Baltic states as well.

The Estonian and Latvian governments had greater success, and their boundary questions were settled by the early 1920s. In addition to boundaries, there was the need for international recognition. Emissaries from the three governments had worked assiduously from 1918 onwards to turn *de facto* into *de jure* recognition by the major European powers. That task was also completed when Estonia and Latvia (in 1921) and Lithuania (in 1922) entered the League of Nations as full-fledged members. In the meantime, all three governments were deeply preoccupied with state-building, which at this juncture involved repair and reconstruction as well as gaining acceptance of the governments' authority. The socioeconomic wounds left by six years of warfare on littoral soil, by the German occupation, and by defensive measures on the part of the Russian government were deep. The refugees who had left the littoral numbered in the hundreds of thousands, and it was not at all clear how many of them would return or even if they would return at all. The first population censuses of the new countries in the early 1920s showed that in aggregate figures the population of the Estonian territories had fallen from about 1.08 million before the war to about 1.05 million in 1920; that of the Latvian territories, from 2.5 million to 1.5 million; and that of the Lithuanian lands from about 4.3 million to about 3.3 million (including the Vilnius territory seized by Poland). The largest city in the littoral – Riga – had lost about half its population, falling from about 517,000 just before 1914 to 250,000 when hostilities concluded; other urban areas showed similar though not quite as dramatic patterns. Population losses of this magnitude played havoc in the short run with the human capital needed for the rebuilding effort, as did the early evacuation of industrial infrastructure into Russia during the first years of the Great War. It is only a slight exaggeration to say that the littoral had undergone a kind of deindustrialization between 1914 and 1920. In addition, some six harvests had been disrupted by repeated military requisitioning of horses and grain, by the rapid growth in the number of abandoned farms, and the consequent reduction in the availability of seed. No incidents of mass starvation were recorded, but continuous hunger, rationing, and certainly undernourishment had become routine, less so in rural than in urban areas.

There were also macro-effects: the establishment of new states had destroyed (in the short run at least) the networks that had tied the littoral economies to the larger Russian market. It was not at all predictable whether a Soviet Russia, in which the market was subordinated to political goals, would readily cooperate in rebuilding economic ties quickly. Although small-scale enterprises oriented to local markets had a chance of rebounding, large numbers of prewar entrepreneurs of this kind were gone, perhaps forever. The transportation systems of the littoral also suffered, especially the rolling stock of the railroads, and estimates place the destruction of rural housing at about 10 percent. Photographs of around-the-clock soup kitchens in urban areas, dug-outs and sod huts in rural areas, wartime trenches serving as temporary housing, and returning refugees milling about became as much part of the pictorial legacy of the 1914–1920 period as group photographs of formally dressed men sitting around tables and making national policy.

Activities to create the machinery for governing began during the year of the independence declarations – 1918 – on the premise that the new governments would survive. The provisional governments of the period, having been drawn from the ranks of politically prominent people, for the time being were functioning *in the name* of Estonian, Latvian, and Lithuanian populations but had not been chosen by them; they lacked the legitimacy that could come only from a constitution. As the period of the independence wars showed, substantial disagreement existed in the three populations on basic questions of who should govern and how governing should proceed. Most of the populations of the three embryonic states literally found themselves included within the announced boundaries of three countries without their consent having been asked directly. Of course, many indicators – support for the provisional governments, support of the new national armies, declarations of various kinds – suggested that public backing for the new states existed, but much of it was latent and had to be fixed in the formal documents and institutions of government that then had to be seen as functioning entities. Inevitably, many of the institutions of governance, especially those of local governments, created in the later imperial period remained in place and entered the new countries as a necessary part of a transition; but at the highest levels, a complete transformation was needed. Although this task was handled differently by the three provisional governments, all were forced to act even though the wars of independence had not concluded.

In Estonia, the provisional government called for constituent assembly (*asutav kogu*) elections in April 1919; they were carried out successfully, with a high participation rate of about 80 percent and the participation of a multiplicity of political parties. The provisional government resigned in May, and the new assembly took over the task of governing through a cabinet headed by Prime Minister Otto Strandman of the Labor Party. A temporary constitution was adopted in June; both the elected assembly and the temporary constitution invested the new Estonian government with considerable legitimacy so that the measures it adopted had weight; and the assembly continued to work on a permanent constitution, which was finally adopted on December 20, 1920.

In Latvia, the provisional government remained active after the proclamation of independence on November 18, 1918, but now it drew its legitimacy from the *Tautas Padome* (National Council) that was created when the declaration was made. This body consisted of representatives of the eight largest political parties formed by that time. Other representatives were co-opted from segments of the population (including Latgale) where parties were only starting to form. Initially, the council had 39 members; by the time its work ended with the election of a *Satversmes Sapulce* (Constitutional Convention) in April 1920, the council had 183 members. Great care had been taken to represent all groupings of the Latvian population. The council adopted numerous state-building measures, confident now that its claim to be speaking for the Latvian people had weight. The elections to the Constitutional Convention in April 1920 involved candidates' lists from some twenty-five parties and groupings, but only sixteen of them received representation. The convention began its work in May 1920, having elected Jānis Čakste as its president. Over the next two years it functioned not only as a kind of pre-parliament, continuing the state-building activities begun by the National Council, but also as the drafting body of a Latvian constitution, which, after much debate and smoothing of party disagreements, was finally adopted in June 1922. The activities of the National Council took place against the background of the independence war; the Constitutional Convention, however, began to meet after nearly all the hostilities had been concluded.

The development of government in the Lithuanian lands went through a similar process. The original *Taryba* (state council) was replaced after the declaration of independence in February 1918, by one with a presidium (a chairman and two vice-chairmen) and a cabinet of ministers. This cluster of power-holders functioned on the basis of a temporary constitution, which was amended in 1919 to increase the functioning offices. These documents called for election of a constituent assembly, which took place in April 1920; the assembly elected Alexander Stulginskis as chair, which also made him *ex officio* head of state. In contrast to the analogous institutions in Estonia and Latvia, the Lithuanian Assembly was young – twenty-nine members were under the age of thirty and only eight were over fifty. In its first meetings, the assembly made changes to the second temporary constitution affecting the office of president. It also set about the task of creating a full-fledged constitution for the country; after considerable debate and revision, this document was passed in August 1922. It stood as the basic law of the land until 1928, when it was changed by President Antanas Smetona, who had become Lithuania's authoritarian leader in 1926.

During the three- to four-year-long deliberations that produced the new constitutions in all three countries, it became abundantly clear that these documents and the machinery of governance would have to satisfy an extremely wide spectrum of opinions to have support in the new political elites as well as in the population at large. The drafters, especially on the left side of the political spectrum, were determined not to have a system resembling the old tsarist autocracy. Consequently, in the new systems, the head of state ("president" in Latvia and Lithuania, "state elder" [*riigivanem*], who was also prime minister, in Estonia) was a relatively weak office since the occupants had been chosen by a vote of the parliament (*Riigikogu* in Estonia, *Saeima* in Latvia, *Seimas* in Lithuania). In Estonia the executive and legislative functions were, in a sense, merged. In all three countries, the parliaments – the legislative bodies – were unicameral and their members were elected by popular vote of all citizens, male and female, aged twenty or twenty-one years and older. The democratic thrust of these three systems was maintained in the regulations governing the formation of political parties, regulations which catered to the existing political divisions in the populations. Parties presented slates of candidates to the electorate, and their representation in the parliaments was proportional to the number of votes they received in a general election. The president (or state elder) asked the leader of the party receiving most votes to form a "government" – a cabinet of ministers – which became the executive and remained answerable to the parliament. From the outset, these systems indeed guaranteed representation in the parliaments of most of the important prevalent political viewpoints, but they also made it almost inevitable that workable cabinets would be based on coalitions of parties (normally three to five). The governments or cabinets could be dissolved upon receiving a no-confidence vote in the parliament. Whether a new election or the formation of a new cabinet followed depended upon the circumstances. These legislative systems placed a premium on consensus and compromise among political parties as well as on the presidents' abilities to persuade party leaders to achieve such temporary unity. They were extremely vulnerable in the face of hard-line stances based on party principles or personal or party ambitions. Whether the newly created systems were workable or not became from the early 1920s onward a much-debated question.

    In Lithuania, the system was already beset by difficulties at the time of the parliamentary elections of 1926, creating a rationale for President Antanas Smetona to establish presidential-authoritarian rule; in Estonia, from 1921 to 1931, the *Riigikogu* had eleven cabinets ("governments") each with the average lifespan of about eleven months; in Latvia from 1922 (the first *Saeima* election) to 1934 (when Kārlis Ulmanis established authoritarian rule) there were altogether four regularly scheduled parliamentary elections, and thirteen cabinets. Even so, during the existence of real parliamentarism in the three countries, the task of state-building continued apace, with much of the needed work being done by the "permanent governments" – the ever-growing professional staffs of the ministries as elected officials and appointed ministers came and went.

    Broadly speaking, the new political elites after 1920 in the three countries consisted of those same people who had helped to bring them into being: members of the provisional governments, the constituent assemblies, and national councils. Recruitment of new political leadership occurred of course, but most of the "founding

29 The *Saeima* building, Riga. After its completion (in 1865), this imposing structure was the headquarters of the Livlandic nobility. From 1918 to 1940 it housed the Latvian parliament (*Saeima*), from 1940 the Supreme Soviet of the Latvian SSR, and in 1991 it reverted to its earlier status as Latvia's parliament.

fathers" (few women among them), who had been in the thirty to fifty age group during the 1914–1920 period, remained at the top, circulating between simple parliamentary membership and ministerial posts. Presidents (or in Estonia, the state elders) and cabinet ministers were Estonians, Latvians, and Lithuanians, although occasionally, when special expertise was needed, cabinets included members of the so-called minority nationalities who were represented in the parliaments with their own parties. The new constitutions forbade discrimination on the basis of nationality, but in actual practice, supported by widespread sentiment in the general population, they demonstrated that the three states "belonged" to the majority indigenous peoples. They now occupied the crucial leadership positions to the exclusion of the prewar elites – Baltic Germans, Russians, and Poles. The political system ensured such outcomes because the parties that dominated the parliaments were both ideological and national in composition. In all three countries, there were broad and very fluid categories of parties, some having been formed before independence while others arose at the time of parliamentary elections. Party leadership consisted for the most part of those with higher education and professional training, with the legal profession dominating. For success at the ballot box, however, appeal had to be made to the differing interests of the electorate. Since the vast majority of the population of each country farmed, the agrarian parties were always prominent in the parliaments of Estonia and Latvia, comprising the core of the political right: the Farmers Party in Estonia and the Agrarian Union in Latvia. Their political philosophy was grounded in the notion that farming was the backbone of the state's economy, and that the virtues of the rural population were at the core of national identity. In Lithuania, religion played a much more significant part in party identity than in the other two states, and the Christian Democratic Bloc (which represented farmers as well) was the most significant grouping on the "right."

The core of the left in all three countries were the Social Democrats, who had been active as organized parties the longest. Gathering their electoral supporters with various modified Marxist slogans, they represented, first and foremost, the industrial workers ("the proletariat"), but also sought to appeal to disadvantaged people of all sorts. The political left remained very strong in Estonia but less so in Latvia, because in the Latvian parliaments the Social Democrats for the most part chose to remain "in opposition" (that is, they did not enter cabinets). In Lithuania, social democracy had little time to prove itself, because a well-functioning parliamentary system ended in 1926.

The third category was composed of splinter parties: some of these came and went in a bewildering variety throughout the parliamentary period, but others – largely those representing minority nationalities – tended to be more stable despite the strong tendency to divide. (In the Latvian parliament, for example, three parties represented the relatively small Jewish population.) By definition the splinter parties – as a bloc – had no unifying political orientation; they tended to be pressure groups more than parties and were forever negotiating with the major parties on behalf of their particularistic constituencies. As a bloc, however, they were numerically large enough to prevent the right and the left from forming long-lasting cabinets; in fact, none of the blocs, however defined, took on the character of a permanent fixture in the political arena. Short-lived cabinets, the coming and going of parties and party formations, and the deal-making that was necessary to move legislation forward easily created the impression, when juxtaposed with an idealized version of an efficient democratic system, that "the parliament wasn't working." The impression was magnified by the fact that in all three countries an active and critical press ensured that all eyes were forever on the central government. After all, it had been the active political elite that personally helped to create the countries, and it was they who were now expected by the populations at large to ensure that progress continued.

In the new states, Estonians, Latvians, and Lithuanians now controlled the political system; sentiment was widespread among them that such an outcome was right and proper. These three peoples comprised the majorities in their countries – in Estonia about 87 percent, in Latvia about 72 percent, in Lithuania (excluding the Vilnius district) about 80 percent. The countries bore their names; the independence wars had been fought with the purpose of gaining political control; and the new constitutions prescribed Estonian, Latvian, and Lithuanian as state languages. But the constitutions also reflected the fact that these new states had minorities defined by nationality, whose treatment was of exceptional concern to the League of Nations, which the new states had joined. Such concern was part of the new order of things in Europe after the war and could not be ignored. Political opinion within the titular nationalities, however, was not unanimous about what special protection of minorities might mean. At issue was the question of what rights beyond those of citizenship the minority nationalities should have, and the question was made more complex by the fact that some of these minorities bore the stigma of having been the prewar political, social, economic, and cultural hegemons.

Also, the proportions of the minority nationalities differed in the three countries. In Estonia, in the early 1920s, proportionately the largest minority was the Russians (8.2%), while in Latvia it was the third largest (2.3%) and in Lithuania, the fourth (2.3%).

Germans (Baltic Germans) in Estonia made up the second largest minority (1.7%), the first largest in Latvia (5.9%), and the third in Lithuania (4.1%). Jews comprised the largest national minority in Lithuania (7.1%), the third largest in Latvia (4.9%), but the fourth in Estonia (0.4%). In Estonia, Swedes were numerically significant (0.7%), but in Latvia and Lithuania they were few and were counted among "others." Similarly, Poles in Lithuania were significant (3.0 percent), but much less so in Estonia and Latvia. These distributions in the early 1920s faithfully reflected the historical experience of the northern and southern halves of the littoral: Germans had been the dominant prewar minority in the Estonian and Latvian lands; Lithuania had been the northern end of the Jewish pale of settlement; Russians had come to settle in all parts of the littoral for a mixture of reasons. The aggregate numbers of all the postwar minority nationalities had been reduced by the wartime experience in the 1914–1920 period, as had the numbers of the titular nationalities. When peace and the new boundaries arrived, however, the proportions of the most important minorities – Germans, Russians, Poles, and Jews – remained relatively high, especially in Latvia. Moreover, several of them – Germans and Jews especially, and to a lesser extent Poles – continued to be economically significant, but not to the same extent in all three of the new countries.

Because the continued international good standing of the three countries depended to a great extent on how the "minority nationality" question was handled, public debate recognized that the new constitutions had to extend protections to them: thus the democratic political systems allowed the formation of political parties based on the nationality principle and their representation in the elected parliaments. The new constitutions created protection of minority language rights, and the new governments subsidized minority elementary schools and cultural organizations. The new postwar *states* were multicultural in the same sense that the Baltic littoral *societies* had been long before the war. But, also as before the war, this multiculturalism took the form of coexistence rather than integration; the latter – intermarriage, the learning of the state language, residential patterns, religious conversion – if it were to take place at all, would have to occur "naturally" without government measures. This general attitude did not sit well with the more nationalistically inclined sectors of the titular populations who envisaged the central purpose of the new governments as being the cultural and economic promotion of the "basic nations." In their view, the "state" and the "basic nation" were separate entities, with the state having a moral obligation to ensure that Estonians, Latvians, and Lithuanians would never again be dominated in any sense by other nationality groups.

Given the scope of such expectations in the general population, it was inevitable that a number of the reform measures introduced by the new governments would center on the redistribution of existing wealth. The continuing attractiveness of the political parties of the left – especially the Social Democrats – lay precisely in their promises before, during, and after the independence wars that some such redistribution would take place; and the postwar governments understood that waiting for economic revival to generate new wealth would be foolhardy. Some measures – such as a progressive tax system that would support social welfare programs – could be promulgated equally throughout the population, but others were bound to affect the population unevenly. The clearest example of the latter was reform measures targeting the concentration of landownership: this question in all three countries had been taken up already during 1918 and 1919 and it was one policy area in which the redistributionist ideology of the left coincided with the "national protection" ideology of the center and right. In all three countries, roughly 40–50 percent of all land was still owned by large landowners, who in Estonia and Latvia were mostly, but not exclusively, Baltic Germans, and in Lithuania, again not exclusively, Germans, Poles, and Russians. With political power passing from these groups – which were being transformed into minority nationalities – it appeared that they were being targeted, and, undoubtedly, the further weakening of the economic power of the traditional hegemonic minorities played a part in the governments' motivations. Just as important, however, was the need quickly to expand the landed property of smallholders and to provide the landless with their own farms: both of these outcomes would give these large groupings of rural people – numbering in the hundreds of thousands – a stake in the new states.

The basic formula of these large-scale agrarian reforms was simple: expropriation by the state of all personally owned land above a certain acreage, the placement of this land into a national land fund, and its redistribution to smallholders and the landless. The process of redistribution was prolonged, lasting into the 1930s, but most of the expropriated lands were redistributed in the first half of the 1920s. In Estonia, what ended up in the land fund comprised something like half of all privately owned land in the country – about half arable and half forests and swamps; the redistribution process had increased the number of farms by some 250 percent by the end of the 1920s. The old owners were given modest compensation in long-term bonds; moreover, they could also apply for restitution of up to 50 hectares of the expropriated land. In Latvia, 3.4 million hectares of expropriated land were transferred to the land fund, and by the end of the 1920s, some 143,000 farms had been newly created or supplemented. The new owners purchased their land from the state through long-term loans guaranteed by the government. The former owners received no compensation; however, the government undertook to pay off whatever debts were owed on the expropriated land, and the former owners were able to keep up to 110 hectares. In Lithuania, which used roughly the same model of expropriation–redistribution, some 38,600 new farms had been created and some 26,190 had been enlarged by the end of the 1930s. Lithuania was the most generous of the three countries in compensating former owners, in part because the expropriation involved a large amount of church properties. By the mid-1930s, the government had paid out some 40 million *litas* in compensation to former owners. As in Estonia, the new owners had to pay the government for their land with payments depending on land quality, and the government extended generous terms as well as loans to the new owners.

In all three countries, veterans of the independence wars and other individuals who had rendered worthy assistance to the creation of the new states headed the list of those persons who received land. In comparison with other postwar countries in Europe, the agrarian reforms in the three Baltic states were quite radical. In reacting to the Latvian reform, Baltic German estate owners took their case of "expropriation without compensation" to the League of Nations, but their complaint was rejected. While the reforms succeeded in the short run in creating a more equitable distribution of land among owners, the thousands of smallholders created by the measures would become a problem for the new states later when a worldwide economic downturn began to affect all of Europe.

THREE AUTHORITARIAN PRESIDENTS

The postwar decades in central and eastern Europe saw the emergence of a host of authoritarian political leaders for different reasons in each country. Some escaped the trend – Czechoslovakia, for example, and Finland – but even there the preservation of liberal-democratic institutions was tied to the influence and charismatic leadership of strong individuals such as President Tomáš Masaryk in the former and Marshal Karl Gustav Mannerheim in the latter. In others – Italy and Germany – the ascendancy of Benito Mussolini (1922) and Adolf Hitler (1933) was to have devastating consequences. Estonia, Latvia, and Lithuania might have avoided this trend had their independence come in less troubled times, but they did join the club of what are sometimes termed the "little dictators" in 1926 (Lithuania) and 1934 (Latvia and Estonia). The three authoritarian presidents who took power in those years – Antanas Smetona (1874–1944) in Lithuania, Kārlis Ulmanis (1877–1942) in Latvia, and Konstantin Päts (1874–1956) in Estonia – had all been deeply involved in the struggle for independence in the 1914–1920 period and in the formation of their countries' constitutions; none of them exhibited any lust for absolute power then and all were willing to practice their leadership within the limits of the new political systems. Yet the political history of the three countries also shows that in a considerable portion of the new political elites and the politically active citizenry impatience with the sometimes cumbersome workings of liberal-democratic political institutions was growing. This impatience should not have arisen. After all, most of the political leadership of the three countries in the post-1920 period were mature men in middle age, and understood from their own prewar experience the political culture of the three peoples. They knew that Estonians, Latvians, and Lithuanians had entered the independence period divided on many fundamental questions, that party politics in the parliamentary arena offered many temptations for further fragmentation, and that success depended on constant negotiations, deal-making, and compromise. Instead, in the minds of many the achievement of independence and the international recognition of the three states produced an idealized image of how their political world would work from that point onward. The disappearance of the "Russian yoke," the "Baltic German yoke," and perhaps also the "Polish yoke," and the emergence of a state framework in which the titular nationalities dominated was to have produced an unproblematic future. Reconstruction and state-building was hard work, to be sure, but the dream of the nineteenth-century national awakeners had finally been realized. This was a results-oriented conception of national independence; problems would be resolved quickly one by one now that independence had arrived. Such political thinking was too ready to accept the notion that a seemingly unsatisfactory political system could be redesigned at will and repeatedly, until a version emerged that would produce the desired results. There were strong utopian elements in these attitudes. The logic of such quasi-utopianism led to the belief – not shared by all, of course – that there had to be a single strong national leader standing above party and factional strife who was capable of cutting through endless political arguments, inconclusive elections, and the enervating polemics that freedom of speech and of the press seemed to produce. Juxtaposed with this ideal, high participation rates in elections, nonviolent transfers of power when cabinets changed hands, and a host of demonstrable legislative accomplishments – all characteristic of the parliamentary period of the three Baltic states – appeared gray and unexciting. Close to the littoral, the successful coup in 1926 against the government of Poland by General Josef Piłsudski and his subsequent "behind the throne" domination of politics until 1935 under the rubric of *sanacja* (regenerative purge) provided food for thought.

The first Baltic country to take the step toward authoritarian rule was Lithuania in December 1926, when a coalition of members of the Nationalist Party, the Christian Democrats, and army officers forcefully took over the political system. The "directorate" leading these insurgents asked Antanas Smetona, the leader of the Nationalists (the *Lietuvju Tautininku Sajunga* or *tautininkai*), to become president, and he was "elected" to that office by a rump parliament. Smetona, then fifty-two years old, had a law degree (1902) from the University of St. Petersburg and had been active in Lithuanian political circles for a long time – in the Great Assembly in 1905, as a journalist and founding editor of several important newspapers, as head of the Lithuanian refugee effort during the war, as a fierce opponent of russification, as chair of the provisional parliament that issued the declaration of independence in February 1918, and as first president during 1919–1920. He also lectured on the Greek classics at the University of Kaunas and translated a number of Plato's works into Lithuanian. A principled anti-Marxist completely

(a)

30a, b, c The three interwar authoritarian presidents of the Baltic countries: (a) Antanas Smetona (Lithuania); (b) Kārlis Ulmanis (Latvia, seated center); and (c) Konstantin Päts (Estonia).

(b)

(c)

30a, b, c (cont).

dedicated to the national cause, Smetona in his long period of public service had appeared committed to the liberal-democratic principles on which the Lithuanian state had been founded and had exhibited none of the ruthless drive for power often associated with authoritarian rulers. But from 1926 until 1940, he presided over the steady increase of presidential power in Lithuania and a severe diminution of the significance of an elected parliament.

Smetona's governing style from 1926 on can be characterized as careful authoritarianism. The more extreme (and younger) wing of the *tautininkai*, led by Agustinas Voldemaras (1883–1942) pushed him to assume all the powers implied in the title of *Tautos Vadas* (leader of the nation). Smetona represented the moderate wing of the nationalist movement, however, and felt compelled to retain reduced versions of the political structures – some would say trappings – of parliamentary democracy. Political party activity was not forbidden outright (except for the Communist Party) but was discouraged, with the result that the *tautininkai* were the only effective political party during the rest of the 1920s and during the 1930s. A rump parliament continued to meet but was completely under the president's control. New constitutions were drafted and promulgated in 1928 and again in 1938, but these only consolidated the powers of a strong presidency. Smetona – like Marshal Piłsudski in Poland – envisaged himself as standing above the fray of party politics and declared the president to be a unifying national figure whose only concern was defending the interests of the Lithuanian nation. Importantly, the nation was defined ethnically by Smetona, apparently, and by the *tautininkai*, definitely. The measures promulgated by his fourteen-year government were not particularly extreme, and most of them were of the kind a strong democratically elected parliament would have approved: economic development, educational reform, agricultural subsidies, promotion of trade, and a hard-line attitude toward Poland over the Lithuanian territory that had been occupied in 1920. There was also a determined effort by the Smetona government to reduce the role of non-Lithuanians (prominently Poles and Jews) in the economy; this followed the logic of national protectionism, that is, the state having as its primary duty the "protection" of the titular nationality. Despite the continuing but somewhat empty institutions of parliamentary democracy, there was no question that important policy decisions originated at the top. While in office Smetona also began to show greater intolerance for disagreement and potential rivals: Voldemaras was driven from political life in 1929; the extreme nationalist organization *Geležinis vilkas* (Iron Wolf), the founding of which Smetona had supported, was closed down in the same year. Smetona rewarded his supporters with salaried offices; government officialdom, especially during the 1930s, expanded very rapidly. He also demonstrated solicitude toward close family members: his wife, wife's sister, and her husband were a kind of informal advisory group – a family clique, in less generous words – and his brother-in-law, Juozas Tūbelis (1882–1939), a man with considerable organizational talents, served as prime minister from 1927 to 1938. The dominance of the *tautininkai* and Smetona had support in the general population – how much is impossible to determine – but, in a larger time framework, there is no doubt that his authoritarian leadership, coming hard on the heels of tsarist autocracy, continued to marginalize the habits of democratic self-government in Lithuanian political culture.

In Latvia parliamentary democracy lasted until 1934, with the first fourteen years of the new state marked by four regular parliamentary elections and frequent changes of coalition cabinets. There was also a progressive electoral weakening of the largest parties – the Agrarian Union and the Social Democrats; the latter chose to remain in opposition because in its view the Latvian "proletariat" was insufficiently developed to require representation. Political competition, already in full view during the elections for the Constitutional Convention in 1919, remained intense, and highly partisan newspapers magnified it. Nonetheless, the "people's business" continued to be done: in the four *Saeimas* (parliaments) from 1922 to 1931 the proportion of introduced measures that became law remained fairly steady at 85% (1922), 84% (1925), 87% (1928), and 78% (1931). So did voter participation in the four elections: 82%, 75%, 79%, and 80%, respectively. At the same time, the very liberal party formation law assured that in each election a substantial portion – about 25% – of those who actually voted would remain outsiders in some form until the next election. In the four elections, the number of candidate lists presented to the voters was 88, 141, 120, and 103, respectively; but the number of parties or party formations that actually received representation by at least one MP was 20, 25, 27, and 27, respectively, and many fewer parties (five or six) actually formed the working cabinets. There were seeds of political alienation in this situation; it lent credibility to the charge from the mid-1920s on that the party system and parliament "weren't working," especially because of the growth of splinter parties in the parliament: the number of MPs who were the sole representatives of their parties or who were part of a two-person representation rose to 17 (of 100 MPs) by 1931. One political leader to whom the situation was becoming increasingly unacceptable was Kārlis Ulmanis, who, by any definition, was one of the "founding fathers" of the new Latvian state and had become the leader of the Agrarian Union by the early 1930s.

Like Smetona in Lithuania, Ulmanis had been a center-right political activist since the post-1905 period, when he had fled the harassment of tsarist officials by emigrating to the United States for a period of six years (1907–1913). His interest then and later lay in agricultural economics, especially dairy science. Even during his exile, he continued to publish in Latvian periodicals on the subjects of agricultural improvements, the cooperative movement, and economic modernization. Serving as head of government during the war years, he found a natural home in the Agrarian Union, the second largest Latvian political party, which he represented in all of the four parliaments. On May 15, 1934, Ulmanis and a group of like-minded Agrarians, supported by elements of the military and the *Aizsargi* (home guard), brought about a bloodless coup, suspending the parliament and all political parties (including his own), and also suspending the 1922 constitution while promising to revise it later. The most prominent leaders of the Social Democratic and other left-of-center parties, as well as other potential opponents of the Ulmanis takeover, were arrested, held in an internment camp for a brief period, and then released. Ulmanis, who was then fifty-seven years old, proclaimed that the country would henceforth be governed by a cabinet of ministers chaired by himself. In 1936, when the term of the sitting president, Alberts Kviesis, expired, Ulmanis assumed the presidency as well. From that point until 1940, he held more power than any single Latvian politician ever had.

Unlike Lithuania, Latvia from 1934 on had no parliament of any kind, organized political parties were not permitted, and Ulmanis never delivered on his early promise to revise the 1922 constitution and present it to the electorate. His rule was personal. Defenders of the coup proposed that it was necessitated by coup plots among disgruntled extremist groups; this assertion was, in fact, reported as the reason for the coup in foreign newspapers such as *The New York Times*. The claim, however, was a pretext; such plots did not exist. What is more likely is that Ulmanis had become impatient with the slow pace (in his view) of parliamentary performance and the seeming chaos of the political system; he and his coterie of supporters could do the job better standing above the fray. Unmarried and something of an ascetic, he nonetheless came to enjoy the cult of personality that surrounded him: the title of *Vadonis* (leader of the nation), the honorary doctorate bestowed upon him by the University of Latvia, the cheering crowds organized for his visits to the countryside. Like Smetona, Ulmanis during the war years and subsequently had given every sign of being committed to parliamentary democracy, and, as in Lithuania, the measures he and his personally chosen cabinet promulgated from 1934 to 1940 would have been passed by a sitting parliament: expansion of the welfare state, promotion of economic growth, subsidization of agriculture and industrial enterprise, and creation of job programs by the state. As in Lithuania, the creation of state monopolies was undertaken in part to expand officialdom and reward Ulmanis' followers with salaried positions. Also, determined efforts diminished the economic power of non-Latvians (principally Baltic Germans and Jews). Ulmanis was a national protectionist; though he had good personal relations with the minority nationalities, versions of the slogan "Latvia for the Latvians" were increasingly popular among his supporters. There is no doubt that he shared with Smetona the view that the principal function of the state was to protect the interests of the *Latvian tauta* (nation). Except for the underground communists, there was relatively little opposition to Ulmanis' one-man rule; the political police kept an eye on potential troublemakers, and the leaders of the now-disbanded political parties (including the Social Democrats) took a wait-and-see attitude.

The claim that a coup was necessary to forestall extremists coming to power had been used already to justify the seizure of political power in Estonia by the sixty-year-old Konstantin Päts in March 1934. Like both Smetona and Ulmanis, Päts had also been a leading politician in Estonia during the world war and the 1920s. He held a law degree from the University of Tartu and had been active in Estonian journalism from 1901 onward. As a member of the *Põllumeeste Kogu* (Farmers Party), he in fact had served as *Riigivanem* (state elder, i.e. president) on five separate occasions before 1934. As it happened, the argument that the Estonian government was threatened by the extreme right was plausible, because an organization called *Eesti Vabadusõjalaste Liit* (Central League of Veterans of the Estonian Independence Wars), led by a lawyer named Artur Sirk (1900–1937), had become a powerful force in Estonian politics by the early 1930s. If organized as a bona fide political party, it would have had considerable electoral support. As the name suggests, the League began as a veterans' organization, but later opened membership to all who supported its ideas. The outward trappings of its members – berets and armbands, Nazi-type salutes – resembled those of the fascist movements of western Europe. Its ideology, though somewhat unfocused, contained large doses of extreme nationalism, anti-Marxism, anti-Semitism, and the leadership cult. Whether the League could have "taken over" the government is debatable, but Estonia had already experienced one serious coup attempt by the Communist Party in 1924. Päts' coup was not as blatantly anti-constitutional and anti-parliamentary as that of Ulmanis in Latvia three months later. In 1933, the Estonian parliament had accepted a new constitution (revising the one adopted in 1920), which enhanced substantially the powers of the head of state (the state elder) and reduced the parliament by half (from a hundred to fifty members). The League of Veterans at this point entered Estonian politics as a full-fledged political party and won impressive victories in the urban elections of January 1934 in Tallinn and Tartu. Keeping up the pressure, the League pushed forward their own candidate – General Andres Larka (1879–1943) – for the position of head of state, and Larka seemed headed for victory. Päts – who was acting president – moved to prevent this by declaring martial law, appointing General Johan Laidoner (1884–1953) as commander-in-chief of the armed forces, arresting some four hundred members of the League, and closing all of its local and national offices. League members were expelled from all other Estonian institutions, including the civil service and the armed forces, and Estonia entered a period termed the "era of silence" (so-called for the silencing of all opposition to Päts and the introduction of censorship). All elections were "postponed" as were meetings of the parliament. In March 1935, all political parties were abolished; instead of them, a new organization called the *Isamaalit* (Fatherland League) was created for the purpose of promoting national unity and ensuring the stability of the state. By contrast to the Ulmanis regime, Päts himself and most of his supporters remained attracted to the ideas of constitutionalism and parliamentarism. A new constitution was promulgated in 1937, and elections were held for a two-chamber parliament. In the parliamentary election of February 1938, the Päts regime, however, forbade activities by all political parties of the pre-1934 years; in spite of this, his own movement, the National Front, which was created for the occasion, won only a weak victory. Manipulating the new constitution and a relatively compliant parliament, Päts brought about his own election as president in April 1938. Though Estonia on the surface was now a parliamentary democracy with elections, Päts continued to act in an authoritarian fashion. There could be no misunderstanding about where the real power lay in the political system. By May 1938, Päts felt secure enough in his presidency to amnesty nearly all of his political opponents – the League of Veterans primarily, as well as the communists. Even though Päts was associated politically with the cause of the Estonian farmers, in 1934 he began to promulgate general policies meant to undergird overall economic development: promotion of industrial growth through state monopolies, continuation of the agrarian reforms started in the 1929s, expansion of the export trade, and expansion of the educational system and the welfare state. Since Päts and his party had been instrumental in formulating similar policies in the years before 1934, his lurch into authoritarianism was meant more to pacify the Estonian political domain than to initiate any major turns in the socioeconomic realm. Minority nationalities (principally the Baltic Germans) were not a major concern for Päts, even though during the "era of silence" great stress was placed on the ideal of national unity and national integration.

Each of these men – Smetona, Ulmanis, and Päts – in his own way thought of himself as steering a middle course and doing battle with "extremists" on the right and the left. To the diverse rightists in their countries, they were a disappointment: Smetona had no sympathy for the kind of conspiratorial thinking that portrayed minority nationalities (especially Jews) as the root of all evil; Ulmanis treated the Latvian *Pērkonkrusts* (Thundercross) organization – a grouping at least outwardly having the trappings of Italian fascism and German Nazism – as he did all troublesome potential rivals, by initially imprisoning them and then marginalizing them politically. Päts' government in Estonia justified its authoritarianism by cracking down on the League of Veterans and by expelling members of the League from all national and local offices. All three presidents viewed communists as potentially a fifth column possibly in service to the Soviet Union and treated them accordingly, and all three disdained ideologies – such as those of the Social Democrats – that placed the true loyalty of industrial laborers in the service of some kind of internationalism rather than the cause of the nation. Their justification for suspending or weakening constitutionalism and parliamentarism was that these "instruments" of government had ceased to serve the purposes of the nation; to venerate such instruments was simply to bow down to formalism; what the three countries needed were strong leaders who retained the original vision of the independence wars, namely, collective action on behalf of the people whose names the three countries bore.

LABORING AGAINST THE ODDS

It is ironic that the postwar turmoil in which Estonians, Latvians, and Lithuanians seized the opportunity of establishing independent countries also gave rise to an international context that increasingly became decidedly inhospitable to small states, especially in the European east. This was not supposed to happen. A host of postwar treaties and the League of Nations were supposed to saturate interstate relationships with principles of international law, defuse rivalries, settle territorial conflicts, and prevent aggressive moves by ambitious regimes. In establishing relationships with other states in the system after being granted recognition, Estonia, Latvia, and Lithuania counted on such protections enduring. Instead, by the early 1930s, international relationships appeared to be moving on two tracks: on the one, postwar countries, small and large, preoccupied with their internal problems, expected the international system to ensure their rights to exist as states; on the other, older and larger countries nursed grievances over the outcome of the Great War and became hosts to leaders promising to change the face of postwar Europe. The probability that the principle of "self-determination of peoples" could survive in this context lessened considerably.

With its original sponsor – the United States – being a non-participant, the League of Nations proved increasingly weaker as a barrier to the predatory behavior of its members; the growing popularity of expansionist ideologies was discounted as inflated rhetoric; and the inward turning precipitated by the worldwide depression of 1929–1933 diminished the desire for any long-term planning for another major conflict. In this general context, small states with weak or virtually non-existent military forces were, in a sense, increasingly on their own. In the Baltic littoral, this meant a growing belief among makers of foreign policy that, somehow, reiteration of the ideas of neutrality and even-handedness would see them through. Efforts at inter-Baltic cooperation led nowhere, largely because the daggers-drawn relationship between Lithuania and Poland over the Vilnius district poisoned the regional atmosphere and Estonia and Latvia did not want to be perceived as endorsing either side. By the late 1930s, it really did not matter that the three Baltic states had authoritarian presidents: had they continued to have vigorous parliamentary systems, their governments would still have had to negotiate their way through the same deteriorating international system. The continuing internal development – economic, cultural, or social – of Estonia, Latvia, and Lithuania, guided by strong parliaments and authoritarian presidents, was unlikely to have any effect on the aspirations of large predatory neighbors; the three states were laboring against the odds, but they had little choice to do otherwise.

The generation of Estonians, Latvians, and Lithuanians who came of age during the 1920s, however, did not think about their lives in these terms. The retention of independence took a back seat to the enjoyment of it, and there was much confidence that the older generation, presumably more experienced in international matters, would do the job well. The momentum of cultural growth already evident in the prewar decades could continue without the threats of germanization, russification, or polonization. Cultural growth could be intensely national, celebrating the physical features of the home-land and glorying in the nuances of the three languages, which were now also the languages of the state. It could also reflect international artistic and literary styles such as symbolism, expressionism, and cubism. The feeling that the national cultures had to prove their worth dropped away; in all genres of cultural expression, a new sense of freedom was created by the economic and social margin-alization of the former self-proclaimed local representatives of alleg-edly "superior" cultures. Those for whom language was the most important medium of self-expression no longer felt that their full intellectual potential could only be realized if they shifted to a lan-guage other than the one with which they had grown up. Generally, creative people could now feel that in doing their work they were expanding cultural domains with a national designator – *Latvian* literature, *Estonian* music, *Lithuanian* painting – and that there were publics that would receive their work as such. A new sense of the national ownership of cultural life was palpable, paralleling the sense of national ownership of territory.

This national culture-building, like state-building, was many faceted. Mandatory public educational systems had to be recreated because the wartime years (both the world war and the independence wars) had brought havoc to systematic education at all levels. At the center of this effort stood Tartu (formerly Jurjew, formerly Dorpat) University in Estonia, the University of Latvia (formerly the Riga Polytechnic Institute), and the University of Kaunas (the ancient Vilnius University was now, of course, on the other side of the Lithuanian–Polish border). Specialized training institutes for stu-dents of music, painting, and architecture were created and staffed. National opera houses were established as well as national theaters. Publishing houses were founded to meet the continuing high demand for literary works in the three languages, and for newspapers, jour-nals, and other kinds of periodical publications.

The main religious faiths of the three countries – Lutheranism in Estonia and Latvia, Catholicism in Lithuania – were "nationalized" through the replacement of German- and Polish-speaking clergy by clergymen who could perform religious services in the three national languages. Scholars at the universities worked at standardization of the three languages, drawing a line between what should be the grammatically correct form of each language and what would be considered dialects. Marketing schemes were devised to bring printed material to the entire population, because such outlets as bookstores were rare except in towns and cities; for this purpose, new postal systems helped a great deal. Most of the population of the three new states still lived in the countryside where communication and transportation remained as slow as in the former century, but the developing technology of radio broadcasting helped to tie the entire population into a nationwide information network. The statistical indicators in all of these endeavors after World War I showed only an upward trajectory through the 1920s and 1930s, thus successfully laying down an institutional and technological base for sustainable national cultures. It was also true, however, that few creative artists could make a living solely within their chosen professions. Many had paying jobs in entirely different fields, and extensive subsidization of the cultural domain by the national governments, especially during the period of authoritarian presidents, also helped. Ivory towers were few and persons of an intellectual bent were expected to deploy their talents in a wide variety of undertakings. A novelist, for example, could easily be a journalist, an editor of encyclopedias for a large publishing house, and even a member of parliament. In many of these fields of culture-building, the three countries did not have to start from zero because prewar cultural growth (before there were states) had been prolific. Many of the writers (poets, playwrights, novelists, essayists) of the prewar period were now becoming canonized. So was the orally transmitted culture of rural areas: it was collected, sorted, printed, placed in museums, transformed into "folklore," and treated as the definitive basis of the new "national cultures."

One important consequence of these endeavors in Latvia was that the Latgalian-speaking Latvians of what had been the western districts of Vitebsk province were now permanently a part of the new Latvian state as a separate region: Latgale. All three states had had the problem of population integration: Estonia comprised the populations of three distinct former Russian provinces, Latvia also of three, and Lithuania of four. But only Latvia had started its new life with so large a population (about 31 percent in 1920 in Latgale) having had a history markedly different from that of the rest of the Latvian territories, as well as with a current political consciousness in which sentiments for full integration (as in the eloquent writings and speeches of a member of the Latvian parliament from Latgale, Francis Trasuns [1864–1926]) vied with expectations of special status (as in the equally eloquent writings of another Latgalian member of the Latvian parliament, Francis Kemps [1876–1951]).

The enthusiasm behind the expansion of national cultures was also evident in economic rebuilding, especially in the immediate postwar years. The economies of Estonia, Latvia, and Lithuania had suffered during the war: economic production had dropped to about 30–40 percent of the prewar level. The loss of human capital (population decline) was also severe, averaging about 20 percent for the three countries. The industrial and transportational infrastructure (factory machinery, roads, railroads) was seriously impaired, and the countryside had been nearly stripped by occupation armies of its principal source of non-human power – the horse. Privation and despair, however, were overridden in the short run by the prevailing feeling that the fruits of prolonged effort would no longer end up in the pockets of Baltic German and Polish landowners or be claimed by a Russian government far away. Even if the rewards would not enrich individuals immediately, they would circulate within a "national economy" and be put to use in other sectors: the psychological boost of working in and for one's own country was a formidable element well into the decade of the 1920s. The upturn of all economic indicators began in the middle years of that decade and lasted into the early 1930s, when the effects of the worldwide depression began to be felt. By that time, however, the problem of economic *survival* had retreated into the background to be replaced by the problem of economic repair of ongoing national economies. The idea of entrepreneurship had taken hold, the agrarian reforms were nearly completed, and the production of foodstuffs remained at satisfactory levels, as did, when measured in the aggregate, the standard of living. After the mid-1930s, the export market expanded especially for agricultural goods, and balance of trade statistics, though fluctuating, were favorable. Revenue flows to the central governments remained steady, allowing for the expansion of various social welfare programs. But there was socioeconomic stratification in all three countries, with the income gap between the richest and the poorest segments of the population exemplified by residential patterns and lifestyles; this division also had an urban–rural dimension. What in the eyes of the political left was a maldistribution of wealth remained a source of its political strength, though with the emergence of the authoritarian presidencies the left was not able to turn social disparities into electoral strength.

Cultural flowering and economic development took place during both decades within the framework of statism – a growing belief among elites and non-elites alike that the central governments of the three states should be the protectors, the movers and shakers, and the initiators of major social and economic policy. It was the central government's obligation to guide, direct, intervene, subsidize, and control. This collective attitude grew out of the wartime years, persisted into the 1920s, and received the strong endorsement of the authoritarian presidents. The free-market philosophy, though present, was not central to the economic thinking of policymakers. The ultimate result was that throughout the 1920–1940 period, under the parliamentary systems and under the authoritarian presidents, ministries enlarged their staffs, developed more expertise in all sectors of life, and correspondingly reduced the role of the private sector without extinguishing it entirely. Officialdom grew in size, sometimes because of merit but just as frequently, especially under the authoritarian presidents, because of political patronage. By the 1930s, economic success frequently meant finding the right ministerial connections, lining up state subsidies, and earning the favor of those at the very top. Continuous subsidization of the agricultural sector, the conversion of shaky private enterprises into state monopolies, politically motivated capital flows from state banks to private individuals, and a determination to favor the undertakings of Estonians, Latvians, and Lithuanians (over those of national minorities) became increasingly more characteristic of all three countries after the middle of the 1930s. Though not quite state socialism, neither was it a system that in the realm of large-scale undertakings had much use for competition and meritocracy. Competition was left to operate freely in the private sector of small-scale enterprises and retail stores. All this produced very mixed economies as well as a mindset in which trust was placed in central governments to make the right decisions to allocate resources in an optimal manner and look after the welfare of all.

Whatever internal policies were being implemented in Estonia, Latvia, and Lithuania from the mid-1930s onward, however, such measures had no chance of affecting the European state-system in which expansionist moves by Mussolini's Italy and Hitler's Germany were encountering few obstacles. In addition to bilateral agreements already entered into with large states, the small states of the littoral sought others – trade pacts, non-aggression agreements, and formal and informal alliances of various kinds – in the belief that the proliferation of such ties, accompanied by the requisite diplomatic niceties and signed treaties, would assure everyone that Estonia, Latvia, and Lithuania intended to live peacefully and be friends to all. These, in fact, were the main tenets of the foreign policy of the three littoral states in the second half of the 1930s: except for Lithuania's wanting to regain the Vilnius territory from Poland, they intended to keep the borders they had and concern themselves only with internal development.

Neutrality seemed to be working for Switzerland (a small state) and the Scandinavian countries (large territorially but small demographically), and the hope was that the Baltic states in the northeastern corner of the continent could also steer clear of the antagonisms now appearing on the continental mainland. The public mood in the three countries appeared to be assuaged by a policy of neutrality, but newspapers in Lithuania expressed the most worry about the future. Hitler's determination to incorporate all Germans into a great Germany directly affected Klaipėda (Memel) over which Lithuania had acquired sovereignty in 1924 with the agreement of the western allies. The population of the Klaipėda territory was about 40 percent German, and Hitler was bound to make it a target just as he was already (by 1937) taking aim at the German population of the Sudetenland in Czechoslovakia. The eastern Baltic littoral, in other words, was not as immune as a policy of neutrality wished to make it. On their side, the Estonian and Latvian governments generally avoided the subjects of Klaipėda and the Vilnius territory when Baltic leaders met; these subjects were considered to be Lithuania's problems.

8

The return of empires, 1940–1991

The year 1939 turned out to be a fateful one for Europe and the world. On September 1 of that year, Nazi Germany's invasion of Poland began a conflict so vast that it quickly received the designation of World War II, requiring that the earlier so-called Great War become World War I. Germany felt confident about its move east, because on August 23, 1939, Hitler and Stalin had agreed to a non-aggression treaty, eliminating for a time the possibility of a two-front war in the east against the USSR and in the west against France and Great Britain (who had come to Poland's defense). The treaty contained secret protocols laying out German and Soviet spheres of influence in eastern Europe, in which the eastern Baltic littoral figured prominently. Germany ultimately declared itself to have no interest in the littoral, in effect giving the USSR a free hand in the region. The Soviet Union responded quickly, invading Poland on September 17 and in fact occupying a slightly larger but less populous section of the country than Germany brought under its control. It might be added that earlier, in March, Poland itself had benefited from Hitler's earlier dismemberment of Czechoslovakia by demanding and receiving that country's Teschen region, with some 240,000 inhabitants. In any event, Great Britain and France declared war on Germany on September 3.

These dramatic events during the middle months of 1939 revealed that the Baltic littoral would not easily escape the effects of this war, but what the appropriate responses by Estonia, Latvia, and Lithuania should be remained very unclear. Information about the

RENDEZVOUS

31 In this drawing, "Rendezvous" in the *Evening Standard* of
September 20, 1939, the British cartoonist David Low
accurately depicted the irony of the Hitler–Stalin Pact of August
23, which permitted Hitler to invade Poland on September 1
and start World War II.

secret protocols had leaked out, but the foreign ministries of the three
countries remained uncertain about what the concept of spheres of
influence would mean on the ground. All three (that is, the three
authoritarian presidents, Päts, Ulmanis, and Smetona) therefore
opted for a reiteration of a policy of neutrality, hoping that an
expression of non-involvement would somehow exempt them from
whatever long-term plans were nursed by the two now-allied expansionist powers. Articulation of foreign policy around any other
theme than neutrality had become impossible. During the past two
decades, flushed by the heady experience of independence, the three
states had done little to create effective regional cooperation, military
or otherwise. Military expenditures in the three states had remained
low during the two decades, and purchases of military equipment was

stymied by bad planning and by foot-dragging on the part of potential suppliers in the east or west. What remained for the three authoritarian presidents was the policy of neutrality, and, for domestic consumption, a policy of reassurance that the political leadership was doing all it could to keep the three states unviolated. Speeches by the presidents warned of hard times ahead but also expressed the confidence that the future could be controlled through careful step-by-step negotiations. The general population of the three countries was not ignorant about what was taking place in their corner of Europe, but the governments discouraged alarmist rumors. The main newspapers reported the international news as though it had little bearing on the future of the littoral. This wishful thinking – in the political elites and in the general population – was to some extent driven by memories: a sufficient number of adults in each country had experienced the ravages of World War I, and they did not wish to believe that the European state-system would once again pitch itself into such a disaster. Nor could they accept the thought that the three Baltic littoral states would once again have to defend their independence, especially after receiving international recognition of it less than two decades ago and in the interim having demonstrated their viability as states in the League of Nations and as signatories of a host of treaties backed by international law.

THE USSR EXPANDS

The German invasion of Poland – *Blitzkrieg* (lightning war) – and the French and British war declarations against Germany did not immediately lead to hostilities in western Europe: wags termed the following months the *Sitzkrieg* (sitting war). In the east, however, the Hitler–Stalin non-aggression pact of August 23, 1939 (also named the Molotov–Ribbentrop Pact for the foreign ministers of the two countries), and its secret protocols, enabled the two treaty partners to finalize their expansion plans and take further steps. For Hitler, this meant consolidation of control over Polish territory through the creation of a *Gouvernment Général* for about 73,000 square miles of Polish territory with a population of some 22 million persons. Since Poles were considered an inferior people in the Nazi racial hierarchy, their political, social, and economic elites were decimated.

The common people were moved about to make room for German settlers who were to inherit the conquered land, while Jews and other "subhumans" were herded into ghettos.

The consolidation of Soviet control over its sphere of interest in the region was more prolonged, because the USSR was dealing with independent states: Finland, Estonia, Latvia, Lithuania. During September and October, the Soviet Union offered so-called mutual assistance pacts (accompanied by veiled threats) to Estonia (September 28), Latvia (October 5), Lithuania (October 10), and Finland (November 26). These pacts were almost identical, and permitted the USSR to place contingents of its army on bases in the territories of the four states. Moreover, the signatories agreed not to enter into coalitions against each other (despite the fact of the USSR having already entered such an agreement with Germany). In return for the military bases, the USSR agreed to supply each republic with armaments and to refrain from using the bases to interfere in the internal affairs of each country. In addition, Lithuania was offered (and accepted) the return of Vilnius territory, which the USSR had just obtained in its share of dismembered Poland. Estonia, Latvia, and Lithuania signed the pacts, while Finland refused. The USSR launched an attack on Finland at the end of November, precipitating the Russo-Finnish War that was to last until March, when Finland accepted defeat and the loss of its Karelian territories, the city of Viipuri, and a naval base (about 16,000 square miles and some 450,000 people).

South of the Gulf of Finland, the sequence of events unfolded very differently. During the months following the signing of the pacts, the three authoritarian presidents oversaw the arrival in their countries of Soviet military contingents that numbered about 25,000 soldiers in Estonia and Latvia and 20,000 in Lithuania. Continuing efforts by the Soviet side to increase that number followed: it was claimed that the bases needed technical personnel and other support staff of various kinds to operate properly and that these were not to be counted in the agreement totals. In the meantime, on October 7 the German government issued a call for all *Volksdeutsche* (Germans not currently residing in the territories of the Third Reich) to "return home." In Estonia and Latvia, this call (which was really a directive) affected the Baltic German populations (53,000 in Latvia, 14,000 in

Estonia), who now had to decide which was their homeland; in Lithuania it affected about 52,000 persons. Most of the littoral's Germans complied with the call and over the next ten months virtually all departed, having disposed of their properties through complicated arrangements with the governments of the countries. This ended the seven-hundred-year presence in the littoral of a minority that for almost that entire period had been the dominant elite in the region. Most of the littoral's Germans were resettled in those western districts of occupied Poland that had been annexed by the Third Reich. Local attitudes toward their departure bordered on indifference, even though more engaged minds worried about what this forced emigration signified about their own future.

The tactics of the USSR in dealing with the three littoral states during these months maintained the illusion that their sovereignty and their declarations of neutrality were being respected. In reality, the base agreements were imposed, accompanied by the massing of Soviet troops on the Estonian border, threats during the Moscow negotiations with the Baltic foreign ministers that the USSR would move even if there were no agreements, and "friendly" explanations advanced about how isolated the three countries really were. Germany, it was said, would not come to their assistance, France and Great Britain were preoccupied in the west, Sweden was neutral, and Poland no longer existed. A flurry of consultations between the Baltic foreign ministers revealed no options, the three authoritarian presidents recognized the military unpreparedness of their countries, and the agreements went forward.

The three governments sought in all ways possible to portray the overall situation as normal, as presenting challenges that could be resolved with appropriate treaties, good behavior on the part of the smaller states, and the avoidance of any war hysteria in the general population. Newspaper reporting in the three republics, following the guidance of the foreign ministries, cooperated in maintaining the pretense of normality. The general public went along with it; rumors swirled, but most people continued with the routines of everyday life. The Soviet contingents in their bases remained on their best behavior, their officers were invited to receptions and balls and were polite. Intelligence reports portrayed Russian officers as being aghast at the well-stocked stores, making large purchases, and sending them eastward; evidently the Baltic republics had been portrayed as containing impoverished, suffering populations under the heel of bourgeois-fascist exploiters. Autobiographies dealing with the period describe people making normal plans for the future – preparing for careers, enrolling in universities, marrying and planning to start families, celebrating Christmas and the arrival of the New Year – as though Germany and the USSR had not partitioned Poland, Great Britain and France had not declared war on Germany, and the Soviet Union had not invaded Finland. Still, the general atmosphere was becoming tenser. In a radio address to Latvians in February 1940 President Ulmanis, without mentioning specifics, warned that "the pressure will become greater and continue to grow," but at the same time balanced this by calling Latvians a "brave people" who "must be ready to stand against hardships, to overcome them, to be victorious over them, so that in the future we can live in our own land and in our state." Dark humor in Lithuania coined the saying:"Vilnius belongs to us, but we belong to the Russians." In commenting on the base agreements, western newspapers began to talk about Estonia, Latvia, and Lithuania as having started to slide into the status of "protectorates" of the USSR.

The leaders of the three Baltic governments were in a quandary as spring 1940 wore on and it became clear to them that good behavior and reiterations of neutrality availed them nothing. In Lithuania, the USSR worked hard to provoke incidents and to interpret them as clear evidence that Lithuania was not observing its side of the base agreement: such incidents became especially frequent during May. On May 16, one of the major newspapers of the USSR, *Izvestia*, published an article observing that "the neutrality of small states, which do not have the power to preserve it, is mere fantasy. Therefore, there are very few chances for small countries to survive and to maintain their independence." Worded as though it were an above-the-fray reflection on the nature of contemporary geopolitics, the article could also be read as a statement of intentions. Another article on May 28, in *Pravda*, the Communist Party's principal organ, accused Estonia of "excessive neutrality." But even though during May Baltic diplomats maintained their belief that almost continous negotiation with Moscow would maintain normality, at the end of the month, the Lithuanian government sent a telegram to its diplomatic corps appointing Stasys Lozaraitis, the country's representative in Rome, as "chief of the residual diplomatic representations abroad" in the eventuality that "a catastrophe occurs here." A similar empowering message had been sent to the Latvian ambassador in London, Kārlis Zariņš, on May 17 by the Latvian government. These diplomats would not be official governments-in-exile, but they would remain independent voices if the governments in the littoral were brought under Soviet control. In Latvia, during the last weeks in May and early June, local choral societies began to rehearse for the national song festival, which was to take place on June 16 in Daugavpils (Russ. *Dvinsk*).

In May 1940, the German army invaded the Netherlands, Belgium, Luxemburg, and France and by the end of June, France asked for an armistice, which was signed on June 22. The British army had withdrawn from the continent by the end of May (Dunkirk). The USSR took advantage of these events to present to the ambassadors of Estonia, Latvia, and Lithuania in Moscow on June 14–16 ultimata that charged the three countries with failure to implement properly the provisions of the base treaties and with conspiring to create an anti-Soviet coalition. It demanded that the governments of Päts, Ulmanis, and Smetona allow the entry of an unrestricted number of Soviet troops and that new governments be formed. Emergency meetings of the three governments judged the situation as hopeless; only Smetona urged armed resistance, but he received almost no support from his ministers and military leaders. Smetona and his family left for Germany, but Presidents Ulmanis and Päts remained in place. The Soviet army crossed the border into Lithuania on June 14, and into Estonia and Latvia on June 17. Three high Soviet officials arrived in the three capitals to supervise events – Vladimir Dekanozov in Kaunas, Andrei Vishinskii in Riga, and Andrei Zhdanov in Tallinn – with the last-named having the task of coordinating the entire takeover. In the weeks that followed, the Soviet plan worked smoothly. Presidents Ulmanis and Päts accepted the resignation of their cabinets, and in all three countries new cabinets (essentially puppet governments) were formed, consisting mostly of Estonians, Latvians, and Lithuanians with no particular expertise in governing but no strangers to the populations at large.

The new governments were headed in Lithuania by the journalist Justas Paleckis (1899–1980), in Latvia by the biologist Augusts Kirchensteins (1872–1963), and in Estonia by the physician-poet Johannes Vares (1890–1946). These three and the members of their new cabinets were political leftists or opportunists who earlier had exhibited considerable friendliness toward the Soviet Union; a few were communists by conviction. The Soviet army contingents had been accompanied by units of the security services, including the NKVD (state security organ), and arrests of potential opponents of the new order began immediately. Antanas Merkys (1887–1955), who had become acting president of Lithuania when Smetona left, was deported to the interior of the USSR on July 17, Ulmanis on July 22, and Konstantin Päts on July 30. Other heretofore prominent people continued to disappear from their homes and workplaces never to be heard from again. During these July weeks, persons likely to be loyal to the new order – members of the Communist Party, crypto-communists who had been "underground" in the three countries, and cadres arriving daily from the USSR – were placed in positions of authority at every level. Throughout, the overall script required that the new national leaders be persons with Estonian, Latvian, and Lithuanian surnames so as to create the illusion of a popular local uprising against previous authoritarian rule (in Soviet parlance, "fascist cliques"). Communists of Baltic origin and their sympathizers, who had left the three countries during the independence wars and in the interim had made careers in the USSR, became very useful. Their ranks in the Soviet Union had been decimated by Stalin's purge of the "Old Bolsheviks" during 1936–1938, and the survivors, now very compliant, were directed to return to their homelands and take on assigned tasks. Some had been sent into the littoral earlier to participate in underground work. These were all very loyal *apparatchiks* with the necessary surnames but frequently with poor, if any, skills in the local languages. Not as prominent in the transition weeks when local communists and communist sympathizers were required, they became more visible later on when the process of sovietization was completed.

Now, however, the main task of the new power-holders was to elect parliaments to reflect the upwelling of the heretofore stifled democratic will of the "working masses." Such elections were held

July 14–15 in all three countries: only one left-of-center slate of candidates was permitted and competing political groupings were peripheralized or arrested. On July 17, it was announced that the "working peoples" list had received 99.2% of the votes in Lithuania, 97.6% in Latvia, and 92.9% in Estonia. Voting was mandatory, and internal passports were stamped to show whether or not one had participated in this alleged outpouring of the popular will. In their first meeting on July 21 the new legislatures proclaimed the three countries to be soviet socialist republics and voted to send delegations to Moscow to apply for annexation to the USSR. This was done, and the Supreme Soviet of the USSR "accepted" Lithuania's request on August 3, Latvia's on August 5, and Estonia's on August 6. Within three months, the three states had been transformed from independent sovereign republics into union republics, constituent parts of a latter-day empire.

The rapidity with which Estonian, Latvian, and Lithuanian statehood disappeared strained belief, and it took some time after early August for the citizenry to realize that ultimate control over their futures had moved to Moscow. This outcome became real enough as one decree after another from the new governments began the process of sovietization. The old familiar terminology of political power – parliament, cabinet, president – was replaced by a new and unfamiliar vocabulary: councils of people's commissars, presidia, councils of ministers, chairmen, first and second secretaries, central committees, and executive committees. A multitude of political parties was replaced by a single omnipotent party – the Communist Party (the self-styled "vanguard of the proletariat"). Each of the three republics retained its own party with a multilayered structure and a presence through cells and bureaus in all non-governmental organizations. The political philosophy of the proletariat state ("the dictatorship of the proletariat") assigned to the party a "leading and guiding role" that, in practice, subordinated the government to the party. These were two parallel structures of power, though in principle an individual could occupy offices in both. The party organizations in the Estonian, Latvian, and Lithuanian Soviet Socialist Republics in turn took their orders from the CPSU – the Communist Party of the Soviet Union and its General Secretary, Joseph Vissarianovich Stalin.

Sovietization proceeded apace in all domains of life in each country. One by one, all other non-governmental organizations were closed unless specifically permitted to continue, and their inventory and property were claimed by the new authorities in the name of the "working people." Religious organizations – especially the Catholic Church – were dealt with more carefully than most, but nevertheless came under special scrutiny and a variety of prohibitions. Large industrial enterprises were nationalized, as were banks and all land. Bank accounts were frozen, and eventually confiscated above a certain level of savings. The value of the old currency – *litas, lats, kroon* – still in use was declared to be equivalent to the Soviet ruble on a one-to-one ratio. An agrarian reform was instituted through which the landless and smallholders received land grants up to ten hectares in size; but talk of agricultural collectivization was discouraged and promises were made about the retention of private farming. Ambassadors of the three states were recalled, and those who did not return were declared traitors and their property confiscated. Educational institutions were placed under new leadership, and mandatory courses in "scientific Marxism-Leninism" were introduced. Newspapers were closed or subjected to strictest censorship; the radio became the voice of the government and the party. Diplomatic representatives of other countries left, and the three republics were in a sense sealed from outside contact. The military forces of the three republics were disbanded or incorporated into the Soviet army; the officers' corps was imprisoned, executed, or deported. The constitution of the USSR and Soviet law were introduced, as befitting three new soviet socialist republics. Initially, most of the labor force remained in place, as did many in the central governmental bureaucracy, but new appointments were made at the managerial and directorial levels. Expertise and talent were not prerequisites for these new supervisors, only correct political attitudes and loyalty to the Soviet Union. By the end of 1940, all major and minor institutions, if not closed, had been purged of their former "bourgeois" leadership. To complete the transformation, in the major cities street names were changed and replaced with those of persons prominent in the Communist Party's past or present.

These changes differed in the three countries in terms of timing, but followed an almost identical overall pattern everywhere. Arrests continued apace, friends and colleagues simply disappeared, and people quickly learned that it was dangerous to ask too many questions about them. An overlay to the new civilian regime was created by the Soviet military: the Baltic Military District was formed with Riga as its headquarters; as a result, the Soviet military presence became a normal part of visible everyday life in the three capitals as well as in the countryside. The reaction of the civilian population to all these changes was mixed, and the feeling of powerlessness pervasive. Some reasoned that the new government would not exhibit the cruelty characteristic of the early Bolshevik regime in Soviet Russia, because it was not being challenged as in the time of the Russian Civil War during 1919–1921. Others played the opportunism card, announcing that they had been oppressed in the independence period and now joined the side of the new socialist order. Some did expect improvement in their lives and enthusiastically endorsed the changes. Since it was virtually impossible to predict who could or could not be trusted, those who disliked the new order, especially those with families, fell silent, complied with the new laws and regulations as best they could, and waited for future developments.

The Hitler–Stalin non-aggression pact of August 1939 had given the USSR a free hand in the Baltic littoral, and Germany offered no opposition to the occupation. Not so the western democracies: the USA refused to recognize the occupation (July 23, 1940) as did Great Britain in 1941; these two countries permitted the continued existence in their capitals of legations of the prewar Baltic republics. The "non-recognition" policy continued after World War II ended and was adopted by other countries, with the result that the prewar republics entered a kind of international limbo: they were no longer independent entities (*de facto*) but they continued to exist *de jure*. In the littoral, the new governments took multiple steps to erase any memory of the interwar states: their symbols (flags, coats of arms) were forbidden; listings of books published before 1940 were compiled and used to remove them from libraries; prewar authors (except for a few serving in the new governments or announcing their loyalty to them) were maligned; and everything associated with interwar independence was denigrated. The history of the first half of the twentieth century began to be rewritten by Baltic Soviet historians so as to characterize the 1918–1940 period as the "rule of bourgeois-fascist dictatorships" and events of the summer of 1940 as the "socialist revolution" that brought the "working masses" into power. The long-term goal of these measures was to silence human memory, to eliminate "bourgeois nationalist" consciousness: after all, in 1940–1941 since the vast majority of the Baltic peoples could easily draw comparisons between the two eras, negative judgments of the new circumstances had to be suppressed.

The transformation of the Baltic states into Soviet republics continued during the first half of 1941, and the growing isolation of the three populations because of the strict control of information produced many rumors. One, possibly born of desperation, was that Germany was preparing to invade the Soviet Union, but hard facts about this possibility were difficult to come by. The extent to which Stalin believed that possibility was real is debatable, but whether for internal or external reasons, the policy of cleansing the Baltic republics of all possible opposition moved to a higher level. Although in the eleven months after June 1940 thousands were imprisoned, executed, or deported, during just one night, between June 13 and 14, 1941, the numbers spiked to tens of thousands. These were the first mass deportations from the Baltic area, designed to remove entire categories of people from the population the new governments had to manage. The action targeted persons (and their families) who had been members of certain prewar organizations (the national guard and Boy Scouts), had occupied important posts in the prewar governments, or had otherwise been in the public's eye nationally, regionally, or locally because of their wealth or influence. The lists communist officials worked from had been compiled by them and local functionaries who were now loyal to the new governments. Those arrested were taken by truck to gathering points at peripheral railroad stations, packed into boxcars, and then taken to different points in the interior of the USSR.

The June 13–14 deportations in Latvia removed 15,424 persons from the population, in Estonia the number was approximately 10,000, and in Lithuania approximately 18,000. The deportations did not involve specific charges against the deportees, hearings, or trials; the appearance of one's name on a list was sufficient. In the series of shocks administered to the three Baltic populations by the new governments, the mass deportations were the most traumatic because they affected the largest number of people, in urban areas, the countryside, and throughout all nationality and occupational groups. As an instrument of terrorization, the technique of the sudden nighttime arrest and deportation of such large numbers as alleged enemies of the working class was most effective, but the new regimes, as it turned out, had no time to enjoy its benefits. On June 22 in an operation entitled *Barbarossa*, the *Wehrmacht* of the Third Reich, numbering about three million, invaded the USSR across a two-thousand-mile front. Army group *Nord* (North), with about 650,000 soldiers, headed for Leningrad, traversed Lithuania, reached Riga by July 1–2, and crossed the Estonian border on July 7. The littoral was being defended by a Soviet force of some 380,000 men, and, just as in World War I, the Baltic littoral became the front for a major conflict between Germans on the one side and Russians (now the Soviets) on the other.

In spite of its overwhelming numerical superiority, the *Wehrmacht* was not able to secure the Baltic littoral until the end of August, but in those two months the German forces gained ground steadily. The Soviet side was also hampered by its lack of preparedness, and by the fact that in all three Baltic republics large numbers of civilians seized the opportunity to form guerilla units that engaged the Soviet forces as best they could. The most effective of these civilian efforts – called the Uprising – took place in Lithuania beginning in June; there it involved an estimated 16,000–20,000 persons and was organized enough to cost the Soviet military a substantial number of soldiers and actually to create a short-lived Lithuanian Provisional Government. In Latvia, the guerillas, who numbered about 6,000–8,000, succeeded in killing some 800 Soviet soldiers and taking some 1,500 prisoners. As the Soviet army and civilian officials fled, "national" irregulars assumed power in some twenty cities and towns and in many Latvian *pagasti* (counties). In Estonia, the guerilla forces numbered about 5,000, killing about 500 Soviet soldiers and forcing the retreating Soviet army into numerous side engagements. The announced intent of all the guerillas was to demonstrate to the German military and civilian authorities that the local populations were as intent on freeing themselves of Soviet control as the Germans were on defeating the Soviet enemy. The incoming German authorities, however, perceived the situation differently; wherever they established themselves, guerillas were quickly disarmed and efforts to establish governmental authority at any level on terms other than those laid down by Germans were rudely brushed aside. If the *Einheimische* (natives) were to exercise any power, they would have to do so in institutions and on the basis of principles created and approved by the Third Reich.

As the Soviet army withdrew from the Baltic, its units were accompanied by thousands of refugees for whom victory by the German forces signaled at least imprisonment if not death sentences. The estimated number of such refugees or evacuees was about 20,000 in Lithuania, 40,000 in Latvia, and 25,000 in Estonia. They included high and low officials of the 1940–1941 Soviet governments, members of the internal security apparatuses, various intellectuals who had expressed their sympathies for the new order, party members of different kinds, and lesser officials who had become prominent in the rural areas. They also included Jews (precise numbers not known) who realized they would be special targets of the incoming regime. Many of them, in fact, had fled to the Baltic states during the German occupation of Poland. The flight of the 1940–1941 Soviet government officials was chaotic: there were many last-minute executions of jailed political prisoners; official papers and files were burned, but not completely; and on the roads leading east the refugees were periodically fired upon by guerilla units. The highest party officials usually fled early by train.

This headlong flight also meant, of course, that sovietization was interrupted; the socialist transformation remained incomplete. Also, many who had found a niche in the 1940–1941 Soviet system could not flee, and such persons were now open to the charge of collaboration. Between June and August as Soviet power in the littoral ended, the region ceased to be a front and became a supply area for the German armies fighting around Leningrad and farther east. The littoral had been simultaneously "liberated" and "reoccupied." Estonian, Latvian, and Lithuanian society had been decapitated – the deportations of June 13–14, 1941 swept away virtually all of the remaining important political leaders of the pre-1940 period, the political elite of the Soviet year had now also fled, and all talk about the renewal of Estonia, Latvia, and Lithuania as sovereign countries fell on the entirely deaf ears of the German occupiers, who had their own plans for the region.

Anticipating complete victory in the east, the Nazi regime in Berlin worked out a reorganization plan for the eastern occupied territories: the three Baltic states, together with Belorussia (Belarus), would become an administrative region called *Ostland* with its headquarters in Riga. Each country was thus reduced to a *Generalbezirk* (district) in this new entity, and each district was further subdivided into subdistricts. The whole of *Ostland* was governed by a *Reichskommissar*, each district by a *Generalkommissar*, and each subdistrict by a *Gebietskommissar*. The city of Riga was a separate entity, governed by an *Oberbürgermeister*. All these officials were Germans appointed by Berlin, and the residents of the occupied territories were entirely excluded from governance at the very start of the German occupation. The entire pyramid was placed under the Ministry of Eastern Occupied Territories, headed by the ambitious but erratic *Reichsminister* Alfred Rosenberg, an Estonia-born and Riga-educated member of Hitler's inner circle.

The Berlin planners understood correctly from the beginning that the hatred engendered by the sovietization policies of 1940–1941 – referred to by the Baltic populations as "the year of terror" – could be put to use in shaping public opinion, and to this end, some leeway was therefore made for symbolic representations of nationalistic sentiments. Thus, for a time, national symbols – the colors of the interwar flags, anthems, and other significant reminders of pre-1940 nationhood – were permitted, but there was a general prohibition against all public reference to the three states by their prewar names. The question of the restoration of statehood (perhaps along the lines of the rump state of Slovakia) was on the minds of even those who viewed the Germans as "liberators," but when the subject came up, the German authorities made it clear that as long as the Reich was at war with the communist enemy and the Baltic littoral remained an important supply region for the front, the future would not be discussed. This was a shell-game, since nothing in the behind-the-scenes planning for the eastern occupied territories indicated any regard for the wishes of the region's residents. Indeed, the plans were reminiscent of the projections by the German Empire during World War I: massive deportations of the local populations to the vast hinterlands of Russia, germanization of the remainder, and colonization of the territory by surplus Germans. The "Germanness" of the littoral, introduced there in the thirteenth century, would thus be restored.

Although on paper the *Ostland* scheme read like a rational way of consolidating control over an occupied territory, in practice the administration of it bordered on chaotic. In addition to the military personnel answering to their front-line commanders and the civilian administrators answering to Rosenberg, a third set of officials was introduced into the region when economic administration was placed under the guidance of *Reichsmarschall* Hermann Göring. From the first moment of the invasion, interwoven throughout the other bureaucratic structures were the functionaries of the SS (*Schutzstaffel*) answering to *Reichsführer* Heinrich Himmler. The turf battles and rivalry of high Nazi officials in Berlin were reflected in the administration of the littoral, with the authority of Rosenberg's officials gradually being diminished. Rosenberg, as it turned out, was not a very talented bureaucratic infighter or administrator, and his *Ostministerium* (Ministry of Eastern Occupied Territories) in Berlin was sneeringly referred to as *Chaosministerium*. These inner struggles of the German administrative apparatus in the littoral were not simply an import from Berlin; locally, the district and subdistrict commissars were constantly warring about overlapping jursidictions as well. The military and the SS were frequently at odds about whether wartime needs or internal security were paramount, and Göring's subordinates sought to impose on everyone various five-year plans for the economic exploitation of the new territories.

Regardless of conflicting jurisdictions and infighting, one set of German occupiers – those involved in state security (the SS and the SD [*Sicherheitsdienst*]) – were quite single-minded about their mission from the moment they entered littoral territory: elimination of "undesirable" elements of the population such as functionaries from earlier communist regimes, Jews, Roma, and the mentally ill. This work involved hundreds of operatives, some organized in special-duty squads (*Einsatzkommandos* or *Einsatzgruppen*), and they succeeded in turning the first six months of the German occupation (June to December) into the most murderous period in the modern history of the Baltic littoral. The general populations were repeatedly told through various propaganda outlets that "communists" and "Jews" were identical; this message resonated with similar anti-Semitic beliefs that had existed in many segments of the general population for a long time. Thus the German security services were able quickly to recruit Lithuanians, Latvians, and Estonians for the "cleansing" process. In most *Aktionen* (actions) – as these organized and bloody activities were designated – Germans were in command and supplied the executioners; in many cases, the native populations acted on their own often without any special organization. The most notorious of these execution squads were *Einsatzgruppe A*, led by the SS *Brigadierführer* Walter Stahlecker, which operated in Latvia, and *Einsatzkommando 3*, under the authority of the Lithuanian SD chief K. Jäger, which operated in Lithuania. In Latvia, perhaps the best known was the *Arājs-Kommando*, a squad of about two hundred Latvian recruits led by Viktors Arājs, a lawyer who in 1940–1941 believed himself to be a convinced communist. After the German invasion, however, he became the principal Latvian executioner of Jews. In Estonia, where there were slightly more than a thousand Jews before the German invasion, the cleansing operations were much more haphazard but also involved local Estonians.

The vast majority of Jewish victims were in Lithuania and Latvia, where the killing started almost immediately after the invasion at the end of June (at Palanga in Lithuania; at Grobiņa, near Liepāja, in Latvia). The general approach of the German functionaries who spearheaded the "actions" was to make it appear that members of the local population were the initiators, but many times no such pretext was necessary. In numerous localities in the littoral where locals had seized power from the hastily departing communist officials, the former undertook "cleansing" operations without having taken any direct orders. The German strategy fed on local emotions heightened by the recent mass deportations, on the sadistic impulses of individuals who suddenly found themselves with absolute power over minorities they disliked, on the merging of the ideas of "communist" and "Jew," on the complete absence of any legal framework that would hold individuals accountable for their actions, and on the reluctance and inability of non-participants to interfere in activities that seemed to be in line with the desires of the new authorities.

The annihilation of Jews in the Baltic littoral – the littoral's Holocaust – was a seven-month-long process involving, initially, the withdrawal of all civil rights from Jews and their shooting in the rural localities where they lived; then came the creation of large urban ghettoes (the largest in Riga, Kaunas, and Vilnius) and many smaller ones, and in the the months of November and December the slaughter of most of the inhabitants of these concentrations. As a result of all the actions, by December 1941 the vast majority of Jews in Lithuania, Latvia, and Estonia had been annihilated (approaching 200,000 in Lithuania, some 90,000 in Latvia, and about 1,000 in Estonia). The number of Jews who were saved from death by Latvians and Lithuanians, by contrast, is relatively small: fewer than 3,000 in Lithuania, and several hundred at most in Latvia. The number in the civilian population who benefited indirectly from these murders cannot be estimated but must have been considerable: personal property was looted, empty apartments occupied, stores pillaged, and valuables confiscated. The German authorities claimed all such Jewish property as their own, but were unable to enforce these regulations with any degree of consistency.

In the other categories of undesirables, the total figures available for the whole littoral are less complete but approached 7,000–8,000. There were also survivors in all categories for many reasons. Substantial disagreement existed among high German officials over the question of keeping able-bodied Jews alive to support the war effort at least until victory, and some remained alive just for that purpose. Other Jews were kept from annihilation by civilians who hid them. Not all Soviet-era functionaries were killed because the German security services "turned" some of them to use for their own purposes; many were merely imprisoned and others went into hiding. There is also reason to think that occasionally lower-level officials sent to their superiors inflated figures about "cleansing" operations. The absence of updated census figures adds to the problem: the last Latvian census was taken in 1935, the only Lithuanian national count was done in 1923, and the last Estonian count was carried out in 1934. Also, there was considerable population movement in and out of the three countries just before World War II and during the period 1939–1941, so that the starting point for calculating survivorship remains imprecise. Nonetheless, the littoral's

Holocaust eliminated some 90 percent of the Jewish populations in the three countries, an estimated 60–70 percent of Roma were killed, and probably almost all of the mentally impaired. With respect to Jews, in less that twelve months mass murder had nearly extinguished an entire population that had been present in the Latvian territories since the nineteenth century and in the Lithuanian territories since the sixteenth.

Throughout the first year of the occupation, the German authorities were not able to work out a hard-line policy on how to deal with the national aspirations of Estonians, Latvians, and Lithuanians, even though they categorically rejected any suggestion that the pre-1940 republics still possessed legal existence. Heinrich Himmler opined that the treatment of the conquered eastern territories should be differentiated: the Baltic peoples, having been subjected to sovietization for only one year, differed in this respect from those who had been under Soviet rule for a quarter century. Also, Nazi racial theory was ambiguous about the Baltic peoples: the Estonians seemed close to the Scandinavian (Nordic) category, the Latvians had felt centuries of German influence, and the Lithuanians, despite having long experienced influence from the racially inferior Poles, were nonetheless related to the Old Prussians and were also staunch Catholics. Still, the littoral was conquered territory and its inhabitants had no right to demand anything of the German authorities; what rights they deserved would be granted to them by the occupation authorities.

Thus, it was thought useful that the chain of command in *Ostland* should have at the bottom a link between the German authorities and the civilian populations. The arrangements for a *landeseigene Verwaltung* (indigenous self-government) were different in each country. In Lithuania, a set of Lithuanian "counselors," headed by General Petras Kabiliūnas, answered to the *Generalkommisar* for Lithuania, Adrian von Renteln; in Latvia, a set of "directors," led by General Oskars Dankers, to the *Generalkommissar* for Latvia, Otto-Heinrich Drechsler; and in Estonia, "directors," led by Hjalmar Mäe, a leader in the veterans movement of the 1930s, to the *Generalkommissar* for Estonia, Karl Litzmann. By the end of 1941, the arrangements in Estonia and Latvia appeared to have a more corporate character than those in Lithuania, but, in any event, the German authorities made certain that none of these quasi-governmental groups evolved into a real self-government. All matters involving Jews, Germans, or the war effort were off limits to the indigenous officials; they could have input in matters of the local economy, communications, ordinary police matters, education, and the administration of law involving "natives," but even in these areas all policy decisions had to be approved by Germans higher in the chain of command. Characteristically, Alfred Rosenberg's pronouncements on self-government, allowing the formation of these entities, muddled rather than clarified lines of jurisdiction. Moreover, in matters involving state security the demands of the security organs overrode the authority of the indigenous institutions. Although the common people of Estonia, Latvia, and Lithuania could take some satisfaction in being able to turn to co-nationals with low-level complaints and problems, any resolution of them independent of German policy was virtually impossible.

Although German administration of the Baltic littoral from 1941 to 1944 was generally guided by long-range plans rooted in ideology, the realities of governance and of military need eventually required various compromises. Regardless of the Germans' assumption of cultural superiority, a native domain of cultural activities continued to exist in all three countries, even monitored for excessive nationalism by the German authorities. There were no special efforts to exclude the use of the three littoral languages from public affairs. Authors who had survived the Soviet year continued to write and publish, the national opera companies performed throughout the whole period, artists exhibited their works, and song festivals took place. High German officials took care to be photographed at these events and to have the photographs appear in the few and strictly controlled newspapers. There was no systematic effort to nazify the content of culture. More than likely, the Germans were motivated by a cynical tolerance of "native" undertakings, believing that the accommodation of local cultural strivings would dispose Estonians, Latvians, and Lithuanians toward helping the war effort.

On their side, the three littoral peoples – those who had not been targeted for immediate extermination – became increasingly disillusioned with their German "liberators," especially as German military successes on the eastern front grew fewer and the front stopped advancing into Soviet territory. Shortages became commonplace in urban areas and the countryside; the officials of the "self-governments" were at best successful in resolving minor problems but made no headway in expanding the scope of national autonomy. A system of mandatory labor service carried young men and women to Germany proper toward an uncertain future. Most of the nationalization measures of the 1940–1941 Soviet period were not rescinded in spite of promises; in this respect, Soviet totalitarianism turned out to be a boon to German economic administrators a year later. Disillusionment became cynicism, and popular opinion, as reported later by those who lived through the period, came increasingly to view the German occupants as no better than their earlier Russian counterparts. The hope for a German defeat in the war and the withdrawal of the Third Reich from the littoral became intertwined with the nearly certain expectation that such an outcome would mean the return to the littoral of Soviet power. Stochastic opposition to German rule was present from 1941 onward but became more organized in 1943 in Latvia and Lithuania and in 1944 in Estonia. But because of the bind in which the littoral peoples found themselves, the goals motivating opponents of the Nazi regime inevitably remained divided: while some worked for the return of national independence, others sought a return to a Soviet littoral – the status quo before the German invasion.

With the fortunes of war beginning to turn against them in 1942, the German planners contemplated the possibility of reversing their initial stance of keeping weapons out of the hands of the local civilian populations. This policy had already been breached earlier through the acceptance into the military effort of so-called "volunteer police battalions," serving mostly within the borders of each country. By 1942, about 20,000 Lithuanians, 14,000 Latvians, and 12,000 Estonians were already serving in this capacity. The newer policy had as its goal the creation of national military units that would be sent to the front to fight alongside the *Wehrmacht*. Organizationally, these units would become part of the *Waffen-SS* (the military contingents of the SS organization); they were to be designated as "volunteers" (*freiwillige*); at the regimental level they were to be commanded by Estonian, Latvian, and Lithuanian officers, but above that by German commanders.

The new policy had different outcomes in each of the three Baltic lands. In Lithuania, no national units materialized because of opposition to the recruitment drive by an active underground movement;

to counter its influence among the young, the German authorities closed Kaunas and Vilnius universities, arrested about fifty activists, and sent them to the Stutthof concentration camp in Germany. The effort in Estonia was only minimally more successful with the formation in 1943 of the 20th Estonian *Waffen-SS* division, which initially was composed of about 5,000 soldiers (the so-called Estonian Legion). In terms of numbers, the most successful recruiting effort took place in Latvia with the formation, also in 1943 and 1944, of the 15th and 19th Latvian *Waffen-SS* divisions which eventually involved more than 100,000 soldiers (the so-called Latvian Legion). The Latvian and Estonian "self-governments" were both actively involved in helping to create these fighting forces, but, in spite of that, avoidance of service became commonplace and quickly the term "volunteer" became a misnomer. Soldiers were conscripted by birth cohort, and not reporting for duty was severely punished. Still, Estonians of draft age continued to flee to Finland (an estimated 3,000) and similar stratagems in Latvia resulted in only about 15–20 percent of the Latvian divisions being true volunteers. As in the war of independence from 1918 to 1920, the Estonians, Latvians, and Lithuanians fought for both sides: the communist partisans and the Red Army had in their ranks an estimated 30,000 Estonians, 75,000 Latvians, and 82,000 Lithuanians. Indeed, several battles in late 1944 and early 1945 involved the "national" units of both sides firing at each other.

By summer 1944, the Baltic littoral populations began to realize that the Third Reich would eventually be defeated. On the eastern front, advances by the German army had ceased long ago; a retreat, though never referred to by that name, had started; the Soviet army began a full-scale counterattack in September. Meanwhile on the western front, after the Normandy invasion on June 6, 1944, the German forces were going on the defensive as well. In the littoral any public expression of worry about the return of a Soviet regime was treated as "defeatism" and harshly punished, but the rumors of a German defeat only became stronger. Signs of desperation among the German occupiers also increased, especially in the area of manpower. Repeated calls for increased conscription became commonplace. There were many instances of abduction of men on the street to complete labor units being sent to Germany; units of sixteen- and seventeen-year-old boys were conscripted into various support units (*Hilfswillige*), and the German civilian authorities became more lenient in discussions about the eventual autonomy (if not independence) of the three Baltic states after German victory. But by autumn 1944, the German authorities had lost all credibility in the eyes of most of the littoral populations; whatever benevolence was demonstrated toward the "natives" was now interpreted as an effort to heighten the spirit of resistance of the local populations while the Germans themselves withdrew to their homeland.

In this context, flight by the littoral's civilian inhabitants who had experienced the 1940–1941 Soviet regime became an everyday subject of discussion, especially when it became evident that the German authorities would create space for refugees on troop ships traversing the Baltic Sea from ports in Ostland to occupied Poland. Alternatively, a land route through western Lithuania into occupied Poland could be used, though this option became problematic since the Soviet counter-attack in Lithuania had as its objective a rapid drive toward the Baltic seacoast. Another alternative was flight to Sweden by fishing boats or trawlers. During spring 1945 the sea routes, however, risked bombardment by the Soviet air force. In fact, all three alternatives were used from summer 1944 until the end of the war with a steady and expanding stream of Baltic-area refugees arriving in Germany proper or in Sweden. Although the absolute numbers will always remain estimates because there is no information about how many were killed in transit, most research agrees that approximately 80,000 Estonians, 160,000 Latvians, and 64,000 Lithuanians left their homeland during the final ten months of the war and headed westward. The vast majority of the littoral's residents, however, did not flee because they did not wish to leave their homelands and be separated from their relatives; because they trusted their ability to survive under any kind of regime, including the returning Soviets; because they actually welcomed the Soviet return; or because the rapidly westward-moving Soviet front caught them behind the battle lines and made flight impossible. The socioeconomic composition of the three refugee streams was mixed, but they all had a large component of the people who had been targeted for repression in 1940–1941: intellectuals, teachers, artists, writers, clergymen, government officials, and politicians who had survived the first Soviet year. Also included were those who expected that the returning Soviet regime would use a very inclusive definition of "collaborator with the forces of fascist Germany."

BACK ON THE SOCIALIST ROAD

In Estonia, the Soviet army took Tallinn on September 22, 1944; in Latvia, the German forces withdrew from Riga on October 13, moving westward toward the Courland coast; in Lithuania, the Soviet drive across the country in October brought the army almost to Klaipėda (Memel) on the Baltic coast. Sporadic fighting continued, however, well into the early months of 1945 in all three countries. In Estonia, the returning Soviets did not establish firm control until December 1944; in Lithuania, fighting around Klaipėda on the Baltic coast continued into January 1945; and in Latvia, about 500,000 German soldiers and members of the Latvian Legion (19th Division) continued to hold out in the northeast corner of Courland – quickly dubbed "the Courland kettle" – until Hitlerite Germany surrendered on May 8, 1945. The months between October 1944 and May 1945 came to seem a kind of *interregnum* – the Germans withdrawing, the Soviets not yet fully in control – and in Estonia and Latvia, desperate though inconsequential efforts were made to re-establish independent statehood. An Estonian National Committee in September 1944 announced the existence of a national government, but this effort fell apart quickly. In the "Courland kettle," a group of determined Latvian officers in the 19th Division, under the leadership of Jānis Kurelis, viewed themselves as the core of a new Latvian army and began to refuse the commands of their German superiors. This was quashed in November 1944 when some 1,300 Latvian soldiers were arrested and eight of their leaders were executed (Kurelis was transported to Germany). In Germany, permission was obtained from the German authorities in February 1945 to form a Latvian National Committee that would become a kind of Latvian government-in-exile; this also remained inconsequential.

All these efforts were guided by the belief that the western Allies – especially the USA and Great Britain – would not permit the Baltic states to be reabsorbed into the USSR; therefore, governmental structures would be needed to establish continuity between the pre-1940 republics and whatever was to emerge after the war. The non-recognition policy enunciated earlier by the western democracies and various international declarations during the war about national-self determination and free elections fed such expectations, but the few surviving Baltic leaders underestimated how much the desires of the USSR – the ally of the western democracies – would shape decisions in the postwar period about the future of the eastern European regions under Soviet army control.

The withdrawal of the German army from the Soviet Union during 1944 created for the Soviet authorities considerable lead time to plan for the reoccupation of the Baltic littoral, even as fierce fighting there continued. Cadres for national and local governmental institutions therefore stood ready to take power as soon as the Soviet army had reoccupied and pacified a given territory, and this process unfolded during the final months of 1944 and the first half of 1945. The three communist parties returned and established their authority; their leadership remained largely the same people who had fled ahead of the German advance, but the situation on the ground now was radically different from that in June 1941. The four-year German occupation of the littoral had taken a severe toll on human and physical resources; also, the returning Soviet army – although believing itself to be "liberating" the littoral – treated the civilian populations as enemies. Even the Communist Party leadership was forced to remind military leaders repeatedly throughout 1944 and 1945 that the three countries were in fact soviet socialist republics and not conquered territory. Still, party leaders had to recognize that even though after May 1945 there existed no real challenges to their authority, they were still operating in a hostile environment.

In all three littoral countries, especially during the final months of the war, thousands of armed men – soldiers and civilians – had taken refuge in the forests and at least for now remained beyond the control of both the Soviet military and civilian authorities. These "forest brothers" – partisans and guerilla fighters – constituted a force to be reckoned with; their numbers (by definition imprecise) are estimated in the immediate postwar years to have been about 10,000 each in Estonia and Latvia, and upward of 40,000 in Lithuania. They were well armed, having brought weapons along from their former military units, and they successfully raided Soviet armories. Referred

Map 9 The Baltic states after World War II. Annexed by the USSR in 1940, the three Baltic countries reemerged as independent states in 1991.

to generically as "bandits" by Soviet auhorities, the forest brothers harassed Soviet functionaries, especially in rural areas; fought pitched battles against the search-and-destroy military units sent to flush them out of their hideouts; and requisitioned or stole food however they could. As long as they received direct or indirect support from the surrounding farming populations, they could survive, but as time wore on such support dwindled. This type of resistance was fueled by the belief that the western democracies and the Soviet Union would soon be at war, which was a misreading of where postwar tensions, soon to become the Cold War, were leading. As hope was abandoned, the most determined of the partisans had nothing more than their burning hatred of the Soviet system to draw upon, and the last of them did not emerge from the forests until the mid-1950s.

In the meantime, the communist parties in Estonia, Latvia, and Lithuania, their dominance having been quickly restored by the Soviet army, took on the multiple tasks of rebuilding the three republics. In Estonia, the party was led from 1944 by Nikolai Karotamm (1901–1969), an Estonian who had been in the Soviet Union during the years of the "bourgeois dictatorship"; in Latvia, by the Latvian Jānis Kalnbērziņš (1893–1986), who had led the Latvian party in 1940–1941, and was therefore an "old hand"; and in Lithuania, by Lithuanian-born Antanas Sniečkus (1903–1974), who had spent the interwar years in the USSR and in Lithuanian jails. These three had managed to sidestep Stalin's purges of the "Old Bolsheviks" during 1936–1938 and therefore understood their principal assignment very well. At lower levels, however, all three parties had a shortage of experienced cadres and therefore appealed to Moscow to help solve the problem. There now began a steady inflow of administrators and specialists from other parts of the USSR which continued well into the 1950s and even beyond. Moscow was not always able to comply with these requests by further tapping the populations of Baltic-born communists living in the USSR; that pool of talent became exhausted relatively quickly. Consequently, the arriving monolingual Russian-speaking cadres were strangers to the Baltic area linguistically and culturally, and the efficiency of the reconstruction efforts was initially impaired by communication difficulties. Most people in the local populations were not fluent in Russian, and the prominence of monolingual

Russian speakers at every level of the renewed power hierarchy fed the impression that the communist parties and the governments were Russian-run. At the highest level this, of course, was the case, but when communist party membership as a whole is considered, the situation was more complicated. The parties were small in 1940, and they had grown somewhat during 1940–1941. Now, in the postwar years, the number of members started a continuous upward trajectory. In Estonia, in 1945 there were 2,400 members, but by 1951 the number had grown to 18,500 (fewer than half were Estonian). In Latvia, membership was around 11,000 in 1946, but by 1953 had reached around 35,000 (perhaps a third Latvian). In Lithuania, party membership in 1945 stood at about 35,000, and by 1953 it had grown to about 36,200 (some 40 percent Lithuanian). Thus, during the 1940s and most of the 1950s, the majority of all three parties was indeed at least Russian-speaking (if not non-native), but each party also had a substantial portion of local members.

Since the party controlled virtually all higher level jobs by virtue of a *nomenklatura* system (in Lithuania, for example, these positions eventually numbered about 42,000 as the party continued to expand), party membership was the rational choice for ambitious people regardless of personal belief. Many party members were, of course, true believers, but others who joined in the postwar decade did so during the pervasive system of double morality that was to last until the collapse of party control. Having been vetted through participation in the communist youth organization *Komsomol* and invited to join, one took the party card, benefited from the advantages party membership offered, and kept one's personal beliefs under wraps when they differed from the "party line." Inevitably, one had to accept partial russification in the linguistic sense, since most of party business at all levels was transacted only in Russian.

There were, of course, many persons to whom party membership was closed. Those with an "unacceptable biography" included people whose relatives had been deported, had emigrated to western countries, had belonged to "anti-Soviet" organizations in the interwar period, and by current definition had "collaborated" with the German occupants during 1941–1945. People with such family connections did not belong in the new elite. Given the relatively small size of the three Baltic-area populations, the pool of native party talent was substantially constricted in the postwar decade. The nature of membership recruitment and composition of the parties would change somewhat after Stalin's death in 1953, especially in Lithuania, but in the meantime, the populations of the three republics had to live with a political elite that was only partially native.

The tasks for postwar reconstruction were formidable. With respect to level of human capital, the three countries had suffered substantial population decrease: an estimated 17 percent in Latvia, 20 percent in Estonia, and 18 percent in Lithuania. But not all those who were left could be permitted to reenter productive activity based only upon their job skills. Loyalty to the new regime became a criterion, and this required normalizing the status of the thousands who had fled their homes but had not left the territory of the littoral; dealing with the other thousands who had served in the German army and fought against the Soviet forces; coping with the many broken families in which some members had fled west, leaving others behind. In addition, foodstuffs and virtually all other material goods were in short supply; the educational system, especially at the elementary level, had to be reinvigorated; housing had to be found for the large number of Soviet army personnel who now became permanent residents of the littoral; and the immediate pasts of the thousands of people whose activities and positions during the German occupation period made their ultimate loyalties suspect had to be vetted. At the level of physical capital, economic reconstruction and development had to be aligned with the centralized plans issued from Moscow; as early as 1946, the three Baltic republics were placed on five-year plans, with the requirements and quotas such plans entailed.

The most demanding task was the rebuilding of industrial capacity. In Estonia, wartime devastation resulted in about a 45% drop in industrial production, and similar declines took place in Latvia and Lithuania. The agricultural sector was equally problematic: foodstuffs had to be provided quickly, but agricultural production was still based on individualized farm ownership. To attempt collectivization immediately could prove disastrous, and the communist parties of the three countries settled in the short run for systems of requisitioning of agricultural products that initially asked each farmer to surrender about 20% of the annual harvest to the needs of the state.

Government propaganda portrayed agricultural collectivization as coming slowly and on the basis of voluntarism.

The recovery and reconstruction that did take place during the immediate postwar years, however, was anchored at least as much, and probably more, in the desire of the littoral populations to lead normal lives than in a conscious enlistment in the government-trumpeted tasks of "building socialism." For a long time, a vast area of mistrust and suspicion continued to exist between the government and the so-called working people in whose name overall policy was now being made. This could not have been otherwise. Adults who had lived through the war years and the two sequential occupations had absorbed the lessons of how to live in a totalitarian system: survival required compliance, making do, a double morality, and a significant amount of resignation and fatalism. None of these survival tactics, however, meant acceptance of the legitimacy of the system or the internalization of its values. Realism required that one recognize where power resided and act accordingly. On their side, the new regimes took it for granted that the Estonian, Latvian, and Lithuanian populations had been corrupted in myriad ways by living for two decades outside the sphere of Moscow's domination. Many knew about the "capitalist west" and its materialistic lures; many had experienced some degree of prosperity under the prewar system; and many had relatives or friends who had fled and were, as far as was known, living in the west. The specter of "bourgeois nationalism" was suspected of lurking everywhere and had to be rooted out with a vengeance. The "people's" thinking had to be redirected toward the leadership of the communist parties, and, most importantly, toward the wise leadership of Josef Vissarianovich Stalin. All memories of better times in the past had to be suppressed and made irrelevant. Reconstruction, in other words, meant not only economic rebuilding but also, and perhaps more significantly, the renovation of the three Baltic peoples' collective psychology.

During the Stalin era, until 1953, the parties attacked the prewar regimes ferociously. A stringent censorship regime was meant to ensure that nothing positive would be said about them, and nothing negative about the post-1945 societies. Censorship operated in all fields of public expression through numerous screening layers. Long lists of "outdated" printed materials – books, periodicals, brochures from the interwar period and earlier – were prepared and the items removed from libraries; these materials were either destroyed or placed into *specfondi* (special collections) accessible only to trustworthy researchers. A new literary canon was advanced, consisting of writers of the past who had had "progressive" credentials, that is, they had demonstrated an interest in or actually advocated socialistic forms of economic organization, had exhibited friendly attitudes toward Russian culture, and had taken a negative stance toward the three national states. Only those military units (including the Latvian rifle regiments) of World War I who supported the Bolshevik cause were lionized. Demonstrations of subservience were demanded of writers, especially poets, through commissioning of poetry in praise of Stalin. Artists could only produce realistic scenes from the 1905 period, Baltic events that connected the littoral to the 1917 revolution, and Lenin's heroism. Specialists in the parties' central committees produced long lists of "suggested topics" in all fields of the expressive arts. The policing of scholarship in the humanities was assigned to the Academies of Science, which were founded shortly after the war on the model of the USSR Academy of Science.

Aesthetic impulses were completely subordinated to the dictates of "socialist realism" as laid out, for the whole USSR, by the hard-line Stalinist Andrei Zhdanov, who was well known in Estonia as the Soviet emissary who supervised its occupation in June 1940. Among the habits of the creative mind zhdanovism aimed to eliminate was "formalism" (art for art's sake, regardless of intellectual content) and, of particular moment for the Baltic littoral, "bourgeois nationalism" (expressions of sympathy for or admiration of the nation-state). Such values did not belong in the new socialist world and had to be extirpated in line with the ideology of Marxism-Leninism-Stalinism. Historians were required to portray the events of 1940–1941 as "inevitable," as a "socialist revolution" during which the "proletariat" of the three Baltic countries, led by the local communist parties as the vanguard and assisted by the fraternal USSR, threw off the "bourgeois yoke," established the "dictatorship of the proletariat," and joined the other fraternal republics of the USSR in the task of building socialism. This scheme of historical developments had the effect of rendering Baltic history as a morality play: all those developments and individuals in the past who were on the correct side of the "class struggle" – the driving force of history – were positive heroes, while the rest were negative or at best irrelevant. This scheme remained mandatory until Stalin's death in 1953, and was incorporated into the curricula of educational institutions at every level, in "official histories" of the three republics written by historians associated with the Institutes of History (components of the Academies of Science) and the Institutes of Communist Party History.

The scheme remained the general framework for all history writing long afterward and provided the new power-wielders – the party, the organs of government, the state security apparatus – with categories of enemies into which to place all population groups that appeared to threaten Soviet power and the state interests of the USSR. The premise was that phases of historical development could overlap, creating people whose thinking was characteristic of an earlier phase but who were nonetheless living in the next, more progressive phase. The guardians of the most recent phase (the dictatorship of the proletariat) had to be alert to all manner of unreconstructed thought because such a mindset could easily turn into deviationism, sabotage, and obstructionist thinking and behavior. The Baltic republics, in this view, were rife with potential enemies who had grown up in a capitalist environment. If such people did not fully cooperate with the requirements of the new order, they had to be removed, in one way or another.

Implementation of policy through physical removal of harmful categories of persons was demonstrated most graphically in connection with the collectivization of agriculture in the three republics. Enthusiasm in rural areas for collective farms of any kind had been minimal in 1940–1941; individualized agriculture was a strong tradition in all areas of the littoral, and it had been enhanced by the agrarian reforms of the 1920s as well as the "reform" of 1940–1941 when the new Soviet governments themselves created a new class of smallholders – the so-called ten-hectare farmers. Since the German occupation did little to change the situation, immediately after 1945 Estonia had 136,000 individual farms, Latvia around 280,000, and Lithuania upwards of 300,000. The pace of enrollment in collective agricultural enterprises – *kolkhozes* and *sovohozes* – remained unsatisfactorily slow in spite of extraordinarily heavy taxation deliberately placed on private farms. By 1947, the party in Moscow had grown tired of waiting, and defined a category of "kulaks" – an obstructionist class of people who were said to be responsible for the delays in collectivization. The category was flexible, but at the center of the definition stood those farmers who were moderately successful and employed other people: these *kulaks* now had to be liquidated as a class. During 1948–1949 about 40,000 were deported from Lithuania to various Siberian locations, and in March 1949 approximately 40,000 from Estonia and about 44,000 from Latvia (estimates vary in all three cases). From the viewpoint of the republics' communist parties, this action was successful: without the harmful influences of the *kulaks* the farming population flocked to collective farms, and by 1950 the transformation of agriculture in the Baltic littoral was nearly completed. As could be expected, agricultural productivity fell rapidly during this period, bringing total production to lower levels than in 1940. The psychological cost of the 1948–1949 deportations was as great as those of June 1941, but whereas the German invasion had permitted some degree of revenge against perpetrators, in 1948–1949 no such opportunity existed.

Taken together, the eight years of Stalinist rule in the Baltic littoral (1945–1953) accelerated hopelessness in the adult populations of the three countries, despite the relentless propaganda that trumpeted the glorious future of a socialist society. Everyday life was marked by shortages of all kinds (ration cards were used until 1947), as the party implemented Moscow directives to focus economic investment in heavy industry. Diminished agricultural output because of collectivization played havoc with food supplies in cities and towns. Housing, especially in larger cities, became tighter than ever, and the shortage of living space resulted in the proliferation of communal apartments. Ordinary people learned quickly not to question a distribution system that allocated more scarce goods to members of the *nomenklatura*, the upper echelons of the party and the government, because the apparatus of state security quickly and effectively created a system of informants and denouncers. Artists and scholars experienced restrictions on freedom of expression most severely; many deserted their calling to take unskilled jobs, others toed the party line and produced ideologically correct art and writing. In any case, the intellectual elites of the three countries had been at least halved through the execution, deportation, and emigration of prewar intellectuals. Contact with the art and literature of western countries – a "western orientation" – was suspect; the mandatory orientation was now toward Russian language and culture as embodied in the official Soviet cultural superstructure. In spite of the "national cadres" – Estonians, Latvians, and Lithuanians – in the three parties and in the structures of government, all these components of the new political elite slavishly followed Moscow's dictates with a mixture of conviction and fear.

AFTER STALIN

The generation of Estonians, Latvians, and Lithuanians who were children during World War II and entered their formative years in the postwar period did not experience the new regime in the same way as their parents and grandparents. Childhood memoirs, while differing from person to person, report the normal pattern of submission to adult authority, conditioned by shortages of various kinds and an equally normal and growing desire to found a stable future: success in school, marriage, and specialized training for a profession. While for adults the contrasts between current reality and the prewar past remained vivid, for most growing children normality was defined by what existed in their own present, including ignorance about what was going on in the rest of the world. Reality meant such institutions as the Young Pioneers, *Komsomol*, and the party, and the understanding that the country to which they belonged was called a soviet socialist republic and that it was part of a larger Union of Soviet Socialist Republics led by a benevolent Stalin. Parents and grandparents tended to keep negative assessments to themselves for their own protection and so as to guard their offspring from missteps. Yet children did acquire fragmentary information about the past from old magazines and newspapers in attics, from curiosity triggered by stultifying preachments of the party line by teachers and other important adults, and from the natural interest in forbidden fruit. As time passed, the likelihood that the world-as-it-was would change radically grew increasingly remote; most of the younger generation internalized the idea that to get along one had to go along, and what one must go along with would inevitably be dictated by outsiders who lived far away. Yet the young were still growing up in entities called Estonia, Latvia, and Lithuania – in their own and their friends' parlance – even though these were not quite the same as the countries that had existed in the past. There were many soldiers about and persons speaking Russian; also, the Russian language was seeping into all nooks and crannies of Baltic society; but the young did not perceive this as an egregious violation of cultural space the way their parents and grandparents did. Rumors circulated that bad things happened to people at odds with officialdom, and the lesson taken from that was that one steered clear of challenges to official persons. There was self-segregation by nationality (through language) among the young, but at least as much crossing of linguistic lines in both directions in search of friendships and even potential marriage partners.

The death of Stalin in March 1953 was less of a shock to the populations of the Baltic littoral than to many others in the USSR who had lived under his leadership much longer and had come to think of him as something close to a deity. The details of the Kremlin power struggle after Stalin's death remained hidden to most people. The emergence of Nikita Khrushchev as first secretary of the central committee of the Communist Party of the USSR did not initially signal new developments. The expulsion in July of Lavrentii Beria – the internal security chief – from the party and his execution did; in the littoral, his name had been associated with extreme repression for a long time, but more recently, after Stalin's death, Beria had urged the party to emphasize the need for "national cadres" in the republics. A much greater shock – in the Baltic littoral and elsewhere – came with the Twentieth Party Congress in 1956, when Nikita Khrushchev condemned Stalin as having institutionalized "the cult of personality" and through that as having led the USSR away from the true path of building socialism as laid down by Lenin. Since the party, by definition, never erred, the policies of recent years that had claimed millions of victims through executions, deportations, and imprisonment were now attributed to Stalin and some steps were taken to reverse the damage. The period from about 1957 to the early 1960s came to be known as the "thaw"; the party – including the republic parties – had to readjust their thinking to the new "party line," which produced disagreements in the littoral over how far the reversals should go. Many decisions of the thaw period, however, were made by the Moscow leadership and required only compliance in the republics. Amnesty ("rehabilitation") was granted to many of those who had been deported during the Stalinist years, producing a drift of littoral populations back to the homeland from outlying areas of the USSR. The returnees were not welcomed by the littoral parties or the state security organs, because they brought with them the problems of reintegration – employment, housing, memories. Through the publication of Aleksandr Solzhenitsyn's *One Day in the Life of Ivan Denisovich* in 1957, Moscow also appeared to be signaling the arrival of a permissive attitude toward public discussion of wrongs of the Stalin period. This shift was attractive to younger literary intellectuals of the Baltic republics, who now saw an opportunity – however small – for creating works of art consistent with their own aesthetic sense. The relaxation of controls had limits, however; the party leaders in Moscow and in the littoral who saw the thaw as an innovation endangering party control did not disappear but were biding their time. In their view, a good example of where permissiveness could lead was the 1956 events in Hungary, where a reformist communist party appeared to want to exit the "Soviet bloc" entirely, following the path of the uncontrollable Josip Broz Tito of Yugoslavia, who had successfully made the move in 1948. Whatever the thaw meant in the realm of cultural activity, it was not to mean reduction of Moscow's control within the USSR and over the so-called satellite communist states of eastern Europe, or of the control exercised by the parties in the individual communist states.

Because of their late entry into the USSR, the Baltic republics and their communist parties were thought to be particularly vulnerable to doctrinal "infections" of various kinds, especially during such transition periods as the thaw, so that Moscow had to be vigilant about the party leadership in the littoral. The membership of the three republic parties had continued to grow throughout the 1950s, reaching, in 1962, about 42,500 in Estonia, 78,200 in Latvia, and 66,200 in Lithuania. This growth trajectory was not without its problems for Moscow, however. The expansion brought into the parties a new generation of members whose loyalty to the idea of Soviet-style socialism was not in doubt, but who at the same time evidently nurtured a streak of independent thinking focused on the welfare of the republics themselves. In the post-Stalinist years, the solution to the problem of bourgeois nationalism could no longer easily be solved by execution; less bloody means had to be found to eradicate independent-mindedness. One way was to ensure that Moscow loyalists remained in charge. Already in Estonia in 1950, a significant purge (including arrests and executions) had taken place, eliminating virtually all of the pre-1940 leadership cadres who were accused of bourgeois nationalism. This action enlarged the power of the Moscow loyalist Ivan (or Johannes) Käbin, who remained in the position of first secretary of the Estonian Communist Party for the next twenty-six years (from 1950 to 1976). Käbin, an Estonian by birth, had grown up in the USSR, and had no particular attachment to the country when the party had brought him back in 1940–1941. Although not a bourgeois nationalist or even a national communist, as first secretary he became an increasingly effective intermediary between Moscow and the Estonian party, maintaining the confidence of both and managing to ward off or soften Moscow directives that seemed unreasonable. A similar role was played by Antanas Sniečkus in Lithuania, who emerged as first secretary of the Lithuanian Communist Party in 1940–1941 and served in that capacity until 1974. Because of his long-standing dedication to the party (since 1920), he managed to retain the confidence of the Moscow leadership during the Stalin years and even long after Stalin's death, developing the reputation of the "squire of Lithuania." His position was secure enough for the changing Moscow leadership to believe that Sniečkus would keep Lithuanian "deviationists" under control. In this Moscow's judgment was correct. These two long-lived party bosses generally kept their parties and the societies they governed from experiencing any dangerous veering away from the party line during the thaw and considerably beyond it, employing for that purpose a substantial amount of ruthlessness.

Latvia, however, was a different situation: there the party's first secretary – Jānis Kalnbērziņš (in office 1940–1959) – was relatively weak. Having successfully survived the postwar Stalin period, Kalnbērziņš during the thaw period presided over a Latvian party within which dissatisfaction with Moscow's strictures was growing, even among many dedicated party members such as Eduards Berklavs, the first secretary of the Riga Central Committee. At issue was the continuing influx of a Slavic-speaking labor force, the accompanying linguistic russification of everyday life, and five-year plans that targeted the republic for further industrialization even in the absence of an adequate labor supply. Questioning whether this was consistent with the "nationality principles" of Lenin, leading figures in the Latvian party advanced plans for development more consistent with Latvia's labor resources. In the view of hard-liners in the Latvian Central Committee such as Arveds Pelše this was "deviationism" of the crudest sort, and they sought Moscow's help and support. A major confrontation occurred in 1959, which even involved Nikita Khrushchev. In a meeting with East German communist leaders in Riga, he heard from the hard-liners in the Latvian party about what they described as "bourgeois nationalists" in its the ranks. A purge followed: an estimated two thousand party members were removed from positions of authority for "serious errors," Berklavs was reassigned (in effect, exiled) to a low-level job in Russia, Kalnbērziņš resigned "for reasons of health," and for the next two decades, the top leadership positions were filled by Latvians who had "returned" to the country after many decades in Soviet Russia. The winner of this intraparty struggle was Arveds Pelše, who remained first secretary from 1959 to 1966. Pelše was not only a typical "Russian Latvian" in his subservience to Moscow, but also exhibited an almost personal animosity toward any and all manifestations of Latvian national culture and traditions.

Nikita Khrushchev's experiments with agricultural modernization and other missteps led to his replacement in 1964 as CPSU general secretary by Leonid Brezhnev, who retained that position until his death in 1982. Brezhnev was considered by the party as a safe but modern leader, not given to the extravagant and unpredictable outbursts that had characterized Khrushchev's leadership, and responsive to the general needs of Soviet society as described by a new generation of the party's *nomenklatura*. In the Baltic republics, the atmosphere created by the thaw continued for a short while after Khrushchev's removal. The period (1956–1964) was long enough to fire the imaginations of Baltic literary intellectuals with respect to both content and form in their writings. This was a triple-generational phenomenon because it involved not only a chronological "new generation" (writers in their twenties) but also the two older generations whose voices had been stilled in the period since

1940. Thus, for example, in 1958 in Estonia, Jaan Kross, aged thirty-eight, published his first major poetry collection, which dealt with a deportee's experience in the coal mines of Siberia; in Latvia, in 1959, Ojārs Vācietis published his first novel dealing with the deportations of 1949; and in Lithuania in 1963, Mykolas Sluckis' novel dealt with World War II and the forest brothers. Some writers published works praising the natural world of their particular part of the littoral; these were really disguised statements of praise for the "homeland." Others wrote realistic descriptions of parent–offspring conflict featuring the offspring of the new political elite; these were really public acknowledgments that under socialism and within the vanguard social conflict continued to exist. Some western literary classics were translated, and some of the pre-1940 writers were republished. In virtually every instance of these departures from the pre-thaw norms, however, there was a struggle to "push" the work through a multilayered system of censorship; often a work stopped midway and had to be withdrawn. Occasionally, if a Russian translation of a short story or poem was published in a Moscow literary journal first, the fear-driven censors of the littoral had to accept its legitimacy. The Baltic writers were after freedom of expression, but they were obliged to probe for it because the full machinery of censorship and punishment was still in place in spite of the thaw. Inevitably, there emerged a "literature of compromise" expressed in indirect language, allusions, symbols, parables, and complicated metaphors. This was a far cry from the socialist realism of the Stalin years – the hackneyed praise of the party, the Soviet future, and friendship with the Russian people – but the heavy hand of orthodoxy was still felt at every step of the creative process. Particularly egregious offenses against prevailing orthodoxy could result in expulsion from the Writers Unions and in a flat-out prohibition against appearing in print; such writers became non-persons and needed exceptional courage to continue to produce their art even, as the saying went, "for the desk drawer."

The literary conflicts of the thaw and immediate post-thaw periods in the littoral signaled that resignation in the face of the new "rules of the game" did not mean that the Baltic republics had become integrated into Soviet society. Everyday life was too full of jarring reminders to everyone of their dependent status; whatever aspirations of republic autonomy had existed were crushed by the elimination of national communist cadres from the republic parties. The littoral's party leaderships continued to live in fear of criticism from Moscow about their mismanagement of local affairs. The influx of Slavic speakers continued, and though the in-migrants thought of themselves as simply changing their residences within "their" Soviet Union, the receiving Baltic republics were confronted with the fact that their native languages were being progressively marginalized in their own homelands. Upward mobility in all organizational and professional hierarchies involved daily and constant communication in Russian, locally or centrally, and the Russian speakers, wherever they lived, showed little desire to learn the local languages.

Similarly, five-year plans continued to subordinate the needs of the republics to the developmental requirements of the USSR as a whole, ignoring the sometimes disastrous impact of large-scale industry on the local environment. The needs of the military remained paramount: not only was the USSR in a Cold War relationship with the capitalist west, but party propaganda made certain that the experiences of the USSR in World War II – invasion from the west – remained fresh in everyone's minds. Consequently, the Baltic republics – comprising a borderland area – came to contain a large number of military bases, storage areas, and training camps, all off-limits to the civilian populations. The center versus periphery problems underscored by the national communists remained unresolved, and their resolution would have to be brought about in ways that did not directly confront Moscow planners or the vigilant guardians of party orthodoxy.

CHANGE AND STAGNATION, DISSENT AND ACQUIESCENCE

During Leonid Brezhnev's tenure as CPSU general secretary time did not stand still either in the Baltic republics or in the Soviet Union as a whole, even though the Cold War framework during those twenty years often resembled a permanent fixture. Possession by NATO and the Warsaw Pact of nuclear weapons forced the two sides to avoid military confrontations, even as they sought by other means to expand their influence into other parts of the world. Western European countries continued to demonstrate a healthy pace of economic modernization, growing more prosperous with each passing year and developing such promising institutions as the European Common Market. In the USSR, however, change had a much more ambiguous meaning, as the CPSU and the republic parties vacillated between accepting certain kinds of modernity (as defined by western development) and wanting to keep absolute control. Though the party at all levels continued to announce successes in the fulfillment of five-year plans, technocrats and high party leaders knew that the public statistics were frequently falsified and that socioeconomic growth was by no means proceeding smoothly. Experimentation became necessary: some loosening of Moscow's control over economic decisions in the republics, the notion of "socialist competition," some bows in the direction of consumer demand, and relaxation of controls over persons who could provide technological innovation were seen as important driving forces for economic improvement. These forms of liberalization began under Khrushchev in the thaw period, but they continued as well during the early years of Brezhnev's tenure. Yet relaxation of central controls was always tentative: though liberally inclined party members urged more of it, the military establishment, the security services, and ultimately the party itself continued to envisage the USSR as on something like a wartime footing that required eternal vigilance and immense investments in the country's defense.

Thus by the end of the 1960s, the pendulum began to swing back toward more centralization. Being at war meant, among other things, controlling the flow of information, particularly of the kind that might reveal the shortcomings of the USSR in comparison with the west. It was particularly important for the party to maintain the fiction that the standard of living in the USSR was as high if not higher than in the "capitalist" world; after all, the party described itself as the vanguard of the masses, and therefore had to downplay information that showed "the masses" in western countries, particularly in Europe, to be outdistancing the USSR in terms of per capita income and other macro-indicators of well-being. New forms of centralization, including higher production quotas and systems of incentive premiums, were supposed to trigger faster growth, but generally failed to do so. By the early 1970s, Soviet standards of living were higher than in the immediate postwar period, but even the communist economies of the eastern European "satellite" countries (especially Poland, Czechoslovakia, and Hungary) appeared to be providing a better everyday life for their citizens than did the USSR. Much more typical of everyday Soviet life were the infamous queue with its own code of ethics, the system of *blat* (colloquial: pull) through which vendors exchanged scarce consumer goods or services for special favors, stores that provided quality consumer goods only for the *nomenklatura*, a thriving black market, and an exchange system in which it was more expedient to trade (cement for radio parts, tires for men's suits) than to place an order and wait endlessly. Since the ruble was not convertible, *valuta* stores appeared in which western relatives with western currencies could purchase for themselves and their Soviet kinfolk high quality goods not available to the common folk. All these informal systems of exchange were meant to circumvent the problems caused by centralized planning: shortages, maldistribution, lack of quality control, production and prices unlinked from demand, and wages and salaries unlinked from performance and set by bureacratic determinations of status. A basic staple such as wheat occasionally had to be purchased in quantity from the USA and Canada because of alleged crop failures due to "bad weather." By the mid-1970s, even internal commentators were coming to refer to the Brezhnev years (though, of course, not publicly) as the "era of stagnation."

In comparative economic terms and in the imaginations of much of the Slavic-speaking population of the USSR, the Baltic republics fell somewhere between the eastern European satellite states and the USSR interior: the region was oftentimes referred to in Soviet publications as "our west." The party *nomenklatura* liked to vacation in Jūrmala – the collection of small beach-front communities on the Gulf of Riga northwest of the city. Baltic cities had the atmosphere of old Hanseatic towns, and monolingual Slavic residents learned very quickly that they needed no other language than Russian to live there. They did not have to experience the feelings of inadequacy that came from being in the real west, or even such highly westernized "fraternal socialist republics" as Czechoslovakia. Though the natives of the three republics spoke some other language, most had learned to speak Russian, and in any event the Russian populations in the Baltic republics by the mid-1970s had grown large enough to create a comfortable pool for Russian speakers to swim in.

By 1965, the number of Russians in the Baltic republics had reached about a million. By the mid-1970s, Estonians in the Estonian republic constituted only 68% of the total population, Latvians in Latvia comprised about 54%, but by contrast the proportion of Lithuanians in Lithuania remained a strong 80%. The most heavily impacted by these migration trends were the urban areas: the proportion of Estonians in Tallinn had fallen to 51.3% by 1979, of Latvians in Riga to about 45%, and of Lithuanians in Vilnius to about 47.3%. The countryside in all three Baltic republics retained a much greater proportion of "indigenous" peoples – around 60–70%. To external observers it looked as though the three Baltic peoples were returning to the status quo of the mid-nineteenth century when city life was dominated by Germans and Poles. Soviet demographic publications of the Brezhnev period dealt with nationality statistics in a gingerly manner, occasionally falsifying the figures to disguise the fact that the Russian incursion into the Baltic littoral had been as great as it had. To Moscow's planners, the population dynamics of these western borderlands were not a source of worry as long as the overall quotas of five-year plans were being met, new industrial enterprises in the littoral were being constructed on time, and their operations meshed with the operations of others throughout the USSR. Concerns over national cadres in the party and the workforce were receding, the Baltic littoral was becoming *Pribaltika* – a region rather than three separate republics – and most of the indigenous population was learning that success in life required the learning of the "international language," Russian. Marxist-Leninist nationality theory was believed to cover these strains: with continuing economic development and the corresponding internal movements of the labor force, nationality differences would be reduced, frictions would be alleviated, and the end product would be the new "Soviet man" who spoke Russian and moved easily from place to place in Soviet space.

By the mid-1970s, the period of national independence (1918–1940) was a living memory only in the minds of the oldest generations of the three Baltic populations; those now entering their post-schooling years had no such personal memories, and the history textbooks in any event painted the independence years in the darkest of colors as a period of exploitation of the working masses from which the Baltic peoples had been rescued by the fraternal assistance of their Soviet neighbor. Many for whom reading about the past was therapeutic leapfrogged the recent past in favor of more distant eras: in Latvia in 1978, when a new three-volume history of Riga went on sale, the first volume, entitled *Feudal Riga*, sold out immediately; the second, entitled *Riga 1867–1917*, did fairly well; but the last volume, entitled *Riga in the Period of Socialism* languished in bookstores for a long time. Such indirect expressions of dislike for the socialist present could not be punished, of course, but they were evidence of attitudes that remained hidden from the communist partry leaders and sycophants of "triumphant socialism."

Starting in the 1960s and throughout the 1970s, there were also somewhat more direct expressions of dislike for the status quo in the Baltic littoral. Probably the most widespread involved pretending in ordinary circumstances that one did not understand Russian. Other such methods of non-violent opposition included placing flowers on the gravesites of important figures of the pre-1940 past or at pre-1940 monuments such as the Freedom Monument in Riga; the "inadvertent" use of the national colors (blue, black, and white for Estonia, crimson and white for Latvia, yellow, green, and red for Lithuania) in various quotidian circumstances (tourist souvenirs, cake decorations, etc.); surreptitious mounting of the old national flags in prominent public places; graffiti calling for Russian departure; cheering for opposition sports teams when they were playing Russian teams. Occasionally the ante was upped: riots – mostly by young people – followed rock concerts in the 1970s and accompanied the Soviet invasion of Hungary in 1956 and of Czechoslovakia in 1968. The authorities blamed these on "outside agitators" and tried to link such manifestations to the influence of western radio broadcasts and the nefarious activities of the western émigré communities. Deeply felt hopelessness was also manifested in violent acts against one's self: in Lithuania in 1972, Romas Kalanta, a nineteen-year-old student, died through self-immolation in front of the Kaunas Musical Theater.

By the 1970s a much more systematic avoidance of official prohibitions appeared in the proliferation of *samizdat* (self-published) literature: forbidden works were copied in typescript and retyped and than passed from hand to hand to interested readers. In Lithuania, the most influential of the *samizdat* publications was the

Chronicle of the Lithuanian Catholic Church (modeled on a similar Moscow publication, *The Chronicle of Current Events*) which started publication in 1972 and had an almost twenty-year run. "Open letters" were smuggled out and sent to western media: one notable example was the "Letter of Seventeen Communists" originating in Latvia; another was a letter originating in Estonia and signed by a group of "Estonian Patriots." All these written variants of dissent focused on what the producers believed to be systematic efforts to russify the Baltic littoral totally, on the persecution of individuals for exercising their freedom of conscience, and on the destructive effects of industrial expansion on the environment. The "environmental" and "ecological" themes were not as prominent in the 1960s, but they assumed much greater importance during the 1970s.

It was entirely possible to build a satisfactory career if one's profession was highly valued by the Soviet state and if in the strict practice of it – the construction of buildings and bridges, experimental science, cybernetics, and the like – there did not exist any kind of challenge to the "party line." Even so, among the "dissident" activists in the littoral during the 1960s and 1970s, there were some prominent cases (such as the chemist Jüri Kukk in Estonia) involving persons in the scientific fields. For the three central committees and party cells in organized institutions, however, the perennial battle from the thaw period onward was with those in the expressive arts – literature, painting, sculpture, the theater, and music. In these fields the communist parties had definitive views, even if these were often rooted not so much in Marxist-Leninist theory as in the personal preferences of high party officials. Not all artists were inclined to be experimental, nor did all party officials dislike artistic innovation. But there were sufficient numbers of defenders of orthodoxy on the one side and rebels on the other for the two sides to be engaged for a period of three decades in what amounted to a cat-and-mouse game, often with disastrous consequences for the mice. Party officials did not understand why the so-called "creative workers" valued freedom of expression when the party was clearly the source of all wisdom concerning the contribution of the expressive professions to the "building of socialism"; the "creative workers" saw party controls as emanating from slavish bureaucrats in whose uninformed minds politics trumped art, and therefore understood their calling to be the circumvention of dictates with subtle methods they hoped the reading and viewing public would understand. Clashes and confrontations were inevitable under the circumstances, especially since the artistic products embodied the same plaints as the more open and direct expressions of dissent: resentment over growing Russian-language hegemony, centralized control of the republics by Moscow, the destructive consequences of hyperindustrialization, fear of the disappearence of Estonian- , Latvian- , and Lithuanian-language culture. For the defenders of orthodoxy, "decadent" artistic styles – symbolism, individualism, impressionism, futurism, expressionism, surrealism, and existentialism – were all unacceptable. But these conservatives were fighting a losing battle in the Baltic littoral as in the larger Soviet centers of artistic creativity, Moscow and Leningrad. There was always a price to pay for innovation, however: disfigurement of the original manuscript through prohibition of poems or a section of prose in it (e.g. the case of the poet Arvi Siig in Estonia), condemnation of entire works by high party officials and the resulting long delays in publication (e.g. Visvaldis Eglons in Latvia), accusations that a particular piece of writing was drenched with negativism and conveyed the meaninglessness of effort (e.g. Romuladas Lankauskas in Lithuania).

Writing with a historical bent was watched carefully for signs that the author was seeking to modify the one and only acceptable interpretation of the past: Russian involvement with the Baltic littoral from the medieval period onward had to be portrayed as positive, German involvement always as negative, the "enemy" could never be portrayed as a normal human being, and the motivations of the "exploiting classes" – aristocrats, merchants, the twentieth-century bourgeoisie – had to be sketched in the darkest of colors. Only party members, people of lower-class origins, powerful Russian state-builders, and Soviet soldiers could become "positive heroes." Violators of party-set limits sometimes paid the maximum price: the poet Vizma Belševica in Latvia was silenced for three years (1971–1974) – nothing by her could be published after she wrote a poem in which, by implication, the presence of the crusading orders in the thirteenth-century littoral was likened to the presence of the Soviet army; Tomas Venclova, the young

Lithuanian poet, was stripped of his Soviet citizenship while visiting the University of California in 1975, for sending an open letter to the central committee in which he declared communist ideology to be "false."

The communist parties of the littoral from the thaw period onward had major difficulties in dealing with the continued existence in western countries of émigré populations within which the post-World War II refugees occupied centerstage. These diaspora populations of Estonians, Latvians, and Lithuanians differed substantially from each other, but in all three, veneration of the prewar republics and their political leaders continued, as did a sprightly cultural life that by the 1960s and 1970s appeared to be somewhat immune to assimilation in their host countries. The main centers of diaspora activity were Sweden, Canada, and the United States for the Estonians (who had numerically the smallest diaspora, about 27,000); Sweden, Germany, and the United States for the Latvians (which was the largest with about 100,000); and Canada and the United States for the Lithuanians (most of whose 64,000 World War II refugees joined the approximately half a million earlier immigrants already present in North America).

After 1945, the high proportion of intellectuals (writers, artists, and academics) among the postwar refugees had led to an active cultural life with schools, publications, and artistic productions even in the refugee (DP – displaced person) camps in Germany; in the period of dispersal, after 1951, when UN-organized refugee camps were disassembled or taken over by the military forces of the USA, Britain, and France, the displaced persons scattered to their new home countries, taking with them the determination to keep alive cultural and religious life in their own languages. By the mid-1960s and early 1970s, it had become clear to the communist parties of the littoral that these communities were not about to assimilate into the millions of English, German, and Swedish speakers among whom they now resided. Repeated castigations of these refugees as "fascist collaborators," "handmaidens of western plutocrats," "shooters of Jews," and "servants of the interwar fascist regimes" did not suffice either. Émigrés published newspapers and magazines, corresponded with their relatives in the Soviet republics, began to visit the Baltic frequently after the early 1970s, and occasionally even accepted invitations (arranged by innocent-sounding but KGB-sponsored cultural exchange organizations) to visit their homelands. In their democratic host countries, they maintained effective and fervently anti-communist lobbying organizations seeking to influence foreign policy, sometimes by having to remind local politicians that such a thing as the "non-recognition policy" existed. Perceiving that the "cultural exchange" and "cultural contact" questions were causing rifts in the refugee communities (most often along generational lines), the strategy of the republic communist parties shifted from wholesale to selective condemnations. Publications appeared in English "naming names" of Baltic émigrés who were alleged to have participated in the Holocaust. These publications were meant to discredit the political efforts of the older generation, while the "cultural contact" gambit continued to target the younger and predictably curious generation. Newspapers were mailed to selected émigrés describing advances in the homeland and urging them to visit or return. Tourists from the west were interviewed during their trips and their comments – often complimentary as befitting their visitor status – were reprinted and circulated in local Soviet newspapers. Eminent émigré cultural figures were targeted for special appeals through invitations to publish in their homelands and to perform concerts. When invitations were accepted, visitors to the Baltic republics were watched carefully, their contacts were noted and conversations with them recorded; cultural delegations to the west normally included at least one KGB informant, and participants were carefully debriefed after their return about which émigrés they had talked to, what was said, and about the internal life of the communities visited.

The strong disagreements in the émigré communities over the "cultural contact" question, however, did not have the divisive consequences desired by the Soviet side; indeed, starting with the late 1960s and the various youth rebellions in the western world, many émigré youths demonstrated that it was possible to be both anti-communist and anti-authoritarian as they lashed out against behavioral rules and restrictions imposed by "the establishment" – their parents and schools at home, the party and its rules when they visited their parental homelands. The give-and-take between the relatively small Baltic émigré communities and the communist parties in the three Baltic states – lasting from the mid-1960s well into the 1980s – was, however, of no major significance for the overall doctrines of the superpowers – the USSR and USA: that relationship had its own dynamic. Internal communications of the Baltic communist parties suggest, nonetheless, that they continued to fret into the 1980s over the persistence in the west of Estonian, Latvian, and Lithuanian communities that were beyond their control and influence and that appeared to be keeping alive the idea of national independence.

During the second half of the 1970s and the first half of the 1980s, Soviet society continued to be fraught with ambiguities, or, to use Marxist jargon, "internal contradictions." Successes in the space program seemed to indicate technological equality with the west, but judging by the inferior quality of many consumer goods (no longer a completely forbidden topic in the press) that equality was illusory. Major investments in massive housing projects were unable to keep up with rural to urban migration; large cities were declared as "closed," which, of course, produced an major increase in illegal urban dwellers. Cramped apartments led to decisions by young couples to limit the number of children or to have none at all: decisions that affected the future size of the labor force. Though statistics about general life expectancy and infant mortality showed improvements during the 1950s, they both began to turn in a negative direction in this period (infant mortality up, life expectancy down). Alcoholism seemed to be endemic, and because of shortages of contraceptives, abortions were a widespread means of birth control. Social dysfunction was more characteristic of Soviet society generally; moreover, widespread knowledge of this fact even by party members enlarged the gap between the reality depicted in glowing propaganda about the "achievements of socialism" and the gray and even dark reality of everyday lives. The party's claim to be an omniscient guide was met with smirks, and increasingly the party's apparatus was perceived as the new "privileged class" which Milovan Djilas, the dissident Yugoslav communist, had warned about in his 1956 book. The Brezhnev regime and its loyalists contributed to the disillusionment by flaunting their privileges and by practicing widespread nepotism.

Those who still believed in the self-proclaimed supremacy of the communist world were shocked when they traveled abroad and discovered that Soviet currency was inconvertible (that is, an inferior kind of money). Even the "mighty Soviet army" – as it pictured itself in school textbooks – seemed to have diminished in strength when, after the invasion of Afghanistan in 1979, it became bogged down in a seemingly unending battle against Afghan guerillas. As the internal communications of party leaders of this period attested, the apparatus of censorship still worked and was put to use, but in the process the party looked increasingly ineffectual because the ideologically dictated methods – centralized production and distribution, long-term planning, and production quotas – no longer seemed to be working; bribery to obtain decisions and scarce goods had become endemic as well.

These features of the USSR were reflected in the Baltic republics to a greater or lesser extent, together with one process that was far more disturbing to the native residents of the littoral than to its more transient populations and to the Moscow *nomenklatura*. This was the diminishing proportion of Estonians, Latvians, and Lithuanians in the three republics, a trend that had started decades ago, then seemed to abate, but resumed by the early 1980s. Since the end of World War II, an estimated 3 million Slavic speakers had come into the littoral, stayed for a while, and had then left because of party reassignments, to look for better jobs elsewhere in the USSR, or for family reasons. Some of each annual group of arrivals remained behind, however, so that by the mid-1980s the proportion of Estonians in Estonia had declined to 62.6% (from 64.7% in 1979), of Latvians in Latvia to 52.6% (from 53.7% in 1979), and of Lithuanians in Lithuania to 79.8% (from 80% in 1979). Although in earlier decades, Lithuania appeared to have avoided demographic denationalization, the trend appeared there as well. The proportion of Latvians in their capital city of Riga diminished to 38.3%, the proportion of Lithuanians in Vilnius to 47.3%, and among the Baltic capitals, only in Estonia's Tallinn did natives make up more than half the population (51.9%) (1979 figures in all cases). The proportion of Russian speakers who were also fluent in the titular language of the republic of residence was 37.4% in Lithuania, 20.1% in Latvia, and 13.0% in Estonia (1979 figures). Few persons were allowed to know such figures precisely, but the memoirs of all littoral residents for whom preservation of the ethnic character of the three republics was important depicted (even in Lithuania) an ever-growing fear that the local languages and cultures were imperiled. This mood was not unlike that of the decades before World War I. Then, however, the three national cultures had not yet developed complete confidence in their ability to survive or acquired states to protect them; now, by contrast, the attitudes of the defenders was much more combative, even though they fully realized and frequently experienced the consequences of being intransigent.

THE BEWILDERED VANGUARD

The CPSU general secretary, Leonid Brezhnev, died in 1982 at age seventy-six, and the party – now solidly ensconced as the vanguard of the proletariat – drew on the principle of seniority to choose Jurii Andropov, age sixty-eight, as his successor. Andropov, who had headed the KGB since 1967, seemed an appropriate leader to handle ongoing problems: economic stagnation; the Afghan war, which appeared to be intractable; and determined opposition to party control in the eastern European satellite states, especially Poland. In the Gdansk shipyards in Poland in 1980, the proletariat had taken the dramatic step of establishing an independent non-communist trade union, *Solidarnošč* (Solidarity). It had been suppressed in 1981 through the proclamation of martial law. Party leaders in Poland and Moscow did not believe, however, that this would be the end of the story, especially given the election of an uncompromisingly anti-communist Polish pope – John Paul II (Karol Josef Wojtila, 1920–2005). A Pole on the throne of St. Peter – an intellectual who had served the church within the Polish communist system and knew how the party worked – spelled trouble. Moreover, two other strong anti-communist leaders had appeared in the western world – Ronald Reagan (1911–2004), the Republican who had been elected to the US presidency in 1980 at age sixty-nine; and Margaret Thatcher (1925–), the Conservative Party leader who became prime minister of the United Kingdom in 1979. Jurii Andropov, however, had only a short time at the helm of the party. When he died in 1984, Konstantin Chernenko (1911–1985), at age seventy-three, succeeded him as first secretary. Chernenko came to the position as a result more of seniority than of demonstrated leadership talents, and died a year later. At this juncture, the CPSU decided to turn to a new generation of party leaders, choosing Mikhail Gorbachev (b. 1931), as his successor.

With Gorbachev, the party had finally extricated itself from what had come to be perceived as a "leadership crisis": he was a faithful *aparatchik* who had worked his way upward in the *nomenklatura*, projected a youthful and energetic image as a voluble leader who stated his ideas carefully, but was also willing to seek new solutions. The very fact of his ascendancy signaled the presence in the party of a substantial component of younger members – technocrats and non-technocrats alike – who saw the need for some kind of basic change. Greater determination in the western political leadership necessitated internal change if the USSR were to retain its position in the two-sided and now seemingly stable configuration of the Cold War. By 1987, Gorbachev had consolidated his power in the CPSU: many of the old cadres were forced into honorable retirement, supporters of the new leadership assumed the majority of important party positions, and terms such as *perestroika* (restructuring), *glasnost'* (openness), and *demokratizaatsia* (democratization) were heard increasingly in party discussions in Moscow. These slogans had in fact become the new "party line" during the Twenty-seventh Party Congress in spring 1986, even though few understood clearly what meaning they were to be given within the hardened structures of the CPSU and in the party organizations of the republics, including the Baltic. A mood of bewilderment grew, anchored in a dilemma: the perceived need for change meant some relaxation of controls, which threatened the "leading and guiding" role of the party. Party leaders in the republics, used to receiving unambiguous directives and interpretations from Moscow, now had to ponder over what was permissible. The habit of toeing the party line was deeply ingrained; the current line appeared to be saying that the fundamentals of the socialist/communist system were basically sound and that the freedoms required by necessary reform could still be channeled in the appropriate directions. In the Baltic republics, the party still had at its disposal the same instruments of control – the KGB, the police, and even the armed forces – but the question now was how to use them selectively and effectively. Hard-liners had no qualms, but they were no longer in full control.

Changes in party leadership in the Baltic republics had already started before the advent of Gorbachev's reforms and thus were not directly linked to the new course. In 1984, Boris Pugo, the republic's KGB chief, became the first secretary, representing a new generation of non-native administrators who had now been prominent in the Latvian party for some thirty years. Pugo spoke some Latvian, but preferred to speak Russian; as KGB chief he had been merciless with Latvian bourgeois nationalist dissidents; but, following Gorbachev's ascendancy, he began to replace aging party figures with men of his own age or younger, promised economic reform, and claimed that advancement in the party would henceforth depend on merit rather than cronyism. Pugo remained in office until 1988, when he left for a higher post in Moscow; by that time, the tempo of *perestroika* in Latvia was building rapidly. In Lithuania, Antanas Sniečkus, the "squire" of the Lithuanian Communist Party, died in 1974 and was replaced by Petras Griskevičius, a Lithuania-born party stalwart who continued Sniečkus' policy of staffing high party posts with native Lithuanian communists, producing a sharp contrast with the situation in Latvia. In Lithuania, some 67 percent of party members were Lithuanian, but in Latvia only an estimated 35–40 percent (no precise figures available). By 1987, when the native-born communist Ringaudas Songaila replaced Griskevičius, the Lithuanian party had not yet exhibited the same kind of generational change as occurred in Latvia. In Estonia, the first secretary since 1978 had been Karl Vaino, a Brezhnev-era appointee, who managed to survive in his post from 1978 until 1988. After Gorbachev's ascendancy, something of a struggle for advancement in high Estonian party ranks ensued between native- and Russia-born Estonians, with the former appearing to gain the upper hand.

By 1985–1987, however, the forces of Gorbachevian reforms had not staged an unambiguous victory in any of the Baltic republics. Just as the general population waited to see what would happen next in Moscow, the republic party leaders and the *nomenklatura* remained a mixture of those who welcomed reform, those who viewed all reform with trepidation, and those who were ready to cast their lot in either direction depending on the flow of events. The party remained a formidable force in each republic none the less: by 1986 Lithuanian membership stood at about 197,000, Estonian at about 110,000, and Latvian at about 172,000. *Komsomol* (the communist youth organization), candidate membership, full membership, inclusion in the *nomenklatura* – these were still the only reliable steps to personal advancement in the three republics, even if during the first two years of the Gorbachev era the policy of *glasnost'* dictated that the party admit and remedy its mistakes, especially with respect to the current economic impasse.

In the littoral, the first systematic and successful steps of overt opposition to party decisions took place in Latvia in 1986, when a young journalist named Dainis Īvāns together with his colleague Arturs Snīps, a computer specialist, launched a letter-writing and petition drive against the building of yet another hydroelectric complex on the Daugava River. The project had already been approved at the highest levels, including Moscow, but by the end of the year, some thirty thousand signatures had been gathered questioning its need and objecting to the projected submersion of the river's natural landscape. The motivation of the opposition was complex: in April 1986, the Chernobyl diasaster (in Ukraine) had taken place; technical expertise of all kinds and judgments based on it were in question; decisions about the Latvian project had been made routinely without reference to public opinion; and the project would disfigure the most revered of Latvian rivers. Ecological protectionism merged with resentment of high-handed party decisions, and these in turn with deep affection for the natural landscapes of the Latvian homeland.

The mixture was an excellent test for *glasnost'* and *perestroika*, and a year later (November 1987), the USSR Council of Ministers canceled the project. What probably went unnoticed (or at least not mentioned) in high party circles (especially in Moscow, where dozens of such projects were being handled) was the extent to which in the Latvian case opposition to a technological undertaking had been fueled by popular sentiments that a short time ago would have been condemned as bourgeois nationalism. The Daugava River had become a powerful symbol for defense of the Latvian homeland against the party and Moscow hegemony. A decade later Īvāns reflected that "the long and activity-full Daugava year, ending in victory, had testified that all was possible, that all obstacles could be overcome, if only hundreds and thousands of people merged into a single fist. A new way of thinking had been born in that year ... the majority was no longer frozen in fear ... The rushing waters of the Daugava were in reality we ourselves, our mission, our hopes and dreams ... one obstacle had been overcome, but a larger and more important one remained in place."

Latvians, however, were not the only littoral people to exhibit such "new thinking." In Estonia, a similar ecological protest had developed over the exploitation of a massive new phosphate lode in the north-central section. At issue here were the potentially harmful effects of mining operations in a particularly rich agricultural region that was also the source of some two-thirds of Estonian rivers; it was feared that radioactive waste from the new mines would poison drinking water and seep into the Baltic Sea. Moreover, the entire project was to require a labor force of about 30,000–40,000 persons, these – presumably Russian speakers – having to be recruited to Estonia from the Slavic parts of the USSR. Opposition stressed the technological dangers, students at the University of Tartu carried the issue into the streets with demonstrations, and opponents underscored repeatedly that protection of a republic's environment was a matter to be decided on by the republic's government even against the wishes of Moscow's ministries (in this case, the Ministry of Mineral Fertilizers). Even some prominent members of the Estonian *nomenklatura* joined public opinion by promising a full review of the whole matter. As a consequence the USSR Council of Ministers in October 1987 decided to stop the development of new phosphorite mines in Estonia. Here was another victory against the bureaucratic planners in Moscow, and again the "defense of the homeland" theme loomed very large.

A summary of events over the next two years can do only scant justice to the remarkable diffusion of new thinking throughout the Baltic littoral as well as other USSR republics. Buoyed by Gorbachev's policies of *perestroika* and *glasnost'* Estonians, Latvians, and Lithuanians, as well as a not inconsiderable number of Slavic inhabitants of the three republics, launched long-term efforts to expand their freedom of public action in the realms of commemoration and center–periphery relations. Mass rallies, starting small but eventually growing to include tens and even hundreds of thousands, were used to create a counter-calendar to government-sponsored celebrations. Official holidays marked the Bolshevik Revolution of 1917, the inclusion of the Baltic republics into the USSR, and victory over Germany in the so-called Great Patriotic War (World War II); the counter-calendar responded by marking the proclamations of independence in 1918, the signing of the Molotov–Ribbentrop pact in 1939, and the deportations of 1941 and 1949. Initially, the communist parties tried blocking the demonstrations by refusing permission for them, detaining demonstration planners, and creating bureaucratic obstructions through the use of the police (*milicija*). None of these worked, and eventually the authorities had to stand by and show cooperativeness. As each event revealed that extreme violence would not be used against participants, the next became even larger. All demonstrations routinely came to include the national flags of the interwar independence republics; in some demonstrations, the prewar republic flags appeared next to the official flags of the three SSRs. Serious discussions were launched about the revival of all the state symbols of the interwar republics, including the coats of arms. If the only heretofore permitted state symbols emphasized membership in the USSR, the new symbolism sought to underline a distancing of each republic from this entity. There was much handwringing among hard-line party functionaries when it became obvious that outright suppression of orderly public demonstrations, including previously suppressed flags and placards, would not be supported by Moscow, and that if violence were used, the republic party leaders were on their own. What was abundantly clear by 1988 was the determination of large numbers of people in each of the Baltic republics to embody their aspirations not only in symbols but also in political, economic, and social action.

The step of converting mass-based demonstrations into mass-based organizations came during the year 1988 also under the heading of *perestroika*: the Estonian Popular Front to Support Perestroika (*Eestimaa Rahvarinne Perestroika Toetuseks*) held its first congress on October 1-2, 1988; the Latvian Popular Front (*Latvijas Tautas Fronte*) on October 10; and the Lithuanian Movement for Restructuring (*Lietuvos Persitvarkymo Sajudis*) on October 22–23. These groupings – eventually referred to generically as popular fronts – did not appear overnight; their organizational meetings came after many weeks of discussion about how they should be structured, and complicated negotiations with the leadership of the republic party central committees about their registration as "informal organizations."

The mood of these first congresses was euphoric; cooler heads, however, saw a difficult road ahead. The communist party leaderships in the three republics were ambivalent: on the one hand, they did not want to tolerate demonstrably popular rival organizations; on the other, the Moscow party leadership appeared receptive to the idea of organizations that would help implement the new "party line" of restructuring. Generally speaking, Moscow appeared to be pulling back from opposition to "informal organizations" of any type, believing them to be the result of the productive ferment – an antidote to stagnation – brought by the new policies. The line between the permissible and impermissible had become unclear, and the party leadership in the Baltic littoral opted for permissiveness.

Party strategists believed that if its own members joined such organizations en masse, the flow of events could be controlled. Indeed, some 22 percent of the delegates to the first Estonian Congress were party members; seventeen of the thirty-five Council members elected in the first meeting of the Lithuanian *Sajudis* were members of the Lithuanian Communist Party; and in Latvia, about a third of the general membership of the Popular Front carried party cards. Believing such overlaps to be morally unacceptable, many activists in all three republics moved "to the right" and founded their own informal organizations (without necessarily exiting from the Popular Fronts): the Latvian National Independence Movement, the Estonian National Independence Party, and the Lithuanian Freedom League. They wanted no communists in their midst and were meant to be independent bases of operations in a political arena that was quickly becoming unusually pluralistic. Pronouncing all informal organizations outside the party to be tainted with "extremism" and "nationalism," hard-line groups within the party, with at least tacit support from many in the party leadership, "moved left" and announced the formation of their own versions of popular fronts: *Vienybe-Yedinstvo-Jednosc* (Unity) in Lithuania, the Internationalist Front in Estonia, and the International Front in Latvia. The base of these organizations consisted largely of persons of non-titular nationalities (Russians, Poles, and others); what united them was the desire to continue the *status quo ante*.

By the end of 1988, the *perestroika*-supporting popular fronts had emerged as the "middle ground" between full-independence seekers on the right and Moscow loyalists on the left. The popular fronts were now a power to be reckoned with: estimates of membership of *Sajudis* ranged from 100,000 to 300,000, of the Latvian Popular Front were about 110,000, and of the Estonian Front about 100,000. In spring 1989, elections to the newly created USSR Congress of Peoples Deputies (an innovation of the *perestroika* policy) resulted in delegations from the three Baltic republics in which about two-thirds of each group were associated with the popular fronts; the other delegates represented the party or party-run institutions. The reformist delegates were now in a position to carry their obstreperousness on a range of questions to a much larger stage (an all-Soviet congress) and to a much larger audience as well, since virtually all the meetings of the congress were carried live on Soviet television.

The interwar period of bona fide national sovereignty was for the activists of the three Baltic republics a reference point: all three had been full members of the League of Nations with their own constitutions, diplomatic corps, and other appurtenances of independent states. But in the early months of 1989, the full restoration of state independence appeared mostly in the public pronouncements of the "right-wing" groups, not the popular fronts. For the latter, the key words were "republic autonomy": the use of the USSR constitution to maximize the freedoms each SSR legally possessed thus separating themselves by distancing themselves from centrally made decisions. This was an interesting reprise of similar discussions in the years before World War I and the crucial year of 1918; then also, more often than not, the goal had been autonomous provinces within a reorganized democratic Russia. Memoirs of the 1988–1989 participants frequently suggest that the intellectual step from republic autonomy to state independence was inevitable given the momentum of events and the continuing intransigence of Moscow and its supporters.

In many meetings held in the three republics – such as the June 1988 Plenum of the Creative Unions in Latvia – the historic fact that in 1940 the Baltic republics had been "occupied" was brought into the open; it followed, therefore, that the republic–Moscow tie had been illegal from the beginning and that complete separation, in line with the provisions of the USSR constitution, was the next logical step. This view seemed obvious and natural to many, just as to others the commonsensical drive for republic autonomy only appeared as much as could be hoped for under current circumstances. To the opposing side – starting with the Moscow government and including its loyalists in the republics – open discussion of such matters bordered on the seditious and threatened the very nature of the larger Soviet state. For the most extreme of them (such as the Interfront groups), even talk of republic autonomy was a disguise for bourgeois nationalist aspirations of total independence, and there were repeated calls for the center somehow to bring an end to such charades. The retired and active Soviet military in the Baltic republics, segments of the Party *nomenklatura*, and many ordinary citizens who were becoming convinced that government in the hands of the "nationalist extremists" would be followed by deportations of all Slavs from the littoral, could not envisage a scenario that would involve a diminution of party monopoly of power and a reduction of the control Moscow had over republic affairs.

The three littoral communist parties remained in a bind during 1988–1989, with their leadership cadres and thousands of members facing hard decisions. In Estonia, Vaino Väljas, a native Estonian, became first secretary in June 1988. From the beginning he advocated extensive republic autonomy and, over the next few months, the entire leadership of the Estonian party came into the hands of reformers. In Latvia, Boris Pugo left permanently for Moscow, and was replaced by Jānis Vagris, a native Latvian, but a colorless figure; the leading reformer in the party leadership, Anatolijs Gorbunovs, became chairman of the Presidium of the Latvian Supreme Soviet (the legislature). In Lithuania, Algirdas Brazauskas, a native Lithuanian, replaced Ringaudas Songaila as first secretary of the Lithuanian Communist Party in October 1988. The appointment of these party leaders, though, of course, approved by Moscow, now had to be made in informal consultation with the leadership of the popular fronts, which could demonstrably speak in the name of tens of thousands of Estonians, Latvians, and Lithuanians. Something resembling a dual-party atmosphere moved into the political arena in all three republics, even though the formal structures of government remained entirely those spelled out in the republics' Soviet constitutions: a supreme soviet with its chairman, a council of ministers with its chairman, and dozens of ministries and directorates. The rank and file members who had joined for reasons of professional advancement rather than dedication to Marxist-Leninist ideas began to quit the party. Sometimes the step was accompanied by a public declaration; more often it was simply a silent decision. But beginning in 1988 party membership numbers fell at a remarkably rapid rate, while the "informal organizations" – especially the popular fronts – continued to grow. A restructuring of elites was unfolding in the Baltic republics. Those who remained loyalists experienced the indignity of having to watch their all-knowing and all-powerful party become a minority organization, as its claims to be speaking for the "masses" rang increasingly hollow. Without the clear backing of the police, security services, and the military, the party was floundering and internally dividing into two factions: the conservative and the reformist. The former continued to call for forceful action by Moscow while the latter sought the best way to survive when surrounded by thousands of politically active persons whose public pronouncements now consisted of calls to rescue the nation rather than proposals for better ways to build socialism.

In the eastern European satellite states, events during 1989 revealed the death of the so-called Brezhnev doctrine – the asserted right of the USSR to rescue communist regimes by using military might. Communist parties throughout the satellites learned from Moscow that they were on their own; Soviet tanks would not roll into Warsaw, Prague, or Budapest as in the old days to help restore single-party rule. By the end of 1989, therefore, Communist Party domination of the governments in the satellites had disappeared and been replaced by multiparty systems, mostly bloodlessly but in Romania with considerable bloodshed. The main question in the Baltic republics by early 1990 had become whether they would be accorded special treatment by Moscow or whether they would be viewed as subversive components of a "one and indivisible" superpower. Public opinion in the Baltic region was in the process of shifting from calls for republic autonomy to demands for renewed independence, a shift not envisaged by the proponents of *perestroika*. Mikhail Gorbachev visited Lithuania in January

1990, and in a jovial manner, sought to persuade Lithuanians that it was in their self-interest – at least economically – to remain part of the USSR. The visit changed no minds, even as it underlined how thoroughly the Moscow party leadership misunderstood the dynamic of Baltic-area nationalism.

In spring 1990, elections to the supreme soviets of all three republics gave moderate majorities – but majorities nevertheless – to independence supporters. Only in Lithuania did the newly elected supreme soviets demand immediate independence (March 11). In Estonia and Latvia, the new bodies declared (Estonia on March 30 and Latvia on May 8) the desire for independence but opted for a prolonged transition period during which the necessary technique of withdrawal would be worked out. On Moscow's side, there ensued declarations about what was required constitutionally for a union republic to withdraw from the USSR. These "rules" foresaw a series of steps that would have made the task virtually impossible. The resulting impasse provided an opportunity for opponents of independence in the Baltic republics to charge that the new supreme soviets – elected legally – were now proposing illegal acts. They argued that the 1940 annexations had come about through the express "will of the people" acting through "people's parliaments" elected in that year and that the new supreme soviets were therefore acting outside the law. Independence supporters countered that the elections of the "people's parliaments" in 1940 – now almost a half-century ago – had themselves been illegal because only one election list had been permitted. The debate about this question was strangely legalistic, almost as though the adversaries believed that they were in a court of law.

Despite the fact that real force remained in Moscow's hands, the now undisguised independence drives in the three republics continued during the summer and autumn of 1990. Appointments to government offices continued to be made, replacing officials responsive to the party with officials responsive to the supreme soviets. Those who were still party members were faced with having to declare their loyalties: to a party half of which now looked to the republic supreme soviets for guidance or to a rump party whose public pronouncements remained loyal to the Moscow line. The beginnings of a split of this kind had already taken place in the

Lithuanian party after December 1989; in Estonia and Latvia, the division came during 1990. Meeting after meeting – scholarly and semi-scholarly – laid out evidence of the harm that membership in the USSR had done to the "basic" nations (Estonians, Latvians, Lithuanians) of the three Baltic states, to the natural environment of the three countries, and to their economies. Counterarguments pointing to the benefits of belonging to a large economy that supplied the littoral with energy resources and distributed its production fell on deaf ears.

In all three republics, the focal point of independence activism remained the elected supreme soviets (or councils); these bodies were increasingly considered transitional until real parliamentary elections could be held under conditions of complete independence. The national activists – having been elected as candidates of the popular fronts – were a diverse group and included many former highly-positioned members of the party who had thrown in their lot with the independence forces. This fact created considerable dissatisfaction among the purists of the independence movements, who stood outside this new elite and believed that a truly legitimate new government should comprise only those untainted by party membership, including those who had suffered repression during the period of Soviet rule. Resentment was building in the new body politic even before independence had been secured. "Cleansing" mechanisms were proposed, but only a few were implemented (focusing on the KGB). The nationalist activists of the extreme right in the new political spectrum were in a sense marginalized and continued to regard the new elite – which was fluid in the extreme – with considerable suspicion. A few claimed that the entire popular front movement was really political theater produced by Moscow and sponsored by the local organs of state security. At the other end of the spectrum, in the Interfront movements, stood those who were calling for an immediate introduction of "presidential rule": Gorbachev should declare a state of emergency and call upon the military to bring about the arrest and punishment of the independence activists, including members of the supreme soviets. The military – symbolized by the headquarters of the Baltic Military District in Riga – stood silently by, remained in contact with the leadership of the supreme soviets, watched events unfold, and awaited orders from Moscow.

THE ASHHEAP OF HISTORY

By early 1991, the eastern European satellite countries were well on their way to becoming post-communist states, and one of them – Yugoslavia – had embarked on a bitter civil war. Other republics of the USSR – some following the Baltic example – were searching for ways of freeing themselves from Moscow's control, and in some there were violent confrontations between the authorities and separatists. There was some violence too in the Baltic republics in January 1991: in Vilnius an attempt by units of the military to seize the main television tower cost twelve civilian lives, and in Riga the events in Vilnius triggered a massive defensive response, as hundreds of citizens created barriers around the main government buildings. Toward the end of January in Riga, four civilians were killed in a shooting incident involving the special forces (OMON) of the Ministry of Interior. Images of these incidents appeared in the international media almost immediately, and the Moscow government disowned them, claiming bad communications and flawed local leadership. The Moscow loyalists in the Baltic republics continued to portray the local situations as heading toward chaos – a huge exaggeration – and reiterated their call for presidential rule from Moscow. The atmosphere over the next several months remained tense because there were no clear signs about what the center was planning, if anything. The Moscow government continued to insist that the path of separation on which the Baltic governments had started was unconstitutional, but the "constitutional" path put forward as an alternative remained unacceptable to the popular fronts. The momentum of public opinion in the Baltic republics was carrying them farther away from any future scenarios other than those of their own devising.

By summer 1991, there was still considerable fear that some sort of crackdown would come, but no one could say when and what shape it would take. On August 19, 1991, however, in a dramatic series of events in Moscow, party conservatives and components of the military launched a badly coordinated and seemingly half-hearted coup against the reformist party leadership, using a moment when Gorbachev was vacationing in Crimea. The coup failed in a matter of days: the plotters were hesitant to use deadly force, they did not have the complete backing of the military, and the president of the Russian Federation – Boris Yeltsin – quickly emerged as a charismatic and persuasive leader of the opponents of the coup.

Baltic reaction to events in Moscow came swiftly: after two days of uncertainty, as the Interfrontists proclaimed themselves in charge and threatened action by the local OMON forces, the Estonian, Latvian, and Lithuanian supreme councils (parliaments) announced complete independence from the USSR. In Tallinn, Riga, and Vilnius, leaders of the Moscow loyalists were placed under arrest on the charge of attempting to overthrow a legally elected government; their mistake was the premature conclusion that the coup had worked. The properties of the once-omnipotent Communist Party were seized by police units pledged to the supreme council governments, and the party itself was declared to be an illegal organization. Within two weeks, the three Baltic republics had been recognized as independent countries by the government of the Russian Federation as well as by most of the governments of western Europe and the USA (September 2).

By September 18, the three republics were accepted as full members of the United Nations, which meant that revanchist moves against them would have to be carried out in full light of international public opinion. The likelihood of such moves, however, became increasingly remote, since the governmental structures of the USSR were in a state of confusion, and political power was shifting from the USSR to the Russian Federation. The Soviet army appeared to be following Gorbachev's lead, and the government of the Russian Federation, under the leadership of Boris Yeltsin, announced its readiness to fill the developing power vacuum. Resigned to the flow of events, Mikhail Gorbachev resigned from the presidency of the USSR on December 25 and in the same speech announced the dissolution of the Union of Soviet Socialist Republics. Shortly thereafter, the Russian Federation assumed legal control over all the assets of the former USSR and those of the nearly defunct Communist Party. Remarkably, one half of the global configuration of the Cold War era had disappeared without a nuclear exchange and without the massive bloodletting that had been expected to accompany such a momentous event. The "ashheap of history," to which Soviet propaganda for decades had been consigning the capitalist countries, had in fact become the final resting place of the Communist Party – the "vanguard of the proletariat" – and its embodiment – the USSR.

The independence drive in the three Baltic republics resulted in success, but the timing of the final act was in many respects ahead of schedule. International recognition of Estonia, Latvia, and Lithuania as independent countries did not amount to certification that three new societies had come into being. Independent statehood was the scaffolding, but the partially renovated house under the scaffolding was still for the most part Soviet-built. The idea that the Baltic states were *renewing* their societies after a fifty-year interruption was not helpful either: the pre-1940 societies were long gone and were barely living memories within the 1991 populations. The new political elites of the popular fronts had to work with the materials at hand.

The shards of the old system were everywhere. Large numbers of Soviet (now Russian) military personnel housed on numerous, jealously guarded bases remained an ominous presence. The currency was the Soviet (now Russian) ruble, so that the three littoral economies were still tied to the fluctuations in its value. The communist parties of the three countries had owned a great deal of real estate that the new governments had confiscated, but a procedure had to be devised to dispose of it. Many laws of the Soviet period remained in place (just as in the transition from tsarist rule to independence after 1918), and these had to be reviewed and corrected.

A full vetting of the legal system could not take place, however, until new constitutions of the three countries were firmly in place. In 1990, Latvia committed itself to renewing the 1922 constitution, which now had to be revised to fit the new times; Lithuania and Estonia, whose interwar constitutional history was more complicated, decided to write new documents, which required the calling of constitutional conventions.

The human side of the transition proved to be wrenching in the extreme. For five decades, the populations of the three new republics had grown accustomed to a Soviet-style welfare state in which most social services were available without cost and monies for a host of different purposes, including pensions, came from a centralized state budget. How much of this social infrastructure could be retained and at what levels became immediate questions not easily answerable because the old allocation system from Moscow had disappeared. The old system had engendered dependency; now, each citizen was to be responsible for his or her own personal income, career path, savings, competitive sense, and ultimate survival.

There was also the potentially explosive question of the ethnic composition of the three populations. Citizenship in the three states had to be redefined, but the question of who was entitled to citizenship was complicated, far more in Estonia and Latvia than in Lithuania. The total population of the latter contained only about 20 percent non-Lithuanians, whereas Estonia had about 40 percent non-Estonians and Latvia close to 50 percent non-Latvians. The independence movements had had as their major theme the protection of the culture of the titular nationality in each country, and a decision simply to grant citizenship to all current residents seemed to many to threaten the goals of the independence drives.

Finally, there was the question of how to deal with former members of the now-illegal republic communist parties. Erstwhile rank and file members could be forgiven, but the energetic and talented *nomenklatura* members were a special problem. Many had adeptly adjusted to the new circumstances by becoming outspoken supporters of independence; others, less vocal, simply remained in their jobs and professional positions, calculating correctly that the renewed republics would need skilled cadres regardless of their backgrounds. Still others had very questionable pasts, containing involvements with the Soviet-era security services. Lessons from the eastern European satellite states were not obvious, revealing no naturally optimal ways of dealing with the problem. The ease with which many high-ranking party officials transformed themselves into equally high-ranking members of the new governments rankled many, who had believed that independence would bring cleansing and the new national government would be led by those who had suffered most during the Soviet period.

9

Reentering Europe, 1991–

Although the three Baltic republics had been part of the European continent even during Soviet times, the "iron curtain" – to use Churchill's words – separated the communist world from western Europe for almost half a century. Indeed, Soviet-era censorship had magnified the psychological impact of the separation. Not all parts of the communist world were equally far removed from the "capitalist west"; the cultural borders of the eastern European satellite states were relatively permeable to western influences of various kinds, and in the Baltic littoral access to Finnish television images, the Voice of America, and other western stations was possible with special equipment in spite of jamming (although illegal). Western sailors brought western magazines and music cassettes to Baltic seaports, and even the Communist Party had become somewhat tolerant of western musical and fashion "fads" among the young from the 1970s on.

By the later 1980s, however, when barriers of all sorts began to fall, a cascade of impressions, revelations, and personal observations merged into a general feeling of socioeconomic and cultural backwardness that was both enervating and inspiring. The reentry into a dynamic and prosperous Europe would doubtlessly place the Baltic littoral at the bottom of European states in terms of socioeconomic measurements – a humiliating position; even so, the move would ensure progress toward "normality," a societal characteristic that was mentioned with increasing frequency in the Baltic media. A half-century of Soviet rule, it was believed, had "deformed" – another frequently used term – the littoral's republics, and now, finally, "normal" developmental processes could start. The juxtaposition of the terms normality and deformation – with the European west as an exemplar of the former and the Baltic republics of the latter – was entirely self-referential, an attempt by Baltic-area opinion-makers to position the region in some kind of larger context now that the framework of the USSR had disappeared. Even among the new political elites few people actually possessed a deep understanding of the costs and benefits of a competitive free-market economic system, of the predominance of law over personal influences, of press freedom, and of the often morally repulsive consequences of freedom of expression; even fewer understood that even in the west all these features of "normality" were aspirations frequently imperfectly realized. The result was a temporary idealization of the west and those who lived there; for the time being at least, the west appeared ready to help and to downplay its economic and strategic self-interest as the three republics entered into its midst.

Interstate relationships on the European continent appeared favorable for such a reentry. The "traditional enemies" of the littoral peoples were preoccupied with their own internal problems, and, besides, a half-century of political evolution had brought into being large-scale multistate organizations that intended to keep their members on their best behavior. For the time being, with the USSR gone, the Russians were too preoccupied with wrenching internal changes to make revanchist moves against the littoral; the Germans too were busy dealing with the problems of reunification; the Poles, who had been the bane of Lithuania's statehood as recently as the decades between the two world wars, were having to cope with their own problems of post-communism. Very promising as future friends and supporters were those countries which in the cataclysms of the twentieth century had shown no territorial interest in the littoral – the Scandinavian countries, the United Kingdom, France, and, of course, the superpower that had emerged as the victor in the Cold War, namely, the United States of America. Diplomatic recognition of renewed independence was easy enough both to receive and to grant, but the really pressing questions revolved around material aid, investment, and advice about how to create institutions that would function as efficiently and productively as those in the west.

In the immediate aftermath of the Soviet Union's collapse, western Europe was careful on the whole not to exploit its obvious advantage over the Russian Federation, being mindful of its functioning nuclear arsenal. The main theme of western foreign policy was watchful waiting until the turmoil of transition – where there was turmoil – subsided. Since the Baltic republics were a relatively peaceful zone, they became candidates for all manner of aid; besides, many of the major western powers now proudly pointed to the fact that they had never recognized the annexation of the Baltic states in 1940/1941 and could therefore be considered special friends. At the same time, Scandinavian, Finnish, German, and Polish companies noticed the prevailing hunger in the Baltic lands for western consumer goods and food products, and they began to establish stores, restaurants, and other retail outlets. This form of westernization was easiest to accomplish and became visible shortly after 1991; western investment capital took longer to arrive and was more circumspect. Within this developing west–Baltic interface, there was an annoying element: the west tended to imagine the three republics as a region or at least a region-in-the-making, referring to them as "the Baltics" just as in the old Soviet Union the littoral was most frequently simply *Pribaltika*. The westerners' obliviousness to differences between Estonia, Latvia, and Lithuania was fed by media stories and images of the 1988–1991 years: the consultations among the three popular fronts, the powerful "Baltic Way" image when tens of thousands of littoral residents linked hands in a line that stretched from the Gulf of Finland to southern Lithuania, and the support the Baltic-area delegates to the Congress of People's Deputies in Moscow gave to each other. This externally created regional identity, however, contrasted with the pent-up desire of the Baltic states to demonstrate national uniqueness culturally, economically, and politically; continuing changes in each of them, in other words, were tending to work against regional integration, and each wanted to enter Europe in its own way.

POPULATIONS IN MOTION

After August 1991, many of the changes that had begun during the past three years continued and grew more pronounced, producing considerable uncertainty in the general populations. Stagnation was replaced by unpredictability, innovation became highly valued, the old hierarchies dissolved, and the everyday world seemed to be in constant, mostly random motion. One type of motion was demographic, as those who could not accept the new order of things began to leave, primarily for Russia but other destinations as well. The populations of Estonia and Latvia fell into a new pattern: if in the Soviet years they had grown somewhat each year, now each year brought negative growth (about –0.2 percent annually), the result of continuing low fertility and the new higher emigration rate. Lithuania did not show the same pattern, since its population continued to increase marginally each year in the post-1991 era (about +0.2 percent annually), in part because its Slavic-language population was smaller to begin with. Emigration from Estonia and Latvia numbered several thousand each year in the immediate post-1991 period, and the bulk of those who truly wanted to leave had departed by 1995–1996. This number by no means included all the "rejectionists": many of them stayed on, hoping that some turn of events would restore the USSR; the activists among them argued that the Baltic republics at the very least should join the CIS (Commonwealth of Independent States), the post-communist organization of former Soviet republics that Moscow began to develop during 1992. Many of those who fatalistically accepted the new governments continued to argue loudly that they were insufficiently represented in the new institutions and that the Russian language had been forced into a subsidiary role. As the outflow subsided and the claims of the stayers were rejected, sufficient disquiet remained alive in the Slavic-language populations to become the basis for political parties that formed before the first election of the post-1991 parliaments.

The littoral populations were in motion not only demographically but also economically, and for many the trajectory was downward. Wage and price controls were removed (though gradually), and personal income as well as normal daily expenditures came to depend largely on individual initiative and on supply and demand. By the mid-1990s an estimated 40–60 percent of the population was living at or below the official poverty level in all three countries. The state-guaranteed incomes of pensioners fell substantially, and the value of personal savings was reduced by inflation and by the transition to new national currencies during 1993–1995. As state-owned enterprises disintegrated, were dismantled, or transformed themselves into privately held corporations, real unemployment levels rose above the officially stated levels of 6–8 percent, and the phenomenon of individuals holding multiple jobs became commonplace. Those who continued to work in state-funded systems – education and medicine, for example – found their salaries reduced to a bare minimum. This reorganization of the workplace and of salaries was all-encompassing, and even heretofore well-protected institutions, such as the research institutes of the Academies of Science, found themselves having to scramble for budgetary supplements by renting out parts of their facilities to various commercial firms. State revenues were reduced, of course, by the disappearance of money inflows from the erstwhile "center" (Moscow), and this was exacerbated by a somewhat chaotic taxation system, which suffered from ineffective enforcement mechanisms. From the understandably negative reactions throughout the general population, it became clear that many if not most people had underestimated the damage the transition from a command to a market economy would do to their personal lives and to the economies in which they lived. The index of per capita gross domestic product (GDP) declined rapidly: from 5.0 in Estonia in 1989 to 3.8 in 1994, in Latvia from 5.0 to 3.2 for the same years, and in Lithuania from 5.5 to 3.4. On this measure, Estonia was the least affected (a 24 percent decline) and Lithuania the most (38 percent).

Inevitably, the targets of popular dissatisfaction were the transitional governments and their political leaders; the euphoria of the 1988–1991 years dissipated and the political elite now in place was expected to provide rapid systemic reforms. Even though public opinion polls showed that most people understood that their homelands were "in transition," such polls also revealed the expectation that the transition would be relatively brief. Many, however, could not tolerate the stress in their personal lives: the suicide rate in Estonia rose from 27.0 (per 100,000) in 1991 to 41.0 in 1994, in Latvia from 28.5 to 40.5 for the same years, and in Lithuania from 30.5 to 45.8. Another indicator of increasing social pathology – murder – was also on the increase – in Estonia from 10.8 (100,000) in 1991 to 28.3 in 1994, in Latvia from 11.4 to 23.0 in the same years, and in Lithuania from 9.1 to 13.4.

For persons of an entrepreneurial bent, the unsystematic and largely unregulated economic transition provided many opportunities, and, as a result, in all three countries a new economic elite began to form. During much of the 1990s, the denationalization of heretofore state-run enterprises – ranging from full-sized factories to small-scale shops providing personal services – put such entities on sale at prices far below their real value; the transition governments handling these transactions appeared to have little time and insufficient expertise to prolong the process. New, privately owned companies proliferated, many of them subsidiaries of equally new holding companies; their creation and registration were relatively easy and rapid. Using hastily raised capital, often of mysterious provenance, such entities became owners of denationalized enterprises and of real estate, at times only with the intention of reselling quickly for profit.

A *nouveau riche* lifestyle became increasingly evident on the streets of Tallinn, Riga, and Vilnius: large western cars, shops selling luxury goods, personal bodyguards, and expensive restaurants. By the mid-1990s, such conspicuous consumption rubbed salt into the wounds of those whose income trajectory was in the opposite direction. Predictably, there was much speculation about the sources of the new wealth: it was said that the more adept members of the former Communist Party *nomenklatura* had simply confiscated parts of the allegedly "immense wealth" of the party and used it to launch themselves into a new capitalist class; other rumors pointed to the "mafia" organizations of the Russian Federation. In contrast to the new political elite – which was very visible – the new economic elite carried with it an atmosphere of shadiness, secrecy, and wealth dishonestly acquired. While the new political elite in principle could be voted out of office (when the electoral system was put into place), the new economic elite appeared to be permanent. The markers and symbols of a "middle class," defined by income, were much less evident. Even so, dispassionate income analysis showed that by the mid-1990s the proportion of the population with mid-range incomes was also growing, but at a relatively slow pace.

Loss of employment or underemployment came as a shock to many, especially to those who had participated in the independence drive from 1988 onward. The rhetoric of demonstrations had included slogans about bearing any price for independence; evidently, the belief had been that the shift from a tightly controlled and planned economy to a free-wheeling one would bring strains rather than shrinkage of economic activity. Western consultants had not been of much help in sketching out the practical results of a transition of this sort since they lacked reliable models of a peacetime shift from a planned to an unplanned economy, and their advice included such hard-to-interpret metaphors as "shock therapy." The sluice gates were open for unending complaint, especially by those with higher education whose standing and employment were also affected by the new situation. In fact, the intellectual class in each republic had taken a very hard fall. If a new political elite was forming from the popular fronts and the institutions of government, and if a new economic elite was coming into being from those who knew how to take advantage of economic opportunities, intellectuals had lost the few centers of influence they possessed under the Soviet regime – the so-called "creative unions" (including the all-important Writers Unions), the Academies of Science with their numerous research institutes, the universities where the salaries for teachers plummeted, and the publishing houses that in the past had virtually guaranteed publication after a piece of writing had been cleared by party censors.

All the institutions that had depended on a steady inflow of funds from state budgets (republic or "center") found themselves scrambling for survival, in the process "reducing cadres" or forcing them into early retirement. In these circumstances, a new intellectual elite was difficult to form and sustain. Publication became a matter of finding sponsors in the new business world – for intellectuals a demeaning process; many research institutes were closed or left to their own devices; support for research from government sources was converted to a competitive grant process; and there were charges that the new governments were seeking to "destroy science." Besides, many intellectuals were appalled by the harshness of this new seemingly business-oriented environment, and said so publicly and repeatedly in now-uncensored periodical publications. Gradually it became very clear that a new intellectual elite would have to come into being, not through membership in system-created and system-supported high-status institutions, but through personal accomplishment: success in publications aimed at a large audience, reputation acknowledged in the media, and international recognition. The spotlight was shifting from "collective" intellectual endeavors to the individual, from publications in which the contribution of each participant was downplayed to individually authored writings that could enhance a person's curriculum vitae (the cv itself being a new phenomenon). Increasingly, for research-oriented intellectuals success meant publication in "western" languages (most often English), a requirement for which many in the older generation were unprepared.

During the post-1991 decade, all three Baltic republics nurtured the expectation that their human resources would be enhanced by returning post-World War II émigrés. Lithuania had a large North American émigré community at least a century old; most Latvian émigrés also lived in North America, but there were important centers as well in Germany, Sweden, and Australia; Estonian émigrés – numerically the smallest of the three – were concentrated in North America (especially Canada) and Sweden. These were the "bourgeois nationalists" against whom the littoral communist parties had been inveighing for decades; they had developed strong centers of anti-communist political activism capped by such cooperative intra-Baltic pressure groups as the Baltic Appeal to the United Nations (founded in 1965). Although assimilation had made inroads into these émigré communities over the past half-century, the efforts of the first post-World War II generation of emigrant-refugees to lay an institutional basis for a continuing cultural life in the Estonian, Latvian, and Lithuanian languages – through churches, Saturday schools, theater groups, newspapers, periodicals, and publishing houses – had paid off. By 1991, there were many in the émigré communities (the children of the first emigrants) whose linguistic, cultural, and emotional ties to the homelands of their parents were deep and potentially useful for the Baltic republics. But after 1991, these émigrés were also faced with the task of redefinition: they could no longer think of themselves as exiles prevented from returning by the hostile regimes in their homelands.

In fact, the anticipated return migration turned out to be minimal – estimated at perhaps several thousand for each country. Those who had left in 1944/1945 as children or young adults were too senior to enter the instability and unpredictability of their former homelands;

the second and third generations were too firmly rooted in the places where they had grown up, married, and started families. Nonetheless, the numbers, though small, were sufficient to make the "émigrés" a continuing factor in post-1991 developments. Some highly motivated individuals returned and stayed, others visited frequently, and still others (principally academics) created half-time arrangements for living in their ancestral homelands. The émigré communities and their homelands developed increasingly multifaceted relationships over the first decade: émigré scholars staffed Kaunas University in Lithuania, activists pushed for the establishment of an Occupation Museum in Riga, and other scholars assisted in creating degree-granting programs at Tartu University. Politics, especially the elections for the first post-communist parliaments in 1993–1994, included a considerable number of émigré candidates. Over the decade, however, the material and symbolic importance of the émigré factor diminished, as the residents of Estonia, Latvia, and Lithuania expanded their own permanent economic and political connections to European institutions and made North American "intermediaries" irrelevant. On the émigré side, many found contemporary life in the Baltic republics to be radically different from what they had idealized: Soviet-era thinking was not disappearing overnight; in Estonia and Latvia, the Russian residents continued to be a prominent factor in daily life, especially linguistically and especially in the urban areas. Speedy reform did not happen. The result of this changing relationship was a continuing lower-level interface of the kind that neither of the two sides had anticipated in the 1988–1991 period.

GOVERNMENT AND PUBLIC OPINION

The 1990 elections of the three Supreme Soviets (Councils) had of course been conducted under the rules of the old system, and, even if in all three cases reformist candidates had been brought to power and had successfully led the three republics to independence, the legitimacy of these political institutions themselves was suspect. They were like the provisional governments of the 1918–1919 period, having a kind of mandate to act in the name of their constituents but also constrained by the knowledge that they were not parliaments in the full sense of the term, and that their actions were not rooted in constitutional law. They were simultaneously legitimate and temporary, acting in lieu of real governments while being careful that their actions should not be perceived as arbitrary. Activism in the popular fronts had been a school for the new political elite; some participants discovered that they had little taste for politics when there was no clear single goal, while others found that they liked to make things happen and wanted to continue doing so. The main political leaders – Edgar Savisaar (b. 1950) in Estonia, Ivars Godmanis (b. 1951) in Latvia, and Vytautas Landsbergis (b. 1934) in Lithuania – had emerged as effective politicians on the path to independence, and for them the next challenge was to remain in the corridors of power. Other important political actors, of varying backgrounds, ages, and temperaments, included in Estonia Arnold Rüütel (b. 1928) and Marju Lauristin (b. 1940); in Latvia Anatolijs Gorbunovs (b. 1942) and Dainis Īvāns (b. 1955); in Lithuania Algirdas Brazauskas (b. 1931) and Kazimira Prunskiene (b. 1943). They understood that with the Soviet Union gone the task of governing was at hand and that the enthusiasm of the "movement" was dissipating; the time for forming political parties that would compete for power had arrived. None of these aspirants had any deep experience with democratic institutions; what they knew they had learned in the transition period. But, in one way or another, events had moved all of them to the top of the new political elite, where the governments they headed retained sufficient trust of the general population throughout the transition period (1990–1993) to deal successfully with reform legislation, handle negotiations with the expiring USSR, prepare (in Latvia's case, renew) constitutions, and work out an electoral system that would lead to real parliaments. In the context of continuing economic turmoil and growing desperation in some parts of the three populations, the transition governments provided an element of stability; they were expected to work out procedures for fully legitimated governments and they succeeded. Many of the numerous people the leaders brought into the new political elite – government ministers, associate ministers, department heads, and technical experts of various kinds – were also new to action at the national level, and were to some extent flying blind, as subsequent autobiographical accounts of the period revealed.

The post-1991 constitutions of the three republics – the renewed 1922 document in Latvia and entirely new fundamental documents in Estonia and Lithuania (in both cases adopted in 1992) – prescribed democratically elected unicameral parliaments: in Estonia, the *Riigikogu* with 101 members; in Latvia, the *Saeima* with 100 members; and in Lithuania, the *Seimas* with 141 members. The term of the MPs was four years; the Estonian *Riigikogu* and the Latvian *Saeima* were elected by proportional representation, while in the Lithuanian *Seimas*, 71 deputies were elected directly and 70 on a proportional basis from party lists. Cabinets, expected to be coalitions, were to be formed from parties that, working together, could assure proposed measures would pass by a minimum of a simple majority. The head of state – the president – was elected by the parliaments in Estonia and Latvia and by popular vote in Lithuania. In principle, the head of state was to stand above party politics and did not have to be affiliated with any party. The presidential term in Estonia was four years; initially three in Latvia but changed to four in 1997; and five years in Lithuania. The parliamentary elections took place in the fall of 1992 in Lithuania and Estonia and in June 1993 in Latvia. The outcomes of the elections underlined how differently the political cultures of the three countries had evolved to this point. To outside observers, the starting point had been about the same for all – a strong popular movement against an entrenched dictatorial party and an external foe – but beneath the headline-grabbing activities of the fronts and the frequent consultations between them, the configurations of active individuals and groupings in each country were decidedly not the same.

In Estonia, where the new *Riigikogu* began work in October 1992, the election had brought into power a coalition of center-right parties, and the new power-wielders were almost entirely of the youngest generation, "untainted" by previous involvements with the Communist Party. For head of state (president), the *Riigikogu* reached into the pre-1940 generation, however, and elected Lennart Meri (1929–2006), a prominent western-oriented scholar and former Siberian exile; Meri turned to Mart Laar (b. 1960), a historian and the head of the Fatherland Party, which had received the largest proportion of the vote (22 percent), to form a cabinet. Laar's government managed to stay in office for almost two years, providing a major spur to continuing economic and institutional reform in Estonia.

In Latvia, the Popular Front began to fragment soon after 1991, and, though it reconfigured itself as a political party, did not achieve even the 4 percent of the vote in the 1993 elections that would have given it parliamentary seats. Over a relatively short time – less than two years – the unity of the independence drive had dissipated, as individuals and groupings sought to differentiate themselves. The new *Saeima* began its work in June 1993 by electing as president Guntis Ulmanis, a grand-nephew of the interwar authoritarian president Kārlis Ulmanis and also a former Siberian exile. He was a member of the Agrarian Union, an interwar party renewed for the 1993 elections. The new President Ulmanis asked Latvia's Way, the party that had received an impressive 32 percent of the vote, to form a cabinet; negotiations produced a center-right minority (forty-eight votes) government as Latvia's Way formed a coalition with the Agrarian Union, the fourth largest vote-getter. In this decision, Latvia's Way was underscoring its centrist credentials, since it did not bring into the coalition the second largest vote-getter – the Latvian National Independence Movement (formed in 1988) – believing its often strident Latvian nationalism to be too far to the "right"; or the third largest – the Harmony Party (more precisely, "Harmony for Latvia, Revival for the Economy") – which during the pre-election campaign had begun to champion, among other things, the non-Latvian minority populations. This strategy at the time appeared to be placing Harmony too far to the left. The Latvia's Way MPs were themselves an odd mixture of generations and biographies. They included the ever-popular Anatolijs Gorbunovs, former ideological secretary of the Latvian Communist Party (who became Speaker of the Parliament); Gunārs Meierovics (1920–2006), son of the very popular Foreign Minister Zigfrīds Meierovics of the World War I era, and one of the most prominent émigré political leaders; and Valdis Birkavs (b. 1942), who had taken a degree in law at the University of Latvia in 1969 and had been an activist in the Popular Front. By choice, Birkavs' cabinet drew heavily on the émigré community: the minister of defense was from the USA, the minister of welfare from Australia, and minister of justice from Germany. As a minority government (commanding only forty-eight votes), the Birkavs cabinet lasted for only one year.

32 Three post-1991 presidents. Left to right: Estonian
President Lennart Meri, Latvian President Guntis Ulmanis, and
Lithuanian President Algirdas Brazauskas as they share a joke
during a meeting at the Hotel Karupcsa in Otepää, Estonia,
some 40 km south of Tartu, May 25, 1997.

In Lithuania, by contrast, the parliamentary elections of 1992 gave
a powerful plurality (42.6 percent) to the Lithuanian Democratic
Labor Party, which was the renamed reform wing of the Communist
Party of the pre-1991 period. The very popular Algirdas Brazauskas
(b. 1931), the former first secretary of the Lithuanian Communist
Party (1988–1990) who had supported the independence drive and
at crucial moments had sided with Sajudis (the Popular Front), was
elected president in October 1992 with about 60 percent of the vote.
In the Lithuanian case, the 1992 parliamentary and presidential
elections had the effect of drawing lines between the Lithuanians in
Lithuania and the émigré community, and between Lithuania and
the other two Baltic states.

The contrasts among the three new states were many. Émigré
Lithuanians voted overwhelmingly for Brazauskas' competitor,

Stasys Lozoraitis (1924–1994; an American-Lithuanian), whereas the voters in Lithuania stayed with the popular Brazauskas. In Latvia, Latvia's Way presented a slate in which émigré Latvians were prominent, but in Estonia few such "outsiders" were featured. Estonian voters were willing to entrust the government to a new generation, but such an impulse was not evident in the Latvian and Lithuanian cases. The Estonian voters at this juncture clearly wanted, at least symbolically, to sever ties with the communist past; in Latvia, they were more forgiving to ex-party members; the Lithuanian electorate had little problem with ex-communists in high office. In Estonia, the voters preferred the "right," in Latvia the new government was "centrist," while in Lithuania it was clearly on the "left." In all three cases, however, voter participation was high – 67.8 percent in Estonia, 89.9 percent in Latvia, and 75.2 percent in Lithuania – suggesting widespread appreciation of the significance of the moment.

From the outset, the democratic political systems of all three countries assumed that a multitude of parties would operate at the national level, just as in the rest of parliamentary Europe; the ideal or even idea of a two-party system was absent from political discourse. The rules of party formation were relatively liberal: parties had to acquire four or five percent of the total vote to have representation in the parliaments; the three systems were not unlike those that were created in the early 1920s during the first period of independence. It was assumed also that no single party would be overwhelmingly dominant, that governments (cabinets) would be coalitions, that coalitions would break down and have to be re-formed, and that in extremis new parliamentary elections would have to be held if a given configuration of parties could not produce a working cabinet.

The 1992/1993 elections showed that these assumptions were warranted and that the largest vote-getting parties could not dominate the legislatures: in Estonia, the Pro Patria Party (headed by Mart Laar) held only 28 percent of seats, in Latvia, Latvia's Way only 32 percent, and in Lithuania, the Democratic Labor Party only 48 percent. Even the overwhelmingly popular Lithuanian Democratic Labor Party needed to reach out to other parliamentary "fractions" to achieve a majority; the Latvia's Way cabinet opted to start with a coalition that commanded only 48 of 100 votes (a minority cabinet); and in Estonia,

Pro Patria had to cobble together a three-party coalition to command 53 parliamentary votes. By contrast with systems in which two parties dominate the political scene (the UK, USA), the multiparty system was by some measures more democratic insofar as it permitted a multiplicity of viewpoints to emerge as organized groups sought power. On the other hand, the system rendered more fragile the work of the legislature: coalitions fell apart when even one partner withdrew; cabinet ministers were chosen not purely on merit but so that all coalition members would have representation; the business of "politics" (deal-making, compromises, and maneuvering) was always on view (in a now-free media), corroborating in the minds of many the image of politicians as self-interested power-grabbers in search of good salaries and the perquisites of office. Continuity in the political domain was provided by the presidents (a relatively weak office in Estonia and Latvia; a relatively strong one in Lithuania) and by the "permanent government," the thousands of bureaucratic officials who worked in the ministries.

In all three countries at this juncture, the number of ministries was being reduced through elimination or combination of functions. The officials who worked in them were being converted to a "civil service" through testing and revision of job descriptions, so that this part of the political domain was also in the throes of change. The continuing turmoil of the long transition period (1988–1993) was not followed by overwhelming peace, stability, and predictability, but the post-election atmosphere did underscore that the "new rules of the game" were widely accepted: external observers declared the elections to have been fair, losers withdrew to plot political comebacks, the Supreme Soviets (Councils) disbanded peacefully, and symbols of high office were transferred between individuals with due pomp and ceremony.

The second post-1991 parliamentary elections in Estonia and Latvia in 1995 and in Lithuania in 1996 repeated the patterns of the first: demonstrable unpopularity of the parties in power (in the first election, they were the popular fronts); proliferation of contenders – existing party formations, new parties, electoral coalitions, single-issue groupings; platforms that were long on promises and short on specifics; reliance on polling; and emphasis in campaign literature on those party members whose popularity ratings remained high. In

Estonia, seventeen parties and electoral coalitions contended for power, in Latvia nineteen, and in Lithuania twenty-seven. The results showed that the electorate was not as accepting of the political turmoil "at the top" as were those directly involved in it. In Estonia the conservative-nationalist Pro Patria lost some two-thirds of its seats, while parties with a populist bent made major gains; in Latvia, Latvia's Way came in second, its parliamentary base dropping from thirty-six to seventeen seats; in Lithuania, the voters turned away from Brazauskas' Democratic Labor Party toward parties on the right, reducing the parliamentary base of the DLP to 50 seats (out of 141).

The second parliamentary elections added another feature to the overall patterns: the readiness of the voters to change directions – even radically – if the coalition in power appeared not to be solving widespread problems, mostly of the economic kind. Public opinion polls suggested the existence of electorates that were simultaneously interested in "reentering Europe" and in quick solutions to transition-linked difficulties: lowered personal incomes, unemployment and underemployment, increased price of foodstuffs, the cost of social services that in the not-so-distant past had been "free" or nearly free (medical treatment, education, public transportation, home heating). Some of these concerns – such as high tariffs on imported foodstuffs – clearly required protectionism. For many, reentering Europe meant simply the arrival of western developmental and investment monies; that the process might also mean painful changes at the personal and institutional level was downplayed by the party platforms and resented by the voting public. The reliance by parties and party coalitions on public opinion polls in the formulation of their platforms was certainly consistent with the democratization of the political arena, yet it made the parties more vulnerable to the temptations of populism.

Moreover, although parties – especially their parliamentary components – could enforce party discipline and tried hard to impose strict discipline among members of coalitions as well, a high rate of defections continued: coalition partners threatened withdrawal of support unless their demands were met; individuals withdrew from parties and became non-party-affiliated MPs; and groups of individuals quit their parties with the intention of forming new ones with themselves in leadership positions. All such political shifting – major or minor – was faithfully reported in the press, impaired the "image" of parties and the legislatures, and promoted cynicism in the voting public about the intentions and motives of the political elite.

Nonetheless, at the time of the third parliamentary elections (1999 in Estonia, 1998 in Latvia, and 2000 in Lithuania) participation rates did not suggest a wholesale disenchantment with the new political system. While rates had dropped from the high participation levels in the first election (from 67% to 57% in Estonia, from 89% to 71% in Latvia, from 75% to 52% in Lithuania), they still remained higher on average than in many established western democracies. The desire among politically ambitious individuals to be heard in the parliamentary arena had not lessened either: in the third post-1991 parliamentary election in Estonia twelve parties vied for the vote, in Latvia twenty-one, and in Lithuania seventeen. By this time numerous prominent individuals had changed party affiliation or had invented party formations more to their liking. In the post-1991 decade in each of the three Baltic republics, a parliamentary democracy had taken shape whose fundamental principles were widely accepted, even though the actors in the parliamentary arena and in political life generally had to deal – almost as a rule – with public opinion that was quick to change from enthusiastic support to condemnation in the darkest terms.

NATIONAL STATES OR WELFARE STATES

Much of public discussion in the post-1991 decade in all three republics revolved around the question of what kind of state should be built now that independence had been acquired. As a thriving multiparty system revealed, there was little agreement on such broad issues; ambitious parties and individuals could easily design platforms so as to attract a fragment of public opinion and then tack on the proclamation that the advocated policies were "in the national interest." In time, three general orientations emerged through which most problems were understood and filtered. There was no perfect correlation between these orientations and the platform of any one party; in the population at large also there were considerable opinion shifts from election to election; outright ideologues in the Baltic republics were marginal and ideologies themselves fluid; placing these positions into the classical spectrum of right, center, and left is difficult. Nonetheless, answers to the basic questions of what the renewed republics essentially were, how citizenship should be defined, what the machinery of the state should be used for, how tight budgets should be divided, and what foreign policies should be adopted reflected an underlying *Weltanschauung* that was itself part historical experience, part sense of ethnic identity, part self-interest, and part an understanding of the meaning of "entering Europe."

Though the popular front movements had splintered and regrouped as political parties – some more successful than others in the parliamentary arena – much of the spirit that had animated the fronts remained alive in the post-1991 decade. Regretting the loss of "national unity" that had prevailed in the 1988–1991 era, persons speaking from this orientation remained ardently anti-Soviet and insisted that the 1940–1941 and 1945–1991 years had been a long, nightmarish, and illegal "occupation" of Estonia, Latvia, and Lithuania by a predatory neighbor. For them, the Soviet era was a modern-day extension of the Russian imperialism that had begun with Peter I in the early eighteenth century and had used Marxist-Leninist ideology as a cover for westward Russian territorial expansion. The current process of reentering Europe was pictured as a restoration of the essential Europeanness of the Baltic littoral, a restoration of heritage. All institutions, norms, and behaviors (including the command economy) produced by the Soviet era had to be expunged; the Russian military (still present until 1994) had to be withdrawn; and most Russian-speaking residents of the littoral had to be persuaded to return to their "ethnic homeland." The discourse of this orientation asserted ownership rights over geographic space; the part of the littoral in which the ancient Estonians, Latvians, and Lithuanians had lived "belonged" to their modern successors; the possessive adjective "ours" proliferated. The principal (though not sole) purpose of the machinery of the state was to safeguard all forms of the national cultures of the "basic nations" (Estonians, Latvians, and Lithuanians), especially the language use of those cultures. Such protectionism was necessary because the carriers of these national cultures were small numerically and therefore vulnerable to overwhelming influences from the "outside" world.

"State" and "national culture" were separable concepts: national culture was of long duration; the state, as recent history had shown, could be lost and regained, and its machinery could be seized by persons inimical to the perpetuation of national culture. Permanent residents of the three countries whose ethnic and linguistic origins were elsewhere could acquire citizenship as long as they passed examinations that certified their loyalty; otherwise, they had the status of resident aliens. The language of the titular (basic) nation was the language of the state; giving equal or similar status to other languages would be a violation of the protectionist purpose of the state. In this view, the continent of Europe was a collection of national cultures (much as Johann Gottfried Herder had pictured it at the end of the eighteenth century), and each of the states that now comprised the European community had a single national culture as its base; the Baltic republics could not be expected to be anything else. In addition, if western civilization truly cared about cultural and linguistic diversity, it should assent to this view of the continent. After all, only in states "belonging" to Estonians, Latvians, and Lithuanians could children truly shape their personalities in terms of these three nationalities and grow up speaking these languages. Only in such states could literary artists develop their talents in these three languages and thus contribute to the cultural enrichment of the whole continent. Survival of these three national cultures, however, could not be left to chance; state policy and oversight had to work hard to protect and promote that survival. In Estonia, in the 1992 parliamentary election, the winning Pro Patria party of Mart Laar expressed many of these views; in Latvia, such viewpoints found voice in the platform of the Fatherland and Freedom Party in 1993; and in Lithuania, the Homeland Union Party – successor to Sajudis – with its still popular leader Vytautas Landsbergis best articulated these positions. Predictably, these parties on the "right" found themselves in competition for conservative votes with splinter parties, which articulated this orientation in even less compromising terms.

In contrast with this general position, a second persuasive world-view took as its starting point the nature of the three littoral societies as they were in the wake of the collapse of the USSR. While it may be true and regrettable that larger predatory neighbors had occupied and annexed the three Baltic states during World War II, the past could not be changed, and the half-century of existence within the USSR could not be treated as simply one long period of unmitigated evil. Having survived conditions of exceptional hardship, the three national cultures and the languages in which they expressed themselves were still very much alive, which demonstrated that they had never been even close to extinction, as some claimed. The fears of literary artists had been individualized reactions and not assessments of the true situation. Within the admittedly harsh constraints of the command economy, talented people still fulfilled themselves; specialists were educated in their fields; modernization (heavy industry, technological growth, urbanization) occurred, even if at a much slower pace that in western countries and with considerably less personal freedom. The communist parties, though claiming undeserved rights for themselves, had valued talent; communism had turned out to be, in spite of its claims of omniscience, simply an alternative path of modernization. The murder, imprisonment, and relocation of innocent people in the Soviet period resulted from mistaken policy; these were not one inevitable byproduct of the system. Besides, ethnic Russians had suffered under totalitarian rule at least as much as the residents of the Baltic countries; all the constituent republics of the USSR had their grievances.

In view of all these things, the Baltic governments in the post-1991 era should each have recognized that the three republics were all entities needing to develop policies befitting the new international situation. European states were now multicultural, multiethnic, and multinational – some because of the influx of immigrants from former colonies, some because of decades-long policies promoting the arrival of "guest workers," and some because of the natural and free migration of labor across national borders in a continent that was receptive to such liberalization. European national states, while nowhere close to disappearing, were gradually redefining the concept of national sovereignty to take advantage of internationalization. A protectionist stance toward "national culture" was bound to fail in the face of worldwide rapidly diffused international popular culture.

In view of these developments, state policies that defined citizenship in terms of language capabilities were undemocratic in the extreme; requirements that schoolchildren learn the language of the state in addition to their family language were ethno-imperialistic;

the seeming exclusion from high office of persons not of the titular nationality was ethno-prejudice. Policies promoting the goal of ethnic and linguistic dominance of one nationality group were a misplacement of time and resources just when national governments should be focusing on economic growth and the reduction of chronic poverty. State policy should concentrate on the creation of welfare states modeled on the Scandinavian experience, which was living proof that small countries could retain their national uniqueness (if this was important) while at the same time providing their residents – citizens and non-citizens alike – with decently remunerated employment, adequate medical care, state pensions, and educational facilities. The resources for the welfare state should come from a reformed tax system aimed particularly at the new wealthy class – the beneficiaries of "shock therapy" and "wild-west, free-market capitalism" – since income inequality had reached intolerable limits. It would make a great deal of economic sense for the Baltic republics to orient themselves both to the west and to Russia, because both represented markets for their goods and services, and, besides, many residents of the Baltic states had historic ties to Russia linguistically and culturally. In the 1992 Estonian parliamentary election, this orientation was most clearly expressed by the United People's Party, which sought to capture the votes of the ethnic Russians; but elements of it were present as well in the platforms of the Rural Party, led by the last Soviet-era president Arnold Rüütel. In Latvia, this orientation appeared in the platform of the Equal Rights and National Harmony parties – both calling for integration of the ethnic Russians into Latvian society – and in the Social Democratic Alliance, which put itself forward as the successor of the interwar Latvian social democracy movement. Unsurprisingly, the social welfare promises of this view also showed up in the People's Movement for Latvia, a blatantly populist and anti-elitist party that did well in the second parliamentary election of 1995. In Lithuania, where all current residents – including ethnic Russians and Poles – had been given the vote by the 1992 constitution, the left was most clearly represented by the Lithuanian Democratic Labor Party (victorious in the 1992 parliamentary elections). Its weak rival, the Lithuanian Social Democratic Party, opposed privatization and remained deeply skeptical of Lithuania's western orientation.

These two viewpoints can be described as the right and the left of post-1991 political thinking in the three republics. Still, no single person or political party espoused all these elements with equal intensity, and many assumed a third – middle – way and sought to present themselves as pragmatists, centrists, and problem-solvers rather than true believers. Reform for such people meant first and foremost transforming the three republics from their current "post-communist" identity into "normal" European countries. In this thinking, "reentering Europe" had to include close attention to the rules, regulations, injunctions, and suggestions of international European organizations that the three republics wanted to join with the accompanying restrictions on absolute freedom of national action. This translated into furtherance of policies that moved in the direction of a free market, but also protection of those who, for various reasons, could not compete. Measures to install a state language and to protect a national culture could not be introduced without similar protections extended to minority languages and minority cultures. Internal policies that appeared to be motivated by vindictiveness toward the Soviet-era political and cultural hegemons – Russians – had to be avoided, just as policies could not be motivated by the desire to settle even older historic scores. Sensible measures had to be rooted in present-day European value systems. Border disputes had to be settled quickly and peacefully through compromise, even if this meant the surrender of some territory.

National sovereignty could not become an excuse for autochthonous behavior, autarchic economic measures, and wholly independent charting of the national future. If the three republics wanted to benefit from European developmental assistance – financial and otherwise – they needed always to act in concert with the value system Europe had incorporated into international organizations during its own half-century of change. The plea of earlier suffering would not in itself earn the Baltic republics special status; many peoples had suffered in different ways. Of much greater interest was how the three republics planned to handle their affairs in the future, even if their desires for righting past wrongs remained partially unfulfilled. They had to work toward the goal of having a spectrum of political and economic opinion that, at the extremes, approximated the spectra of other European states. Moderation, compromise, pragmatism, negotiation, rationality, centrism, and exclusion of extreme ideological positions were to be the watchwords. By definition, parties that sought to straddle orientations hoped to attract voters by projecting an image of moderate, competent, and recognized leadership. In Estonia, this strategy did not work well for centrists (primarily the Center Party, led by Edgar Savisaar, the founder of the Estonian Popular Front) in the 1992 elections, but it was effective in 1995 and especially in 1999, when the Center Party was the biggest vote-getter (Pro Patria coming in second). In Latvia, the centrist Latvia's Way triumphed in 1993. In 1995, however, the voters found the centrist orientation frustrating, and moved either toward a newer left-of-center party called the Democratic Party Saimnieks ("boss") or toward the populist, protectionist, and opportunistic People's Movement for Latvia. In 1998, they moved back to the center by giving the most votes to a new centrist party (People's Party) or to Latvia's Way. In Lithuania, the popularity of the left had faded by the 1996 parliamentary elections: the Social Democrats were ousted by the somewhat more moderate sounding but still nationalistic Homeland Union and its smaller allies, the Christian Democrats. In the 2000 elections, Homeland Union was itself ousted. Even though the Social Democrats now held more seats than other parties, the government was formed by a makeshift coalition of centrist parties, some of which were brand new. Landsbergis, the leader of the defeated Homeland Union, called this centrist government "a soup where every sort of ingredient can be found."

During the first post-1991 decade, the new political elites came to realize that none of the philosophical orientations with which they sympathized offered any rapid solutions to the continuing problems associated with economic growth. Budget shortages confronted whichever parties won elections, and campaign promises remained unfulfilled to the frustration of parties and electorate alike. The problems were identifiable enough, but they were linked and thus delay or partial reform in one sector frustrated progress in others. The enlargement of the free market – good in principle – appeared to have no other immediate consequence than the creation of a new wealthy class while leaving the wage and salary levels of most others far behind. Much of the new wealth remained untaxed as a result of badly drawn tax laws, imperfect collection mechanisms, and the fear of creating disincentives to the entrepreneurial spirit. The privatization of real estate, land, and industrial enterprise – already started before 1991 and continuing apace in all three republics during the 1990s – lacked effective oversight by the government and seemed to favor only those who had quickly learned the techniques of financial manipulation. Many normal citizens remained dubious about anything that smacked of the "speculation" that had been condemned in the old command economy.

Not wanting to quash the risk-taking that was so essential to entrepreneurship, the three governments were hesitant to regulate, opening the way to charlatanry in the form of various pyramid schemes. New banks promised huge interest to attract depositors, who were enriched in the early stages by pay-outs from new deposits, but then crashed when all depositors demanded their money together with the enormous interest. Such machinations lay behind the "banking crisis" in Latvia in 1995/1996 when a cluster of major banks either collapsed or needed to be bailed out by the Bank of Latvia. Businesses and consortia were formed overnight, promised enormous investment opportunities, attracted some risk-takers, and just as quickly disappeared together with the investors' money. Reform-minded cabinets appeared always to be a step behind the quickly changing marketplace, realizing the need for rules and regulations after the damage had already been done. Frequently the brake to reform came from the existing ministries, where officials, still with a mindset close to their Soviet-era training, were uncertain about how to implement new laws; civil service reform had not yet started or at best was slowly coming into being. Running throughout all the economic turbulence was the red thread of criminality, allegedly carried out by local or Russia-based "mafias" that appeared to be taking advantage of badly written import-export regulations, corrupt customs officials, and poorly equipped police forces. Political leaders themselves frequently revealed a poor understanding of ethical norms when they awarded themselves and one another various kinds of prizes and premiums, accepted "scholarships" from prominent industrialists, used their parliamentary living allowances to rent apartments from relatives, and placed family members on the public payroll. The idealized Scandinavian welfare state remained a distant goal, and even the political parties that most directly shared its ideological premises – such as the Lithuanian Democratic Labor Party – seemed unable to take major irreversible steps in its direction. It was of little solace to most people that the per capita GDP began to reverse its downward slide in 1994–1995 in Estonia and Latvia, and slightly later, in 1997, in Lithuania. This dry statistic did not immediately translate into an improved standard of living for most people. By this measure, Estonia by 1995 was far ahead of the other two Baltic states, with Latvia in second place, and Lithuania last. All three, however, were substantially ahead of the Russian Federation, which explains why the out-migration of Russian speakers from Estonia and Latvia had been reduced to a trickle by the second half of the 1990s.

The economic downturn accompanying independence prevented a deep feeling of satisfaction from settling in, and those who wanted to see signs that independence was irreversible had to be satisfied with symbolic acknowledgments of the fact. Acceptance for membership in a host of international organizations (including the United Nations) was an important symbol, as was the final withdrawal of the Russian military contingents from the three countries in 1993–1994. Considerable pride was taken in the fact that by the end of the 1990s all three countries had carried out a series of parliamentary and presidential elections in the manner of "normal" democratic countries: the losers triggered no mass demonstrations, and very few charged that the elections had been rigged or corrupt. No less significant was the disappearance of the irritating reminders in everyday life that the three countries had once been component parts of a Russian-speaking larger entity. Statues of Lenin and memorials to other Soviet-era worthies were long gone, and the changing of street names began even before 1991; the new names were largely those of the pre-1940 period. The Cyrillic alphabet disappeared in signage of all kinds, and language laws, though imperfectly enforced, pressured those who attended to the needs of the general public – clerks, streetcar conductors, waiters, and bureaucrats – at least to try to communicate with their customers in the state language.

All such changes signified the return of "ownership" by Estonians, Latvians, and Lithuanians of the countries that were their primary homes. Moreover, the returning sense of ownership meant that the guardians of the national culture (primarily artists and literary intellectuals) could work at the restoration of cultural wholeness by reintegrating the experiences of the 1944/1945 émigré populations into the "national story," by uncovering and investing with value the multiple experiences of the Baltic populations deported in 1941 and 1948/49, and by expelling from that story the elements inserted in it by party dictates during the Soviet era. The émigrés were no longer viewed as "bourgeois nationalists" or "fascists," nor were the Siberian exiles "enemies of the people." The "heroes" of the Soviet period were to be understood as perpetrators of a half-century of brutal "occupation." The insertion into school textbooks of this historical paradigm symbolized the return of ownership of the "national past" and the rescue of that past from servitude to the historical philosophies of Marxism-Leninism and Russian chauvinism.

Important symbolism was also conveyed by the three presidents who by the year 2000 represented the Baltic countries to the outside world. In Estonia, Lennart Meri, elected in 1992 and reelected in 1996, a literary scholar and former Siberian exile, was an uncompromising "European." In fact in 1998 the French newspaper *La Vie* named him "European Man of the Year." In Latvia, Vaira Vīķe-Freiberga (b. 1937), elected in 1999 and reelected in 2003, was a 1944 émigré born in Latvia but raised in Germany, Morocco, and Canada. She had been professor of psychology at the University of Montreal and, though she spoke no Russian, she addressed international gatherings in fluent English or French. In Lithuania in 1998, the voters elected as president Valdas Adamkus (b. 1926), an émigré from the United States, who for many years headed the Great Lakes District of the Environmental Protection Agency before becoming active in post-1991 Lithuanian politics. Each president in his or her own way represented the "national healing" process: the "nation" that had remained behind was bringing back those who had been exiled by coercion or desperation. All were also indubitably western-oriented.

NETWORKING AND ITS CONSEQUENCES

The turbulent internal politics of the renewed Baltic republics after 1991 unfolded against a background of steadily expanding connections with international organizations, particularly those with a European base. Some involvement, such as that with the United Nations, took the form of full membership from the very beginning, while most required a period of candidate or associate status until current full members decided that membership criteria had been met. This was a very different "internationalism" than had been permitted in the Soviet period; then, the term was used to describe involvements only with the socialist states or with organizations controlled and directed by the USSR. Now the door was wide open, and for most residents of the Baltic littoral, internationalization meant, in principle, westernization. To be sure, diplomatic relations were established with all the post-communist states, including the Russian Federation, but none of the Baltic republics joined the Commonwealth of Independent States launched by Russia in 1992, fearing continued subordination. Such concern was not entirely absent either in the unfolding formal and informal relationships with the west, when the realization arrived that membership in western organizations would also mean self-imposed constraints on absolute freedom of action. Just having emerged from a half-century in a "union" in which one member was dominant, the public doubted the wisdom of joining others – no matter how democratic – in which a handful of well-established and economically powerful states played key roles. Discussion over these issues in the early 1990s became a dialogue between the political leadership and a skeptical public. Most of the leading political parties in all three Baltic republics supported the moves toward the west; among the Russian-speaking populations and among the parties that reflected their interests, however, there was hesitation and doubt, in some instances outright animosity. Some doubts could be found among the parties of the right wing as well, though here it was more a fear of the unknown mixed with a romanticized view of national sovereignty.

Yet the desire to reenter Europe remained a powerful sentiment, and by the mid-1990s the phrase became accepted as meaning that they would join international organizations in which all other – normal – European states held membership. On their side, western countries were receptive, even encouraging, and informal sponsorship of Baltic membership was undertaken by those European states that had historic connections to the littoral – Germany, Sweden, and

Finland – and by the North American countries – United States and Canada – that had active Baltic émigré communities. Western interest in the littoral, of course, had its economic side: the three countries could potentially offer investment opportunities and become markets for western consumer products. There were geopolitical motives as well, still cast in now-fading Cold War terms: to remove the Baltic republics from the Russian "sphere of interest" and add them to the "free west." The mixed motives and hesitations on both sides never disappeared entirely, but they did not remain strong enough in the general population to block governmental decisions to join such organizations.

An important role in the early stages was played by the Council of Baltic Sea States formed in 1992; this organization educated the representatives of the three republics in the view that cooperation, coordination of policy, compromise, and negotiation were not inimical to national sovereignty. When, also in 1992, the European Community (now the European Union [EU]) expanded its program of transformational aid to include the Baltic states, additional proof was forthcoming that coordination of developmental plans with the funding sources was also not injurious. Such interactions required continuing dialogue and compromise, but not surrender of national uniqueness. Representatives of the Baltic republics, conditioned for decades by the need obediently to follow orders from the "center," learned that centralized organizations were not all alike. In 1995 Estonia, Latvia, and Lithuania applied for membership in the European Union and became associate members. One byproduct of this membership was the reorientation of trade away from the eastern markets toward the west, and a corresponding increase in the number of western firms entering the "Baltic market." EU commissions appointed to guide the Baltic republics to full membership began to instruct their political leadership on how to continue working toward the goal of a free market, to avoid protectionist legislation, and to continue necessary internal reforms.

Security connections to Europe were as important as economic ties, and almost immediately after 1991, the three republics began to lobby for inclusion in the North Atlantic Treaty Organization (NATO). This was a far more complicated goal because it involved not only the security interests of European states but also the United

States of America and, of course, the Russian Federation with which NATO was seeking to work out an appropriate post-Cold War relationship. For the governments of the Baltic republics, only NATO could bring relief from a revanchist Russia; from the NATO perspective, inclusion of former Soviet satellites and Soviet republics would be a hazardous step that would very likely be interpreted by the Russian Federation as a threat to its security. Besides, NATO was a defensive alliance, predicated on the assumption that each member state would be able to make a significant contribution to the defense of all other member states.

In the early 1990s, the Baltic republics had no significant armed forces, Soviet (now Russian) military contingents were still present on their territories, and some articulations of Russian security interests suggested that the Baltic republics would remain part of Russia's "near abroad," that is, within its interest sphere. Also, public opinion in the Baltic republics was not unanimous: the same population segments who were skeptical about closer economic ties with western Europe were adamantly opposed to membership in a military organization that for decades during the Cold War had symbolized opposition to the USSR. Those who reflexively took Russia's side in all controversial matters were joined in the NATO dispute by those who did not want the Baltic republics to have any military force at all, those who believed that the Baltic rim countries should be a nuclear-free zone, and those who on principle admired neutrality. All the post-1991 governments in the Baltic republics, however, held fast to eventual NATO membership as a foreign policy goal. By 1998 the question of membership was temporarily tabled when the USA created a Charter of Partnership, which declared that the USA endorsed the Baltic republics' integration with such European and transatlantic institutions as the European Union, the Organization of Security and Cooperation in Europe, the World Trade Organization, and, eventually, NATO itself. NATO partnership would be replaced by membership when the new members demonstrated readiness to assume all responsibilities and obligations of membership, which, among others things, meant an increase in the national defense budgets of each potential member and the creation of credible national armed forces. In the meantime, NATO members, especially the USA, worked hard to include Russia in various NATO activities to demonstrate that the organization had no offensive intentions.

A European organization joined by the Baltic republics in 1991, soon after they regained independence, was at the time called the Conference on Security and Cooperation in Europe (CSCE). It became the Organization on Security and Cooperation in Europe (OSCE) in 1995. Convened in 1975 to resolve disputes before they became conflicts, the conference with more than fifty participating states had expanded its mission to include arms control, human rights, protection of national minorities, democratization, policing, and economic and environmental activities. Its programs were meant to be an early warning system to member states that their policies might be heading them into crises that required conflict prevention and crisis management. Though membership in the CSCE/OSCE was a logical step, public opinion over the next decade often questioned the organization's intentions when its High Commissioner on National Minorities, Max van der Stoel (commissioner 1992–2001), during frequent visits to the Baltic littoral sought to steer the three governments toward what the OSCE regarded as fair treatment of the Russian-using minorities in Estonia and Latvia and the smaller minority populations in Lithuania. Particularly incensed were people who believed the national governments to be instruments for defending national – Estonian, Latvian, and Lithuanian – culture and the constitutionally mandated languages of the three states. The very thought that minority and language policy would be monitored by "outsiders" was offensive. The OSCE, of course, could not dictate internal policy, but it could remind the Baltic republics that membership in European institutions as well as financial and advisory assistance entailed an obligation to international norms, and that inevitably reports from such organizations as the OSCE would be read by other organizations that were not concerned as directly with minority rights. "Europe" expected its constituent states to implement a system of laws reflecting general and evolving concepts of "human rights." The settling of old scores with formerly dominant minority populations was not a sound basis for a wholly European state.

The elected governments of the three Baltic republics soon recognized that reentering Europe would be a lengthy, multifaceted process involving more than simply acquiring membership cards in a host of organizations. Popular opinion by contrast was slower to accept this fact; evaluations from "outsiders" were often taken as strictures and commands, giving rise occasionally to populistic slogans such as "Europe will never understand us" and to conspiracy theories. Even so, during the 1990s the three Baltic countries never withdrew from an international organization once membership had been secured. International norms were successfully incorporated into the laws of the three states in a stepwise fashion through the normal political process. A new law proposed by the cabinet of ministers would be sent for vetting to a group of specialists at the relevant ministry; these persons, knowing international norms and consulting with international advisors, would suggest needed alterations; the proposed law would then be returned to the cabinet, which would discuss it and send it on to the parliament for a discussion and vote. Changes made in the parliament might or might not be adopted, and if a passed law were sent to the president he or she might return it to parliament for reworking. This process, largely invisible to the general public, provided numerous points at which a government could exercise state "sovereignty" in the creation of a new law or regulation that was of interest to international organizations such as the OSCE. Most new laws and regulations, of course, continued to be relatively uncontroversial and gave to international observers no reasons for intervention.

Rapidly growing involvement in the established system of diplomatic representation and in international organizations brought to the fore in all three Baltic republics the question of qualified personnel. During the last years of the Soviet period, there had been a proliferation of ministries and sub-ministries dealing with internal matters – the economy, culture, social welfare, transportation, finances, public services, and internal affairs: all of these seemed then to be necessary if the three republics were to become autonomous within a reformulated Soviet Union. A ministry to deal with "foreign affairs" at the republic level was irrelevant, since these relationships were undertaken by the Moscow government. With independence, however, a new set of priorities soon appeared – not only did a foreign affairs ministry become absolutely mandatory, but, with a constricting national budget, ways needed to be found to reduce the total number of ministries and the staffing of those that were retained.

Even ministries that did not deal directly with foreign relations needed staff oriented toward the outside world and with the necessary foreign language skills, especially English. Such people were to be found most readily in the universities and research institutes, and from the early 1990s people from academic disciplines – especially the humanities and social sciences – began to flow toward governmental service. Older cadres with technical knowledge but without second-language skills other than Russian were disadvantaged, and those without any language skills except Russian were disadvantaged most of all.

The general reorientation toward the west in fact affected the entire working population, especially in the service sector of the three economies. Fast-food chains entered the Baltic market, competing with local entrepreneurs who had begun to establish food outlets of a similar sort. Large commercial enterprises from the Scandinavian countries and Germany looked for investment opportunities, and department stores and hotels with well-known names were built in Tallinn, Riga, and Vilnius. The lackadaisical attitudes of service personnel during the Soviet period were well known, and these behaviors had to be reversed. The language question became germane: language laws required that personnel dealing with the general public be able to communicate in the state language if needed, regardless of whatever other languages were required to do the job well. Foreign language skills (beyond Russian) became a part of job descriptions, and service personnel also had to learn and practice such western nostrums as "the customer is always right"; they also had to learn that continuous employment was related to the quality of their work, a notion that often did not sit well with the belief, learned in the Soviet period, that all persons were entitled to income-yielding jobs regardless of the quality of their work. Such behavioral transitions came hardest to those who were older; the new requirements seemed "normal" to the younger generations entering the economic marketplace. Besides, "western" ways of doing things had a cachet that made them even more attractive.

The management of western-owned enterprises in the Baltic republics necessitated training in the west of managerial personnel, who sought such training through in-house programs of various kinds, university summer courses created specifically for these purposes, as well as short-term employment in western companies to learn "the tricks of the trade." Personal connections and friendships established by these means meant, in a sense, the emergence of a long-term "mentoring" system that was facilitated by the parallel appearance of easier and more rapid communication through fax machines and computer-based email systems as well as the rapidly growing use of English as the international language of the business world. Westernization, once started, had the effect of a large stone dropped in a small pond: the ripples spread outward and covered the entire surface. Numerical characterizations of the economies of the three republics were inserted into international rating systems meant to inform potential investors about potential profitability and the relative safety of their investments. Internal publications of national statistics had to conform to established international precedents and had to be calculated according to established norms. Donors of funds for humanitarian assistance expected accountability for how those funds were spent and what proportion of them ended up as salaries of administrators. In order to accept students from the Baltic republics, western educational institutions insisted on knowing the intellectual content of academic degrees granted by Baltic institutions of higher learning. Reentering Europe had come to mean hundreds of different rites of passage in which "transparency" was valued – a norm that oftentimes clashed with the prevailing secretiveness in public affairs and private relationships that had pervaded the old Soviet system. For many, the psychological stress of having to re-adjust was unbearable, and the proportion of persons in the older age groups who left the workforce voluntarily was high, contributing to the absolute numbers of "economically inactive" persons. In Latvia, for example, this category, which did not include unemployed persons seeking jobs, jumped for all age groups from 8,600 in 1991, to 22,500 in 1992, to 75,800 in 1993, to 95,500 in 1994.

For some time after 1991, the European networks in which the Baltic republics were becoming enmeshed viewed them and all the erstwhile European communist societies through the prism of "post-communism," making the same allowances that parents make toward teenage children. The expectation was that, after passing through this difficult phase of maturation, these countries would emerge capable of assuming adult responsibilities according to size and economic promise. Since no models for a post-communist "transition" could be scrutinized for lessons, the moment at which allowances would no longer be needed could not be specified with any clarity. Drawn-out processes that involved continual judgments about readiness for various memberships ensued and continued in the early years of the new millennium. In 2004 the Baltic republics were judged to be mature enough to be accepted as full members of the European Union and of NATO. Both memberships meant that national independence had once again received reaffirmation by the larger system of existing states. For most of the Baltic populations such reassurance was welcome, but, as public opinion polls suggested, a significant proportion of the three populations continued to have doubts about these steps. Some doubters questioned the wisdom of increasing the symbolic distance between the Baltic republics and Russia, some feared entanglements that curtailed national freedom of action, and some were irked by the unending stream of "standards" that western international organizations continued to heap upon new members. Nonetheless, the milestones of EU and NATO membership had been reached through the activities of elected governments, and though public support was not overwhelming, it was certainly commanding.

REDISCOVERING THE PAST

Membership in the most important western economic and military organizations signified that the post-communist phase of the recent past was being left behind. These geopolitical processes were paralleled by efforts among historically minded intellectuals of the three countries to make sense of what had happened and what was still happening. Any long-lived Balt born in, say, 1910, would have lived through two world wars, two declarations of independence, occupation by Nazi Germany and the USSR, deportations and emigrations, massive population losses and replenishments, and now unprecedented reorientations toward the west. This fragmented story had to be made whole, if only for the reason that schoolchildren needed to be imbued with an easily understood story of the country in which they were growing up. The task was far more difficult to carry out than to envisage, because the twentieth-century histories of the three

Baltic countries contained no single coherent story agreed upon by adults. In addition, the distant past – the centuries before the twentieth – offered no unambiguous tale either. Envious glances were cast at the national states – France, the United Kingdom, the USA, the Scandinavian countries – whose history, though punctuated by civil wars and strife of all kinds, had long-established frameworks and boundaries within which their complex national story could be placed. The Baltic republics had no such frameworks for the longest term. They were products of World War I, and their recent reemergence as sovereign states was the result of the unexpected outcome of a Cold War between global superpowers. It was important, however, to demonstrate that the three Baltic republics – as political entities – were more than accidental byproducts of historical processes in which Estonians, Latvians, and Lithuanians were not the prime movers. The three peoples had to be shown as having had "agency" – that is, they had in fact made their own history within the constraints imposed by circumstances.

This was the third time in the twentieth century that history writing in the Baltic littoral had changed course. The first was the period after 1918, when historians challenged the triumphalist historiography of the Baltic Germans and Poles in which these minorities were presented as the movers and shakers of the littoral, while Estonian, Latvian, and Lithuanian "peasants" were relegated to the role of passive observers. The second had come after 1945, when the Communist Party had created a rigid schema within which Russians and the Russian Empire were portrayed as having brought untold benefits to the littoral peoples from the medieval times onward, and, in the twentieth century with its class conflict, the Soviet Union had helped the "proletariat" of the three peoples to achieve its historical mission after 1940. These interpretative schemes were now, in the 1990s, a dead letter, and the dozens of textbooks, monographs, and articles flowing from the Soviet-era historical professions – organized in the universities and research institutes – were in disrepute for the time being. The needed reorientation was psychologically trying for several reasons. The post-communist era had arrived quickly, and many historians and historical writers now facing the task of producing a "new" history had been actively engaged in their profession during the Soviet period, writing within acceptable guidelines, some with more enthusiasm than others. Colleagues sat in judgment on each other, deciding to what extent each had "sinned" and who could continue to work. Retirements ensued. Some practitioners left the history profession for other work, some began to write the "new" history with even greater fervor than they had brought to the "old," while others continued to work in the expectation that their "sins" would be understood and forgiven. There was also a generational change: younger scholars who began their training in the mid-1980s and had yet to publish did not need to apologize for earlier intellectual products. Moreover, practitioners of the "new" history came to understand that the "national story" they now produced could not be simply a throwback to the interwar period and a continuation of the historical style that had ended in 1940. Celebratory national histories would not pass muster with western colleagues, because the western professionals had themselves changed since the mid-twentieth century. There was no single western way of doing history; competing interpretations of the past had become legion. Since the 1960s, history writing in the west had come to focus not only on the wealthy, successful, and powerful, but also on marginalized populations, particularly minorities of various kinds. It required that "national histories" make room for women, the imprisoned, the sexually unorthodox, and the destitute. The arrival of intellectual freedom after 1991 coincided with the arrival of western expectations about "national history" that now had to be incorporated into published work. This seemed grossly unfair to some, but, since the organized history profession from 1991 placed a high value on westernization of various kinds, the changes in western ways of doing history – some called them fashions – could not be ignored. Estonian, Latvian, and Lithuanian historians had to devise ways of doing their work with at least two audiences in mind: readers in their home countries who, after a half-century of browsing through heavily ideologized historical accounts, were truly interested in what really happened in the past; and the larger international historical profession in which national histories, though continuing to be written usually as textbooks, were not generally regarded as contributing much to human knowledge. In addition, in the western intellectual landscape the past in general was being overshadowed by a much more immediate and exciting popular culture that was particularly appealing to the young. Passive reading skills seemed to be fighting a losing battle with an interactive cyberspace culture.

The new national histories that began to appear during the 1990s were in fact different than those of the Soviet period and of the first independence decades. Virtually absent from them was the notion of inevitability: that change in all centuries before the twentieth was working toward the appearance in 1918 of the Estonian, Latvian, and Lithuanian states; or that such change was pointing toward the "triumph of the proletariat" in 1940. These events were treated like other historical events rather than as predestined outcomes. The idea that historical change was produced by "prime movers" – the land-owning nobilities in the distant past, grand dukes and tsars, the "working masses," the Communist Party, "progressives" – was replaced by a much more inclusive idea of how historical change occurred. All residents of Estonian, Latvian, and Lithuanian territories had produced noteworthy events: all were actors in the centuries-long historical drama, regardless of what social status they occupied, languages they spoke, or cultural norms they followed. This more inclusive sense of the past shifted the focus from the activities of any single population grouping within the littoral territories to the interaction of all of them. Historical description became more the story of the littoral territories and their human populations and less the history of any particular population. At least in principle, it was the job of the historian to describe all that had happened in the past – the interaction of human populations, the interaction of human populations and impersonal force such as technological innovations, the interactions of the littoral's populations and the peoples adjacent to the littoral. Such an approach to the past was intended to reduce the boundaries between the littoral's past residents, as well as the notion that the past was an unending story of exploitation, mistreatment, and victimization. All these were part of the story, but not its whole.

The appearance, disappearance, and reappearance in the twentieth century of sovereign states named Estonia, Latvia, and Lithuania ensured, however, that even within the more inclusive sense of the past the question of state formation in the littoral remained of major interest. In dealing with this question, historians were led to other more difficult questions: was it the case, for example, that the continuous use of the Lithuanian language in the Lithuanian territories implied the continuous presence, at some level, of a Lithuanian national consciousness? Did this consciousness shape itself around the memory of an independent Grand Duchy of Lithuania? Was this medieval state formation therefore a lineal ancestor of the independent Lithuania of the twentieth century? Since Estonians and Latvians had no state formations in the distant past, when in the more recent past did their national consciousness originate – during the national awakenings of the nineteenth century, the events surrounding the 1905 revolution, or the near-chaos of World War I? Questions of this nature had no easy answers, but in the new histories it was evident that in discussions of state-consciousness there was a strong preference for long-term continuity. If there was no direct evidence that Estonians and Latvians thought in terms of their own states before the twentieth century, such a desire could still be imputed in the continuous use of vernacular languages, in the oral tradition, and in social conflicts between peasants (Estonian- and Latvian-speaking), landed nobilities (German-speaking), urban patriciates (German-speaking), and imperial administrators (Russian-speaking). This continuity was easier to project back into Lithuanian history because of Lithuanian participation in the so-called Polish insurrections against Russian rule in 1830 and 1863.

Historical inclusivity reawakened questions that had been marginalized before, and a significant set concerned the World War II period. They were pushed to the forefront of public attention by a clash of viewpoints: the insistence by most Estonian, Latvian, and Lithuanian historians that the periods of 1940–1941 and 1945–1991 be called occupations, the equally strong retort by political leaders of the Russian-speaking minorities that what had happened in 1944–1945 had been the "liberation" of the littoral from fascism by the Soviet army, the understandable desire to document fully the 1941 and 1949 deportations, the equally understandable desire to clarify the participation of the local populations in the extermination of Baltic Jews during the 1941–1945 German occupation, and the desire by the republic governments to change the official calendar of national holidays by downgrading those of the Soviet era and replacing them with commemorations of greater emotional significance to the titular nationalities.

By the end of the 1990s, all these and similar, fundamentally historical questions had became knotted together, giving rise to charges and countercharges about "efforts to rewrite history," "a desire to hide crimes against humanity by Soviet-era power-holders," and about how the term "genocide" was to be applied to the events of the World War II period and subsequent decades. The popular press in the Russian Federation and some Russian lawmakers weighed in on the side of those who insisted that Estonians, Latvians, and Lithuanians wanted to "rewrite" history. In response, Baltic writers charged the Russian Federation with meddling and accused it of wanting to be the legal successor to the USSR without taking responsibility for the atrocities committed by that now-extinct state. To dampen the interlocking controversies, the presidents of all three republics (Lennart Meri of Estonia, Guntis Ulmanis of Latvia, and Valdas Adamkus of Lithuania) agreed in 1998 to create special presidential commissions in each country and to assign them the task of impartially documenting the events of 1940–1945 and subsequent decades. These commissions would consist of Baltic-area historians and knowledgeable specialists from other countries, hold periodic conferences, and publish their findings. Special attention would be paid to the fate of the Jewish populations of the littoral, to the role of the local populations in the murder of Jews, and to the clarification of such emotionally laden terms as genocide. The work of these commissions would continue until their members concluded that the available archival sources had been exhausted. The Estonian commission submitted its findings in 2006 but in Latvia and Lithuania, where the Holocaust had involved the murder of tens and hundreds of thousands of Jews, the two commissions continued their researches.

Controversies about the meaning of World War II events and the subsequent half-century, however, would not be stilled; they flared up periodically, sputtered out, and flared up again, especially when politicians in the Baltic republics and in the Russian Federation manipulated such controversies for their own purposes. As if this were not enough, new facets of the past revealed themselves as, over time, publicists in the Baltic republics and the Russian Federation presented calculations about how much each "owed" to the other for "damages" during the Soviet era; and as the Baltic governments sought ways of compensating people who had suffered injustices during the

World War II period. For those members of the public who wanted the three Baltic states to have forward-looking and future-oriented images, the continual intrusion of the past into the present was frustrating and would continue to be bothersome for some time to come.

THE TRAVAILS OF NORMALITY

The 2004 accession of Estonia, Latvia, and Lithuania to membership in the European Union and NATO signaled the growing irrelevance of the descriptive category "post-communist." Having met a host of demanding criteria for admission, the three Baltic republics could now consider themselves "normal" European states. They would continue to wrestle with socioeconomic problems, some of which dated from the Soviet period, but, then, no member states were problem-free. Comparative international rankings might classify member states as richer or poorer, having more or less corruption in the private and public sectors, and being more or less observant of their citizens' human rights. But such rankings were too fleeting a criterion for judging a country's fundamental characteristics: all evidence had to be considered in making such a judgment, and the three Baltic republics could now take satisfaction in having passed the multiple tests for normality. Residual feelings of unworthiness, inferiority, and "poor cousinship" might still be present in the general population, but these were now "internal problems" that did not alter the Baltic states' overall status.

Becoming members of the EU and NATO meant that these organizations considered the political systems of the three Baltic countries sufficiently stable to be entrusted with the obligations of membership. Parliamentary elections in all three continued at regular intervals (Estonia: 1999, 2003, 2007; Latvia: 1998, 2002, 2006; Lithuania: 1996, 2000, 2004, 2008). The victors in each created coalition governments, and the losers withdrew to wait until the next election. In all three countries, coalition governments dissolved regularly and had to be re-formed, but this was accomplished without the call for early parliamentary elections. The multiparty political system virtually ensured that even the largest vote-getting party never held an absolute majority of parliamentary seats. Presidential elections (by parliament in Estonia and Latvia; by popular vote in Lithuania) generally continued to place at the head of each country reliable persons, some of whom were political leaders, while others had to receive on-the-job training. In Estonia, the popular Lennart Meri, first elected to the presidency in 1992, remained in office until his retirement in 2001, when he was replaced by Arnold Rüütel, an agronomist, who had had a series of high positions in the Estonian Communist Party from the 1970s onward, but had supported independence from the USSR and had already been the titular head of state during the transition period. In 2006, however, the Estonian parliament turned to a former American-Estonian émigré, Toomas Ilves (b. 1953), who had already established an effective record as an Estonian diplomat and western-oriented foreign minister during the 1990s and in the years after 2000. In Latvia in 1999, President Guntis Ulmanis was replaced by Vaira Vīķe-Freiberga, a Canadian-Latvian recently returned to Latvia, an academic at the University of Montreal and by profession a psychologist and folklorist, unaffiliated with any Latvian political party. After reelection in 2003, she was followed in the presidential office in 2007 by Valdis Zatlers, a prominent Riga orthopedist who had not been active in Latvian politics before this time. Only in Lithuanian presidential elections was there a misstep. In 1998, the Lithuanians had elected an émigré, Valdas Adamkus, an American-Lithuanian. The next election in 2003 brought into office a much younger man, Rolandas Pakšas (b. 1955), a celebrity and former mayor of Vilnius, but he was impeached after a year for shady economic dealings, and the country turned again to Adamkus in 2004. In judging people in high office, popular opinion was quick to change from brief enthusiasm after an election to negativism soon thereafter. Even popular presidents came under fire by the critical media for "meddling" in politics (that is, exceeding their constitutionally mandated and relatively limited roles). None of the seemingly negative events of Baltic littoral politics marked the three systems as extraordinary: the short life-span of multiparty coalitions was characteristic of some of the oldest members of the European Union, the United States had had its own experience with presidential impeachment in 1998, and the low esteem in which voters held their political leaders seemed to have become typical of the political cultures of many western democratic societies.

The relative political stability in the three Baltic republics was joined after 2003 by statistically significant economic growth, as measured by annual expansion of the gross domestic product (GDP). Annual growth averaged 6–7 percent (in Estonia shooting up to 10 percent in some years); thus, in 2004 the European Union was admitting not three new impoverished members but ones in which the value of the total amount of goods and services in circulation was increasing, and some enthusiastic advocates of EU membership began to talk about the "three Baltic tigers." Aggregate economic measures, of course, if used by themselves could disguise chronic problems. Some 50–60 percent of the GDP growth was due to an expanding service sector in all three republics, which not only reflected a "modern" growth pattern but also signaled that the Baltic countries were seeking their proper niche in the overall European economy. None of them was as yet associated with a single economic sector (or a group of linked sectors) in which performance and productivity were truly outstanding. Moreover, various "human development" measures showed substantial differences in regional economic development in each country: urban areas were doing much better than rural, some regions (for example, Latgale in Latvia) remained "poor" by contrast with the rest of the country, and even in urban areas a wide disparity continued between layers of the population as defined by annual income. Conspicuous consumption among those newly enriched by the market economy reminded the rest of the population (especially many in the public sector) that their incomes were only creeping upward. Fortunately, inflation rates remained relatively low (4–5 percent) and the central national banks showed heightened awareness in their policies of the dangers of high inflation. None of these economic characteristics, however, made the Baltic republics unusual in the entire EU membership; wide income disparities and uneven regional development could be found especially in many of the members located in the southern part of the European continent.

Another set of disparities that after 2004 began to generate worry – from the viewpoint of national self-confidence – involved the mismatch between the relatively stagnant salary and wage levels in the three Baltic republics and levels in other older members of the European Union. Movement of labor across national boundaries became easier after 2004, and, as a consequence, a small but steadily growing outflow of working-age people (especially younger persons) began in search of employment elsewhere in Europe. Statistics for this trend were never precise, but educated estimates by 2007 placed the total number of emigrating Estonians (in the age group 15–64) at about 20,000–30,000 (to Finland, the United Kingdom, and Ireland), the number of Latvians at about 80,000–100,000 (to Sweden, the United Kingdom, and Ireland), and about 200,000 Lithuanians (to Poland, Germany, the United Kingdom, and the United States). By contrast with the *Gastarbeiter* who came from southern Europe to West Germany during the 1950s and 1960s, this Baltic migration involved educated people, often with degrees in specialized fields, who nonetheless were willing to work at better-remunerated manual labor abroad than at low-paying jobs consistent with their education at home. Their long-range plans remained unclear: some wanted to earn substantial sums quickly and return home; others evidently planned to relocate permanently. Interviews revealed not only dissatisfaction with low wage and salary levels but also a psychology of "not being wanted" or "not being valued" in their home countries. Although national governments worried about this out-migration (numerically the largest since World War II), there was little they could do to stem it because the free movement of labor was one of the premises of the European Union.

Another source of worry, particularly in Estonia and Latvia, was the possible negative consequences for a "normal" state of a large proportion of resident non-citizens (elsewhere designated as resident aliens), most of them ethnic Russians. The naturalization process that had been created in the post-1991 years eventually received the approval of the Organization for Security and Cooperation in Europe and other international bodies, but in later years the process yielded a relatively meager return: a few thousand naturalizations each year. By the second decade after 1991, the workings of the naturalization process still left about 278,000 Russians and Russian speakers without citizenship in Latvia (363,000 in this population category were citizens), and about 100,000 in Estonia (about 150,000 had citizenship). Few problems were as readily exploitable by various controversy-needing activists as this: discussions of it, no matter how rational at the start, quickly tapped deep emotions fed by very different understandings of the past half-century of Baltic history. Many of the ethnic Russians felt discriminated against by overly harsh citizenship rules; on the Estonian and Latvian side, modifications in naturalization policy were often perceived as nothing but tribute that had to be paid to other Europeans to improve Baltic "image." The charges of "ethnocrat" and "occupant" were heard in these debates frequently, with European observers weighing in periodically with comments about how "troubling" the situation was.

Public opinion polls showed that the events of World War II and the subsequent Soviet era were perceived very differently by Latvians or Estonians on the one hand and by Russian speakers on the other. The ongoing controversy was periodically fueled by statements of politicians in the Russian Federation about the obligation of Russia to "protect" its compatriots no matter where they lived. Experts on citizenship questions could offer no easy solutions to the dilemma: "normal" states should not have a large proportion of "stateless" citizens, but states had the right to define the rules of citizenship. Though no solution was at hand, it was entirely possible that the problem would resolve itself over time. Microprocesses were at work in both countries that reduced the emotionalism attached to the problem. Many parents of young children among the Russian speakers did not object to curricula in the schools that had classes in Estonian or Latvian; learning the state language was not perceived as objectionable. A decade and a half into restored independence, most Russian speakers employed in jobs requiring contact with the general public seemed at least to understand the state language, and could exchange basic information in it. Relatively high intermarriage rates (especially in Latvia) formed kin networks that contained both Estonian and Latvian speakers and Russian speakers. Among those of the older and middle generations who refused to learn the state languages on principle or out of the habit of regarding the Russian language as superior to Latvian or Estonian, non-citizenship, while irksome, was not an obstacle to economic survival. In Latvia, for example, an exaggerated catchphrase was that "the Latvians owned the political system while the Russians owned the economy." Participation by ethnic Russian citizens continued to produce in each parliamentary election considerable support for parties that had a protective attitude toward the Russian-speaking population. Such parties were never invited to join coalition governments, but neither were they marginalized; the Latvians in their leadership and the ethnic Russians who had learned the state languages fluently succeeded in keeping them as viable alternatives for voters.

The problem of the integration of ethnic minorities continued to be treated seriously by the governments of the two states: in 2000, Estonia launched the program "Integration in Estonian Society 2000–2007" and renewed it in 2008, and in 2004, Latvia created a special assignments minister for social integration in the ministry of foreign affairs. These efforts recognized that at issue was more than simply *social* integration; economic, educational, and social processes had to be promoted that would discourage the perpetuation of geographically defined *enclaves* of Russian speakers (in Estonia, in Tallinn and in the northeastern Narva district; in Latvia, Riga, other large cities, and Latgale). In Latvia, a question seriously debated at this juncture concerned granting non-citizens the right to vote in local (city and county) elections.

By 2001 the three Baltic republics, together with most of the other post-communist states of the European east, had become sufficiently integrated with most of the important international organizations of the European continent for the residents of these countries to feel fully that they were Europeans. The internationalization of Baltic geographic and cultural space was continuing at a brisk pace. Self-advertisement in European media by Baltic governments expanded tourism, and flights were offered at attractively low fares from Riga, Tallinn, and Vilnius to other parts of the continent, as well as to points east in the Russian Federation. For those with means, vacations in famous continental locales had become normal, and the businesses in the littoral that catered to the tourist trade were among the most rapidly growing sectors of the three economies. Media outlets in the three countries allocated as much space to reportage of "foreign" as to domestic news, thus furthering among readers and listeners the feeling that they belonged to a greater whole. The absorption and emulation of "western" popular culture had been rapid, with one consequence being the virtual disappearance of a boundary between specifically Estonian, Latvian, and Lithuanian variants of popular culture and the larger international corpus. Public and private institutions, ranging from government ministries and academies of science to small private enterprises, manifested a presence in cyberspace, making information about themselves available worldwide. Also, the growing popularity of blogging appeared to be equalizing the views of everyone with those of everyone else. There were signs, however, of a generation-linked divide in this new computer-oriented world between those who could afford to participate in it and felt comfortable in a polyglot, international, multicultural and fast-moving environment and those to whom it felt like alien territory. National identity was being redefined, this time not by predatory neighboring states but by an impersonal culture-driven force within which enemies were harder to identify.

Internationalization of popular culture, membership in international organizations that appeared to demand increasing standardization and homogenization, and the deep penetration of the so-called information revolution continued to provoke in all three Baltic states discussions in the intelligentsia about national uniqueness. Was it possible for small countries to survive as identifiable entities in a world where globalization promoted the free flow of everything – people, information, goods – across national borders and indeed seemed to be looking to a future in which such borders would be of minimal relevance?

33 The differences in the religiosity of the three Baltic states is symbolized by the famous Hill of Crosses in Lithuania.

How likely was it that the age-old habit among outsiders to think of the three Baltic states as a natural set – "the Baltics" – would turn out to be an unintentional prediction of the littoral's future? Post-1991 national sovereignty had created the opportunity once again for Estonians, Latvians, and Lithuanians to transform into multiple regulations the cultural protectionism that had been central to their national identities for a century. Language laws, signage, the conceptual separation of ethnic nationality from political nationality, and doubts about the advent of multiculturalism all suggested that the desire to be unique remained alive and sought to present itself to the eye of the beholder. The cultivation of uniqueness was to a great extent history-based and expressed itself in countless specifics. The Hill of Crosses in Lithuania, for example, suggested a mystical, perhaps Catholic, religiosity not to be found in Estonia or Latvia with their Lutheran traditions. A cultural orientation of Estonia toward Scandinavia and Finland, and of Lithuania toward Poland, found no equivalent in Latvia. The celebration of Riga as a centuries-old European regional capital provided for Latvians a component of the national image that could not be claimed by either Estonia or Lithuania, where an urban duality (Tallinn–Tartu, Vilnius–Kaunas, respectively) was more prominent. Lithuania's historical memory contained a grand duchy, no less, while those of Latvia and Estonia could speak only of seven hundred years of subordinated peasanthood. Only Latvia contained a large region – Latgale – where the spoken variant of the national language was for many much more than simply a dialect. The Estonians seemed to be more successful at internationalizing their literature through translation – the novels of Jaan Kross are a good example – while Latvian and Lithuanian writers continued to believe that their works were being read only by their compatriots. Political resolution of the "Russophone" question differentiated Estonia and Latvia, where large non-citizen resident populations continued to exist, from Lithuania, where citizenship was granted to all residents during the early 1990s. Sociopolitical integration appeared to have made more headway in Lithuania than in the other two countries, but the proper measures for this process remained contested. The long-term results of the dynamic interaction of europeanization, globalization, and sociocultural efforts at preserving national uniqueness remained very difficult to predict even two decades after regained independence.

SUGGESTED READINGS

GENERAL

Flint, David. *The Baltic States: Estonia, Latvia, Lithuania.* Brookfield, Conn.: Millbrook Press, 1992.

Hiden, John, and Patrick Salmon. *The Baltic Nations and Europe: Estonia, Latvia, and Lithuania in the Twentieth Century.* Reading, Mass.: Addison-Wesley, 1995.

Kiaupa, Zigmas. *The History of Lithuania.* Vilnius: Baltos Lanka, 2002.

Miljan, Toivo. *Historical Dictionary of Estonia.* Lanham, Md.: Scarecrow Press, 2004.

O'Connor, Kevin. *Culture and Customs of the Baltic States.* Westport, Conn.: Greenwood Press, 2006.

The History of the Baltic States. Westport, Conn.: Greenwood Press, 2003.

Plakans, Andrejs. *Historical Dictionary of Latvia.* Second edition. Lanham, Md.: Scarecrow Press, 2008.

The Latvians: A Short History. Stanford, Calif.: Hoover Institution Press, 1995.

Raun, Toivo U. *Estonia and the Estonians.* Second edition. Stanford, Calif.: Hoover Institution Press, 1991.

Rubulis, Aleksis, ed. *Baltic Literature: A Survey of Finnish, Estonian, Latvian, and Lithuanian Literatures.* Notre Dame, Ind.: University of Notre Dame Press, 1970.

Smith, Inese, and Marita V. Grunts. *The Baltic States: Estonia, Latvia, Lithuania.* World Bibliographical Series No. 161. Oxford: Clio Press, 1993.

Suziedelis, Saulius. *Historical Dictionary of Lithuania.* Lanham, Md.: Scarecrow Press, 1997.

THE PEOPLES OF THE EASTERN BALTIC LITTORAL

Bojtár, Endre. *Foreword to the Past: A Cultural History of the Baltic People.* Budapest: Central European University Press, 1999.

Gimbutas, Marija. *Ancient Symbolism in Lithuanian Folk Art.* Philadelphia: American Folklore Society, 1958.

The Balts. New York: Praeger, 1963.

The Slavs. New York: Praeger, 1971.

Greimas, Algridas Julien. *Of Gods and Men: Studies in Lithuanian Mythology.* Translated by Milda Newman. Bloomington: Indiana University Press, 1992.

Mallory, J. P. *In Search of Indo-Europeans: Language, Archeology, and Myth.* New York: Thames and Hudson, 1989.

Saks, Edgar V. *The Estonian Vikings.* Cardiff: Boreas, 1985.

Spekke, Arnolds. *The Ancient Amber Routes and the Geographical Discovery of the Eastern Baltic.* Stockholm: M. Goppers, 1957.

The Baltic Sea in Ancient Maps. Stockholm: M. Goppers, 1957.

Velius, Norbertas. *The World Outlook of the Ancient Balts.* Vilnius: Mintis, 1989.

THE NEW ORDER, 1200–1500

Blomkvist, Nils. *The Discovery of the Baltic: The Reception of a Catholic World System in the European North (1075–1225).* Leiden: Brill, 2005.

Burleigh, Michael. "Scandinavia and the Baltic frontier: The Military Orders in the Baltic." In *New Cambridge Medieval History.* Vol. V. Edited by David Abulafia. Cambridge University Press, 1999.

Christiansen, Eric. *The Northern Crusades: The Baltic and the Catholic Frontier 1100–1525.* London: Macmillan, 1980.

The Chronicle of Balthasar Russow: A Forthright Rebuttal by Elert Kruse; Errors and Mistakes of Balthasar Russow by Heinrich Tisenhausen. Translated and edited by Jerry C. Smith, Juergen Eichhoff, and William L. Urban. Madison, Wis.: Baltic Studies Center, 1988.

The Chronicle of Henry of Livonia. Edited and translated by James A. Brundage. Madison, Wis.: University of Wisconsin Press, 1961.

Gieysztor, Aleksander. "The Kingdom of Poland and the Grand Duchy of Lithuania, 1370–1506." In *New Cambridge Modern History.* Vol. VII. Edited by Christopher Allmand. Cambridge University Press, 2000.

Halecki, Oscar. *Borderlands of Western Civilization: A History of East Central Europe.* New York: Ronald, 1952.

Jadwiga of Anjou and the Rise of East Central Europe. Boulder: East European Monographs, 1991.

Salomon Henning's Chronicle of Courland and Livonia. Translated and
edited by Jerry C. Smith, William Urban, and Ward Jones. Dubuque,
Iowa: Kendall Hunt, 1992.

The Livonian Rhymed Chronicle. Translated by Jerry C. Smith and
William Urban. Bloomington: Indiana University Press, 1977.

Mänd, Anu. *Urban Carnival: Festive Culture in the Hanseatic Cities of the
Eastern Baltic, 1350–1550.* Turnhout: Brepols, 2005.

Rowell, S. C. "Baltic Europe." In *New Cambridge Modern History.* Vol. VI.
Edited by Michael Jones. Cambridge University Press, 2000.

"Eastern Europe: The Central European Kingdoms." In *New Cambridge
Medieval History.* Vol. V. Edited by David Abulafia. Cambridge
University Press, 1999.

*Lithuania Ascending: A Pagan Empire within East-Central Europe,
1295–1345.* Cambridge University Press, 1994.

Urban, William. *The Baltic Crusade.* First edition, Dekalb: Northern Illinois
University Press, 1975; second edition, Chicago: Lithuanian Research
and Studies Center, 1994.

The Livonian Crusade. Washington, D.C.: University Press of America,
1981.

THE NEW ORDER RECONFIGURED, 1500–1710

Andersen, N. K. "The Reformation in Scandinavia and the Baltic." In *The
New Cambridge Modern History of Europe.* Vol. II. *The Reformation.*
Edited by G. R. Elton. Cambridge University Press, 1990.

Dembkowski, Harry E. *The Union of Lublin: Polish Federalism in the
Golden Age.* Boulder: East European Monographs, 1982.

Frost, Robert I. *After the Deluge: Poland-Lithuania and the Second
Northern War 1655–1669.* Cambridge University Press, 1993.

*The Northern Wars: War, State, and Society in Northeastern Europe,
1558–1721.* Harlow: Longman, 2000.

Kirby, David. *Northern Europe in the Early Modern Period: The Baltic
World 1492–1772.* London: Longman, 1990.

Kirchner, Walther. *The Rise of the Baltic Question.* Newark, Del.:
University of Delaware Press, 1954.

Kurman, George. *The Development of Written Estonian.* The Hague:
Mouton, 1968.

Lindquist, Sven-Olof, ed. *Economy and Culture in the Baltic 1650–1700.*
Visby: Gotlands Fornsal, 1989.

Lisk, Jill. *The Struggle for Supremacy in the Baltic, 1660–1725.* New
York: Minerva Press, 1968.

Renner, Johannes. *Livonian History 1556–1561.* Translated by Jerry
C. Smith and William Urban. Lewiston: Edwin Mellen Press, 1997.

Roberts, Michael. *The Swedish Imperial Experience.* London: Cambridge University Press, 1979.

Ross, Kristiina and Pēteris Vanags, eds. *Common Roots of the Latvian and Estonian Literary Languages.* Frankfurt: Peter Lang, 2008.

Stiles, Andrina. *Sweden and the Baltic 1523–1721.* London: Hodder Arnold, 1992.

Stone, Daniel. *The Polish-Lithuanian State 1386–1795.* Seattle: University of Washington Press, 2001.

INSTALLING HEGEMONY: THE LITTORAL AND TSARIST RUSSIA, 1710–1800

Berkis, Alexander V. *The History of the Duchy of Courland, 1561–1795.* Towson, Md.: Harrod, 1969.

Brakas, Martin. *Lithuania Minor: A Collection of Studies of Her History and Ethnography.* New York: Lithuanian Research Institute, 1976.

Hundert, Gershon David. *Jews in Poland-Lithuania in the Eighteenth Century: A Genealogy of Modernity.* Berkeley: University of California Press, 2004.

Kaplan, Herbert H. *The First Partition of Poland.* New York: Columbia University Press, 1962.

Lord, Robert H. *The Second Partition of Poland: A Study in Diplomatic History.* Cambridge, Mass.: Harvard University Press, 1915.

Lukowaski, Jerzy. *Liberty's Folly: The Polish Lithuanian Commonwealth in the Eighteenth Century, 1697–1795.* London: Routledge, 1991.

Peterson, Claes. *Peter the Great's Administrative and Judicial Reforms: Swedish Antecedents and the Process of Reception.* Stockholm: Nordiska Bokhandeln, 1979.

Rosman, M. J. *The Lord's Jews: Magnate–Jewish Relations in the Polish Lithuanian Commonwealth during the Eighteenth Century.* Cambridge, Mass.: Harvard Ukrainian Institute, 1990.

Shulvass, Moses A. *From East to West: The Westward Migration of Jews from Eastern Europe during the 17th and 18th Centuries.* Detroit: Wayne State University Press, 1971.

Stone, Daniel. *Polish Politics and National Reform 1775–1788.* Boulder: East European Monographs, 1976.

REFORMING AND CONTROLLING THE BALTIC LITTORAL, 1800–1855

Klier, John Doyle. *Russia Gathers Her Jews: The Origins of the "Jewish Question" in Russia.* Dekalb, Ill.: Northern Illinois University Press, 1986.

Leslie, R. F. *Polish Politics and the Revolution of November 1830.* University of London, 1956.

Raun, Toivo. "The Development of Estonian Literacy in the 18th and 19th Centuries." *Journal of Baltic Studies* 10 (1979), 115–126.

Starr, S. Frederick. *Decentralization and Self-Government in Russia: 1830–1870.* Princeton University Press, 1972.

Thackeray, Frank W. *Antecedents of Revolution: Alexander I and the Polish Kingdom, 1815–1825.* Boulder: East European Monographs, 1980.

Thaden, Edward C. *Russia's Western Borderlands, 1710–1870.* Princeton University Press, 1984.

Yaney, George. *The Systematization of Russian Government: Social Evolution in the Domestic Administration of Imperial Russia.* Urbana: University of Illinois Press, 1973.

Wandycz, Piotr. *The Lands of Partitioned Poland, 1795–1918.* Seattle: University of Washington Press, 1974.

Weeks, Theodore. "Managing Empire: Tsarist Nationality Policy." In *The Cambridge History of Russia.* Vol. II. *Imperial Russia 1689–1917.* Edited by Dominic Lieven. Cambridge University Press, 2006.

FIVE DECADES OF TRANSFORMATIONS, 1855–1905

Henriksson, A. *The Tsar's Loyal Germans: The Riga German Community: Social Change and the Nationality Question, 1855–1905.* Boulder: East European Monographs, 1983.

Kirby, David. *The Baltic World 1772–1993: Europe's Northern Periphery in an Age of Change.* London: Longman, 1995.

Krapauskas, Virgil. *Nationalism and Historiography: The Case of Nineteenth Century Lithuanian Historicism.* Boulder: East European Monographs, 2000.

Loit, Aleksander, ed. *National Movements in the Baltic Countries during the 19th Century.* University of Stockholm, 1985.

Senn, Alfred E. *Jonas Basanavičius: Patriarch of Lithuania's National Rebirth.* Newton, Mass.: Oriental Research Partners, 1980.

Staliunas, Darius. *Making Russians: Meaning and Practice of Russification in Lithuania and Belarus after 1863.* New York and Amsterdam: Rodopi, 2007.

Thaden, Edward, ed. *Russification in the Baltic Provinces and Finland, 1855–1914.* Princeton University Press, 1981.

Tobias, Henry Jack. *The Jewish Bund in Russia from its Origins to 1905.* Stanford University Press, 1972.

Whelan, Heide. *Family, Caste, and Capitalism among the Baltic German Nobility.* Cologne: Böhlau Verlag, 1999.

STATEHOOD IN TROUBLED TIMES, 1905–1940

Crowe, David. *The Baltic States and the Great Powers 1938–1940: Foreign Relations.* Boulder: Westview Press, 1993.

Graham, M. W. *The Diplomatic Recognition of the Border States: Latvia.* Publications of the University of California at Los Angeles in Social Sciences 3. Berkeley: University of California Press, 1939–1941.

Hiden, John W. *The Baltic States and Weimar Ostpolitik.* Cambridge University Press, 1987.

Hiden, John W., and Aleksander Loit, eds. *The Baltic in International Relations between the Two World Wars.* University of Stockholm, 1988.

Hovi, Olavi. *The Baltic Area in British Policy 1918–1921.* Helsinki: Finnish Historical Society, 1980.

Kasekamp, Andres. *The Radical Right in Interwar Estonia.* New York: St. Martin's Press, 2000.

Mansbach, S. A. *Modern Art in Eastern Europe: From the Baltic to the Balkans, ca. 1890–1939.* Cambridge University Press, 1999.

Page, Stanley W. *The Formation of the Baltic States: A Study of the Effects of Great Power Policies on the Emergence of Lithuania, Latvia, Estonia.* Cambridge, Mass.: Harvard University Press, 1959; reprinted New York: Howard Fertig, 1970.

Parming, Tönu. *The Collapse of Liberal Democracy and the Rise of Authoritarianism in Estonia.* Beverly Hills: Sage, 1975.

Rauch, Georg von. *The Baltic States. Estonia, Latvia, and Lithuania: The Years of Independence 1917–1940.* Berkeley: University of California Press, 1974.

Rogers, H. I. *Search for Security: A Study in Baltic Diplomacy 1920–1934.* Hamden, Conn.: Archon Books, 1975.

Sabaliunas, Leonas. *Lithuania in Crisis: Nationalism to Communism 1939–1940.* Bloomington: Indiana University Press, 1972.

Lithuanian Social Democracy in Perspective 1893–1914. Durham, N.C.: Duke University Press, 1990.

Senn, Alfred E. *The Emergence of Modern Lithuania.* New York: Columbia University Press, 1959.

The Great Powers, Lithuania, and the Vilna Question. Leiden: Brill, 1966.

Simutis, Anicetas. *The Economic Reconstruction of Lithuania after 1918.* New York: Columbia University Press, 1942.

Tarulis, A. N. *Soviet Policy toward the Baltic States 1918–1940.* University of Notre Dame Press, 1959.

Tuskenis, Edvardas, ed. *Lithuania in European Politics: The Years of the First Republic 1918–1940.* New York: St. Martin's Press, 1997.

Vardys, V. Stanley, and Romuald J. Misiunas, eds. *The Baltic States in Peace and War 1917–1945*. University Park: Pennsylvania State University Press, 1978.

THE RETURN OF EMPIRES, 1940–1991

Allworth, Edward, ed. *Nationality Group Survival in Multi-Ethnic States: Shifting Support Patterns in the Soviet Baltic Region*. London: Praeger, 1977.
Clemens, Walter C., Jr. *Baltic Independence and Russian Empire*. New York: St. Martin's Press, 1991.
Eksteins, Modris. *Walking since Daybreak: A Story of Eastern Europe, World War II, and the Heart of our Century*. Boston: Houghton Mifflin, 1999.
Ezergailis, Andrew. *The Holocaust in Latvia, 1941–1944: The Missing Center*. Riga: The Historical Institute of Latvia, in association with the United States Holocaust Museum, 1996.
Gordon, Harry. *The Shadow of Death: The Holocaust in Lithuania*. Lexington, Ky.: University Press of Kentucky, 1992.
Hiden, John, and Martyn Housden. *Neighbors or Enemies: Germans, the Baltic, and Beyond*. New York and Amsterdam: Rodopi, 2008.
Hiden, John, and Thomas Lane, eds. *The Baltic and the Outbreak of the Second World War*. Cambridge University Press, 1992.
Karklins, Rasma. *Ethnic Relations in the USSR: The Perspective from Below*. Boston: Allen and Unwin, 1986.
Kavass, Igor I., and Adolph Sprūdžs, eds. *Baltic States: A Study of their Origin and National Development, their Seizure and Incorporation into the USSR*. New York: William Hein, 1972.
Loeber, Dietrich A., V. Stanley Vardys, and Laurence P. Kitching, eds. *Regional Identity under Soviet Rule: The Case of the Baltic States*. Hackettstown, N.J.: AABS, 1990.
Lumans, Valdis. *Latvia in World War II*. New York: Fordham University Press, 2006.
Maley, William. *The Politics of Baltic Nationalism*. Canberra, Australia: Research School of Pacific Studies, 1990.
Misiunas, R. J., and Rein Taagepera. *The Baltic States: Years of Dependence 1940–1980*. Berkeley: University of California Press, 1983; expanded and updated edition, 1993.
Nikzentaitis, Alvydas, Stefan Schreiner, and Darius Staliunas, eds. *The Vanished Worlds of Lithuanian Jews*. New York and Amsterdam: Rodopi, 2004.
Parming, Tönu, and Elmar Jarvesoo, eds. *A Case Study of a Soviet Republic: The Estonian SSR*. Boulder: Westview Press, 1978.

Rosenfeld, Alla, and Norton T. Dodge, eds. *Art of the Baltics: The Struggle for Freedom of Artistic Expression under the Soviets, 1945–1991*. New Brunswick, N.J.: Rutgers University Press and Jane Vorhees Zimmerli Art Museum, 2002.

Senn, Alfred E. *Lithuania 1940: Revolution from Above*. New York: Rodopi, 2007.

Swain, Geoff. *Between Stalin and Hitler: Class War and Race War on the Dvina, 1940–1946*. London: Routledge, 2004.

Taagepera, Rein. *Softening without Liberalization in the Soviet Union: The Case of Juri Kukk*. Lanham, Md.: University Press of America, 1984.

Thomson, Clare. *The Singing Revolution: A Political Journey through the Baltic States*. London: Michael Joseph, 1992.

Vardys, V. Stanley. *The Catholic Church, Dissent, and Nationality in Soviet Lithuania*. Boulder: East European Quarterly, 1978.

Vardys, V. Stanley, ed. *Lithuania under the Soviets: Portrait of a Nation, 1940–1965*. New York: Praeger, 1965.

Vizulis, J. I. *The Molotov–Ribbentrop Pact of 1939: The Baltic Case*. New York: Praeger, 1990.

Yekelchyk, Serhy. "The Western Republics: Ukraine, Belarus, Moldova, and the Baltics." *Cambridge History of Russia*. Vol. III. *The Twentieth Century*. Edited by Ronald Grigor Suny. Cambridge University Press, 2006.

REENTERING EUROPE, 1991–

Alanen, Ilkka. *Mapping the Rural Problem in the Baltic Countryside: Transition Processes in the Rural Areas of Estonia, Latvia, and Lithuania*. Aldershot: Ashgate, 2004.

Bager, Torben, and Helene Oldrup. *Farm Structure and Farmer Attitudes in Estonia, Latvia, and Lithuania*. Esbjerg: South Jutland University, 1997.

Clemens, Walter C., Jr. *The Baltic Transformed: Complexity Theory and European Security*. Lanham, Md.: Rowman and Littlefield, 2001.

Dreifelds, Juris. *Latvia in Transition*. Cambridge University Press, 1996.

Galbreath, David. J. *Nation-Building and Minority Politics in Post-Socialist States: Interests, Influences and Identities in Estonia and Latvia*. Stuttgart: Ibidemverlag, 2005.

Hansen, Birthe, and Bertel Heurlin, eds. *The Baltic States in World Politics*. New York: St. Martin's Press, 1998.

Hood, Neil, Robert Kilis, and Jan-Erik Vahlne, eds. *Transition in the Baltic States: Micro-level Studies*. New York: St. Martin's Press, 1997.

Karklins, Rasma. *The System Made Me Do It: Corruption in Post-Communist Societies*. Armonk, N.Y.: M. E. Sharpe, 2005.

Kelertas, Violeta, ed. *Baltic Postcolonialism*. New York and Amsterdam: Rodopi, 2006.

Lieven, Anatol. *The Baltic Revolution: Latvia, Lithuania, Estonia, and the Path to Independence*. New Haven, Conn.: Yale University Press, 1993.

Mourtizen, Hans, ed. *Bordering Russia: Theory and Prospects for Europe's Baltic Rim*. Aldershot: Ashgate, 1998.

Riislaki, Jukka. *The Case for Latvia. Disinformation Campaigns against a Small Nation*. New York and Amsterdam: Rodopi, 2008.

Schwartz, Katrina Z. S. *Nature and National Identity after Communism: Globalizing the Ethnoscape*. University of Pittsburgh Press, 2006.

Senn, Alfred E. *Gorbachev's Failure in Lithuania*. New York: St. Martin's Press, 1995.

Lithuania Awakening. Berkeley: University of California Press, 1990.

Silova, Iveta. *From Sites of Occupation to Symbols of Multiculturalism: Reconceptualizing Minority Education in Post-Soviet Latvia*. Greenwich, Conn.: Information Age Publishing, 2006.

Skultans, Vieda. *The Testimony of Lives: Narrative and Memory in Post-Soviet Latvia*. London: Routledge, 1998.

Smith, David J., Artis Pabriks, Aldis Purs, and Thomas Lane. *The Baltic States: Estonia, Latvia, and Lithuania*. London: Routledge, 2002.

Smith, Graham, ed. *The Baltic States: The National Self-determination of Estonia, Latvia, and Lithuania*. New York: St. Martin's Press, 1994.

Subrenat, Jean-Jacques, ed. *Estonia: Identity and Independence*. New York and Amsterdam: Rodopi, 2004.

Van Arkadie, Brian, and Mats Karlson. *Economic Survey of the Baltic States*. New York University Press, 1992.

Vihalemm, Peeter, ed. *Baltic Media in Transition*. Tartu University Press, 2002.

INDEX

Page numbers in **bold italic** refer to photographs and illustrations.

CAMBRIDGE CONCISE HISTORIES